Rabbi Israel Salanter and the Mussar Movement

Seeking the Torah of Truth

Rabbi Israel Salanter and the Mussar Movement

Seeking the Torah of Truth

IMMANUEL ETKES

Translated from the Hebrew by Jonathan Chipman

THE JEWISH PUBLICATION SOCIETY

Philadelphia   Jerusalem

5753 / 1993

Originally published in Hebrew under the title
Rabbi yisra'el salanter ve-reshitah shel ha-mussar
Copyright © 1982 by The Magnes Press,
The Hebrew University, Jerusalem

This edition copyright © 1993 by Immanuel Etkes
First English edition   All rights reserved
Manufactured in the United States of America

Designed by Arlene Putterman
Typeset in Meridien by Ruttle, Shaw & Wetherill, Inc.
Printed by Haddon Craftsmen

The publication of this book was made possible
by the trustees of the Gloria and Sidney Danziger Foundation,
Rabbi Benjamin Z. Kreitman, Stanley T. Miller, Robert E. Fischer,
in memory of Gloria and Sidney Danziger.

Contents

Significant Dates

1810   Israel Lipkin born in Zager. Known later as Israel Salanter.

1822   Sent by his parents to study Torah in Salant.

1840   Moved to Vilna, where he was invited to serve as head of Yeshiva.

1845   Took first initiative toward establishing the Mussar Movement in Vilna.

1848   Fled Vilna for Kovna in order to be free of the pressure of the authorities to serve as a Gemara teacher in the rabbinical seminary then established in Vilna. In Kovna, he actively disseminated the ideas of the Mussar Movement.

1851   Began teaching Torah in Nevyozer *Kloiz* in Kovna.

1857   Left Lithuania and settled in Prussia, intermittently in Memel, Koenigsberg and Berlin.

1861   Began publishing the periodical entitled *Tevunah*.

1880   Left for Paris in order to rehabilitate the Jewish community made up of Russian and Polish immigrants.

1882   Led a public struggle against the initiative to re-establish the rabbinical seminary in Russia.

1883   Died in Koenigsberg.

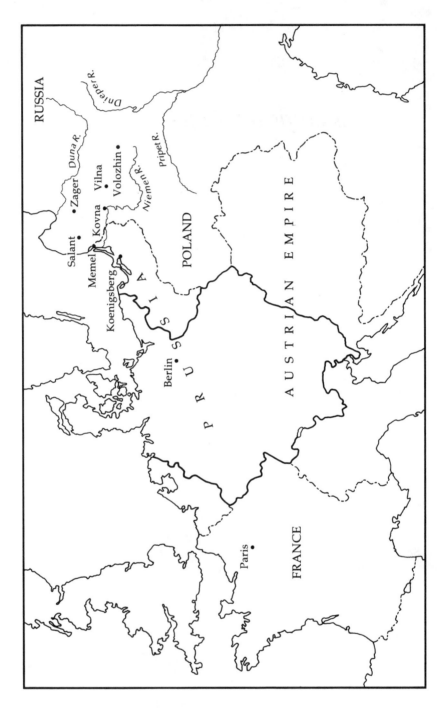

Rabbi Israel Salanter's Europe, including cities where he lived and spread his teachings.

Rabbi Israel Salanter and the Mussar Movement

Seeking the Torah of Truth

Introduction

THE PRESENT volume is devoted to the thought and life-work of Rabbi Israel Salanter,[1] who, in the 1840s, began to disseminate the message of his Mussar movement. While the term *Mussar* has had a variety of meanings in Hebrew literature and historical periods,[2] in Salanter's writings the term is used to denote both the effort and the means employed to attain religio-ethical self-perfection and self-restraint. Through this movement, Salanter hoped to foster a spiritual and ethical renewal within Lithuanian Jewry. His message had three components: the demand that ethical self-perfection be a priority of the Jew, the identification of the ethical weak point in the realm of human relations, and the creation of a new and promising system of religio-ethical improvement.

It would be difficult to find another such instance in the history of Eastern European Jewry during the modern period in which the labor and initiative of a single individual could be credited with the birth and initial growth of a new movement. Salanter originated the theoretical basis for the Mussar movement, organized its first cells while spreading its message to the public, and headed the movement until his death in the early 1880s, at which time his disciples took over his efforts. It is therefore not surprising that the history of the Mussar movement overlaps, to a large extent, the biography of Rabbi Israel Salanter.

The present work is therefore limited to the relationship between the Mussar movement and its founder and first leader. I do not discuss here the development of the Mussar movement following the death of Salanter, nor those manifestations of it that took place during his lifetime that were not directly related to him. On the other hand, I have attempted in this work to encompass the main facets of Rabbi Israel's

3

public activity, including those that were not specifically connected with
the Mussar movement.

ISRAEL SALANTER was raised and worked within the Lithuanian sociocultural context of Mitnaggedic society, which is generally
portrayed in terms of its negative message—that is, the negation of the
Hasidic movement—and as no more than that. This image calls for
certain qualifications and additions. One may distinguish two main
stages in the history of Mitnaggedism. During the first stage, which
began in 1772, the phenomenon was indeed "Mitnaggedism" in the
literal sense of the word—that is, "opposition" to Hasidism. This response was primarily articulated in the organized struggle led by Rabbi
Elijah, the Gaon of Vilna, and carried out by the community organization. Explanation and analysis of the motivations of the Mitnaggedim
during this stage would take us too far afield in our present discussion.
Let it suffice to say that they were not interested at that point in
conducting a polemic with Hasidism. From their point of view, Hasidism
was understood as a deviant sect, whose heretical nature was to be
publicly exposed and uprooted by use of all available means—at least
within the borders of Lithuania.

At the beginning of the nineteenth century, it became clear that the
Mitnaggedim had suffered a decisive defeat in their struggle with Hasidism. Not only was their hope of completely eliminating Hasidism not
realized, but during the latter third of the eighteenth century the Hasidic
movement continued to gather strength and to grow. Indeed, many
young men from the ranks of the learned elite were swept up by the
influence of the new movement, so much so that the persecuted sect
became a threat to its persecutors.

The transition to the second stage in the history of Mitnaggedism
came about against the background of that development. At that point,
Mitnaggedic society in Lithuania became crystallized as a movement
with a positive self-image, in which the all-out war against Hasidism
was supplanted by intellectual confrontation and social competition
with the rival movement.

The central figure in the formulation of Mitnaggedism as a constructive and creative movement was Rabbi Hayyim of Volozhin, the
leading disciple of the Gaon of Vilna. In his well-known work, *Nefesh
ha-hayyim* (1824), Rabbi Hayyim offered not only an articulate and
profound polemic against the Hasidic approach, but he created a systematic doctrine that may be construed as a response to that of Hasidism. Alongside his theoretical work, at the beginning of the nineteenth
century Rabbi Hayyim founded a yeshiva (academy for advanced tal-

mudic studies) in the Lithuanian town of Volozhin, which he headed until his death in 1821. He thereby laid the foundations for the reconstruction and renewal of the institutions of Torah study in Lithuania.

It was in this milieu of Mitnaggedic Lithuanian Jewry that Rabbi Israel Salanter grew up and toward which he directed the major part of his public activity. Moreover, in the person of his teacher, Rabbi Zundel of Salant, Rabbi Israel had a direct connection with the school of the Gaon of Vilna and of Rabbi Hayyim of Volozhin—the two most important figures in shaping the image and path of Mitnaggedism. For this reason, I have chosen to devote the opening chapters of this book to a description of the teaching and path of these three personalities— the Gaon of Vilna, Rabbi Hayyim, and Rabbi Zundel—and to Rabbi Salanter's relationship with them. By this means, we shall attempt to determine whether and in what sense the teaching and activity of Rabbi Israel Salanter was a natural continuation of his Mitnaggedic roots, and in what respects they reflected elements of innovation and change that went beyond the influence of those roots.

SEVERAL chapters of this book are devoted to the description and characterization of Rabbi Israel Salanter's ethical teaching, known as the "Mussar system." This system of thought revolves around two main focii: the relationship between Torah (that is, the study of Jewish religious law, or halakhah) and *yir'ah* (the fear of God),[3] and the individual's psychological motivation in Divine service.

The problem of the relationship between Torah and *yir'ah*—that is, between the value of religious study in the intellectual-scholastic sense, and that of religio-ethical perfection—is one that appears repeatedly throughout the history of Jewish thought. The dialectical tension between these two values already appears in the classical Rabbinic tradition. On the one hand, the Sages were unsparing in their praise of the unique importance of Torah study. On the other hand, they qualified this central value by saying that the study of Torah cannot be separated from the desire for ethical perfection. This tension raises the question of the relative weight to be attached to each of these two values: whether, and in what sense, a reciprocal relation exists between the effort invested in Torah study, on the one hand, and that devoted toward ethical improvement, on the other.

In addressing these questions, Rabbi Israel Salanter expressed his own opposition to what he saw as the neglect of *yir'ah*, joining a long line of individuals and movements, including Hasidism itself, that protested against such phenomena in earlier ages. The criticism lodged by the leaders of Hasidism against the learned elite included complaints against the conspicuous gap between its accomplishments in the scholarly realm and its failures as far as fostering *yir'ah* were concerned. In reacting to the Hasidic critique, Rabbi Hayyim of Volozhin attempted to formulate an approach that would, in his view, present a balanced and proper combination of the values of Torah and *yir'ah*. Salanter, however, did not find this approach, which was extremely influential within Lithuanian Mitnaggedic Jewry, satisfactory. His call for a reevaluation of the relationship between Torah and *yir'ah* therefore expressed a challenge to the accepted view and a call for a new way.

More than any other question, that of the role of psychological motivation within religious life drew the interest and study of Rabbi Israel. While this subject is addressed in historical Mussar literature with varying degrees of attention and emphasis, the discussions devoted to it in Salanter's thought differed from that of his predecessors in two respects. First, he attributed such crucial importance to the question of motivation in human ethical improvement that, in effect, he transferred the discussion of Mussar from the theological to the psychological plane. Second, his analysis and explanations concerning this question were based upon a model of the human psyche that may be characterized as modern, within the conceptual framework and language of his time and place. Thus, in those chapters dealing with Rabbi Israel's theories regarding ethical education, I attempt to note primarily those features that are unique to this line of thinking, as against those that are characteristic of Jewish ethical literature generally. I likewise attempt to identify the source of inspiration for Salanter's new doctrine of the psyche.

Salanter did not leave a comprehensive, systematic work on ethics. His views were primarily expressed in sermons delivered in public, in letters addressed to individuals and to groups, and in some isolated published writings. The various articulations of his views concerning matters of ethical education are spread over a period of forty years. Moreover, even when he did express his views on these matters, he did not primarily function as a thinker who wished to impart a systematic body of thought. Salanter was first and foremost an educator, all of whose expressions in the realm of ethics, whether verbal or written, were intended to accomplish an educational mission within a certain specific context. All of these factors prompted me to organize the presentation of Rabbi Israel's thought chronologically, thereby enabling us to trace the developments that took place in his thinking over many years of activity. Moreover, this approach assists us in taking note of the interaction between developments on the theoretical plane and Salanter's concrete activity as leader and educator.

IN THE chapters describing Salanter's public activity, I have attempted to elucidate and to interpret this activity in terms of the circumstances of his time and place. Rabbi Israel took his first steps as a *rosh-yeshiva* (head of a yeshiva) and as a communal leader during the last fifteen years of the reign of Czar Nicholai I (1840–55). During that time, there was an intensification of the tendency of Nicholai's government to interfere in the internal life of the Jewish community in order to bring about their cultural assimilation within the general Russian population. To the earlier edict of compulsory conscription into the Russian Army and censorship of Hebrew printing houses was added, in the 1840s, the policy known as "compulsory enlightenment": that is, the attempt of the government to impose a reform upon the traditional system of Jewish education. An additional step taken by Czar Nicholai's government during those years was the order abolishing the *kahal*, the Jewish community organization. The practical consequence of that step was the drastic restriction of the authority of the communal organization.

This policy of Nicholai's government had significant implications for the balance of power within Jewish society. The scope of the Jewish communal organization's authority was severely limited, and the traditional rabbinate lost its official recognition (henceforth given over to the government-appointed "puppet rabbis," whose function was largely restricted to registering births and deaths). Simultaneously there was a distinct strengthening in the public impact of the Maskilim, the followers of the enlightenment who worked to foster cultural, economic, social, and political integration of the Jews into general society. As a result of the pattern of cooperation with the government, which came about during the course of "compulsory enlightenment," the Maskilim were transformed from a persecuted and powerless minority into a self-confident entity, capable of struggling for its approach aggressively and firmly. The traditional camp, on the other hand, was now exposed for the first time to the phenomenon of Enlightenment as a palpable threat to the tradition. These circumstances lead one to the conjecture that Rabbi Israel Salanter was motivated to found the Mussar movement, at least in part, by the wish to strengthen the tradition in light of these threats to it. Since circumstantial hypothesis is in itself inadequate to prove the point, I have attempted to determine whether evidence for this interpretation can be found within the writings and activity of Salanter from that period. I have further attempted to ascertain whether and in what sense the founding of the Mussar movement can be interpreted in relation to the economic and social problems that plagued Russian Jewry during the decade of the 1840s.

The subsequent stages of Salanter's public activity took place during the reign of Czar Alexander II (1855–81). During this period, major changes occurred in the life of Russian Jewry. The abolition of the restrictions of the "Pale of Settlement" for selected groups within the Jewish population, as well as the resultant economic opportunities for educated Jews, encouraged the enrollment of Jewish youth in gymnasia and institutions of higher learning. Thus there began to emerge a new class of Russian-Jewish intelligentsia, rooted in Russian culture by education and emotional predilections, while being alienated from the Jewish tradition. Simultaneously, a process of radicalization began in the character of the Hebrew Haskalah. The latter's critique of the traditional milieu and of the rabbinic leadership became more severe, and its demands for changes in the Jewish way of life more aggressive and far-reaching. Although these developments were characteristic of only a small percentage of the Jewish population, they represented a very significant change with regard to Jewish society in general. During the 1860s and '70s, there was a progressive weakening in the resistance of the tradition to these changes, a process that left its mark upon the majority of Russian Jewry, who continued to be loyal to the tradition. It is therefore not surprising that the struggle between those who supported various kinds of innovation and those who supported the traditional way of life was the central theme in the life of Russian Jewry during those decades.

In the face of these developments, Israel Salanter was one of the outstanding activists on behalf of the strengthening of tradition. Geographically, his activity encompassed the Jewish communities in Lithuania as well as a number of centers of Russian Jewish immigrants in Germany. It took many varied forms: he was a *rosh-yeshiva* who devoted himself to developing traditional scholars and rabbis; a thinker, guide, and educator in the realm of ethical-spiritual development; an initiator and organizer of Torah classes for artisans and university students; a publisher and editor of a religious journal; and an activist involved in various public issues, such as the struggle to establish a Western-style rabbinical seminary in Russia. All that does not exhaust the list.

In a certain sense, Salanter's public activity was a chapter in the history of the formation of Orthodoxy within Russian Jewry—the term *Orthodoxy* being used here in the sense of a traditionalist community that has become conscious of factors challenging the hegemony of the tradition, and that is prepared in the mental, ideological, and organizational sense for a struggle against these factors. By this definition, I wish to take exception to the generally accepted image of Orthodoxy, in which it is seen as a kind of fossil cut off from the processes of change and transformation taking place over the course of time. Indeed, the very act of marshaling oneself to the defense of the tradition entailed an element of innovation and change. If this is so with respect to the emergence of Orthodoxy in general, it is even more so regarding Salanter's public activity. The unique character of this activity was determined by a combination of Salanter's great sensitivity to the changes wrought by the times, his independence and nonconformity in relation to institutions and accepted forms, and his flexibility and openness, which enabled him to initiate and develop new forms in response to the challenges of the times. It is worth noting another unique feature of Rabbi Salanter's character compared with that of other Orthodox leaders in Russia: as one who had lived for several decades in Germany and had contact with the leaders of neo-Orthodoxy in that country, he was able to take a stand on issues concerning Russian Jewish society from the perspective of one who recognized the synthesis of Jewish traditionalism and modern European culture.

THE PRESENT work combines an attempt to reconstruct the biography of Rabbi Israel Salanter—as far as the scant available sources allow—with a discussion of his thinking on questions of ethical education, and a description of his public activity, which I interpret within the context of historical events. It may well be that each of these three areas deserves a monograph in its own right. However, the underlying assumption of my research is that, in seeking to understand the historical dynamic of phenomena in the cultural and social realm, it is necessary to take note of the inter-relationships of the personal, social, and ideological dimensions. It is my hope that the effort I have made in this direction has been fruitful.

PART ONE

The Theoretical Roots of Rabbi Israel Salanter's Teaching

1
The Genealogy of the Mussar Movement

IN ORDER to understand the historical background of the emergence of the Mussar movement, we must address the question of the sources from which Rabbi Israel drew within Mitnaggedic society in Lithuania, in which he was raised and educated and in whose framework he was active. As a point of departure for our discussion of this question, we shall analyze the commonly held view within the Mussar movement itself as to the sources from which it evolved.

The literature of the Mussar movement tends to place the movement's founder within a distinguished spiritual genealogy beginning with the Gaon of Vilna. Israel Salanter himself testified to his close connection to Rabbi Joseph Zundel of Salant.[1] Rabbi Zundel was in turn among the favorite students of Rabbi Hayyim of Volozhin,[2] who was known as the outstanding disciple of the Gaon of Vilna. Rabbi Isaac Blazer, a disciple of Salanter and one of the outstanding figures in the Mussar movement, describes the interrelationship of these four individuals as composing a chain in which each one transmitted to his disciple his way in matters of *"yir'ah* [fear of God] and Mussar."[3] Thus, Rabbi Israel Salanter's approach in this matter has its roots in Rabbi Zundel, while the latter received it from Rabbi Hayyim. While the Gaon is not explicitly mentioned in this passage, for Blazer the Gaon's authority and personality radiate over the entire chain, the powerful connection of Rabbi Hayyim of Volozhin to the Gaon being so well known as to require no proof or mention. Nevertheless, Blazer elsewhere mentions the Gaon's relationship to this chain, citing various statements in his name in praise of the study of Mussar.[4]

Several later authors followed in the wake of the disciples of Salanter, the outstanding example being Rabbi Dov Katz. In his book *Tenu'at ha-mussar* [*The Mussar Movement*, 1945], Katz unhesitatingly

13

accepts the claim set forth for the "pedigree" of the movement; moreover, he explicitly includes the Gaon within the genealogical chain. However, he does not claim to present to the reader a systematic, comprehensive analysis of the position of Rabbi Hayyim and of the Gaon with regard to the proper relationship between Torah and *yir'ah*, or of the nature of *yir'ah* and the manner in which it is acquired. Instead, he is satisfied with some fragmentary quotations from which it follows that, in his opinion, "the Gaon behaved in accordance with the system of the Mussar movement" and that "also in his earliest and closest disciple, Rabbi Hayyim of Volozhin . . . we find the same system."[5]

In the course of his discussion, however, Rabbi Katz somewhat qualifies his initial remarks, drawing a distinction between the Mussar "system" and "movement." While the system per se was received by Rabbi Israel from the Gaon of Vilna, via Rabbi Hayyim and Rabbi Zundel, "Rabbi Israel was the one who established the movement. He took the Mussar system out of books and brought it into life." Katz concludes in an additional qualifying remark: "Rabbi Israel also expanded the Mussar system . . . he paved new paths for it, in accordance with the soul of the generation, and the conditions of that place and time. . . ."[6]

A severe criticism of this claim for the pedigree of the Mussar movement, as expressed in the remarks of Rabbis Isaac Blazer and Dov Katz, is made by Norman Lamm in his study of the thought of Rabbi Hayyim Volozhin, *Torah li-shemah*.[7] Following a detailed discussion of R. Hayyim's position regarding the study of Mussar books,[8] Lamm writes:

> On the basis of the above, exception must be taken to the efforts of some of the leading figures of the *Mussar* movement in the nineteenth century, followed by some contemporary historians of the movement, to identify Rabbi Hayyim as one of the forefathers of *Mussar*. The search for distinguished antecedents is an expected and respected part of any new impulse and changing perspective within the Jewish tradition . . . [however] the evidence for the theory of the Gaon as the founder or even a precursor of the ethicist movement is meager indeed. Dov Katz briefly points to the fact that the Gaon recommended meditation in devotional works. . . . But this hardly makes the Gaon a *Mussarite*; . . . such stray remarks are totally inadequate to identify him as the originator or architect of the *Mussar* movement, still three generations away.[9]

Further on, Lamm concentrates upon disproving the arguments proposed by Rabbis Isaac Blazer and Dov Katz concerning the role played by Hayyim of Volozhin in the lineage of the Mussar movement. In principle, Lamm argues, these two read the writings of Rabbi Hayyim in a tendentious and partisan manner, relying upon fragmentary and selective quotations taken out of context. Lamm argues that while Isaac Blazer and Dov Katz try to create the impression that Rabbi Hayyim supported study in the spirit of the Mussar movement, the overall impression gained from Rabbi Hayyim's writings is the definite tendency to limit the study of ethical texts.[10]

Lamm's observation that the pride taken by the Mussar movement in the lineage headed by the Gaon and Rabbi Hayyim is motivated by the wish and need to find a distinguished precedent for the Mussar system seems correct. Further, as to his remark that this tendency is characteristic of every new stream within a traditional society, we should note the particular circumstances under which this rule applied to the Mussar movement. One must remember that several of the leading figures of his generation took exception to Rabbi Israel's activity during its earliest stages. Moreover, what began as reservations about the path of the Mussar movement became, during the latter half of the 1890s, a severe struggle that agitated the Jewish public in Russia.[11] *Sefer or yisra'el*, the classical book of the Mussar movement in which the above claim for the pedigree of the movement is formulated by Salanter's disciples, was published by Rabbi Isaac Blazer in 1900. There is reason to assume that, both in the timing of its publication and in its contents, this book was intended to counter the attacks that were then issued in public against the Mussar movement.[12] Thus, the claim of Salanter's disciples concerning the sources for his system was part of a more comprehensive apologetic attempt aimed at legitimizing the Mussar movement in the eyes of Mitnaggedic Orthodoxy.

Lamm's argument against the tendentious interpretation given by Salanter's followers and by Dov Katz to Hayyim Volozhin's position regarding the study of Mussar literature is similarly justified. Critical comparison of the respective stances of Rabbi Hayyim and of Salanter concerning this question indicates a significant gap between the two. But even if they agree with Lamm's critique, historians cannot be content with this. From the standpoint of historical research, the problem is not just whether there is an identity between the Mussar system of Salanter and the beliefs of the Gaon and of Hayyim Volozhin. No less important is the question of whether, and to what extent, the thought and activity of these personalities prepared the ground for Israel Salanter's lifework. In other words, can one find the historical roots of the Mussar movement in processes and tendencies operating in Mitnaggedic society during the first half of the nineteenth century? Neither Dov Katz nor Norman Lamm poses a question in this spirit. The former adhered to the rather naive reading of the Mussar movement, to the point of representing the continuity among these different personalities as unidimensional and simplistic; Lamm is satisfied with a theoretical, almost "technical" comparison, of the positions of Rabbi Hayyim, on the one hand, and of Salanter, on the other, denying the identity between the two. The common denominator of both is that neither of them paid attention to the dynamic, and in a certain sense even dialectical, character of the historical process.[13]

In the following chapters, I examine the views of the Gaon of Vilna, of Rabbi Hayyim of Volozhin, and of Rabbi Zundel of Salant regarding the nature of *yir'ah*, the means by which it is acquired, and the desired relationship between it and the study of Torah. On that basis, we shall be able to critically weigh the claim for a relationship connecting the work of Rabbi Israel Salanter with this sequence of persona. Furthermore, in examining the teaching and activity of the Gaon and of Rabbi Hayyim, both of whom played a decisive role in forming the spiritual image of nineteenth century Lithuanian Jewry, we shall be able to note not only the sources of Rabbi Salanter's inspiration within Mitnaggedic society, but also the tendencies toward transformation and change that characterized his own work within the framework of the forms and values of this society.

2
The Fear of God in the Thought of Rabbi Elijah of Vilna

THE "GAON" —Rabbi Elijah ben Solomon of Vilna (1720–97)—did not leave in his writings a systematic doctrine concerning *yir'ah*, its acquisition, and the appropriate balance between it and the study of Torah.[1] He makes, however, fragmentary reference to these topics in his commentaries to the Bible and to kabbalistic works, as well as in the ethical will that he left to his family, and in oral remarks recorded in his name and in the name of his disciples. In addition to his explicit statements on these matters, the Gaon's heritage in this area was embodied in the example he set by his way of life, as it was understood and described by his disciples. In this chapter, I attempt to reconstruct the Gaon's views on these subjects, insofar as it is possible to do so from the available sources.

The Nature of *Yir'ah* and the Mode of Its Acquisition

The unique position of authority enjoyed by the Gaon was not based solely upon his accomplishments as a scholar, but rested upon the combination of these attainments with his embodiment of piety and asceticism. That is to say: the personality and way of life of the Gaon were understood as the ideal expression of the combined values of Torah and *yir'ah*. His contemporaries' awareness of that combination is reflected in the pair of titles by which they habitually referred to him: *ha-Gaon he-Hasid*, the term *gaon* being used to refer to an individual of unusual attainments in Torah learning, while *hasid* refers to his extraordinary religio-ethical qualities.[2]

While the Gaon's scholarship was depicted by his contemporaries and by those who followed him as striking both in its breadth and profundity, his greatness in Torah was not only the product of a genius intellect and an extraordinary memory. No less important were his constant effort and persistence in the pursuit of learning.[3] The Gaon's way of life, as portrayed by his sons and his students, was characterized by the maximum channeling of the powers of body and soul to one, exclusive goal: the study of the Torah. In practice, the Gaon understood absolute devotion to Torah study as one side of the coin; the other side was the value of asceticism and withdrawal from society as a guiding principle and way of life.

In stressing the value of asceticism in the service of God, the Gaon followed in the path of ethical teachers of previous generations; however, the Gaon's uniqueness can be seen in his understanding of the purpose of this withdrawal. Unlike his predecessors, who saw asceticism as freeing the soul for complete devotion to love of God,[4] the Gaon saw the main significance of asceticism in its channeling of the majority of an individual's physical and spiritual resources toward the purpose of Torah study. He therefore particularly stressed the value of separation from the society of other people, as social contact brings in its wake the loss of time from Torah study, while isolation from society assists in constancy of study.[5] One may therefore say that the Gaon adopted the ideal of asceticism as it was formulated in Mussar literature, and particularly in kabbalistic Mussar, except that its purpose is redirected: The contemplative act, whose goal is the attainment of attachment to God, is supplanted by the study of Torah.

The ideal of separation from the life of this world for the sake of Torah study reflects an outlook that denies all autonomous value to things of this world or to worldly activity. To this was added the quality of *bitahon*—trust in God—which relied upon the fatalistic assumption that "all of a person's sustenance is fixed from Rosh Hashanah . . ."[6] and that human effort within the economic realm is thus to no avail.[7] However, the realization of this philosophy in practical life constitutes a difficult test, requiring one to ignore the hardships of the members of one's own family. It is therefore not surprising that, when he comes to describe a sublime quality in Divine service, the Gaon combines withdrawal for the sake of Torah study with the quality of trust in God:

> "And men of valour"—these are the strong-hearted ones of perfect trust, who constantly perform the mitzvot and engage in Torah day and night, even though in his house there is neither bread nor raiment, and his children and the members of his household cry out to him, "Bring us sustenance to keep [us] alive and to sustain us." But he does not heed them at all and does not fear their voice . . . for all of his loves are abnegated in the face of love of God and His Torah and commandments. . . .[8]

Even though the Gaon saw as the principal value of asceticism its freeing one's time and energy for the study of Torah, he also attached great importance to it as a protection against the Evil Impulse. The Gaon believed that contact with the world, and particularly social contact, is filled with temptations and obstacles. Asceticism is therefore a secure shelter for those who tend to be tempted by their desires.[9] Moreover, it may serve as a preventive measure for any person who does not wish to undergo difficult trials. In the spirit of this outlook, the Gaon advised the members of his family to minimize their own social contacts as far as possible—even when these are for the sake of a good deed.[10]

More than anything else, the Gaon's commitment to the ideal of asceticism for the sake of Torah study was expressed in his own way of life. The Gaon's separation from society, as it is described in the testimony of his students, is striking in its strict and uncompromising character. During his youth, he studied Torah in isolation. After he married, he went into self-imposed exile, during the course of which he wandered about the communities of Prussia.[11] During this period, the Gaon was also accustomed to engage in ascetic practices, although over the course of time he refrained from outright self-affliction, because those who engage in self-mortification are unable to properly fulfill their obligations with regard to Divine service. There was likewise a fear that excessive self-affliction may violate the Torah's commandment to "take heed of your selves" (that is, one's physical health). Nevertheless, the Gaon justified his youthful self-affliction with the claim that he was then sufficiently strong so as not to fall into these dangers.[12]

Upon return to his city and his home following the period of exile, the Gaon continued to maintain his practice of withdrawal from the world. Almost to the point of total isolation, he avoided any contact with anything outside the parameters of halakhah. Even if we admit a certain degree of exaggeration in the hagiographic descriptions that have come down to us concerning the Gaon, who shut himself off from the entire world beyond the sealed shutters of his study room,[13] there is no reason to doubt that these descriptions do, in principle, reflect the truth. The strictness with which the Gaon limited his contact with other people is also reflected in the small number of his disciples. Only a few were privileged to spend time in his presence and to be counted among those "who saw his face."[14] The Gaon's asceticism seems to have reached its peak in his relations with his family. He suppressed his natural feelings toward his offspring, refrained from interesting himself in the situation of their livelihood, and spent very little time in their presence.[15]

Insofar as we can tell, the Gaon approved of and encouraged the

desire of some of his disciples to withdraw from the world, instruct-
ing them that those who wish to separate themselves ought not to
worry about being perceived by others as arrogant or vain—"for today
the prohibition against such vanity does not apply; on the contrary, it
is preferable that it be well known." Moreover, "one who wishes to
separate himself from the world shall cry out in the marketplace that
he wishes to separate himself and to be a righteous person, for without
this he cannot free himself of them [that is, his corporeal appe-
tites]. . . ."[16] The public proclamation is thus seen as aiding those who
seek to separate themselves from the world to overcome the attraction
toward earthly pleasures—probably because social pressure constitutes
a powerful motivating factor upon the individual. When Rabbi Joel of
Amzislaw approached him to request guidance in acquiring this attribute, the Gaon answered, "If he is stubborn, he will succeed."[17] In the
wake of these guidelines are two reservations: "One should not exag-
gerate in one's withdrawal, that one seem separated from the world;
the essential thing is that it be for the sake of heaven."[18] Also, it is
doubtful whether the Gaon intended withdrawal from the world as a
path for the multitude; however, it seems that he related positively to
the adoption of an isolated way of life by those whose main activity
was the study of Torah.[19]

The Gaon's piety was also expressed in the meticulous manner in
which he performed the mitzvot. His path in this respect was marked
by uncompromising obedience to the demands of the halakhah. He
invested great effort in fulfilling mitzvot, even under extremely difficult
circumstances, even laws that it had become customary to neglect. The
uniqueness of the Gaon in this area seems to have lain in reviving
forgotten laws and correcting mistaken customs, even if these errors
were already widespread in Jewish communities. According to one of
his disciples, the Gaon objected to the title *hasid*, which many people
attached to him, arguing that:

> . . . the term *hasid* only refers to one who does kindness with
> his Creator, and goes beyond the letter of the law incumbent
> upon him according to the Sages. But one who does not deviate
> from [performing] anything explicated in the Talmud and in the
> four sections of the *Shulhan 'Arukh* is not to be described as a
> *hasid*, but simply as a proper Jew. . . .[20]

One might say, then, on his own terms, that the Gaon's piety did
not express itself in going over and beyond the law, but in his effort to
realize the halakhah in life in the maximal manner, on the basis of its
primary sources. The Gaon's piety in the realm of observance of the
commandments was therefore connected with and dependent upon his
unusual intellectual attainments and his authority as a scholar.

The Gaon ascribed considerable importance to the perfection of one's ethical attributes. This is expressed in his relation to the schema in which the worship of God is based upon three pillars: Torah, mitzvot, and *middot* (traits of personality expressed in one's ethical behavior).[21] The unique importance of proper character traits, and their advantage over Torah and mitzvot, were seen by the Gaon as forming a first line of defense against sin. While study of Torah and performance of mitzvot likewise protect one against the Evil Impulse, the influence of the *middot* in this respect is far more comprehensive and profound, because proper character traits "teach man the path by which he is to walk. . . ."[22] In other words, as these qualities are rooted in the soul, the proper traits dictate forms of behavior that remove human beings from the realm of sin. The Gaon noted that the converse is likewise true: Those who neglect the improvement of their ethical qualities will not be aided by the "restrictions" and "fences" they impose upon themselves in order to subdue their appetites. Even the "fence" that they have built around themselves by study of Torah is thereby destroyed and is unable to save them from sin.[23] Another expression of the importance of character improvement in the Gaon's view is found in his statement that only those who have purified and refined their *middot* may merit the revelation of the secrets of Torah in the course of their study.[24]

The great weight attached by the Gaon to character improvement would seem to be based, among other things, upon his understanding of the place of the *middot* within the soul. Following in the wake of kabbalistic Mussar literature, the Gaon drew a distinction between the intellective soul and the vital or animative soul. The body serves as a garment—that is, as a wrapping or receptacle—for the vital soul, which is in turn a garment for the intellective soul. The character traits are located within the vital soul, which is closer to the body, and therefore determine the forms of behavior relating to bodily appetites.[25]

The correction of character was understood by the Gaon as a fierce struggle, involving self-control and restraint:

> For the wicked person himself knows that his path is bitter and evil, but it is difficult for him to separate [from it]. And this is all of man's purpose [in life]: that he not be left to [satisfy] his own desire, but to be constrained in with bridle and bit [cf. Ps. 32:9], and until his dying day man must chastise himself, not by fasts and self-afflictions, but by restraining his mouth and his appetites. . . .[26]

The Gaon points here to the tension between consciousness, which distinguishes between good and evil, and the appetite, which is rooted in the wicked attributes. The imposition of moral-religious judgment upon the appetites is a process in which people are liable to be engaged

their entire life, entailing much suffering of the soul. The Gaon understood the *middot* as a dualistic system: every good attribute has an evil
attribute, which is its counterpart and opposite.[27] The improvement of
character therefore involves two aspects: the acquisition of good attributes and the breaking of evil ones. Following the dominant outlook
in ethical literature, the Gaon suggests habit as an important tool for
correcting one's personal traits: ". . . for character requires habituation,
and habit rules all things, and all beginnings are difficult."[28] Thus, the
primary difficulty is encountered in the initial stage of the process of
character improvement, so that the more consistent a person is in
behaving in an ethical way, the more deeply rooted, and therefore
easier, such behavior becomes. The strict and punctilious observance of
the commandments was seen by the Gaon as the practical method of
acquiring good qualities by means of habit. Repetition and persistence
in the performance of mitzvot implant positive traits in the soul. The
opposite is also true: contempt for the mitzvot strengthens bad qualities
within oneself.[29] There is thus a relation of mutuality between the
commandments and the character: On the one hand, the character
guarantees that a person will be able to fulfill the commandments even
when under pressure from the temptation of the appetites; on the other
hand, good traits are themselves acquired by punctiliousness and con-
sistency in the fulfillment of the mitzvot.

The eradication of bad characteristics is seen by the Gaon as a
gradual and continual process:

> For a man who wishes to break his appetites cannot jump
> immediately to seize the opposite extreme and the contrary to
> what he had been accustomed, but must gradually separate
> himself until he reaches the opposite extreme; and then he
> should break his appetite until he stands on the correct
> path. . . .[30]

It is illuminating in this context to note the distinction drawn by the
Gaon between the positive and negative aspect of character improvement:

> . . . In order to walk in the ways of God, one must take counsel
> with wise and righteous men who already walk in God's way
> and have not stumbled upon the obstacle, which is the Evil
> Impulse. For in order to wage war against the Evil Impulse, one
> must oneself exercise cunning, and counsel alone does not help
> in this matter without cunning.[31]

Thus, with regard to the adoption of positive behavioral patterns,
the advice of "wise and righteous men" is useful—for these are the

people whose behavior is to be imitated. However, their advice alone is insufficient to save the person who is struggling with the Evil Impulse. We, as individuals, stand alone in this battle, and it is incumbent upon us to find the appropriate "cunning" or "tricks" to fit our own personal circumstances.

An important aid in the battle to conquer and restrain the appetites was found by the Gaon in the study of words of rebuke and Mussar.[32] Included in a pamphlet describing the daily routine and customs of the Gaon is the directive: "Mussar books several times every day."[33] In the ethical will that he left to his family, the Gaon advised study of Mussar works and likewise instructed them to read regularly the biblical books of Proverbs and Ecclesiastes and the talmudic tractates *Avot* and *Avot de-Rabbi Nathan*. Writing of the value of the Book of Ecclesiastes, the Gaon states, "It makes vain all things of this world. . . ."[34] The vanity of this world is evidently one of the most important lessons to be drawn from the study of Mussar works as well, but it is not enough. The Gaon warned against the study of Mussar books whose purpose was solely "[the act of] reading, for from this alone a man does not become [spiritually] aroused, for many people read Mussar works and do not become aroused. . . ."[35] The experience of "arousal" (*hitpa'alut*) which the Gaon considered the main benefit of the study of Mussar works, evidently refers to the combination of emotional excitement with feelings of regret and purification, that has the power to motivate individuals to change their behavior. (We shall see below that the study of Mussar works "with arousal" was to play an important role in the system of Rabbi Israel Salanter.) The Gaon, however, qualifies the value of the study of Mussar books, making its power dependent upon separation from society. Those who gain the sense of spiritual arousal from the study of Mussar books, but do not restrict their contact with other people, are like one who "sows without plowing, for the wind will scatter [the seeds] and feed them to the chickens . . . and this is because he is unable to restrain and limit himself. . . ."[36] We therefore find that, while Mussar works can awaken the psychological motivation that is helpful in the process of restraining the lusts, separation from society continues to serve as a bastion, without which the positive influence of Mussar works has no lasting result.

The Relationship between Torah and *Yir'ah*

In our discussion thus far, we have seen how the values of Torah and *yir'ah* were intermingled in the approach and way of life of the Gaon. Asceticism, which expressed negation of the value of worldliness and simultaneously constituted a protection against the enticements of the Evil Impulse, is primarily intended to free the major part of a person's time and energy for the study of Torah. At the same time, the Gaon's quality of *yir'ah* was likewise expressed in the strict observance of the mitzvot and in the correction of his character traits. We may now ask the following questions: What did the Gaon understand as the proper balance between Torah and *yir'ah*? Does the study of Torah in itself constitute a means of religio-ethical elevation? Are the study of Torah and the cultivation of *yir'ah* interdependent, and— if so—to what extent?

In the Gaon's commentaries on the Bible, and in those sayings attributed to him by his disciples, one finds a decided tendency to give the study of Torah preference both over the performance of mitzvot and over the battle with the Evil Impulse and the improvement of one's character traits. He expressed the superiority of Torah study over the mitzvot by means of an analogy:

> . . . The Torah is like bread, upon which man's heart feeds . . . and it is needed constantly, like bread; therefore, "You shall meditate upon them day and night" [cf. Josh. 1:8]. But the mitzvot are like a confection, which is good periodically and in the proper time, like a confection which one eats from time to time. . . .[37]

A more extreme assertion of the superiority of Torah study over the performance of mitzvot is expressed in the formulation that every word a person learns is as valuable as all the mitzvot together.[38] A translation of this approach into practical terms may be found in the statement quoted by Rabbi Hayyim of Volozhin in the name of the Gaon: "Our teacher said that it is not good to pursue the mitzvot, and he said in the name of the Gaon that it is better to walk about one's private study room with folded hands than to go to the market-place seeking a mitzvah."[39]

In addition to the primacy he gave Torah study over the pursuit of mitzvot, the Gaon thought that study constitutes an important defense against the Evil Impulse. In this spirit he interpreted the words of the Mishnah, "Turn it over and turn it over, for everything is in it" (Avot 5:22): "That is to say, through the Torah he will merit all of the acts . . . as it is known, that when a person studies Torah in his youth, then the 'Evil Impulse' cannot have hold over him thereafter. . . ."[40]

The relationship between Torah and *yir'ah* was also expressed by the Gaon in a homily: ". . . If there is no wisdom, even though there is fear of God, this is nothing, for the fear of God in itself is nothing

. . . but a storehouse for wisdom, as is said [Isa. 33:6], 'The fear of God is his treasure-house.' "[41] From the image of the fear of God as a storehouse, whose purpose is to preserve wisdom, it follows that *yir'ah* in and of itself is worthless when not combined with the study of Torah. Moreover, "the fear of God comes from the Torah, and if he does not study, he will not have fear of God."[42]

Alongside these expressions indicating the superiority of the study of Torah, and that study is itself an important means of acquiring fear of God, one finds in the Gaon's writings other statements that reverse the dynamic, making Torah study dependent upon the relationship to *yir'ah*. For example, we read in the following that when study is motivated by the fear of God, it brings about a qualitative superiority in the nature of the study itself:

> . . . If a person has the fear of God, he will learn [in order to] know . . . from what [acts] to guard himself. And it is the nature of man that, when he desires a certain thing and finds it, it is precious to him and he guards it. But if he does not have the fear of God, and does not fear sin, even though he repeats it several times, he will not find it, for he does not study in order to know what to take care of. . . .[43]

A more far-reaching expression of the dependence of study upon *yir'ah* is implied in the statement that the influence of the study of Torah upon a person's soul may even be negative, for study "irrigates" the soul and strengthens all of its powers, including the negative ones. Therefore, the Gaon states that both before and after the act of study one must learn "to expunge the refuse from [within] oneself, by [means of] fear of God and good deeds. . . ."[44] Finally, one should again mention the Gaon's comments concerning the value of character improvement: They who do not bother to improve their character will find that even the fence that they have built around themselves through the study of Torah is destroyed, and cannot save them from sin.

This rendering of the value of Torah study conditional upon the relation to *yir'ah* found expression in an additional area—namely, the demand that study be *li-shemah* (for its own sake); that is, the value of Torah study is dependent upon the psycho-spiritual motivation of the student. The importance of Torah study "for its own sake" had been universally accepted since the time of classical Rabbinism: The uniqueness of the Gaon's position is in the severity with which he relates to those who study for other motivations—that is, not "for its own sake." Various halakhic scholars addressed this problem in their attempts to resolve the contradiction between the strict statements made by the

Rabbis in condemnation of learning for some ulterior purpose—for example, "For whomever engages in Torah not for its own sake, it becomes a deathly poison" (Ta'anit 7a)—as opposed to such well-known sayings expressive of a more tolerant view as, "Let a man always engage in Torah and commandments even not for their own sake, for [as a result of] doing them not for their own sake, he will come to do them for their own sake" (Pesahim 50b). Both Rashi and the Tosafists resolved this contradiction by drawing a distinction between two different kinds of ulterior motivation: legitimate ones, such as the wish to be called "rabbi" or to be honored by others, and those that are totally rejected, such as one who studies for self-aggrandizement.[45]

The Gaon's strict position offers a striking contrast to those of Rashi and the Tosafists: ". . . There is a person who studies in order to enjoy the learning or in order to be called Rabbi, and this is a very bad lot. . . ."[46] He gives two reasons for his condemnation of those who study in order to achieve honor: first, that such study is marred by the very fact of the improper motivation that underlies it, and second, such study may be described as "love which is dependent upon something else" (compare Avot 5:16)—that is, it is unreliable; because of its dependence upon some extraneous factor, a change in outer circumstances is liable to lead to its abnegation—in this case, the cessation of Torah study. Whether for these or additional reasons, the Gaon does not mince words in his condemnation of those students who wish to acquire honor and social prestige by means of their scholarship.[47] He interpreted the talmudic justification for the study of Torah for ulterior reasons—that is, "that as a result of doing so not for its own sake he will come to do it for its sake"—as referring to one who studies, not because of any concrete ulterior purpose, but simply because of a certain upbringing—but certainly not as referring to one who studies in order to receive honor.[48] The extent to which the Gaon objected to study motivated by extraneous factors may be seen from his directive that a small amount of Torah without interests is preferable to quantitatively superior study that is improperly motivated.[49]

We may summarize by saying that, both in terms of their specific value and in terms of the energies to be devoted to each one of them, the Gaon gave decisive preference to study of Torah over the pursuit of mitzvot and the cultivation of *yir'ah*, at the same time making the value of Torah conditional upon a strong relationship to *yir'ah*. Just as *yir'ah* without Torah is an empty vessel, so is it impossible to imagine study of Torah without *yir'ah*; the two are interconnected in a relation of dependence and mutual fructification. The ideal is thus a combination of Torah with *yir'ah*, wherein the primary effort is focused upon

Torah study, with *yir'ah* constituting both a means toward study and a consequence thereof.

The Kabbalistic Element

The place of Kabbalah in the inner world of the Gaon, like that of the Gaon in the history of Kabbalah, has not yet been examined by historical scholarship; nevertheless, there can be no doubt concerning the great importance of Jewish esoteric teaching in his life. He himself thought that he had achieved unusual attainments in this area,[50] considering himself among those few individuals who properly understood the teaching of Rabbi Isaac Luria.[51] In fact, the acknowledgment of the Gaon's greatness as a Kabbalist was among the more important components of his public image and one of the foundations of his charismatic authority.

A portrait of the Gaon as a Kabbalist was given by his disciple, Rabbi Hayyim of Volozhin, in his introduction to the former's commentary on *Sifra de-zeni'uta*. Rabbi Hayyim there described the Gaon as one who was sent by Divine Providence to illuminate the secrets of Kabbalah to his generation.

According to Rabbi Hayyim, the Gaon differed from other scholars in that he understood how the details of kabbalistic teaching, as these are explicated in the later and more fully revealed levels, are alluded to in the earlier and more obscure levels. Further on, Rabbi Hayyim notes the structural resemblance between the Gaon's method in his interpretation of mystical books and that of his well-known glosses to the *Shulhan 'arukh*—that is, the attempt to discover the roots of later halakhic ruling in its earlier sources in Rabbinic literature. Moreover, just as in the realm of halakhah the Gaon corrected numerous corruptions in the text, so did he do in kabbalistic works.

Rabbi Hayyim's testimony regarding the Gaon's method in his kabbalistic study cannot serve as a substitute for critical study of the Gaon's writings in this field; nevertheless, it seems reasonable to assume that the characterization given by Rabbi Hayyim was not only based upon his own impression, gleaned from a reading of the Gaon's works, but upon what he heard from the Gaon's own mouth. Thus, on the basis of both Rabbi Hayyim's testimony and that of an examination of the Gaon's kabbalistic writings—if not on the basis of a disciplined scientific study thereof—one may state that the most salient feature of his involvement in Kabbalah was not the desire to receive further mystical revelations, but the wish to uncover the thread of inner connections within the kabbalistic teaching, as these had been revealed and formulated earlier. The activity thus bore more of an intellectual character than that of contemplation leading to a mystical vision.

Rabbi Hayyim's testimony concerning the various revelations enjoyed by the Gaon has been widely publicized. However, the Gaon firmly rejected these very angelic guides (*maggidim*) who wished to reveal "the secrets of Torah" to him "without any labor." The revelations sought by the Gaon were only those that a person may receive as the fruit of intellectual labor, and not as a result of bypassing it. To quote the formulation of H. H. Ben-Sasson, in his illuminating analysis, "the intellect must dominate, because only by that which he learned through his own labor did Rabbi Elijah feel that God spoke to him 'from His mouth' [that is, directly] and not by means of an intermediary."[52]

It should therefore not be surprising that, both in the testimony of Rabbi Hayyim of Volozhin as well as in other sources describing the Gaon's activity as a Kabbalist, we do not find the longing for mystical attachment to God. It would seem that the Gaon saw the essence of a person's attachment to God precisely in constant devotion to the study of Torah for its own sake. That was quite different from the *devekut* (attachment to God) for which kabbalistic Mussar literature wished to prepare people, and which the Gaon's Hasidic contemporaries placed in the forefront of their own interest.

We now summarize the conclusions to be drawn from our discussion. Certainly, the Gaon's own outlook concerning the subject of *yir'ah* was influenced by his deep relation to Kabbalah. This fact was expressed in several ways: in the understanding of the components of the soul and the manner of its functioning; in the understanding of the Evil Impulse as the agent of forces in the demonic realm (*Sitra ahra*); in the assumption concerning the influence of human acts upon upper realms, and consequently the metaphysical significance of the act of mitzvah, on the one hand, and of transgression, on the other; and, finally, in the emphasis upon the value of asceticism and withdrawal from society, while denying the values of this world. All of these points correspond to the dominant tendencies of kabbalistic Mussar literature. One ought to note two reservations concerning the relationship of the Gaon to the world of Kabbalah. First, his guidelines in the realms of *yir'ah* and Mussar do not constitute a doctrine of kabbalistic Mussar similar to that found in kabbalistic Mussar literature—that is, an ethical teaching whose primary goal is to prepare human beings for the mystical experience of attachment to God. Second, even though the Gaon's expressions concerning matters of *yir'ah* include a not-insignificant number of allusions to the realm of Kabbalah, in the final analysis he preferred to formulate his ethical instructions in more conventional terms. In that respect, he remained loyal to the principle that one is not to reveal to the public those teachings that are appropriate only to the select few, who are on a higher spiritual level. It is quite interesting that Rabbi Hayyim Volozhin was to depart from the path established by his master in both these matters, not because he wished to deviate from the legacy of the Gaon, but precisely because he wished to defend it and fortify it under new and different circumstances.

3

Torah and the Fear of God in the Thought of Rabbi Hayyim of Volozhin

RABBI Hayyim of Volozhin (1749–1821)[1] was considered by his contemporaries to be the first and foremost disciple of the Gaon of Vilna, and heir to his mantle as unofficial leader of Lithuanian Jewry.[2] His fame is primarily associated with the yeshiva of Volozhin, which he founded at the beginning of the nineteenth century and which he headed for twenty years.

Rabbi Hayyim's Thought as a Reaction to Hasidism

Unlike his teacher, Rabbi Hayyim developed a systematic and detailed doctrine with regard to the method of Divine service. In his major work, *Nefesh ha-hayyim*,[3] he discussed at length such questions as the role of Torah study, the proper balance between the study of Torah and the cultivation of *yir'ah* and the means of integrating the two, the relationship between intention and deed, and other problems. The impulse toward formulating a systematic and comprehensive doctrine on these subjects was rooted in the confrontation between Mitnaggedic society and Hasidism in the late eighteenth and early nineteenth centuries.[4] At first glance, this statement seems surprising: the Gaon likewise participated in this confrontation, and in fact led the Mitnaggedic camp. Why then was it left to Rabbi Hayyim to formulate the response to Hasidism through the creation of a system of thought?[5] This could be explained by noting that the literary expression of the Gaon's thought was primarily of a homiletical, exegetical character; however, the difference between the reactions to Hasidism of the Gaon and of Rabbi Hayyim was in fact rooted in factors that go beyond mere differences in style of written expression. Fundamentally, despite the

deep admiration in which Rabbi Hayyim held the Gaon and the closeness between master and disciple, Hasidism had a different meaning
within the spiritual world of the Gaon and that of Rabbi Hayyim.[6] In
the Gaon's view, Hasidism was an heretical sect that had gone outside
the proper bounds of Judaism and shaken the very foundations of the
tradition; therefore, all possible means of destroying and uprooting it
available to the communal organization were permissible.[7] The Gaon
certainly did not see Hasidism as a suitable partner in ideological debate.
Heretics are to be "brought down,"[8] not legitimated through distance.
The Gaon was adamant in his refusal to receive delegations from the
Hasidic camp, who besieged him with requests to meet him in order to
explain and defend their path.[9]

Rabbi Hayyim of Volozhin, by contrast, saw Hasidism as a mis-
guided and unsuccessful attempt to attain certain goals that were in
themselves worthwhile. In other words, while Rabbi Hayyim saw the
methods and practices introduced by Hasidism as being fundamentally
mistaken, so that the damage they caused was greater than the benefit,
he believed that the motivations of Hasidism were pure and that their
deepest longing was "closeness to God."[10] Rabbi Hayyim's reaction to
Hasidism may be understood in terms of this evaluation: instead of the
series of condemnations and curses that typified the writings of the
Mitnaggedim in general, we find in Rabbi Hayyim's work a polemic
essentially moderate and restrained in style, though powerful and profound in its contents. Rather than addressing himself to external manifestations and hurling ungrounded accusations, Rabbi Hayyim exposed
what seemed to him to be the fundamental weaknesses in the Hasidic
system, in a manner revealing familiarity with and understanding of
their teachings.[11] Moreover, in his book *Nefesh ha-hayyim*, going beyond
mere polemic, Rabbi Hayyim presented a comprehensive system of
religious thought clearly intended as a response or counterweight to
the Hasidic path.

The question naturally arises: What caused this striking gap between revered teacher and devoted disciple, both in terms of their
evaluation of the nature of Hasidism and their choice of the response
to be taken toward it? One could of course attempt to explain it in
psychological terms. Such is the approach taken by Norman Lamm,
who argues that Rabbi Hayyim's stance toward Hasidism was rooted
in his fundamentally moderate character.[12] One might add that, in
contrast, the Gaon was noted for his stubbornness and fanatical devotion to his understanding of truth. One might also suggest an explanation rooted in the respective ways of life of the two. The Gaon, who
lived as a recluse, presumably derived most of his information con-

cerning Hasidism from secondary or tertiary sources—that is, from what he was told or written by his intimates.[13] Rabbi Hayyim, on the other hand, who was more involved in direct contact with others, had far greater opportunity to become acquainted with Hasidism firsthand, and at close quarters. It therefore seems likely that doubts and fears that shaped the Gaon's position regarding Hasidism were shattered by Rabbi Hayyim's unmediated acquaintance with the reality.[14]

While the above explanations, based upon the personality and way of life of these two figures, are richly suggestive, I consider them to be conjectural. In my opinion, a more solidly grounded explanation is one based upon the historical background and context. The Gaon's position with respect to Hasidism took shape in the early 1770s, when that movement had just taken its first public steps in Lithuania and White Russia. At this stage, one might still imagine that, given a firm and energetic battle, the spread of the sect could be halted or even uprooted altogether. Rabbi Hayyim's reaction, on the other hand, was formulated at the beginning of the nineteenth century. By that point, the balance of forces was entirely different: the attempt to suppress Hasidism had failed, and the new movement had even broadened and deepened its position within the public. Moreover, even individuals from within the circles of the *lomdim* (the learned)—particularly among the younger generation—were attracted by the Hasidic path.[15] Thus, over the course of time, the persecuted and excommunicated sect had been transformed into a movement that challenged the future of Mitnaggedic society. Rabbi Hayyim formulated his own reaction in light of these circumstances, and based as well upon a more knowledgable, clearer reading of the spiritual power inherent within Hasidism. He correctly understood that the influence of this movement could not be stopped by bans and condemnations, and instead chose the path of intense and profound ideological confrontation.

Another possible explanation combines the historical-chronological with the personal dimension. When the Gaon first encountered Hasidism, his was a fully developed ideological and spiritual personality. That was not the case for Rabbi Hayyim, who was still only in his early twenties when the great polemics concerning Hasidism of the 1770s erupted. In effect, the same metamorphosis described by Rabbi Hayyim[16] in the lives of those youths who were numbered among the students at the yeshivot and became caught up in the waves of influence of Hasidism, occurred to Rabbi Hayyim's own contemporaries. It would not be unreasonable to assume that Rabbi Hayyim, as a young man during the period of the great expansion of Hasidism, himself gave serious thought to the nature of this new doctrine, appreciated its attractions, and possibly even considered it as a personal option. Rabbi Hayyim's own teaching seems to me to indicate that such a possibility is more than mere conjecture. From its thematic foci and general tendency, it is clear that this doctrine was shaped through direct confrontation with the Hasidic system, and with a clear awareness of its drawing power. For this reason, there is substantial ground for the assumption that the doctrine formulated by the mature Rabbi Hayyim as a *rosh-yeshivah* and communal leader who sought to assist his students and contemporaries to resist the influence of Hasidism, was born out of his own searching and struggles many years earlier, when he had himself confronted the Hasidic challenge.

In brief, the encounter with Hasidism would seem to have been a major formative experience for Rabbi Hayyim, which it was not for the Gaon. Whereas the Gaon's outlook concerning the role of Torah study, the nature of *yir'ah*, and the relationship between the two was formulated without any significant reference to the Hasidic phenomenon, Rabbi Hayyim's positions on these subjects took shape and were formulated in the course of a direct confrontation with the ideology of this movement. It seems to me that the innovative elements and nuances in the thought of Rabbi Hayyim, as distinguished from that of the Gaon, must be interpreted in light of this fact.

The Value of Torah Study

At the center of Rabbi Hayyim's thought lies the attempt to strengthen and restore the position of Torah study as the highest religious value. In placing the mystical ideal of *devekut* (attachment to God) as the central goal of Divine service,[17] Hasidism brought about an essential change in value. As a result, Torah study was displaced from the preferred position that it had hitherto enjoyed. The status of the *lomdim* (those whose main occupation was Torah study) and their position of authority in community leadership was similarly affected. From the point of view of Mitnaggedic society, the fact that many of the younger generation of *lomdim* were captivated by the influence of Hasidic propaganda was particularly serious, as these potential scholars abandoned their devotion to talmudic study in favor of Divine worship in the Hasidic manner.[18]

What gives Rabbi Hayyim's system its unique flavor and its power is the fact that it is woven out of concepts and ideas borrowed from kabbalistic literature. It is nevertheless clear that Rabbi Hayyim did not address himself to kabbalistic virtuosi, nor did he wish to transform the Jewish people into a community of Kabbalists in the traditional sense of the term. His use of the Kabbalah may rather be described as a deliberate attempt at popularization, expressed in his emphasis upon general principles while ignoring the weight of details. On the one hand, he wanted every Jew to be aware of the tremendous impact of his actions upon the upper worlds; on the other hand, he does not make this influence dependent upon detailed knowledge of the Divine secrets or upon practical use of kabbalistic *kavvanot* (mental intentions underpinning ritual observance and prayer), nor does he demand deep involvement in the study of esoteric teachings.[19] It would appear that Rabbi Hayyim was primarily interested in bolstering his system with the authority of the Kabbalah, as a counterweight to Hasidism, which likewise drew extensively upon the Kabbalah.[20]

In attempting to restore the supremacy of Torah study above all other forms of Divine worship, Rabbi Hayyim developed a series of arguments that attribute a mystical significance and character to the traditional activity of Torah study. This approach is applied to the study of halakhah, unaccompanied by kabbalistic *kavvanot* of any sort. While the Kabbalah attributes to the Jewish individual's Divine worship an influence upon the upper worlds and makes the claim that the flow of the Divine emanation that enlivens and sustains all of the worlds, including our own earthly, corporeal world, depends upon this influence,[21] Rabbi Hayyim argues that it is the act of Torah study that brings about the release of this emanation:

> And the undoubted truth is that were the entire world, from one end to the other, to be, God forbid, empty of our study and contemplation of the Torah for even one single moment, all the worlds, upper and lower, would be destroyed in an instant, and would become as nullified and vacuous, heaven forfend.[22]

In effect, Rabbi Hayyim assigns to the scholarly elite the cosmic task that had hitherto been restricted to the kabbalistic elite.[23] Thus, the *lomdim*, whose main activity is Torah study, fulfill a universal mission of the highest order, powerfully reinforcing the traditional ideal of constant Torah study—the dependence of the very existence of the "worlds" upon the study of Torah requires almost uninterrupted devotion to this study.

In addition to its decisive influence upon the sustenance of the worlds, Torah study is also the surest path of spiritual ascent for the individual Jew. Through Torah study, the student is able to form an attachment to God, the Torah being an embodiment of God. Moreover, direct unmediated contact between the soul of the student and the divine realm is facilitated by the intellectual process of study itself: students of Torah may at times enjoy an influx of "sparks of light" into their souls, carrying with it a certain intellectual fructification enabling them to overcome various difficulties in the course of their study.[24] Thus, the actualization of the experience of revelation, which is among the distinctive signs of mysticism, is manifested here in an intellectual form, wherein the revelation enjoyed by the student of Torah is not that of a vision or a "secret," but rather the enrichment of the student's own intellectual powers and abilities.

Rabbi Hayyim's discussion of the possibility of attaining *devekut* through Torah study constitutes a clear response to the argument of Hasidism that Torah study, as generally practiced in the circles of the *lomdim*, is religiously barren. Indeed, in the method of study taught by the Baal Shem Tov (Rabbi Israel ben Eliezer, 1698–1760, the founder of Hasidism), the devotee becomes attached to the Divine light or vitality concealed within the letters of Torah, disregarding the ideational meaning of the particular text. In practice, the Baal Shem Tov poured new content into the vessel of Torah study, replacing the traditional understanding of study with an ecstatic experience of *devekut*. For him, only this form of study is deserving of being called "study for its own sake" (*Torah li-shemah*). The barb of this statement was directed against scholars of the traditional school, whose study was therefore not to be considered as *Torah li-shemah*.[25]

Rabbi Hayyim rejects the Hasidic interpretation of the concept of *Torah li-shemah*, arguing that it completely uproots the practice of study in the traditional sense.[26] Against the Hasidic view, he proposes his own interpretation, based upon a clear distinction between Torah study, on the one hand, and prayer and practical mitzvot, on the other. In the case of the latter two activities, the accompanying spiritual *kavvanah* must indeed be directed toward God, but the opposite is true with regard to Torah study. As the Torah studied is an earthly embodiment of the supernal Torah, understood as a transcendental entity, those engaged in study "for its own sake" must direct their thoughts toward the Torah itself, their *kavvanah* being to acquire knowledge and depth in Torah. There is thus a certain overlap between the nature and goal of study in the traditional sense and the religious intention that ought to accompany it.[27]

To summarize, it is specifically Torah study in the traditional sense—that is, study directed toward intellectual attainments in the

knowledge of halakhic literature—that constitutes the royal road toward the religious elevation of the Jew. The more students broaden
and deepen their knowledge of Torah, the more do they find themselves
clinging to God, as embodied in the Divine will. In the course of such
study, they may even enjoy direct Divine intervention, expressed in the
influx of "sparks of light" upon the soul. Finally, Torah study in this
sense is an act through which the student may come to realize the
value of "Torah for its own sake."

Torah and *Yir'ah*

The question of the respective roles of Torah study and
yir'ah—the "fear of God"—occupied an important place in Rabbi
Hayyim's thought. These discussions take place against the background
of the Hasidic critique of the alleged lack of *yir'ah* in the camp of the
learned (*lomdim*). A typical example of such criticism appears in the
work by Rabbi Meshullam Feibush Heller, entitled *Yosher divrei emet*.
The central assumption is that the study of Torah ought to be a means
of attaining *devekut*. The attainment of *devekut*, however, is in turn
predicated upon the cultivation of *yir'ah*. Rabbi Meshullam argues:

> The people of our generation, even those who are great masters
> of Torah, have ignored those conditions mentioned in Mishnah
> Avot, Ch. 3,[28] and have imagined that they have already at-
> tained all or part of them, so that it seems to them as though
> they are really masters of Torah. . . . But in truth, if they would
> briefly examine these conditions, and would examine them-
> selves carefully, they would realize that they have not acquired
> even the smallest part of them. . . .[29]

The *lomdim*'s religio-ethical mediocrity is also reflected, according
to Rabbi Meshullam, in their motivation for studying Torah. An individual who wishes to approach God through Torah study must cultivate
the attributes of modesty and humility, for pride and the pursuit of
honor separate people from God. But he asserts the opposite is true of
these *lomdim*, whom he categorizes as "unworthy disciples" whose only
goal is to be renowned as extraordinary scholars. Thus, their very
intellectual attainments in the study of Torah themselves become a
stumbling block, because they are simply a means of acquiring social
prestige.[30] The widespread assumption that the act of study in the
traditional way in itself automatically brings about spiritual elevation
is rejected by Rabbi Meshullam: He cites the existence of known *lomdim*
who are adulterers or guilty of other sins, arguing that it is impossible

for such people to cling to God.[31] The phenomenon of great *lomdim* whose fear of God is at best suspect proves, according to Rabbi Meshullam, that intellectual attainment in Torah study is not per se a guarantee of the individual's religiosity or spiritual level.

In response to this Hasidic critique, Rabbi Hayyim presented his own understanding of the desired relationship between Torah and *yir'ah*. He begins by offering a certain historiographical scheme, describing the origins of this problem and the desired direction toward its solution:

> The earlier generations used to devote all their time to study of and meditation upon our holy Torah, dwelling in the tents of the study of Talmud with Rashi and Tosafot. And the love of the holy Torah burned in their hearts like a flame, with pure love and fear of God, and their only wish was to magnify its honor and to adorn it. They flourished with many earnest disciples, that the earth might be filled with [Divine] knowledge.[32]

This description of the manner of study of the "earlier generations" is rooted in the traditional ideal of the combination of Torah and *yir'ah*, as understood by Rabbi Hayyim. On the one hand, the *lomdim* devoted all their energy to the study of halakhic literature; on the other hand, their study was motivated and accompanied by the fear and love of God, their only aim being the honor of the Torah, rather than personal aggrandizement. From there, Rabbi Hayyim goes on to describe the second stage, that of decline and deterioration.

> As time passed, such is the way of the [Evil] Impulse to be jealous of these people of God who walk properly in the way of the Lord, and to implant in them poison—some of the students spent all of their time and energy solely on *pilpul* [that is, labored argument divorced from concrete outcome] of Torah and nought else; but, as we learn in the Mishnah, where there is no fear of God, then there can be no wisdom.[33]

The spiritual decline expresses itself, then, in the concentration of the *lomdim* upon the intellectual side of study, while neglecting *yir'ah*. These words seem to imply an indirect acknowledgment of the accusation leveled against the scholars in the Hasidic critique that Torah study had become divorced from *yir'ah*. The emergence of an ethical literature within Jewry is portrayed by Rabbi Hayyim as an attempt to restore the distorted balance between the two:

> For this reason, several of their eminent men, the eyes of the community, whose sacred way it is to be alert for the improve-

ment of the public, aroused themselves . . . and composed works relating to the fear of God, to set straight the hearts of the people, that they might engage in the holy Torah and in Divine service with pure fear of God.

However, as Rabbi Hayyim stresses, these spiritual leaders did not intend the study of books of Mussar and *yir'ah* to supplant or displace the study of Torah:

> Their intention was noble—that the principle fixed times for study by the holy people shall be exclusively in the holy Written and Oral Torah and in the many *halakhot*, which are the essence of Torah, as well as in the pure fear of God.[34]

Following his statement that the authors of Mussar works only intended their books to be an addition and accompaniment to the main subject of study—namely, halakhah—Rabbi Hayyim discussed the crisis in Torah study that took place following the advent of Hasidism:

> But now, in these generations, the situation is reversed due to our many sins. What was high is now low. Many people have made works of *yir'ah* and *Mussar* their primary subject of study most of their days. They declare that such is the function of man in this world—to be involved with them constantly—for they arouse the hearts, that one's heart may be humbled, to subjugate and break the Evil Impulse of its desires, and that one may become upright and of good character. But the crown of Torah is left in a corner. With my own eyes I have seen this become widespread in a certain region to the extent that in the majority of their study-houses they possess an abundance of Mussar books but not a single complete set of the Talmud. And their eyes are blind to see . . . that this is not the path which God has chosen, for it is undesirable. In the course of time, they may come, Heaven forfend, to be without a guiding teacher; what then will become of the Torah? . . . [35]

Rabbi Hayyim thus interprets the crisis in Torah study in his own generation as a distortion of the proper balance between Torah and *yir'ah*, in which the secondary has become primary. The obligation to study Torah can only be fulfilled through the study of halakhic literature. The study of Mussar works does not come under this category. Moreover, the study of Torah being the principal component of Divine service, not only in terms of value, but in terms of the amount of time to be devoted to it, the main purpose of *yir'ah* is to guarantee the positive intention motivating the act of study and the consciousness that accompanies it. Study of Mussar books can assist this, but under no circumstance can such study become a substitute for the study of Torah proper.

The proper relationship between Torah and *yir'ah* is explained by Rabbi Hayyim by means of an interpretation of the Talmud's remarks in Shabbat 31a:

> Resh Lakish said: "What is the meaning of the verse, 'And the faith in your times shall be strength, salvation, wisdom and knowledge' [Isa. 33:6]? 'Faith' refers to the [Mishnaic] Order of *Zera'im*; 'your times' refers to the Order *Mo'ed* [Festivals]; 'strength' to the Order of *Nashim* [Women]; and so forth. Even so, [the verse concludes] 'the fear of the Lord is His treasure [*ozar*].'"[36]

The word *ozar* (treasure) is interpreted by Rabbi Hayyim in the sense of a storage vessel; thus, the Torah is compared to a harvest, while "fear of God" is compared to a storehouse, whose function is to protect and preserve the crop. It follows that, "If a person did not first prepare the storehouse of *yir'ah*, then his harvest of Torah is so-to-speak left out in the field, to be stepped upon by the the ox and the donkey, God forbid, so that it is not preserved by him at all."[37] This metaphor clearly shows that the study of Torah is the essential thing, with *yir'ah* as a means, albeit an indispensable one; the study of Torah is impossible without it.

Actually, this metaphor has a double meaning and is a barbed polemic directed against Hasidism: Would anyone think that because the storehouse preserves the harvest, one should spend all or most of one's time on building it and never gather the harvest? Likewise, how can anyone think that *yir'ah* is the supreme ideal of the individual Jew so that a person's entire study is invested in building the "storehouse of the fear of God," which is then left empty?[38]

While the Hasidic critique stressed the lack of correlation between Torah study and *yir'ah*, and the intellectual processes of study and the acquisition of *yir'ah* are two seemingly unrelated psychological phenomena, nevertheless, Rabbi Hayyim wishes to argue for a certain relationship between success in Torah study and the student's degree of fear of God. He posits that success in Torah study depends upon the same Divine inspiration that enriches and fructifies the student's comprehension, seeing God's "hand, so-to-speak, constantly open to infuse each one of his chosen people with great wisdom and exceeding understanding." However, the privilege to merit this intellectual inspiration, as well as its dimensions, depends upon the "storehouse of *yir'ah*" that each individual has prepared. "For if a person has prepared for himself a great storehouse of pure fear of God, God correspondingly grants him abundant wisdom and understanding . . . according to the capacity of his 'storehouse.' "[39] Thus, the very success in the process of study is dependent on the degree of *yir'ah* on the part of the student.

There is still another aspect to the interdependence of Divine inspiration and Torah study. The very effort at understanding invested by a person in the process of Torah study causes "an additional increment of holiness to descend to the source of his soul. . . . From that holiness and light it devolves and flows into his spirit and being, to perfect and complete them."[40] Hence, one whose main occupation is Torah need not undertake any special additional activity in order to attain *yir'ah*, "for the Holy Torah shall itself clothe him with the fear of God, in a short while and with little effort to this end. Such is the way and the special quality of the Holy Torah. . . ."[41] Based upon the above-cited talmudic lesson from Shabbat 31a, Rabbi Hayyim proposes an exact quantitative formula for the balance between Torah study and those activities that are specifically directed toward the acquisition of *yir'ah*: One who studies Torah fifteen hours a day need devote no more than five minutes during the course of that day to acquiring *yir'ah*.[42]

We have thus far discussed the question of the relative weight to be allotted to *yir'ah* as opposed to Torah study. However, we have not yet established the nature of that *yir'ah*, nor how it is to be integrated in practice within the process of study. Rabbi Hayyim alludes to this problem in the following comments:

> Thus should a person prepare himself each time before he begins to study: to think for a while of his Creator, blessed be His name, with purity of heart and fear of God, and to purify himself of sin with thoughts of repentance. In this way he will be enabled to have close contact, while engaged in the study of the Holy Torah, with His word, and His will, may He be blessed. He should also take upon himself to perform and to fulfill everything recorded in the Written and Oral Torah, that he may see and understand his way and behavior from the Holy Torah. Likewise, when he wishes to study words of halakhah, he should pray that God may enable him to resolve the discussion in accordance with [correct] practice, to seek the truth of the Torah.[43]

The *yir'ah* that Rabbi Hayyim sought to combine with the study of Torah is therefore a certain state of consciousness that must serve as a framework for the process of study. This state is acquired via a spiritual effort to purify one's mind of sinful thoughts, accompanied by self-examination and the atonement of sins based upon repentance. The consciousness of *yir'ah* is a necessary precondition for attachment to God during the course of study.

There is a striking similarity between Rabbi Hayyim's proposal that one prepare oneself with the consciousness of *yir'ah* prior to commencing study, and the system of preparations prior to prayer introduced by Hasidism. This technical similarity highlights the basic difference in values between the two systems: in Hasidic literature, in which mystical cleaving to God (*devekut*) is seen as the essential, Torah study is occasionally presented as one of the ways of preparing oneself for prayer; for Rabbi Hayyim, for whom Torah study is the essential, it is *yir'ah* that provides a necessary preparatory stage to study.

Rabbi Hayyim adds two additional demands to this consciousness of *yir'ah*, which are likewise intended to guarantee the religious value of study. First, the Torah student is required to apply in active life all practical conclusions that may arise from the study of Torah. In light of the context within which Rabbi Hayyim articulates this demand, that would seem to refer not just to those acts that are codified in the works of the *poskim* (legal decisors) and in collections of halakhah, but would also require the student to fulfill in practice everything "that he sees and understands to be his way and behavior in accordance with the Holy Torah." This evidently refers to any fresh conclusions that the student might derive from studying that are not yet incorporated within the standard halakhic literature. To be precise, he has in mind those practical conclusions that the student might reach through studying the Talmud, including its aggadic sections, as well as the midrashim. During the period under discussion here, as in previous generations, *lomdim* in Eastern Europe tended to concentrate upon the theoretical aspect of the halakhah, the main subject of study being the Talmud with its commentaries. This demand of Rabbi Hayyim's was intended to add to the theoretical study of halakhah a dimension of practice-oriented study, not by changing the text studied, but rather by being sensitive and alert to the practical consequences to be derived from the sayings of the classical Sages.[44] This lent added weight to the religious value of Torah study. At the same time, it provided a certain response to the Hasidic criticism that portrayed the *lomdim*'s method of study as intellectual exercises of dubious spiritual or religious value.

A second demand presented by Rabbi Hayyim to the Torah student was the attempt to arrive at the truth of Torah. This was evidently directed against extreme *pilpul,* or casuistry, which tended to go far beyond the *peshat* or the plain meaning of the passage being studied.[45] In this respect, Rabbi Hayyim followed his teacher, the Gaon, who attempted to reinstate the understanding of the straightforward meaning of the text as the main task of halakhic studies. The demand that one direct oneself toward the truth of Torah was likewise motivated by the wish to cleave to God via Torah study; if such *devekut* is possible because the halakhah is the embodiment of the Divine will, then one who becomes alienated from the true meaning of Torah likewise forfeits closeness to God.

Thus far, we have been concerned with understanding Rabbi Hayyim's approach to *yir'ah* as a consciousness that accompanies and guides the act of Torah study. However, he also gives considerable weight to the cultivation of *yir'ah* in the context of good deeds and prayer. In this respect, as well, his position implies a certain response to Hasidism. The latter movement greatly stressed the importance of the religious intention (*kavvanah*) that must accompany prayer and the performance of mitzvot, prayer with *kavvanah* being understood by it as a central avenue for the pursuit of *devekut*. For that reason, the Hasidic masters devoted special efforts to overcoming the "alien thoughts" (lustful or mundane notions) that destroy a person's concentration during prayer, thereby damaging the attempt to draw close to God.[46] To this end, the Hasidim preceded their prayers by various preparations, the main purpose of which was to purify and refine the soul to make it fit for the effort of *devekut* during the course of prayer. Hasidism likewise understood the practical mitzvot as a means of cleaving to God, by virtue of the intention meant to accompany them. The extreme importance given by Hasidism to *kavvanah* is reflected in its innovative notion of *'avodah be-gashmiyut* (Divine service through corporeality)—that is, the idea that even secular acts, such as eating and drinking, may be considered as acts of Divine service if accompanied by the proper intention.[47]

Rabbi Hayyim's attitude to these tendencies was an ambivalent one. On the one hand, he saw in a positive light the attempt to elevate Divine service to a higher level by the cultivation of *kavvanah* and of the consciousness accompanying the religious act. At the same time, he saw certain dangers to the integrity of the halakhah in the methods of Hasidism. Rabbi Hayyim had particularly severe reservations concerning the idea of "worship through corporeality," because it could undermine the foundations of the halakhah, which is based upon objective distinctions between the realms of impurity and holiness, of the forbidden and permitted, and so forth, as these are defined by the Divine command.[48]

Rabbi Hayyim held certain reservations concerning the Hasidic demand that every mitzvah or prayer be performed with purity of thought and *devekut*—attachment to the Divine. In the final analysis, making the religious value of prayer and the performance of mitzvot conditional upon the achievement of purity of thought and *devekut* is liable to harm the halakhic framework of that same prayer or mitzvah, because an individual imbued with the awareness that "any Torah or mitzvah in which there is no cleaving to God is worthless" will prefer prayer with *kavvanah*, but not at the proper time required by halakhah, to prayer recited at the proper time without *devekut*.[49]

The solution recommended by Rabbi Hayyim is an intermediate one, avoiding both extreme spiritualization, with its inherent dangers, and Divine worship lacking in any inner religious consciousness. His path is based upon three basic assumptions: (1) that any religious activity must of necessity be defined within the limits of halakhah; (2) that prayer and other acts of mitzvot have religious value even when not accompanied by *kavvanah*; and (3) that the way toward perfection in Divine service is one of ascent on a graduated scale, progress that depends upon the individual qualities of each person. The first of these assumptions underlies the alternative that Rabbi Hayyim proposed to *'avodah be-gashmiyut*. In a response to one of his disciples, Rabbi Hayyim declared that such service was indeed legitimate prior to the giving of the Torah, and that even today non-Jews may serve God in any manner they see fit. For Jews, however, who have been given the Torah as a lucid, precise, and all-comprehensive guide, "the definition of piety is to be meticulous about [the mitzvot] to the utmost degree, and to avoid even the slightest danger of violating that which is prohibited, and to pay heed to all the restrictions of the rabbis and their admonitions. . . ."[50] There is nothing particularly new in the presentation of punctiliousness in the mitzvot and the prohibitions as an act of piety per se; such an approach had been a common one in the tradition for generations. However, in specifically stressing its legitimacy as a framework for acts of piety, and in educating his disciples to act this way in practice, Rabbi Hayyim attempted to avert the danger implicit in "worship in corporeality," and simultaneously to prod his disciples to perform pious acts in the traditional sense.

To counter the danger inherent in the Hasidic accentuation of the importance of *kavvanah*, Rabbi Hayyim drew a clear distinction in principle between the realm of the obligatory and that of the permitted in the performance of mitzvot. The halakhic obligation applies to the very act of the mitzvah per se; this is a basic demand from which one cannot move. The *kavvanah* accompanying the act is an extremely desirable addition, but is not, strictly speaking, essential; that is to say, the absence of intention does not abrogate the value of the act of mitzvah as such. Rabbi Hayyim finds the theological grounding for this statement in the kabbalistic outlook concerning the influence of human actions on the upper worlds. According to this view, when a person performs an act of mitzvah properly—that is, according to its explicit definition in the halakhah—this act affects the upper worlds even when unaccompanied by *kavvanah* or knowledge of the secrets of mystical intentions: "For the Creator, may He be blessed, set the nature of the worlds that they should act in accordance with man's deeds. And every mitzvah ascends by itself to accomplish the effect unique to it."[51] Thus, Rabbi Hayyim relies upon the kabbalistic principle of the mechanistic-causal relationship between people's actions and the upper worlds in order to halt the extreme spiritualistic tendencies that threatened traditional modes of Divine worship. Indeed, the principle that the performance of an act of mitzvah has value in its own right, and that *kavvanah* is a desired but not essential addition, is applied by him to the act of prayer itself.[52]

As I have noted, the statement that acts of prayer and of mitzvah influence the supernal worlds even without proper intention was only meant to counter the danger inherent in the Hasidic emphasis upon the importance of *kavvanah*. Nevertheless, Rabbi Hayyim wished to stimulate the Jew to serve God on a higher level insofar as possible, a tendency reflected in his principle of gradation in the service of God. This principle is based upon psychological insight, taking into account the following factors: the continuous and gradual nature of the educational process, the fluctuations in the emotional life of the individual, and the differences in the basic makeup and psychological capabilities of each individual. Rabbi Hayyim concludes from this that the path toward perfection in the religious life is a many-runged ladder, the ascent of which is a slow and extended process, which differs from one person to another. By depicting Divine worship as a path that, by its nature, has many rungs, a certain religious legitimation is given to the lower levels of this scale. This approach served to hold in check the dangers implicit in the radical position of Hasidism, which seemed to demand all or nothing.[53]

The dilemma confronting Rabbi Hayyim concerning the relationship between deed and intention in the context of mitzvot again arose with regard to the study of Torah and the *kavvanah* meant to precede or accompany it. Just as Hasidism made the value of the performance of the mitzvot conditional upon the accompanying *kavvanah*, it held that Torah study that is not *li-shemah* is valueless. Rabbi Hayyim viewed that statement with extreme concern because of its potential to weaken the devotion of the *lomdim* to study;[54] his reaction was marked by the same dialectical approach that we have already noted. On the one hand, he was extremely tolerant toward Torah study that was not precisely Torah "for its own sake"; on the other hand, he spoke in glowing terms of the value of study "for its own sake." These two extremes are bridged by the same graduated process of self-education, in which all individuals progress in accord with their own personal makeup and efforts.

For his justification of the study of Torah not for its own sake, Rabbi Hayyim relies upon the Rabbinic dictum in Babylonian Talmud Pesahim 50b: "Let a person always engage in Torah and mitzvot even if not for their own sake, for through doing them not for their own sake he will come to perform them for their own sake." This well-known dictum, which is generally interpreted as granting limited, temporary permission to study Torah "not for its own sake," is explained by him in a new light:

> For in truth, it is almost impossible for a person properly to arrive at the level of studying "for its own sake" immediately on beginning his studies. For study of Torah "not for its own sake" is a stage, from which he may [thereafter] be able to ascend to the level of [studying] "for its sake," just as one cannot ascend from the ground to the attic except by the rungs of the ladder. Therefore, he [that is, the one studying "not for its own sake"] is also beloved before Him, may He be blessed . . . and of this they [that is, the Sages] said (Pes. 50b), "Let a person always engage in Torah and mitzvot 'not for their own sake.' " They used the term "always"—that is, in a fixed manner; in other words, on commencing his studies, he is only required to study regularly, day and night. And even if there should enter his mind certain ideas concerning himself, such as that this [study] is for the sake of honor and the like, he should still not consider desisting or slackening his study on account of it, Heaven forfend. On the contrary, he should strengthen himself greatly in the study of Torah, and let his heart be firmly set on it, that he will certainly arrive at the level of doing for its own sake.[55]

We therefore find that study that is "not for its own sake" is no longer viewed as a blemish, to be justified only retroactively, but as an almost indispensable stage in the path toward study "for its own sake." This stage is therefore not only legitimate, but valuable in its own right. Moreover, Rabbi Hayyim finds in this rabbinic dictum a promise that one who persists in devotion to studies "not for their own sake" will ultimately, as a result of that very persistence, come to study Torah "for its own sake." As the justification of study "not for its own sake" is

rooted in its being a "level" leading toward study "for its own sake,"
Rabbi Hayyim proceeds to expand his permission even further:

> Even if it seems that throughout his entire life, from his youth
> until he became a hoary-headed elder, his study was "not for
> its own sake," you must even then treat him [that is, the Torah
> scholar] with respect, and certainly not treat him with contempt,
> Heaven forbid. For as he has constantly engaged in Torah study,
> there is no doubt that on many occasions his intention must
> also have been "for its own sake," for our sages have promised
> that through study "not for its own sake," one comes to [study]
> "for its own sake." This does not mean to say that he will come
> to do it for its own sake—to the extent that thereafter, through-
> out his entire life, he will engage in it only for its own sake.
> [Rather,] that each time he studies . . . for several consecutive
> hours, even if his intention was generally speaking "not for its
> own sake," it is utterly impossible that there did not enter into
> his heart in the middle of his study, even if only for a short time,
> the desired intention of "for its own sake." It follows from this
> that everything he has studied thus far "not for its sake" is
> sanctified and purified by that small moment during which he
> intended to study it for its own sake.[56]

It must again be noted that Rabbi Hayyim's repeated efforts to
affirm the value of Torah study even when it does not reach the level
of *li-shemah* were exclusively intended to halt the serious threat that he
perceived in the Hasidic position on this question. At the same time,
he did not spare words in extolling the great value of Torah study that
is *li-shemah*:

> The individual who takes upon himself the yoke of [learning]
> the holy Torah for its own sake in truth . . . is elevated above
> all worldly matters, and is guarded by Him [God], may He be
> blessed, with specific Providence, above natural law, because he
> clings to the Torah and to the Holy One, blessed be He, as it
> were, literally. . . . To the contrary, the forces of nature are given
> into his power when he declares a decree upon them, and he
> may bend them to whatever he wishes, and fear of him is upon
> them.[57]

Rabbi Hayyim's Teaching as the Educational
Program of the Volozhin Yeshiva

To a great extent, the public impact of Rabbi Hayyim's
teaching stemmed from the fact that it became the educational program

of the Volozhin yeshiva, which he founded in 1803 and led over a period of nearly twenty years.[58] The pamphlets compiled from the answers and advice that Rabbi Hayyim gave to his students show this yeshiva to have been more than an institution for the dissemination of Torah in the narrow sense.[59] It was an educational institution that sought to develop a religious individual, a *lamdan-hasid* (scholar-pietist),[60] who would combine in his personality and way of life the values of Torah and of *yir'ah*.

The demand for and striving toward maximum devotion to Torah study shaped the environment of the Volozhin yeshiva, where an unceasing struggle took place for the utilization of every hour and every moment of the student's day. Rabbi Hayyim led his students in this struggle by advice and guidance intended to assist them in overcoming the impulse toward idleness. These instructions testify to the rabbi's sensitivity and psychological penetration, varying from case to case, depending upon the makeup of the individual student.[61]

The ideal of maximal devotion to Torah study was also reflected in his stance concerning the proper allocation of time between study of Torah and economic activity. He suggested that ordinary householders divide their day in two, devoting half to remunerative work and the other half to study of Torah.[62] His closer disciples, who bore the yoke of their own livelihood, were asked to devote most of the day to Torah study and only two hours a day to earning a livelihood.[63] These guidelines are based upon the assumption that a person's livelihood is determined by Heaven on Rosh Hashanah,[64] so that even if one exerts a greater effort toward work, that person will earn no more than has been predetermined.[65] His approach was thus a fatalistic one, based upon the ideal of trust in God.

Along with prodding his students to maximal devotion and constancy in their Torah studies, Rabbi Hayyim guided them in the way of *yir'ah*, particularly regarding care and punctiliousness in the performance of mitzvot, stating that "the definition of piety is to be punctilious in them [that is, the mitzvot] to the extreme, and to keep oneself apart from even the seventy-first part of that which is forbidden, and to be careful of all the strictures of the rabbis and their warnings. . . ."[66] The definition of piety thus consists neither in supererogatory acts of piety nor in service in corporeality, but rather in the perfect observance of the halakhah. What made this a novel approach was the attempt to base the performance of mitzvot upon the maximal development of the implications of the halakhah by thorough reexamination of its primary sources. The example that presented itself to Rabbi Hayyim and his followers was, of course, that of the Gaon of Vilna.

The Gaon attempted to reexamine the established, codified hala-khah practiced in his own day in light of talmudic and midrashic sources.[67] As a result, his own personal behavior deviated on certain points from the accepted norm. For a number of his disciples, the Gaon's customs served as an example to be emulated. This attempt to turn the Gaon's customs into a normative model was expressed in the book *Ma'aseh rav*, compiled by Rabbi Issachar Baer ben Tanhum, one of the Gaon's disciples.[68] The author recorded the Gaon's customs and rulings, together with a commentary in which he attempted to identify the Gaon's sources in Rabbinic literature. In the introduction to this work, Rabbi Issachar begins by citing evidence for the fact that, when the talmudic sages disagreed concerning some halakhic matter, they would sometimes refer to the custom or practice of one of the great rabbis. The assumption was that these outstanding scholars, because of their sublime individual level and their greatness in Torah, were above sus-picion of error in halakhic matters. Rabbi Issachar then applies this principle to the personality of the Gaon:

> In our own day God wished Israel to have meritorious deeds
> . . . and there descended from heaven an angel, a rabbi similar
> to an angel of the Lord of Hosts . . . the Gaon and pious R.
> Elijah, who lifted up the yoke of Torah. . . . And he restored
> them [that is, the proper deeds] to their original place, as they
> were in the days of the sages of the Talmud, and all his deeds
> were carefully weighed and considered, based upon the source
> of the Law, as explained in the halakhic discussion, and all his
> *middot* and practices are based upon the Sages, as expressed in
> the Talmud and *aggadot*, not deviating from their path either
> right or left. . . .[69]

Rabbi Issachar thus views the Gaon as a messenger of Divine Prov-idence, sent to restore the ancient crown of Torah and correct the mistakes that had accumulated over the course of generations. The unique level of the Gaon—that described here by the author as pos-sessing a charismatic character—is rather expressed in his ability to reconstruct the halakhah from its primary sources, while correcting the mistakes that stemmed from incorrect reasoning of the later authorities.

Rabbi Issachar's comments concerning the Gaon have been quoted at some length because they typify the way of thought of Rabbi Hayyim and his disciples.[70] Indeed, in the eyes of these disciples Rabbi Hayyim was himself a model to be emulated, for two reasons. First, as an intimate disciple of the Gaon, he knew his master's rulings and customs well, and could therefore also serve as a reliable source concerning this subject to his own students.[71] Second, Rabbi Hayyim himself continued in the path of the Gaon in that he likewise attempted to base his behavior upon a careful examination of the primary sources of the halakhah. An explicit expression of this appears in his introduction to the Gaon's commentary upon *Shulhan 'arukh*, section *Orah hayyim*. Rabbi Hayyim claims that, *ab initio*, all practical halakhic rulings should be based upon examination of the words of the Sages. The fact that later generations of rabbis saw fit to compose halakhic codes only stemmed from the "burden of Exile" and the decreased numbers of those who "taught [directly] from the Talmud." However, the existence of these codes in no way justifies the subsequent development in the approach to halakhic ruling:

> For many people erred in casting off the burden of [exerting] effort in the study of Talmud, in order to infer *halakhot*. And they said that only the *Shulhan 'Arukh* is to be studied [as a guideline] for practice. And even if they study *gemara* [Talmud], they do so only in order to sharpen their intellects. . . . And this is not the straight path [for] which God has given us intellect to penetrate the depths of the Talmud. . . . But the righteous who walk in the straight path make their primary [source of] ruling the Talmud, and the *Shulhan 'Arukh* is [only] studied to help them remember the laws. . . . For this is the essential fruit of the study of Talmud—to derive from it practical halakhah.[72]

These remarks by Rabbi Hayyim combine two distinct demands in one fell swoop: first, that all instruction in practical halakhah ought to be grounded in direct study of the relevant talmudic passages; second, that all of one's study of the Talmud should be directed to the practical consequences that follow from it.

Following the Gaon, Rabbi Hayyim attempted to ground his own approach to the observance of mitzvot upon study of the primary sources of halakhah, and in this same way he guided his disciples who turned to him with questions, and attempted to behave in accordance with his own personal example and instructions. This phenomenon is documented in the pamphlets in which Rabbi Hayyim's disciples recorded his answers to their queries, and described his religious behavior as they had witnessed it. It is interesting to note here that he imposed a certain limitation upon those of his students who wished to adopt the customs of the Gaon: "The practices of our teacher, the Gaon, of blessed memory, are to be observed in private. But concerning those things which are performed in public, about which there is difference of opinion . . . if one is unable to observe them in private, one ought not to perform them in places where they would cause controversy— even if such a view is brought in the Talmud as well."[73] The fact that Rabbi Hayyim saw the need to restrict the observance of the Gaon's customs indicates that his disciples had a certain tendency to follow them.

The example and instructions that Rabbi Hayyim gave his disciples concerning the performance of mitzvot included a demand for punctiliousness regarding matters that exceeded even the awareness of the majority of the community. For example, Rabbi Hayyim took care to avoid eating *hamez* (foodstuffs containing leavening) after Passover even if it had been sold to a non-Jew because, in addition to being sold, *hamez* requires total renunciation of ownership—a condition that many people were unable to fulfill.[74] Generally speaking, one may say that the scholar-*hasid*, who attempted to base his practice upon expert knowledge of the primary sources of the halakhah, developed an awareness of situations in regard to which the broader public was not aware of the relevancy of the halakhah.[75] In addition, Rabbi Hayyim taught that one must be careful not to endanger the property of others even when the damage is so minimal that most people would not even notice it. This conclusion may be drawn from a certain incident recorded by one of his students:

> Our teacher once travelled to Vilna and, since there was no Torah scroll to read in the inn, he asked them [the students] to go to a nearby lodging place where there was one. On the way there was a puddle of water, and his disciple, the rabbi of Chalitz, placed a tree-trunk upon the puddle for them to walk over it. Afterwards, on their way back, he ordered all of the entire quorum to return to their inn, while he and the rabbi of Chalitz returned to the inn and asked the owner of the place whether he forgave them, and he stated explicitly that he forgave them [for using the tree-trunk].[76]

In taking the trouble to go to a neighboring place so as not to forego the public reading of the Torah, Rabbi Hayyim also set his students an example of punctiliousness in observing the mitzvot. His disciples specifically mentioned his practice of praying with a *minyan* (quorum) even when this entailed considerable trouble: "He said that, from the day that he reached the age of discretion, he never prayed save with a community [that is, a *minyan* of ten]. Once he was in an inn, and sent carriages to the nearby villages that they might come to pray the Afternoon Prayer in public."[77] Training for *yir'ah* in the Volozhin yeshiva was not limited to guiding the students toward punctiliousness in mitzvot. From the questions of the students and the rabbi's replies, we learn that *yir'ah* was understood in the broadest, most inclusive sense: namely, as a constant struggle for purification of body and soul. One student, disturbed by the dire punishments threatened in kabbalistic Mussar literature against those guilty of the sin of nocturnal emission, sought his master's advice and was calmed by Rabbi Hayyim with the statement of the *Tikkunei Zohar* that study of Torah protects one from suffering in such a case.[78] As for the question of how to guard oneself against alien thoughts, Rabbi Hayyim answered that one simply ought to ignore them, "and thereby he breaks down the [power of the] *Sitra Ahra* ("Other Side"—Satan) but if he thinks about them, it is a grave evil."[79] This response is clearly aimed against the teaching of the Baal Shem Tov that one ought to elevate alien thoughts rather than to reject them. Rabbi Hayyim likewise advises his students as to how to avoid licentious thoughts associated with looking at women. Utilizing down-to-earth psychological insight, he takes exception to the approach that advocates one to avoid looking at women as far as possible, because "the more one restricts oneself and avoids looking, if one afterwards looks and sees, he will burn like fire. . . ." Therefore, Rabbi Hayyim advises: "When he intends going to the marketplace, he should pray and ask for mercy that he not stumble, Heaven forfend, in the slightest sin or licentious thought."[80]

Not only in the above-mentioned contest but, in general, Rabbi Hayyim accepted prayer as an important weapon in the battle against the Evil Impulse—a position clearly based upon the assumption that one requires Divine assistance in order to overcome the temptation. In addition, however, Rabbi Hayyim would appear to have thought that the act of prayer itself exerts an important influence upon the person praying; it provides a kind of inner decision not to fall prey to that particular sin, and may also serve to calm the person from fear and worry lest he stumble.[81] Rabbi Hayyim's response to the student who asked how to be saved from anger and gossip was based upon the same consideration:

> He answered that first of all he should always anticipate trouble by prayer. Before going among people or travelling somewhere, or when rising in the morning, he should say, "Master of the Universe: behold, I walk in the valley of darkness; save me from the Evil Impulse and save me from these sins." And he should enumerate them, and weep greatly from the walls of his heart [during the *Elohai Nezor* (the personal petitionary prayer recited at the end of the Amida]. . . .[82]

The subject of pride occupied an important place in the ethical guidance that Rabbi Hayyim gave to his students. In several places, he calls attention to the enormous power of the desire for honor, and particularly warns against the quest for pride entailed in filling a rabbinic office.[83] The atmosphere of *yir'ah* that existed in the Volozhin yeshiva may also be seen in the request of one of his students for guidance as to how to achieve humility of spirit.[84] At times, these appeals of the students to their rabbi bear a note of personal confession, which would seem to indicate an intimate fabric of relationship between teacher and student.[85] An additional ethical quality that Rabbi Hayyim wished to instill in his students was trust in God, which he generally addressed during instruction concerning the laws of charity.[86] Finally, among other matters in which he guided his students were the laws of repentance and instruction concerning the *kavvanot* of prayer.[87] Like other Mussar teachers, Rabbi Hayyim warned that the struggle with the Evil Impulse demands constant vigilance;[88] moreover, in order to struggle effectively against the Evil Impulse one also needs craftiness. In this respect, an interesting comment is found in his interpretation of the dictum in *Pirkei avot* 1:6:

> "Acquire a friend" . . . with whom one can take counsel also concerning matters of Divine service. For if you are wise in your own eyes, the Evil Impulse can blind your eyes and make the crooked and the hilly [to appear] straight. Therefore, you must take counsel with a friend, for your own evil impulse is not so close to him, as to be misleading.[89]

It must also be noted here that, even in the guidance he gave his students concerning the various aspects of *yir'ah*, Rabbi Hayyim expressed considerable hesitation regarding the actual study of Mussar books! Such study is recommended to "householders who are always involved in business"; however, the *lomdim*, who were his main concern, would do better to derive ethical lessons from the study of midrash and *'Ein ya'akov* (a collection of aggadot from the Babylonian Talmud), and not focus upon later Mussar works, because these "take away time from study." Rabbi Hayyim added one reservation to this general rule:

> If one who studies Torah constantly sees that he begins to be overcome by the Evil Impulse in a certain matter, God forbid, he is commanded and obligated constantly to study Mussar works which address this particular item—lest his uncircumcised heart submit—and there will not be any evil left in him.[90]

The fact that both Hasidism and the *lomdim* who joined it preferred involvement in Mussar books to halakhic studies led to a reserved and suspicious attitude on his part toward involvement in this literature. Due to his fear that the primary thing (that is, normative Torah study) would be displaced by that which was secondary, Rabbi Hayyim recommended aggadot and midrashic literature of the classical talmudic Sages as vehicles of study in the area of Mussar. One who studies these texts, even if not engaged in halakhah per se, still remain within the limits of the Oral Law. Rabbi Hayyim nevertheless did not ignore the special power of persuasion possessed by Mussar literature, and therefore he required their study in those special cases where the Evil Impulse was strong.

Similarities and Differences between the Teachings of Rabbi Hayyim and the Gaon

Having surveyed the teachings and educational path of Rabbi Hayyim of Volozhin, we may now consider the degree of continuity between his outlook and method and those of his teacher and master, the Gaon of Vilna. A comparison will reveal that in many matters there was indeed a great deal of similarity or even identity between the two; nevertheless, in certain areas Rabbi Hayyim took a new and independent stance.

First and foremost, the continuity and similarity between master and disciple may be seen in their common view about the centrality of Torah study and its overwhelming importance in comparison with the other components of Divine service. Both advocated the maximum degree of devotion to Torah study, while ignoring and rejecting all worldly values and acquisitions. Like the Gaon, Rabbi Hayyim thought that involvement in "the way of the world"—that is, economic activity—possessed no autonomous value and that one ought not be involved in it except for lack of any alternative, and even then only on a very limited scale, in order to provide the absolute minimum requirements of one's sustenance. This position was based upon a certain economic fatalism, rooted in a particular understanding of the quality of "trust in God."

The closeness between the Gaon and Rabbi Hayyim is likewise expressed in their respective understandings of the proper relationship between Torah and *yir'ah*. Both agreed that study of Torah is of primary importance and that *yir'ah* is of secondary importance; study is the end, and *yir'ah* the means toward that end. Nevertheless, both shared in the opinion that fear of God is an indispensable accompaniment to the study of Torah, and that Torah study that is not accompanied by the cultivation of *yir'ah* is faulty.

One may likewise note the points of contact between Rabbi Hayyim and the Gaon regarding the nature of *yir'ah* and the "Battle with the Impulse." Following the Gaon, Rabbi Hayyim stressed the importance of the relationship between study and the practical performance of mitzvot. The *yir'ah* of master and disciple was also reflected in the extraordinary efforts that each made to fulfill the mitzvot even under extremely difficult conditions. As for their understanding of the nature of the Evil Impulse, both the Gaon and Rabbi Hayyim accepted the image widespread in certain Mussar works, whereby the Evil Impulse is portrayed as a crafty and dangerous personality; therefore, struggle with it demands commensurate craftiness and sophistication. Moreover, following the kabbalistic view, they both thought of the Evil Impulse as the messenger of the demonic forces of the *Sitra Ahra*, and while they both emphasized the enormous power of Torah study as a defense against it, at the same time, they agreed that activities over and above Torah study, specifically directed to this purpose, are necessary in the struggle against it.

The continuity between the Gaon and Rabbi Hayyim may be attributed both to the common religious and cultural heritage of Lithuanian Jewry and to the admiration that Rabbi Hayyim felt toward the Gaon. There is no doubt that Rabbi Hayyim perceived the teaching, personality, and way of life of the Gaon as the ideal model of Divine service, which one ought to adopt and follow. In a certain sense, Rabbi Hayyim's teaching may be understood as an attempt to translate the image and way of life of the Gaon into a systematic doctrine, which could be presented as a theological manifesto and educational program to the community of *lomdim*. But even if we agree that the Gaon constituted a source of inspiration and influence of the highest order for Rabbi Hayyim, we must not be surprised to find certain points of innovation and independence of the disciple with respect to his master, alongside this continuity and closeness. There is no reason to interpret these points as deliberate deviations on the part of Rabbi Hayyim from the path of the Gaon. By the nature of things, a disciple of prominent stature, even when continuing in the teacher's path, adds new elements to it. Indeed, at times it seems as though it was precisely the desire to defend the heritage of the Gaon under new and different circumstances that led Rabbi Hayyim to adopt these new and innovative positions.

A particularly striking feature of Rabbi Hayyim's innovation is the tendency toward what can be designated as "mystification of Torah study." While he may have expressed here certain ideas that were also held by the Gaon, a significant innovation is implicit in the presentation of these ideas to the broader public per se. As mentioned earlier, Rabbi Hayyim wished to restore the centrality of Torah study by means of a theological structure drawing upon the concepts and directives of the

Kabbalah, and addressed to the general public. Such a tendency, which was rooted in his confrontation with the Hasidic influence, is entirely absent from the Gaon's thought. Moreover, Rabbi Hayyim's attempts to integrate the value of *devekut* within Torah study is also an innovation with respect to the Gaon. Of course, there is room to wonder about the extent to which this experience of *devekut*, which according to Rabbi Hayyim could be acquired only by means of traditional Torah study, resembled that experience of *devekut* that was at the summit of the desires of the Hasidim. In any event, there can be no doubt that Rabbi Hayyim's intensity on this point was a response to the challenge presented by Hasidism. And whether or not we assume that when he referred to *devekut* attained through the act of study of *Torah li-shemah*, Rabbi Hayyim had in mind the spiritual exaltation in which the Gaon was enveloped while studying Torah, one must still credit him with innovation on this subject. By focusing upon the subject of *devekut*, as well as by his substantive discussion of the possibility of integrating this value within the study of Torah, Rabbi Hayyim went beyond what we find in the writings of the Gaon and the oral traditions ascribed to him.

He also took an independent and somewhat different position from that of the Gaon concerning the relationship between intention and act. As mentioned, Rabbi Hayyim viewed this question in terms of the great danger inherent in the Hasidic stress upon *kavvanah*, to the extent that it threatened the wholeness or integrity of the act itself. He proposed a dialectical approach that, on the one hand, posited the act of mitzvah as possessing value even when unaccompanied by *kavvanah* and, on the other, prodded and stimulated one to attain a higher degree of integration of intention and act. As against this dialectical complexity, we find a stricter and more unequivocal position in the Gaon. Thus, the Gaon sternly condemns Torah study that is not "for its own sake," while Rabbi Hayyim goes to considerable lengths to justify it.

In the context of the present work, there is particular interest in the differences between the two relating to the acquisition of *yir'ah*. While the Gaon gives considerable weight in his writings to the subject of character improvement, this subject hardly appears in Rabbi Hayyim's writings. Though according to some accounts, Rabbi Hayyim did warn his disciples against the pursuit of honor and encouraged them to acquire the characteristic of modesty, nevertheless, neither in his writings nor in the verbal instructions attributed to him do we find any reflection upon the topic of the improvement of character traits as deserving of special attention. Rabbi Hayyim was likewise hesitant regarding the study of Mussar books, suggesting that one study instead the dicta of the Sages. The Gaon, by contrast, saw the study of Mussar works as an important and effective tool to be used in the struggle against the Evil Impulse.

Once again, the difference between the two on these matters is rooted in Rabbi Hayyim's confrontation with Hasidic influences. As we have noted, he viewed the emphasis upon the study of Mussar works by Hasidism and its followers at the expense of halakhic studies as one of the serious signs of the harm caused by this movement. His reserved attitude toward study of Mussar books flowed from this view. For the same reason, he discouraged excessive concentration upon character improvement, as this matter was likewise greatly overemphasized among those who had abandoned the study of Torah to devote them-selves to Divine worship in the Hasidic manner. The Gaon, whose views concerning the question of Torah and *yir'ah* were not formed in relation to the Hasidic context, did not share those fears that motivated Rabbi Hayyim and left their impression upon his stance.

Finally, one must note one more striking difference between the master and his disciple. Asceticism and withdrawal from society, which played such a great role in the way of life and worldview of the Gaon, did not form a part of Rabbi Hayyim's approach. He was himself in-volved with other people and spent considerable time with communal affairs. Even in his writings, we do not find that he advocates asceticism or isolation from others. Rabbi Hayyim's attitude on this matter may also have been rooted in his confrontation with Hasidism. Since that movement presented a new model of leadership, which stressed the element of direct contact with the public, and in light of the vitality and power of attraction displayed by the Hasidic leadership, it would appear that Rabbi Hayyim thought the time no longer propitious for the learned elite to shut itself off from the community.

4

Rabbi Zundel Salant as the Embodiment of the Educational Ideal of the Volozhin Yeshiva

AN EXAMINATION of the figure of Rabbi Zundel of Salant (1786–1866), as reflected both in his writings and in the extant traditions about him,[1] will indicate that his worldview and way of life were seen as a kind of exemplary fulfillment of the educational ideal of the yeshiva of Rabbi Hayyim. Rabbi Zundel is portrayed as the personal embodiment of the *lamdan-hasid*; Rabbi Hayyim's influence is evident, not only in the combination of Torah and *yir'ah* as such, but in a number of details of both of those traits. That is not to say, however, that a total similarity existed between Rabbi Zundel and Rabbi Hayyim. Even the existence of a close relationship between teacher and disciple does not preclude the option of innovation and individuality on the part of the disciple. As we shall see below, Rabbi Zundel's path in Divine service carried a deeply personal stamp.

There is no extant documentation pertaining to Rabbi Zundel's accomplishments in Torah study. However, the fact that, during the period he lived in Jerusalem, many people turned to him with halakhic queries and that he, in effect, served as an halakhic authority there indicates that he was deeply revered by his contemporaries and considered as a great Torah scholar.[2] Rabbi Israel Salanter testified to Rabbi Zundel's approach to learning in the following comments:

> His primary effort in study was devoted to what was required for practice. He studied the Talmud . . . *Bet Yosef* [a comprehensive commentary by R. Joseph Caro] and all the later authorities in depth, and paid the greatest attention to the glosses of the Vilna Gaon, of blessed memory. And when he studied a section in *Shulhan 'Arukh* or a given subject in all its implications, it was as if that subject had arisen in practice. . . . All of his study of Bible, Talmud, Midrash and Zohar was based upon the principle of seeking knowledge of [proper] practice. . . .[3]

Rabbi Zundel's method of study was thus marked by emphasis upon the relation between study and practice. That approach reveals one aspect of his *yir'ah* that betrays the influence of Rabbi Hayyim. This is particularly true with regard to the attempt to derive practical conclusions even from the study of works that were not generally considered as a source for halakhic rulings.[4]

While relatively little is known concerning his accomplishments and method in Torah study, there can be no doubt as to the great value given to Torah study by Rabbi Zundel. Like his teacher, Rabbi Hayyim, he saw Torah study as the principal and most sublime means of serving God. Under his teacher's influence, he was imbued with the consciousness that the sublime status enjoyed by Torah study within the service of God requires maximal devotion to study in everyday life. A characteristic expression of this appears in a letter of Rabbi Zundel to his son, who traveled far and wide in order to seek a cure for his wife's illness. In attempting to encourage his son, he repeatedly emphasizes that one engaged in a mitzvah that cannot be performed by another person is exempt from the commandment of Torah study. He nevertheless warns: "But when you have free time, you must learn constantly. . . ."[5]

The ideal of maximal devotion to Torah study, as understood by Rabbi Zundel, is reflected in a brief pamphlet he wrote, *Hanhagah yesharah ve-hizzuk ha-torah* (*Upright Behavior and the Strengthening of Torah*). He begins this pamphlet as follows:

> As soon as one awakens from sleep one should immediately get out of bed, even if it is very cold . . . and one should straight away wash and insofar as possible immediately go and study a book. One should not interrupt study save for some urgent need, and with one deliberation—for example, to prepare oneself for prayer. And while in the midst of studying, even if it be "as difficult as death" to study, one should nevertheless study, for the Torah is only preserved by those who mollify themselves for its sake, and by constant self-afflicted pain. . . . For a single letter of the Torah is worth more than the entire world and than all the mitzvot (JT Peah, beginning), and the sin of neglecting Torah study is greater than all others, and earns the designation "heretic" (*apikoris*) with forfeiture of the World to Come (Sanhedrin, Helek). The world is sustained by the Torah, as is explained in Tractates Pesahim and Avodah Zarah and elsewhere, and were it not for the Torah, one could not be saved from the dominion of the Evil Impulse (Kiddushin 30). When one needs to attend to one's essential physical needs, such as to eating and so forth, one should reflect upon matters of Torah and *yir'ah*, and should attempt to do so [that is, eat, etc.] as briefly as

possible, and at all times think to oneself, "When will I be able to study?" . . .⁶

One of the striking expressions of Rabbi Zundel's piety was the fact that he did not utilize his Torah scholarship to earn a livelihood. Despite the fact that, considering his knowledge of Torah, he would have been expected to serve in a rabbinic position, he preferred to forego this possibility. He likewise refused to accept any financial support from the community or from individuals, as was customary among those *lomdim* who did not serve in the rabbinate,⁷ but he preferred to earn his own modest living as an ordinary householder. Moreover, Rabbi Zundel attempted to hide his unusual piety and Torah knowledge from others, disguising himself as one of the simple folk by his form of dress and behavior.⁸

Several anecdotes about Rabbi Zundel revolve around his practice of hiding his identity. A typical example is the following:

> I heard from rabbi . . . Gershon Amsterdam, of blessed memory, of Vilna, that he did not know the aforementioned pious man [that is, Rabbi Zundel], but that once this *hasid* happened to come to Vilna, bringing a letter to the said Rabbi Gershon from a person in Salant. The *hasid* entered . . . and stood by the doorway and gave him the letter. Rabbi Gershon thought that he was a simple person, a wagon-driver or the like, and wished to pay him for his trouble. He called him into his room and offered him a glass of liquor and begged him to drink. . . . Afterwards the rabbi said to him, "Are you not from the town of Salant? How is the *hasid* Rabbi Zundel?" And he answered him what he asked. Afterwards the rabbi began to speak with him at length about the *hasid*, and he began to be hesitant in his answers, in order to belittle himself. From his replies, he [Rabbi Gershon] began to suspect that perhaps this person was the *hasid*, even though it was not apparent from his speech. Rabbi Gershon said to him, "Tell me in truth what your name is." He said, "My name is Zundel." Rabbi Gershon said to him, "God executes the will of those who fear Him. For one would not at all recognize you by appearances."⁹

While it is difficult to determine the reliability of other stories in a similar vein,¹⁰ this account seems reliable, as Rabbi Isaac Blazer states that he heard it directly from the person to whom it occurred. In any event, even if we assume that some of these stories are legendary, there is no reason to doubt the veracity of their common core: that Rabbi Zundel in fact behaved with great modesty, so that to those who did not know him personally he seemed to be an ordinary man.

Fundamentally, Rabbi Zundel's way of life was shaped by the value of asceticism and separation from the world, first and foremost, upon the total negation of the value of this world and its pleasures. Rabbi Zundel consequently refrained from enjoying the economic and social advantages that would have been his were he to have served in the rabbinate, concealing his spiritual level from the eyes of the world. His practice of "exiling himself" to another city in order to study Torah in an atmosphere of social isolation and economic want must be seen in the context of his asceticism.[11] He was accustomed as well to go out and meditate in the fields in order to be isolated from other people.[12] Explicit remarks in praise of isolation are recorded in the above-mentioned pamphlet by Rabbi Zundel: ". . . and he should see to it that one is separated from the company of other people as far as possible, and that one love solitude. . . ."[13] These remarks were made within the context of the matter of constancy in Torah study; it would therefore seem that isolation was intended to prevent wasting time from Torah study. It also seems likely that, following in the path of the Gaon of Vilna and of other Mussar writers, Rabbi Zundel saw limitations upon social contact as a means of defense against sin.

The asceticism advocated by him did not go so far as requiring self-affliction; he nevertheless saw great value in accepting suffering out of love:

> Man was not created to enjoy pleasure in this world, which is full of pains and followed by death, after which he is no longer remembered; but [he is created for] the World to Come, and in accordance with the suffering is the reward. . . . And he should accept his sufferings with love. . . . For it is better to suffer somewhat in this world than to suffer greatly in the World to Come, which is eternal. He should therefore rejoice greatly that his sins are atoned for in this world.[14]

We may infer from this that the asceticism advocated by Rabbi Zundel was based upon the principle that it is impossible for human beings to enjoy both worlds. Reward in the next world, which is the true goal of our existence, depends upon maximal sacrifice of pleasure in this world, especially as suffering in this world atones for one's sins. Rabbi Zundel himself acted in accordance with the spirit of this rule,[15] and preached to his son to do likewise.[16]

Further edification concerning the nature of Rabbi Zundel's religious consciousness may be gained from a "prayer made up of [biblical] verses," which he composed for himself.[17] This prayer gives one a striking sense of the nothingness of the human being, as against the greatness of God. However, the verses chosen by Rabbi Zundel for this prayer concentrate more on the portrayal of human guilt and sinfulness than on the greatness of God. One may perhaps conclude from this that Rabbi Zundel tended more toward examination of the self, focused upon his failures in fulfilling the Divine command, rather than upon deep theosophical contemplation. The intense sense of guilt, based upon the laziness and lack of wholeness in one's fulfillment of the mitzvot, indicates that Rabbi Zundel saw our response to the Divine command as the essence of Divine service. Though his study included kabbalistic literature, the image of God as immanent did not seem to play a major role in his religious consciousness, nor did the associated value of *devekut*. Instead, he tried to see the hand of Divine Providence as shaping and guiding people's destiny in this world. The attribute of *bitahon* (trust in God) was doubtless one of the major elements of his religious consciousness and a striking expression of his *yir'ah*.

Rabbi Zundel's *bitahon* was based upon a strict reading of the idea of Providence. According to this view, Divine Providence not only tracks human behavior and metes out reward and punishment, it is even involved in the detailed guiding of the individual's destiny. In a letter to his son, Rabbi Zundel wrote: "Know and believe that a man's steps are guided by God, and what can man know of His ways? Everything is decreed from Heaven, in every moment and in whatever place he may be, and at whatever time, and with whatever people he may be. . . ."[18] Underlying Rabbi Zundel's understanding of the attribute of trust was the assumption that God rewards with goodness those who trust in Him: "For this is the secret of trust, that the Holy One, blessed be He, performs the will of the person who trusts in Him with a full heart, and provides him with all his needs in every place and every time, even if he is not a *zaddik* [a fully righteous person]. . . ."[19] The conclusion to be drawn from this is the limitation of human effort within practical life. A certain degree of effort is permitted and even desirable, so that Divine Providence need not operate only through explicit miracles; however, in principle, humankind's destiny is determined by the extent of their trust in God.[20]

The concept of trust in God also affected Rabbi Zundel's stand concerning the ideal relation between study of Torah and involvement in practical life. He held that, since an individual's economic success in any event does not depend upon the quantity of that individual's effort, the amount of time devoted to one's occupation ought to be limited, and one ought to devote the majority of one's time to Torah study. The attribute of *bitahon* therefore demanded a fatalistic attitude toward economic activity, even if a certain amount of human effort is both permissible and desirable. On this question, Rabbi Zundel followed the guidelines given by Rabbi Hayyim to his disciples, and which he himself taught to his followers.[21]

What made Rabbi Zundel's approach to the attribute of *bitahon* unique was the attempt to implant within one's soul the awareness of the nothingness of human beings, the lack of value of all their efforts, and their total dependence upon Divine will and mercy. Among Rabbi Zundel's writings, we find a list of "verses of trust" from the Book of Psalms, which he was accustomed to repeat[22] and which is in keeping with his order to his son: "[C]onstantly repeat verses of trust and of salvation. . . ."[23] It would therefore seem that Rabbi Zundel was aware of the gap between intellectual awareness of the principles of Divine Providence and trust in God as theological axioms, and the application of these principles as forces guiding the soul in everyday life. By means of the repetition of these verses, Rabbi Zundel hoped to internalize the principles of providence and trust, transforming them into points of reference that would guide one's everyday acts.

Rabbi Zundel's *yir'ah* was likewise reflected in his punctilious care over the observance of mitzvot. Following the rulings and customs of the Gaon of Vilna and of Rabbi Hayyim,[24] Rabbi Zundel's pious deeds may be understood as a continuation of a tendency characteristic of his teachers. As Rabbi Naphtali Amsterdam attested:

> Once he was speaking with people during the days of Hanuk-kah, and in the course of conversation one of them mentioned a sad matter. He said to them, "Silence! One may not mention sad matters during these days, as the Sages prohibited the giving of eulogies during Hanukkah." . . . He once walked in a place where there were gardens and fields belonging to Jews, and when he passed by the gardens and fields they observed that he pressed his finger to his nose at which they were astonished. Afterwards he explained the reason for this act, following his custom in all his study, to seek out knowledge [pertaining to] practice . . . [namely,] that the rabbis stated at the beginning of tractate Bava Batra that it is forbidden for a person to stand in his neighbor's field when it is in full bloom; and Rashi explained . . . that [this is] so as not to damage it with the evil eye. . . . Since at times it is impossible to avoid glancing at it for a moment, [one may do] as it states in Berakhot 55b: "One who ascended to a certain place . . . and he fear the evil eye, let him grasp his left nostril." That is why for this reason he so acted. Once they found him standing near a small door in his courtyard with hammer and nails in his hand, banging the hammer and nails very energetically, and afterwards they discovered the rea-

> son for this: The lock had become broken and [the door] closed
> by itself, so that the beggars who go from door to door were
> unable to open the door, which violated the statement in the
> Talmud, Bava Batra 7b. . . .[25]

The above acts deserve the title of "acts of piety" because they are
unusual acts, which the majority of people would not even consider
performing. Nevertheless, they were not pictured as acts of extra-
exemplary piety—to the contrary, one is struck by Rabbi Zundel's tendency to base all his actions upon specifically halakhic considerations.
His acts of piety are thus similar to those of Rabbi Hayyim, as described
by the latter's disciples, the common element of both being the attempt
to apply the halakhah to situations to which the average person would
not at all consider it applicable. All this is based upon the attempt to
derive practical applications from the direct study of the talmudic discussions, including those of the aggadah and midrash.

A description of Rabbi Zundel's piety would be incomplete without
mentioning his stand concerning the Evil Impulse and the means by
which one may struggle against it. It is the nature of the Impulse to
continuously tempt people and to attack them every day, first trying to
deceive them and then attempting to draw them close. It especially
tempts talmudic scholars, because "whoever is greater than his fellow,
his Impulse is likewise greater." Rabbi Zundel sees the principal dangers
of the Impulse's activity in those areas that he considers to be the main
focus of Divine service: "the main thing is that the Impulse tempts one
to neglect Torah and to pursue honor and money. . . ."[26] In other words:
The primary area of struggle and conflict with the Evil Impulse lies in
the area of devotion to Torah study and separation from worldly pleasures. In the Rabbinic dicta cited by Rabbi Zundel concerning this
matter, as well as in his own remarks on the subject, the Evil Impulse
is portrayed as a crafty and dangerous persona, the struggle against
whom requires devotion of considerable energy. Even though he does
not state so explicitly, it would appear that, following the kabbalistic
outlook, Rabbi Zundel saw the Evil Impulse as the agent of the forces
of the *Sitra Ahra*—the "Other Side."

Rabbi Zundel was imbued with the awareness, based upon Rabbinic
dicta and various Mussar works, that people need Divine assistance in
order to overcome the Evil Impulse, being unable to do so by their own
powers.[27] That assistance, of course, depends upon the degree of arousal
and effort on the part of the individual person. There are two ways by
which one can overcome a personal Impulse. The first path, which
does not involve any frontal confrontation with it, is that of Torah
study. Rabbi Zundel cites the words of the Midrash in *Avot de-Rabbi*

Nathan, chapter 2, on this point: "Whoever places the words of Torah upon his heart removes from himself thoughts of the sword and thoughts of famine, thoughts of foolishness and thoughts of lewdness, thoughts of the Evil Impulse and thoughts of [adultery], thoughts of vain things. . . ." He also cites the remark of the Talmud in Kiddushin 30b: "If you involve yourselves with Torah, you are not given over to it [the Evil Impulse]."[28] On the basis of these rabbinic dicta, he states that the very act of Torah study protects the student from the onslaughts of the Evil Impulse. (One ought to mention here that this principle was already accepted by Rabbi Hayyim, who taught it to his disciples.) But although Rabbi Zundel saw the study of Torah as an important means of protection against the Impulse, he did not consider it adequate. Following the prominent Mussar work by Rabbi Moses Hayyim Luzzatto (1707–46), *Sefer mesillat yesharim*, Rabbi Zundel recommends daily self-examination:

> The cure for this [is to do] as written by the *hasid*, the author of *Mesillat Yesharim* . . . [namely,] that a person must examine every day and every time the straight path that he shall choose for himself according to his time and nature and occupations, and search his deeds, [to see] if he is walking in the upright path or if he needs to correct his actions. . . .[29]

We find that even those who devote themselves to Torah study have no guarantee that their actions will be ethically correct; it is therefore incumbent upon them periodically to interrupt their routine in order to examine themselves and their actions. This self-examination has a distinctly personal cast: only individuals themselves, who are aware of the ethical tests that they are likely to encounter in their own specific life situations, can find the right tactic to anticipate difficulties, and thereby avoid or overcome them. This self-examination serves as a framework for a personal stock-taking of what the individual has done in the past and the best way to correct any errors that were made.

At this point, we must address the question of the function and weight given to the study of Mussar works per se by Rabbi Zundel. His remarks concerning the need for self-examination are followed by his assertion that: "[O]ne must learn *Mesillat Yesharim* several times"; further along, he mentions several sources in the midrash, as well as in *Hovot ha-levavot* and *Sefer ha-zohar*, concerning matters of Mussar. He concludes: "[A]ll these and their like cause a person to examine his affairs, and it then goes well with him both in this [world] and [in] the next."[30] The study of Rabbinic dicta concerning matters of Mussar, as well as of such Mussar works as *Mesillat yesharim* and *Hovot ha-levavot*, was therefore perceived by him to be factors stimulating and encouraging a person to engage in self-criticism.

In this context, we should properly note the considerable stress that Rabbi Zundel placed upon the study of Rabbinic dicta concerning matters of *yir'ah* and Mussar. This point may be seen from the large number of Rabbinic sayings quoted in his writings, whether from the Talmud or from the midrash, and particularly from *Avot de-Rabbi Nathan*. Further support for this is given by Rabbi Naphtali Amsterdam:

> It is clear that all the force of righteousness and piety of this exalted person only [came about] through the study of Mussar. . . . [He would] repeat a certain verse or Rabbinic dictum several times, with great concentration, as our master and Teacher of blessed memory [that is, Salanter] related of him.[31]

This testimony, based upon what Rabbi Naphtali had heard from Rabbi Israel Salanter, also indicates the method used by Rabbi Zundel to study these Rabbinic sayings. It did not consist of straightforward study whose purpose was knowledge of the religio-ethical ideas cited in Rabbinic sayings, but of repetition of certain specific dicta. Note his practice of repeating certain verses of "trust," which we have already mentioned. The aim of the repetition was identical in both cases: the creation of an intense psychological effect, sufficiently powerful to influence a person's reactions and patterns of behavior.

Alongside his involvement in Rabbinic dicta, Rabbi Zundel did not neglect Mussar works. We quoted above his remarks that one should "learn *Mesillat Yesharim* several times. . . ." Rabbi Naphtali Amsterdam likewise records what he saw concerning this subject in the writings left by Rabbi Zundel. On the eve of his departure from Volozhin, Rabbi Zundel asked Rabbi Hayyim: "What Mussar book ought one study?" His master replied: "Every Mussar book is good to learn. But *Mesillat Yesharim* should be your guide."[32] (Note that neither Rabbi Zundel's question nor Rabbi Hayyim's reply concern the amount of time to be allotted to Mussar study; moreover, he seems to distinguish between *lomdim* in general and unusual individuals among his disciples, upon whom he relied to find the proper balance between Torah study and study of Mussar. Clearly Rabbi Zundel belonged to the latter category.)

Having attempted to reconstruct Rabbi Zundel's path in Divine service, we now examine the degree of continuity between his path and that of Rabbi Hayyim. Having viewed Rabbi Zundel as a kind of living embodiment of the ideal toward which Rabbi Hayyim wished to educate his disciples, I have attempted to demonstrate that the continuity between master and disciple was expressed, not only in the combination of Torah and *yir'ah* as such, but in several specific aspects of both. That continuity was primarily expressed in the valuation of Torah study as the main element in Divine worship; in the struggle for maximal commitment to Torah study in daily life; in the emphasis upon the relation between study and practice; in the evaluation of *yir'ah* as a necessary accompaniment to Torah study; in the awareness of the power of the Evil Impulse and the need for constant struggle with it; in the understanding of Torah study as a means of defense against the temptations of this Impulse; in the recognition of the need for devoting special effort toward the aim of ethical improvement, through forms of activity not incorporated in Torah study; in the evaluation of the study of Rabbinic dicta concerning matters of *yir'ah* and Mussar as an important means of religio-ethical improvement; and in the great weight given to the attributes of humility and trust in God (*bitahon*).

Despite the points of similarity and of continuity between Rabbi Zundel and Rabbi Hayyim, we must recognize the uniqueness of Rabbi Zundel, whose piety bore a distinctly personal stamp from several points of view. Though he did not deny the supremacy of the study of Torah, the relative weight he gave to the cultivation of *yir'ah* seems to have been greater than that given by Rabbi Hayyim. While such a statement cannot be proven by exact measurements, such is the impression gained from study of the writings of Rabbi Zundel and various accounts that have been preserved about him. This uniqueness may also be seen in the way of life he chose for himself, which may be described as one guided by the value of asceticism and self-effacement. By refusing to hold rabbinic office, and by his efforts to conceal his unusual qualities from other people, Rabbi Zundel realized something of the ideal conception of the "hidden *zaddik*." He differed in this respect both from Rabbi Hayyim himself as well as from the majority of his prominent disciples, who served in rabbinic offices or as teachers of Torah in yeshivot. In a certain sense, one may even point to a contradiction between the teaching of Rabbi Hayyim and Rabbi Zundel's behavior. In a reply to one of his students who was uncertain as to whether it was preferable to accept financial support in order to study Torah all day, or to forego such support and devote part of the day to earning his own living, Rabbi Hayyim stated that it was clearly preferable to accept support and devote all of one's time to study.[33] Rabbi Zundel did not accept this approach. By choosing to support himself by his own labor rather than benefit from the crown of Torah, he expressed a certain preference of *yir'ah* over and above Torah study.

The specific quality of Rabbi Zundel's *yir'ah* may also be seen in the unique path that he established for himself: prayer by means of recitation of verses; the repetition of verses of *bitahon* and of Rabbinic dicta; and isolation from people by walking in the fields, all of which bore a strictly personal stamp. If we add to these his intense consciousness of sin, his periodic self-examination with the aim of ethical perfection, and his study of Mussar works, we find that Rabbi Zundel's *yir'ah* had a distinctive character, as well as bearing greater relative weight than it did in the teaching of Rabbi Hayyim.

It would be incorrect to interpret Rabbi Zundel's path as a deliberate departure from the teaching of Rabbi Hayyim; rather, it was the result of a process whereby the disciple developed certain tendencies that had in principle existed in the teaching of his master. While the distinctive character of Rabbi Zundel's *yir'ah* obviously stemmed to a great extent from his own personal makeup, it seems to me that his increased emphasis upon *yir'ah* may be explained as well in terms of certain changes that took place over the course of time in the status of Torah study. As has been mentioned, Rabbi Hayyim's reservations against the excessive involvement of *lomdim* in the study of Mussar works stemmed from his fear that Torah study would suffer. That fear, of which Rabbi Hayyim was aware when he wished to determine the status of *yir'ah* generally in relation to Torah study, no longer troubled Rabbi Zundel, because by his day the status of Torah study had greatly improved as the result of Rabbi Hayyim's own activity.[34] Under these circumstances, the ground was set to develop further the realm of *yir'ah*.[35]

5

The Encounter Between Rabbi Israel Salanter and Rabbi Zundel Salant

RABBI Israel Lipkin, known as Salanter, was born in 1810[1] in the town of Zager, in the district of Kovna (Kaunas).[2] His father, Rabbi Zeev Wolf Lipkin, who was descended from a rabbinic family,[3] served as a Talmud teacher in that town, and later as rabbi in Goldingen and in Telz. Rabbi Zeev Wolf was renowned in the world of talmudic learning for his work *Hagahot bet aryeh* on the Talmud, Maimonides, and the *Turim*. Israel received his earliest training in Torah from his father. It is related that, as a boy of ten, he was already renowned for his intellectual acumen and was known as "the Zager *'Iluy"* (prodigy). His father, who was not happy with his convoluted pilpulistic method of study, sent him to study Torah with Rabbi Zvi Hirsch Broide, the rabbi of Salant, known for his devotion to the straightforward (*peshat*) method of study.[4] While in Salant, Rabbi Israel married the daughter of Rabbi Jacob Eisenstein and continued his studies while being supported by his father-in-law.[5]

Salant was a center of Torah study during the years in which Rabbi Israel studied there. Gathered around Rabbi Zvi Hirsch Broide was a circle of young scholars, several of whom were later to become noted rabbis, including Rabbi Samuel Salanter, who was to become the leading Ashkenazic rabbinic figure in Jerusalem, and Rabbi Alexander Moshe Lapidus, who was to become the rabbi of Reisin.[6] This circle of scholars was joined by the young Rabbi Elijah Kartinga, whom Rabbi Israel Salanter taught and befriended. Some years later, Rabbi Elijah became known as an activist in community affairs and a militant opponent of Haskalah. He maintained his connection to Salanter throughout those years, and even acted as his emissary.

During the time that he studied in Salant, Rabbi Israel was renowned for his talents, becoming one of the chief disciples of Rabbi Zvi Hirsch Broide. We learn of this from a student of Rabbi Alexander Lapidus, who also studied with Rabbi Zvi Hirsch. He states that "during the period that he studied in Salant, Rabbi Israel headed a yeshiva in Salant and studied *Seder Nezikin* with his students, and when he had completed this [talmudic] order, the *gaon* Rabbi Zvi sent my above-mentioned teacher to hear the concluding lecture and to report to him on what he heard."[7] We therefore learn that, evidently during his twenties, Rabbi Israel began to teach Torah to his own students, who were probably young boys, as the more advanced young married students continued to be guided by Rabbi Zvi Hirsch. From the above-cited testimony, it would appear that the latter followed with interest the teaching activities of his outstanding student.

Rabbi Zundel also lived in Salant during the period of Rabbi Israel's sojourn. The meeting between the two brought about a far-reaching change in the direction of young Rabbi Israel's life, about which we learn from the account of his students, including that of Rabbi Isaac Blazer:

> When our master and teacher, *ha-gaon he-hasid*, a saint in Israel, may the memory of the righteous and saintly be a blessing, was in the flower of his youth . . . and was already renowned as a great *gaon*, the glory of Israel, he was close to his saintly teacher, *ha-gaon he-hasid* Rabbi Joseph Zundel, and would come and go constantly, like a member of his household. He observed the ways of his master in his holy service and he carefully followed his footsteps. When his teacher went into the fields to study and to repeat matters of *yir'ah* and *Mussar*, our teacher secretly followed him, to observe and to hear his good words of *Mussar*. The Gaon, Rabbi Joseph Zundel, saw and understood that this delightful flower would grow like a cedar in Lebanon. . . . He took him under the wing of the glory of his righteousness. . . . And as the first step, he saw fit to instruct him about the study of Mussar. I heard in particular that once he spoke to him as follows, "Yisrael, learn Mussar and be God-fearing." These words penetrated the chambers of his heart like an arrow from a bow, and he began . . . to study every day works of *yir'ah* and *Mussar*. And his soul was greatly aroused in the fear of God, may He be blessed. . . .[8]

Underlying this description are the basic facts that Rabbi Israel was drawn toward the unique personality of Rabbi Zundel, clung to him and became his disciple in the realm of *yir'ah*. The study of Mussar is, so to speak, the quintessence of Rabbi Zundel's message to Rabbi Israel, having brought about the immediate and revolutionary change in his manner of serving God.[9]

In addition to Rabbi Isaac Blazer's testimony, with its combination of rather naive contents and stylized presentation, Rabbi Naphtali Amsterdam gave the following account:

> . . . When he was in his prime, in the full force of his greatness and genius, he began to pour water over the hands of [that is, to serve] his master, the *hasid* Rabbi Zundel, of blessed memory. And from him alone did he receive wisdom and this great learning, which is the study of Mussar, to study and to repeat Rabbinic dicta and Mussar works many times, with great concentration. He served him, and accepted him as his foremost teacher, who he used to say that he had set him on his feet in the service of God and on the path of holiness. And when his teacher, the *hasid*, travelled to the Holy Land, our teacher [that is, Rabbi Israel] escorted him three parsangs [about eight miles], as one is required to do by law for one's principal teacher. And our master and teacher of blessed memory related to us that when he heard the voice emanating from his teacher commanding him to study Mussar, it was as if a burning fire descended into the chambers of his heart, and he began to involve himself in this study.[10]

The tendency to emphasize the value of Mussar study also appears in Rabbi Naphtali Amsterdam's words;[11] he similarly testifies to the powerful psychological impact upon Rabbi Israel of the "command to study Mussar."

It is important here to avoid the mistaken impression that Rabbi Zundel's influence upon Rabbi Israel was specifically centered upon the demand to learn Mussar. It seems more likely that the young scholar was attracted to the personality of this *lamdan-hasid* because of the totality of his personal qualities, of which the technique of Mussar study as a means of ethical perfection was only one component, albeit one of considerable importance. This assumption seems to me to be strengthened by what Rabbi Israel Salanter himself wrote concerning Rabbi Zundel:

> I poured water over the hands of [that is, served] my master, Rabbi Joseph Zundel, who dwells in Jerusalem, may it be speedily rebuilt, and thus far I have not even reached his ankles. He was a ladder standing upon the ground, [a reference to Gen. 28:12], troubled by thoughts of commerce, seeking his livelihood in the manner of the householders whose livelihood

weighs heavily upon them. But his head reached the heavens, with great effort on behalf of the life of his soul. His study was mainly involved with those things needed for practice. He studied the Talmud, *Bet Yosef* and all the later authorities with great concentration, and most especially *Bi'urei ha-Ger'' 'a* [the glosses of the Gaon of Vilna]. And when he studied a passage in the *Shulhan 'Arukh*, or a given topic with all its scholarly apparatus, it was as if this law had come before him for a ruling in practice. . . . All his study of Bible and Midrashim and *Zohar* was based upon the aim of knowing how to practice, and above all, there was a great effort to correct the character traits and obligations of the heart. . . .[12]

One is struck here by the fact that Rabbi Israel, in the few short lines that he wrote concerning Rabbi Zundel, did not refer at all to the subject of Mussar study. Rather, his remarks express amazement and admiration of the remarkable combination embodied in the personality of Rabbi Zundel: of hard work for one's livelihood, of relentless cultivation of one's ethical character, and of devotion to Torah study while emphasizing the close relation of study to practice.

In light of what we know about Rabbi Zundel and on the basis of the statements of Rabbi Israel Salanter and his disciples, one may sum up the influence of Rabbi Zundel upon the latter as follows. Rabbi Israel found in the personality and way of life of Rabbi Zundel a living example of the integration of Torah and *yir'ah*. As a scholar, who had hitherto concentrated his main efforts upon acquiring knowledge of Torah, he now viewed *yir'ah* as an area requiring special awareness and deliberate activity. The transformation wrought by the influence of Rabbi Zundel upon the soul of Rabbi Israel may be described as a transformation of values, in the sense that the relative weight of *yir'ah* became infinitely greater than it had been until that time. The components of *yir'ah* that Rabbi Israel found to be embodied in Rabbi Zundel were the following: (1) the effort toward the maximal realization of the halakhah, while attempting to derive practical conclusions even from the tentative arguments raised within the talmudic discussion and the Rabbinic midrashim; (2) sensitivity and alertness to the power of the Evil Impulse, which constantly schemes against a human being (his oppressive sense of sinfulness, whose source lies in the tendency toward severe self-criticism, is also related to this); (3) the assumption that, for purposes of the struggle with the Impulse and for ethical improvement, it is insufficient only to study Torah, but that one must also engage in some separate, distinct activity; and (4) self-examination and Mussar study as means of ethical improvement. Those are the general qualities that characterized Rabbi Zundel, most of which are found in Rabbi Israel Salanter as well.

We have no exact chronological landmarks indicating Rabbi Israel's age when his connection with Rabbi Zundel began to develop. Rabbi Israel Salanter's disciples state that this occurred when their master was quite young, albeit already known as an outstanding scholar. On the basis of these statements, one may conclude that Rabbi Israel's personality was already fairly well developed when he started to attach himself to Rabbi Zundel. If such was in fact the case, then the change that took place under the influence of his new teacher was a fairly sharp one, if not revolutionary. The intensity of that change may be seen in Rabbi Israel's remark, preserved by Rabbi Naphtali Amsterdam, that it was Rabbi Zundel who "put him on his feet in the service of God."

Something of the fabric of the relations that were woven between Rabbi Israel and Rabbi Zundel, who was some thirty years older than the former, are suggested by the sources quoted here.[13] The expressions that repeat themselves are service to the master by his disciple, pouring water over the hands of the master, the clinging of the disciple to his master, and so forth. All of these expressions indicate the intimate relationship between Rabbi Israel and Rabbi Zundel. The former followed intensely Rabbi Zundel's path in the service of God, and must have discussed with him matters of Torah and *yir'ah*.

There is some extant documentation from the period of Rabbi Israel's sojourn in Salant pertaining to a number of events in his life that seem to be connected with the influence of Rabbi Zundel. One such event concerns Rabbi Israel's decision to change his approach to the study of Torah: "In my youth, when I was involved in the study of Mussar and its laws, I forced my Impulse (which longed to show off my *pilpul* [casuistry] against my contemporaries) completely to abandon the path of *pilpul*, so that my gaze might be [directed] only toward the truth. . . ."[14] Thus, Rabbi Israel's decision to abandon *pilpul* was not primarily motivated by methodological, but rather by ethical, considerations. The *pilpul* method of study cannot be considered as "Torah for its own sake," because it serves the desire for honor and recognition. Rabbi Israel explains the change in his own method of study as the result of his study of Mussar. Indeed, the connection between this development and the influence of Rabbi Zundel is alluded to in his wording, for those few lines in which Rabbi Israel portrays the character of Rabbi Zundel appear as a note to the sentence quoted above. As mentioned, Rabbi Hayyim stressed that all those who wish to study Torah "for its own sake" must direct themselves toward the truth of Torah. He guided his students in the Volozhin yeshiva in this same spirit. It would seem that it was Rabbi Zundel who prodded the young Rabbi Israel to abandon the method of *pilpul* and to study Torah "for its own sake"—that is, in the pursuit of truth.[15]

Rabbi Zundel's exemplary influence may also explain Rabbi Israel's decision to take no formal rabbinic position. It is related that Rabbi Israel and his close friend, Rabbi Samuel of Salant, took upon themselves three restrictions: not to serve in the rabbinate, not to write books, and not to study Kabbalah.[16] Both Rabbi Israel and Rabbi Samuel were in fact offered the position of rabbi in Brisk, and they both rejected the offer.[17] One of Rabbi Israel Salanter's disciples relates that his teacher had "hidden reasons" for his refusal to serve in the rabbinate,[18] while another records that Rabbi Israel had thirty different reasons for this decision.[19] It is difficult to determine with any accuracy the degree of truth of these various traditions, though the latter, which speaks of thirty separate reasons, clearly seems like hagiographic hyperbole. In any event, it seems likely that, under the influence of Rabbi Zundel's example, Rabbi Israel saw greater value in devotion to Torah study without being supported by the public. He perceived the rabbinate as an exploitation of the Torah as a "spade with which to dig," not only because of the financial income it involved, but also because of the accompanying honor and power it provided.[20] His decision not to write any books may likewise be perceived as an expression of the attempt to cultivate the attribute of modesty and to shun honor.[21]

As one of the manifestations of how Rabbi Israel's *yir'ah* became strengthened in the wake of his closeness to Rabbi Zundel, Rabbi Isaac Blazer relates his plan to take upon himself a life of asceticism and withdrawal. According to this account, Rabbi Israel intended to move to a place where he was unknown so that he might hide his qualities from other people.[22] The second generation of his disciples relate the details of the preparations he undertook in order to advance this plan.[23] However, Rabbi Israel changed his mind and decided to forego becoming a recluse because he would be unable to act for the public good were he to withdraw from the community.

Rabbi Blazer describes an incident that occurred several years later, when Salanter was already living in Vilna, which sheds light on this later decision. His students heard of a certain person who supported himself by planing boards of wood, who wore *tefillin* all day and whose lips were constantly moving. Out of curiosity, they urged their teacher to invite this man to find out what he was all about. Rabbi Israel's reply was that he could not believe that a person who was truly on a high spiritual level could, in such a historical situation as theirs, choose to live the life of a "hidden saint [*Tzaddik*]" while ignoring the pressing needs of the public.[24] This would seem to support Rabbi Blazer's essential testimony—namely, that when Rabbi Israel lived in Salant he had intended to become a recluse, but had changed his mind because of the above-mentioned consideration. It would also make sense that, because of Rabbi Israel's closeness to Rabbi Zundel and his admiration for his way of life, the young student should have wished to imitate his master in this respect as well. If we accept Rabbi Isaac Blazer's testimony, then even during the period that he lived in Salant, Rabbi Israel set himself the goal of acting on behalf of the public and within it. However, this does not justify Dov Katz's statement that when Rabbi Israel still lived in Salant, he already developed the idea of bringing about a revolution among the Jewish people on the basis of "Mussar teaching."[25]

Among the second generation of disciples of Rabbi Israel Salanter, followed by Dov Katz, an internal tradition circulated that describes the activities undertaken by Rabbi Israel to prepare the ground for his public mission in the realm of Mussar, as follows:

> Rabbi Israel knew that without the authority of a Torah giant [*gaon*] he would have no access to Lithuanian Jewry, and after a difficult struggle within himself he decided to reveal himself before the people. In order to begin his activity, he went about the neighboring towns preaching *pilpul* of Torah. Wherever he went, his audience was astonished at his genius and acuity, and his name was on everybody's lips. Before long, the news spread in the camp of the *lomdim* that a great *gaon* had arisen in Israel. . . . Rabbi Israel utilized this opportunity, at the same time preaching to the public about matters of admonitions and Mussar, rousing them to spiritual awakening and winning souls over to his approach. He was graced with great talent in public speaking, a strong voice breaking into flames of fire, and he aroused the fear of God in their hearts and brought them close to their Heavenly Father.[26]

Further on, Dov Katz adds that, because of difficulties in the situation of his wife's business, Rabbi Israel sought a position that would provide him a source of livelihood, and at the same time constitute an appropriate framework within which to fulfill his public mission. Among other options, he considered the possibility of serving as a *maggid*—an itinerant preacher. He later thought that the position of *mashgiah* (model and guide in Mussar education with higher status than even the yeshiva head) in a yeshiva would be the proper solution, but finally responded to the proposal that he serve as a *resh metivta*, heading one of the yeshivot in Vilna.[27]

Suggestive though these stories are, they appear to have no basis in fact; they all took shape in the world of legend created by the second generation of Salanter's disciples and neither confirmation of them nor an echo of them is found among the members of the previous generation, who were his contemporaries. These stories reflect a tendency typical of all hagiographical legends surrounding a historical personality—namely, the attempt to fill a lacuna in our knowledge of an earlier period by means of what is known from the later time. Since Salanter later became renowned as a Torah *gaon* throughout Russia, the legend asserts that he must have gone from one community to another attempting to establish his brilliance before the public. Moreover, because the office of *mashgiah* became of central importance in the Mussar yeshivot that were established at a much later period, he is said to have intended to serve in such an office already when he lived in Salant, when, in fact, this institution—as it developed in the Mussar yeshivot— had not yet existed.

It has been necessary to quote and analyze these traditions due to the importance of the question as to when, in fact, the idea of founding a movement centered around issues of Mussar first originated in Rabbi Israel Salanter's mind. The internal tradition of the Mussar movement would bring this development forward to the period of his residence in Salant, with the intention of stressing the connection between the founding of the movement and Rabbi Israel's relationship with Rabbi Zundel, and thereby indirectly with Rabbi Hayyim of Volozhin and the Gaon. There is no reason to cast doubt upon the fact that Rabbi Israel's personality was indeed strengthened and took shape during the years that he spent in Salant, including his position regarding the status of *yir'ah* and the proper means of acquiring it. In this sense, the Salant period was one of preparation and training for his initiative and activities during later periods. But one may not conclude from this that he had, during the Salant period, already attempted to transform his own personal path in Divine service into the ideological platform of a broad movement. The first reliable information concerning Rabbi Israel's public activity in the area of Mussar appears several years after his move to Vilna. Indeed, as we shall see below, it was no mere coincidence that the idea of founding the Mussar movement originated and developed specifically in Vilna.

PART TWO
Vilna, 1840–49

6

The Dissemination of Torah and Laying the Foundation for the Mussar Movement

IN 1840, at the age of 30, Rabbi Israel Salanter left Salant, along with his family, and moved to Vilna.[1] This change of location signifies the beginning of a new chapter in his life: No longer a young student who spent his days studying Torah, he became a Torah teacher and a leader, who labored to spread his own teachings. Whereas the years spent in Salant were devoted to the formation and crystallization of his personality and the acquisition of intellectual tools, the period in Vilna gave him extensive opportunities to act within and on behalf of the public.

Vilna in the early 1840s, with its Jewish population of about 30,000,[2] was a metropolis whose unique character derived not only from the large number of its Jewish inhabitants, but from the caliber both of its traditional scholars and of its Maskilim (enlightened intellectuals). The large number of "confraternities" for Torah study that populated its study houses, the yeshivot that attracted talented young men from both within the city and outside, as well as the large number of outstanding Torah scholars who resided there, gave Vilna the prestige of a major center of Torah.[3] During this period, there was also quite an active and well-defined group of Maskilim concentrated in Vilna, which, because of its size as well as the personal prominence of several of its number, was a focus of leadership and inspiration to the Haskalah movement in Russia generally. The unique status of Vilna in relation to other communities within the Pale of Settlement, as well as the prominence of its Maskilim, made it the main battlefield in the 1840s in the struggle between advocates and opponents of reform in the spirit of the Haskalah.[4]

An additional characteristic of Vilna during that period was the great number of simple artisans, day laborers, peddlers, and petty merchants who, taken together, constituted an extensive proletariat. The size and social character of this class were determined not only by the fact that Vilna was a large population center, but also by the severe economic depression that weighed upon the Jews of Lithuania generally, and those of Vilna in particular, during this period. It is extremely doubtful whether this class constituted a "proletariat" in the sense of a group with a developed class consciousness. However, there is no reason to doubt that the milieu of this class, upon whose faces were written poverty and want, was strongly felt in the life of the city.[5]

Thus, in the Vilna of Rabbi Israel, the social experience of Lithuanian Jewry as a whole was manifested in concentrated form, with all of its streams, uncertainties, and struggles. It seems reasonable to assume that he, who by nature was aware of and sensitive to matters concerning the public, was aroused by the encounter with this reality to define and identify the areas and challenges around which his future public activity was to be centered. In very broad terms, one can say that the orientation of Salanter's activity was shaped by a combination of two factors: the Torah, which he learned in Salant, and the problematics of Jewish existence, which he came to know in Vilna.

Shortly after his arrival he was invited by the trustees of the yeshiva of Rabbi Meile to serve as *rosh-yeshivah.*[6] Rabbi Isaac Blazer later recorded that his teacher answered this request only under duress: his wife's business in Salant had failed.[7] Rabbi Blazer used the argument of economic necessity to justify Rabbi Israel's decision to earn his living from a Torah position rather than following in Rabbi Zundel's path. But even if we concede that he relocated under economic pressure, it is difficult to agree that this was the only, or even the main, reason for the move to Vilna and his acceptance of the position in Rabbi Meile's yeshiva.

Since in those days Vilna was a mecca for outstanding *lomdim* from all of Lithuania,[8] it is not surprising that Rabbi Israel should also have been drawn there. It is more than likely that, after many years spent studying Torah in Salant, Rabbi Israel felt that he had exhausted the potential represented by that town, and that he hoped that the encounter with the scholars of Vilna would enrich and fructify his own scholarship. At the same time, it seems likely that he hoped to find a new source of livelihood in Vilna. He first went there by himself, in the hope that his household would join him there at a later date—once he would be settled. The invitation to serve as a teacher in Rabbi Meile's yeshiva was indeed a convenient solution to the problem of a livelihood, but was first and foremost an exciting challenge: Teaching Torah in a yeshiva was an appropriate avenue of expression for an outstanding scholar of the likes of Rabbi Israel. Furthermore, his public awareness and his natural propensity toward education, characteristics that were to be repeatedly revealed during the course of his life over the following years, must have made the office of *rosh-yeshivah* seem an exciting and attractive challenge.

Rabbi Meile's yeshiva, which was founded in 1827, was among the most prestigious and well-established Torah institutions in Vilna. During the first years of its existence it had no permanent building, but wandered from place to place; in 1831, it was given a spacious building in the courtyard of Rabbi Meile—hence the name "Meile's yeshiva." The yeshiva was divided into "stages"—that is, individual classes graded according to level. From 1831 on, Rabbi Mordecai Meltzer was the head of the highest "stage," while Rabbi Eliezer Teitz served alongside him as second *rosh-yeshivah*.[9] While the background of the invitation to Rabbi Israel to serve as *rosh-yeshivah* instead of, or alongside, Rabbi Mordecai Meltzer, is not altogether clear, the fact emerges that to his detriment, and probably also without his knowledge, Rabbi Israel became embroiled in a dispute between the trustees of the yeshiva and Rabbi Mordecai. In one version of the dispute, Rabbi Mordecai left Meile's yeshiva over an insult to several of his students. The trustees then turned to Rabbi Israel with the suggestion that he take the vacant position. Rabbi Israel agreed after being reassured by Rabbi Zvi Hirsch Broide that this was not considered trespassing upon another's rights. Suddenly, after Rabbi Mordecai had been absent from the yeshiva throughout the summer of 1840, the trustees proceeded to "restore him to his former place."[10]

This explanation for Rabbi Mordecai's abandonment of the position of *rosh-yeshivah* seems naive and unconvincing; moreover, this version takes pains to refute the rumors that a certain enmity or tension existed between Rabbi Mordecai and Rabbi Israel Salanter—Rabbi Mordecai's disciple both emphatically denies these rumors and fiercely denounces those who spread them. He argues that "only a few immature students had spread these rumors, and that the two principal figures involved admired and respected one another, and that on a number of occasions both were invited together to various festive occasions in Vilna, where everyone could clearly observe the close relationship between the two."[11]

A more balanced and reliable account of the course of events appears in the writings of Hillel Noah Maggid Steinschneider. According to him, several of the leading Torah scholars in Vilna were jealous of Rabbi Mordecai, who was considered one of the sharpest scholars in the city. They exploited the fact that Rabbi Eliezer Teitz, Rabbi Mor-

decai's second-in-command, had left his position and had advised the
trustees of the yeshiva to appoint Rabbi Israel in his place, "as he is
also sharp and expert—and will also be ahead of Rabbi Mordecai
Meltzer." Rabbi Mordecai, who was slighted by this appointment, took
his students and moved to another *bet midrash* (house of study). Steinschneider adds that "throughout this entire year, there were controversies between these great scholars, [fostered] by those who spread
deceit and lies, and it was impossible for these two rabbis to serve with
one crown [that is, in one place], as both of them were tremendous
geonim in Talmud, and each was affected by the prestige of the other."
In the end, "Rabbi Israel waived his own honor, left this place, and
went to study by himself in the precinct of Zarzecze in Vilna, and before
long he established a new yeshiva there. And Rabbi Mordecai Meltzer
returned to Meile's yeshiva as previously. . . ."[12]

Confirmation of the accuracy of Steinschneider's version appears
in the text of the appointment of Rabbi Israel Salanter as head of Rabbi
Meile's yeshiva:

> We, the trustees of the great yeshiva here in Vilna, located in
> the courtyard of Rabbi Meile . . . have hereby agreed to call by
> name the honorable Rabbi, the great light, the sharp-witted and
> erudite, the noted Rabbi Israel, may he live long, from Salant
> . . . to appoint him to be first *rosh-yeshivah* in the above yeshiva.
> And we have sent a letter signed by our hand to the above-
> mentioned great rabbi, upon his being appointed *rosh-yeshivah*
> of said yeshiva, and it is now about one-half year since the
> above-named rabbi has come here, and been appointed by said
> letter. Now we, the trustees, have gathered together with the
> above rabbis-overseers to reinforce the matter by means of a
> written appointment of the great light . . . Rabbi Israel, that he
> may be the first *rosh-yeshivah* in that yeshiva, to be an officer
> and commander of Torah and knowledge in that yeshiva, for a
> period of five years from today, to teach suitable students to be
> chosen by the trustees, to sit at the head of the highest grade in
> the yeshiva. . . .

The trustees go on to enumerate the conditions of his employment with
a salary fixed at four silver rubles per week, and eight rubles on those
weeks in which there is a festival. The trustees likewise agree to provide
him with an apartment near the yeshiva premises.[13]

It is thus clear that this appointment, in which it is explicitly stated
that Rabbi Israel will serve as the "first" *rosh-yeshivah*, followed an
earlier appointment issued about half a year earlier. Why was a new
appointment necessary? It was probably because Rabbi Israel was ini-

tially appointed as second *rosh-yeshivah* to Rabbi Mordecai, the senior man, while now, after Rabbi Mordecai left, he enjoyed the status of "first" *rosh-yeshivah*. It seems likely that this step exacerbated the injury to Rabbi Mordecai and that the dispute concerning the leadership of the yeshiva intruded into the personal relations between the two rivals. In the final event, Rabbi Israel decided to leave the office of *rosh-yeshivah*, thereby removing the cause of the controversy.

He thus acted over and beyond what was expected of him. In the final analysis, he was not responsible for the dispute between Rabbi Mordecai and the trustees of the yeshiva and his appointment was valid for another four and a half years; moreover, the office of *rosh-yeshivah* not only entailed an interesting occupation and a position of prestige, but assured him a respectable income during a period of general economic hardship. We do not know the exact considerations that caused Rabbi Israel to abandon all this. It may be that it became clear to him during that year that the trustees of the yeshiva had done an injustice to Rabbi Mordecai, and that he himself had served as an instrument to this end. It may also be that Salanter was repelled by the controversy itself and its accompanying manifestations. In any event, by this act Salanter was revealed as a personality whose steps were guided by fine ethical considerations.[14]

After leaving Meile's yeshiva, Rabbi Israel began to teach Torah in the *bet midrash* located in the Vilna suburb of Zarzecze, where his needs and the needs of his family were from then on supplied by the wealthy philanthropist Hayyim Baskas.[15] His decision to establish himself in the Zarzecze *bet midrash* came in the wake of the appeal of a number of "outstanding" young men who studied Torah there, asking him to be their teacher.[16] Among this group were Hillel Milikovski,[17] who was later to become rabbi of Salant and other communities; Alexander Moshe Lapidus, who became well known as the rabbi of Rosain; and Rabbis Samuel Lovtzer and Bezalel ha-Kohen, who were both later to serve as halakhic authorities in Vilna. In brief, these were talented youngsters, the future outstanding rabbis of nineteenth-century Lithuania. Two of them, Hillel Milikovski and Alexander Moshe Lapidus, continued to maintain contact with Israel Salanter and cooperated with him in communal matters even many years later. This group of young men was later joined by other *lomdim* who wished to hear Rabbi Israel's teaching. Thus was founded Israel Salanter's yeshiva in Zarzecze.[18]

The lectures given by Rabbi Israel during the years that he served as a teacher in Vilna brought him prestige as an unusually talented scholar. Hillel Milikovski described his acuity as similar to that of Rabbi Jonathan Eybeschutz (a famous eighteenth-century Polish rabbi), and

noted that he suffered a headache for several weeks due to his own
desire to completely follow the profundity of Rabbi Israel's analysis.[19]
Rabbi Isaac Blazer likewise relates that the Gaon Rabbi David Luria of
Bichove,[20] on the occasion of a visit to the city of Vilna, attended
Salanter's public lectures, and was greatly impressed by the latter's
depth of intellect and acuity.[21]

Another testimony relating to Rabbi Israel's method of study and
his influence among the *lomdim* is cited in the name of Rabbi Samuel
Lovtzer, who was one of his students during that same period:

> In 1840, a new star appeared on the horizon of Talmudic studies
> in Vilna, when the great and wondrous *gaon*, the Salanter, ar-
> rived there. His light shone upon the paths of study in that city.
> This Gaon displayed wonders of acuity and dialectical subtlety,
> drawing nigh ingeniously matters as distant as east and west.
> He, with his mighty spirit, and by the power of his marvelous
> intellect, brought them together as one, and made of them
> delicacies of acuity and clarity which astonished the minds of
> all who heard them, and the whole city was astounded that
> such a sharp Gaon had come to it. His contemporaries, the
> young men who were outstanding in halakhah, were jealous of
> him, and tried with all their strength to follow his method and
> to compose sharp dialectical novellae as he did—but they were
> not all successful in their wish.[22]

As far as we can tell, Rabbi Israel's skill was primarily expressed in
his ability to argue and demonstrate that a common principle underlies
seemingly unrelated halakhic matters, and that one can therefore draw
conclusions from one for the other. This method of study was unusual
in its sharpness, and thus attracted and enthused the outstanding students among the younger *lomdim*, who attempted to imitate it.

Further details of Rabbi Israel's method of study appear in the
remarks of his son, Rabbi Isaac Lipkin:

> In 1848 he delivered a *shi'ur* [lesson] in the *kloiz* [study house]
> of Rabbi Hayyim Parnas on the tractate *Hullin*, and during the
> entire semester he taught only seven or eight folios, and likewise
> in the second half of the year he studied it without the [standard
> commentaries of] Rashi and *Tosafot*, but for each *shi'ur* he would
> need [to refer to] the entire Talmud, or at least to half the
> Talmud. . . . And when I was in Krinik for several days with my
> great father . . . he told me apropos of the *shi'ur* which he said
> . . . that he regretted he had not then written them down. And
> as I heard, he said the lesson for a long time without Rashi or
> *Tosafot*, and without raising a contradiction from any commen-

tator, and without any change in the reading, and without any
on the earlier or later commentaries.[23]

Rabbi Isaac Lipkin's comments refer to 1848—the ninth year spent
by his father in Vilna. It would appear that, after he became widely
known as an outstanding scholar, Salanter was invited to teach a *shi'ur*
in other study houses in Vilna, and thus came to the *kloiz* of Rabbi
Hayyim Nahman Parnas in 1848. The latter was one of the most important public figures in Vilna; in addition to being a talmudic scholar
in his own right, he served for many years as trustee and important
communal leader.[24] It is therefore reasonable to assume that a number
of the superior *lomdim* and important householders of the city were
concentrated in this *kloiz* and that, in the invitation extended to Rabbi
Israel to "say a *shi'ur*," there was an acknowledgment of his stature by
the social and intellectual elite of Vilna.

Isaac Lipkin's testimony also includes several points that characterize his father's method of study. The small quantity of material
studied reflects an extremely deep and thorough approach. This is
reinforced by the comment that in every lesson he made use of the
entire Talmud, or at least half of it. It follows that the particular page
of Talmud that was the ostensible subject of the lesson merely served
as a point of departure for a complex speculative structure, in which
were woven together citations from many different talmudic discussions. As the study of the commentaries of Rashi and the *Tosafot* are
considered in the world of the *lomdim* as the usual point of departure
for any talmudic study, the fact that Salanter deliberately refrained from
relying upon the approaches of Rashi and *Tosafot* would indicate a high
degree of original creativity. Finally, also notable is the fact that the
original system built by Rabbi Israel did not conflict with the interpretations of the standard, authoritative commentators. In other words,
Rabbi Israel's ability to create a harmony between "his system" and
the various other interpretations, and to resolve every difficulty, again
testifies to the power of his acuity. Rabbi Israel himself evaluated his
own *shi'urim* from that period as an outstanding scholarly accomplishment, which was evidently the reason for his regret at not having
recorded them.

Laying the Foundation for the Mussar Movement

Beginning in 1844–46, alongside his activity as *rosh-
yeshivah*, Rabbi Israel began to engage in efforts that may be seen as
laying the foundation for the Mussar movement. These efforts included

(1) initiatives in the printing of Mussar works; (2) sermons on the subject of Mussar; (3) the founding of a "Mussar House"—that is, a special place for the study of Mussar works; and (4) the attempt to pass on the main elements of his doctrine to a group of close disciples, which was to become the initial cell of the Mussar movement.

It seems no accident that Rabbi Israel's public activity in the realm of Mussar did not begin prior to the year 1845, the sixth year of his sojourn in Vilna. That period was needed for him to become acclimatized personally and for him to become acquainted with the Jewish community, with all its groupings and problematics. During the course of those years, his position became more firmly established by virtue of his fame as a scholar and his teaching activity. Now, when he enjoyed the status and authority that Lithuanian Jewry customarily granted to an outstanding scholar, and having reached the age of thirty-six, Rabbi Israel felt himself ready to set out upon a course of public activity that departed from the normal models accepted among *gedolei torah*—"great Torah scholars."

One of Salanter's early public efforts is documented in Steinschneider's history of the city of Vilna.[25] He relates that, "at the advice of Rabbi Israel, there were published here the book *Heshbon ha-nefesh*, by Rabbi Mendel Satanower, in 1844, as well as *Sefer goren nakhon*, and *Tikkun middot ha-nefesh* of Solomon ibn Gabirol in 1845." Steinschneider, who does not state the source of this information, presumably relied upon traditions current in Vilna, for in fact the three titles mentioned were published without any reference to Rabbi Israel's role in their publication.[26] Even so, Steinschneider's version would seem to be strengthened by the very choice of books. Despite the profound difference between them in terms of period of composition, style, and contents, *Heshbon ha-nefesh* and *Tikkun middot ha-nefesh* nevertheless share a common denominator: neither was among the most widespread and popular Mussar books, so that their publication itself arouses our curiosity; and both books concentrate upon "improvement of character traits," based upon identification and knowledge of the components of the soul and their manner of functioning—subjects that were of central interest to Salanter, as elaborated below. It therefore follows that Salanter initiated the publication of these books because of their rarity and the special importance that he attached to them.[27]

During the period 1845–46, Rabbi Israel preached about matters of *yir'ah* and Mussar in the study house at Zarzecze. Among those who heard his preaching was the young student, Shneur Zalman Hershowitz, who recorded these sermons "as they were given, in their form and image, stature and shape, as they emerged from his holy mouth, literally, without any change, in clear language." His notes, published in 1883 with Salanter's permission as *Sefer even yisra'el*,[28] reveal the earliest expression of Rabbi Israel's views on matters of religio-ethical improvement. The contents of these sermons are discussed below; for the moment, we shall confine ourselves to the facts pertaining to his activity as a preacher.

To what sort of audience did Rabbi Israel preach? Steinschneider's remark that Salanter "awakened to Mussar those who were young in years by means of his impassioned words and clarity of language . . ."[29] evidently refers to young *lomdim*, his own students, and other young men. This latter group included the individual who recorded the sermons—Shneur Zalman. Important information concerning the character of his listeners is implicit in the nature of the sermons themselves. One who reads them in the hopes of finding fiery words of denunciation and direct admonitions calling for the changing of one's character and for repentance is likely to be disappointed. In form, these sermons resemble nothing so much as an halakhic discourse. Most of them are built upon a complex structure of apparent contradictions and solutions, interwoven with quotations and proof-texts from the Bible, the midrash, and especially from the Babylonian Talmud. Reading these sermons one is likely to wonder at times at what point he crosses the line separating halakhah from aggadah and Mussar. That is so, not only because Rabbi Israel works into his sermons explicitly halakhic discussions, but because he also applies the formal models of halakhic discussion to biblical stories and Rabbinic dicta, subjects that, in terms of their contents, belong to the realm of aggadah.[30] Taken as a whole, his sermons have a definitely learned character. They would therefore seem to be addressed to an audience that is able to follow and find pleasure in intellectual challenge—that is, an audience of *lomdim* and of *ba'alei batim* (householders) with a background in Torah learning.

From the period 1845–46, Rabbi Israel followed the common practice of his age in giving a learned cast to his sermons, the Jewish sermon having long been influenced by the intricate forms of halakhic discussion. If the learned element seems excessively prominent in Rabbi Israel's discussions, it was evidently the natural result of his training and activity as an outstanding scholar who still made use of the accepted norms of expression. Only later, and by stages, did he develop and crystallize his own forms, appropriate to his unique personality and activity. These forms are discernible in the letters to his disciples, the earliest examples of which were written in 1849, and in the famous "Mussar Epistle" (*Iggeret ha-mussar*), published in 1858;[31] but in the sermons published in the periodical *Tevunah* during the years 1861–

62, the learned-halakhic element is no longer prominent at all. Instead, these sermons focus upon matters of Mussar in a straightforward manner, the homiletical attempt to "dress" these ideas in Rabbinic dicta becoming distinctly secondary. Alongside our assumption that the learned style apparent in the sermons published in *Even yisra'el* reflect an early stage in Rabbi Israel's career as preacher, it may well be that this very style more successfully blunted the sharpness of his departure from the expected norm as a Talmud teacher. In the eyes of his audience, whose relation to Rabbi Israel was primarily based upon his great reputation as a talmudic scholar, the learned style of these sermons may have lent a certain authority to his ideas in the religio-ethical realm as well.

Thus far, I have described Salanter's initial activity as a preacher, based upon the evidence available and upon the sermons themselves. But in those works that focus on the internal traditions of the Mussar movement, quite a different picture is portrayed, as can be seen from the description by Rabbi Yehiel Yaakov Weinberg:

> Rabbi Israel spent seven years in Vilna. . . . During this time he held great public assemblies in the large synagogue as well as in other synagogues and study houses in the city, where he gave sermons on Mussar with burning passion. The mighty power of his speech, added to his fine and strong voice, made him the favorite of the community. . . . Masses of people, artisans, coachmen, and peddlers were heartily grateful to him for coming down to the simple folk from his exalted scholarly genius and for not delivering sharp casuistry and fragments of philosophical speculation, as did the other *geonim*. Rather, he spoke to them in simple terms about ordinary spiritual matters. They were devoted with heart and soul, and followed him . . . and they would gather en masse, filling the study house. . . .[32]

Neither Rabbi Weinberg, nor Dov Katz, who writes in a similar vein,[33] indicates sources or testimony to support their version. It would seem that Rabbi Weinberg, who was one of the students of Rabbi Nathan Tsvi Finkel of Slobodka, bases his description on what he heard from the second generation of Rabbi Israel Salanter's students. Since it is reasonable to assume that if Salanter acted in Vilna according to the scope and form described, it would have left its imprint on the memories of that generation, yet, in the sources known to us, one cannot find even a single allusion that corroborates that description, we can only conclude that it contains a certain measure of exaggeration. It looks like we have before us a typical instance of filling a gap in the biography of a revered historical personality by retrojection from a later period.

While it is true that Rabbi Israel took pains to be active and to influence wide sections of the community, and it is also true that he adopted the sermonic style intended to capture the audience and arouse their emotions, that course of action characterizes his latest activities, after he had left Vilna.[34] His earliest activity in the realm of Mussar concentrated on a relatively restricted circle of students and close acquaintances to whom the sermons printed in the book *Even yisra'el* were directed. As we shall try to see later on, Rabbi Israel wanted to draw this circle of his students and close acquaintances into the nucleus of leadership that would work to disseminate his ideas among a broader public.

One of Rabbi Israel Salanter's initial activities in the realm of Mussar in Vilna was the establishment of a Mussar house. Steinschneider, our only source on this, states that Salanter "awakened to Mussar those who were young in years by his impassioned words and clarity of language," and he adds, "he also established a special place for this purpose in the courtyard of the *zaddik* Zalman Rabbi Oris, and those who heard his Mussar went there regularly, and each one studied with his neighbor *Mesillat Yesharim* and *Hovot ha-Levavot.*"[35] We thus learn that the Mussar house was founded approximately the same time that Rabbi Israel gave his first Mussar sermons—that is, around 1845–46. Presumably, this new institution was attended by the same group of disciples and friends before whom he preached, who numbered no more than a few dozen. The nature and educational function of these Mussar houses is explained below; however, we may already state here that the very act of establishing this institution entailed a considerable innovation in principle. The setting aside of a special *bet midrash* for the study of Mussar works doubtless reflected a radical change in the importance and gravity attached to this kind of study. Morever, it was only natural that a Mussar house should be a social and organizational center for those people who rallied around the ideas of Rabbi Israel. From the point of view of Mitnaggedic society, which in the wake of the struggle with Hasidism was naturally suspicious and sensitive to the introduction of any new forms and institutions, the establishment of a Mussar house clearly called for explanation. It would seem that, whatever the motivations of its founders, in the specific situation of Lithuanian Jewry during this period, the establishment of a special *bet midrash* for the study of Mussar was bound to be interpreted sooner or later as a step competing with the "old" *bet midrash*, and against the study of Torah as it had been conducted since time immemorial.

Thus, Rabbi Israel Salanter's activities during the years 1844–46, including the initiation of the publication of Mussar books, the delivery of sermons related to matters of *yir'ah* and Mussar, and the establishment of a special Mussar study house, were the first practical steps toward the establishment of the Mussar movement.

I have thus far concentrated upon ascertaining the factual framework of these activities. But what was their significance? What was the "message" that took root and matured within Rabbi Israel's soul, that he wished to convey to the broad public? For what reason did Rabbi Israel see fit to establish a special *bet midrash* for the study of Mussar works that had been widespread and known for generations? We can answer these and other questions only by studying and discussing those sources that express Rabbi Israel's educational theory during the period under discussion.

7

Salanter's Mussar Doctrine—The Points of Departure and the Initial Stages

THOSE scholars who have so far discussed the doctrine of Rabbi Israel Salanter have presented his ideas systematically,[1] their assumption being that his was a systematic approach to Mussar and that it was therefore appropriate to define his principles as a total, coherent system.

The need to describe the system underlying Rabbi Israel's thought is self-evident, particularly in light of the fact that all of his writings were formulated in a fragmentary and diffuse manner. However, in their preference for systematic presentation, most of these authors, whether consciously or not, tended to ignore the chronological aspect; they generally failed to distinguish between earlier and later elements within Salanter's thought,[2] which is spread over a period of nearly forty years.

The chronological presentation of Salanter's thought in this work has two important advantages in terms of historical research: (1) it allows one to determine whether substantive changes occurred in his thought over the course of time; and (2) it enables one to trace the relationship between Salanter's views and concrete historical events. This relationship seems to me to be of particular significance, as Salanter was not an "ivory tower" thinker, but a leader and educator who lived in the heart of a society that he ceaselessly attempted to influence and shape. His goal was not to teach his Mussar doctrine to an abstract public; every sermon, letter, or article of his was first and foremost an educational act, intended to achieve a particular purpose within a particular context.

The fragmentary character and the limited number of available sources require a division of Salanter's philosophical activity into several secondary periods, each one of which is discussed as a more or less coherent whole. The first period, to which the present chapter is devoted, spans the years from 1845 to 1849, overlapping his initial public activity in the realm of Mussar. Our discussion is based upon two main sources—namely, Salanter's sermons given in the *bet midrash* in Zarzecze during the years 1845–46 and the five letters that he sent to a circle of his disciples-followers in Vilna in 1849, after he moved to Kovna.

The earliest source reflecting Salanter's views on questions relating to religio-ethical improvement are the sermons that were not recorded by Rabbi Israel himself, but by Rabbi Shneur Zalman Hirshowitz. This young Vilna scholar testifies that he took extreme care to pass Rabbi Israel's words on exactly as he heard them; indeed, the accuracy of his notes is confirmed by the fact that Salanter himself agreed to their publication.[3] Unlike the sermons, which were delivered to a relatively large public, the five letters that Rabbi Israel sent from Kovna to Vilna in 1849 have a more intimate and personal flavor. They were intended, in effect, to encourage the core of his followers to continue their activity on behalf of the dissemination of his Mussar ideas even after Salanter himself had left Vilna. These letters thus have an "internal" character, revealing far more of Salanter's thought than he saw fit to disclose to those who heard his sermons. Even though these letters were written during the first year after Rabbi Israel left Vilna, they rightfully belong to the period during which he lived there, not only because of their proximity in time, but also because the language and the context of the letters reflect ideas that are not seen as innovative but that had already been expressed orally to these disciples and reflected in his activities.[4]

The Theological Framework and the Definition of the Field of Mussar

Before we begin to discuss Rabbi Israel Salanter's Mussar teaching per se, we ought to devote some attention to the theological framework within which this system took shape. Such a discussion is required because the very definition and religious significance of the Mussar system are based upon its overall outlook concerning the relationships among God, human beings, and the universe. While Salanter did not specifically discuss his theological outlook within his writings, it is nevertheless possible to infer its general outlines from the context of his remarks on ethical matters.

Study of Salanter's writings reveals that, not only is his underlying theological position completely lacking in innovation, but it even entails a certain degree of retreat. His approach is essentially a return to the classical Rabbinic thought of the Mishnah and the Talmud. The image of God in his writings is a strictly transcendent and personal one: He is the God Who reveals Himself to humankind in His Torah and His commandments; who is providential; who rewards and punishes. Just as He is not the God of the philosophers, the object of speculation and of intellectual apprehension, so is Salanter's image of God remote from that of the Kabbalah. The attempt to influence the upper worlds or the desire to cling to God in the mystical sense play no role in his religious thought. Religious activity and meaning are defined by the concepts of commandment and transgression, reward and punishment, this world and the World to Come. The essence of Divine service thus consists in response and obedience to the mitzvot per se.

By ignoring the entire complex of questions and solutions pro-pounded by the major theological movements in post-Rabbinic Juda-ism—that is, rationalistic philosophy on the one hand, and Kabbalah and Hasidism on the other—Salanter retreats, as it were, from the later, more sophisticated stages of Jewish thought to an earlier, simpler stage. In principle, this retreat reflects a certain "theosophic apathy" on his part, curiosity and examination of theosophic questions in themselves being of no interest to him. Neither philosophical knowledge of the godhead nor contemplative meditation upon its secrets are understood by him as a religious value or goal. To the extent that he does concern himself with questions of the nature of Divine rule, such as that of reward and punishment, he does so only because of its implications for people's moral education.

From an historical point of view, it is not surprising that Salanter's thought was not significantly influenced by medieval philosophical speculative literature, as its influence within the social-religious context in which he grew up was extremely limited. What is surprising is his attitude of distance toward the Kabbalah, not only because of the central role that it played in Jewish thought from the sixteenth century onward, but because one might have expected him to follow in the footsteps of his forebears in this matter. It will be remembered that Kabbalah played a central role in the spiritual world of both the Vilna Gaon and of Rabbi Hayyim of Volozhin; there is also some evidence that Rabbi Zundel of Salant was attracted to it.[5] For this reason, Rabbi Israel's position concerning the Kabbalah may properly be described as a conscious retreat. This is even more striking in light of the fact that he specifically studied Rabbi Hayyim's book, *Nefesh ha-hayyim*, even citing it in his sermons. Interestingly enough, whenever he paraphrases Rabbi Hayyim's words in one of his sermons, they lose their kabbalistic coloration and are, so to speak, assimilated to the conceptual world of the rabbis.[6]

These matters must be portrayed accurately. I am not arguing here that Salanter denied, or even doubted, the authority and authenticity of the Kabbalah. On the contrary, he almost certainly accepted the assumptions that had been accepted for generations as to the antiquity, sanctity, and sublimity of the Kabbalah. However, he distanced himself from its influence, so that it no longer played a role in his religious outlook, and there is justification for the assumption that this was the result of a conscious and deliberate choice; in fact, one tradition states that in his youth, while still living in Salant, he took upon himself not to study the Kabbalah,[7] and traditions of later periods in his life confirm this assumption and shed some light upon it. When one of his acquaintances asked why he did not study Kabbalah, he replied, "What practical difference does it make in which heaven the Holy-One-Blessed-be-He sits? One thing is clear to me—that they will beat one with whips! And that it will hurt very much! And the beatings will be fierce! This I know clearly—so what else do I need?"[8] Those remarks, whose general tendency and style lead one to think that they are authentic sayings of Rabbi Israel, indicate the connection between "theosophic apathy" and his involvement in questions of Mussar. Rabbi Israel does not repudiate the value of theosophic speculation, but simply gives it a low position on his own scale of priorities. He argues that, from the point of view of an individual who is potentially subject to punishment in Hell, theosophic speculation on esoteric matters seems entirely irrelevant.

The conflict between involvement in esoteric thought and the attempt to shape human behavioral patterns may also be seen in the following saying of Rabbi Israel: "The *MaHaRal* of Prague created a *golem*, and this was a great wonder. But how much more wonderful is it to transform a corporeal human being into a *mensch*. . . ."[9] Rabbi Israel preferred moral education, not only as the more urgent of the two goals, but as a more significant and difficult religious challenge. Clear proof of his position regarding involvement in Kabbalah appears in a passage from his letter to a friend and disciple, Rabbi Elijah of Cartinga: "[Moses Hayyim] Luzzatto's work on the Kabbalah is not pertinent to me, because I do not study this subject and I do not know at all if the time is ripe for it."[10]

There seems to be a relationship between Rabbi Israel's self-imposed separation from the world of Kabbalah and his discussion concerning the structure of the human soul and the means of its moral improvement. The activities of the human soul are understood in kabbalistic literature in terms of contact with metaphysical forces. Hasidic literature displays a tendency to psychologize certain concepts that are metaphysical in origin; however, as Hasidic thought was molded by kabbalistic terminology and rooted in the theological assumptions of the Kabbalah, it could not cut itself off from the kabbalistic doctrine of the soul. On the other hand, because he separated himself both from the theological assumptions and the terminology of the Kabbalah, Salanter was both open to and able to absorb and to develop approaches that saw the human soul as an autonomous unit, whose components and the mechanism of whose actions can be explained rationally.

Salanter's "theosophic apathy" is likewise expressed in his understanding of the problem of Mussar. The uniqueness of this approach, which seems to me to be the most innovative aspect of his thought, may be understood against the background of the ethical thought of previous generations. Despite the wide spectrum of approaches in earlier generations of Mussar literature,[11] the majority of those ethical works that enjoyed wide circulation and influence nevertheless shared a common characteristic: a normative religio-ethical message. That is, the authors of these books wished to present their readers with a framework of actions, behavioral norms, and levels of religio-ethical norms that are deserving of execution. Thus, for example, Rabbi Bahya ibn Paquda presents an entire system of "obligations of the heart" in addition to the "obligations of the limbs."[12] The implicit message of this system is the demand for spiritualization and internalization of the religious life. On the other hand, the religio-ethical message that follows from *Sefer hasidim* is expressed in the concept of "the will of the Creator"—that is, that a special system of religious obligations, over and beyond the demands of the halakhah incumbent upon every Jew, is imposed upon the *hasid*, in responding to which he follows the will of his Creator.[13] The Mussar works belonging to the philosophical stream, on the one hand, and those belonging to the kabbalistic trend, on the other hand, each reflect a message of normative significance, the ethical way of life that these works wish to foster being derived from the ideational tendencies and religious ideals of each stream.

Thus, the value of asceticism reflects the attitude of the Kabbalah to earthly reality, at the same time constituting a prior and necessary condition for realization of the mystical ideal of *devekut*.[14] Also, those parts of Hasidic literature that are within the ken of Mussar literature, such as Hasidic *hanhagot* literature,[15] reflect a religio-ethical message in the normative sense. The common denominator of all these Mussar works, reflecting the ideational and spiritual tendencies of the various movements within the history of Judaism, is that the religio-ethical message implicit therein is seen as an addition to or completion of the halakhah. But even in those Mussar works that do not belong to any one of these specific streams and that may be identified for the purpose of our discussion as having a rabbinic orientation, a stress is generally placed upon normative contents. This is accomplished by focusing upon particular areas within the system of the mitzvot, taking note of their significance, discussing their details, and, at times, explaining them in a new light.[16]

To summarize, the majority of thinkers and authors in the realm of Mussar literature saw their task as the clarification and detailed depiction of ethical norms. Underlying this enterprise was the assumption that an important, if not decisive, step had been taken on the path leading the reader toward ethical perfection by one's very exposure to correct ethical norms. Many of the authors of ethical treatises also devoted attention to the problem of motivation in Divine service and to the psychological pitfalls lying in one's path. Nevertheless, discussions of this aspect of Mussar were generally connected and secondary to their primary concern of presenting the normative contents of Mussar. Moreover, even those authors who discussed Mussar within its psychological context, such as Maimonides in his *Shemonah perakim* (an essay in his *Commentary on the Mishnah*), did not isolate the question of motivation from the normative question, but defined the ethical norm itself by means of psychological concepts.

Rabbi Israel Salanter's understanding of the problem of ethics presents a striking innovation in contrast to those that are characteristic of Mussar literature.[17] His main innovation lay in transferring the focus of the problem of Mussar from the theological to the psychological realm. The problem with which ethics must deal is not which ethical norms an individual ought to fulfill—these are explained and codified in halakhic literature, and require no elaboration. The true problem of Mussar is the gap between cognitive knowledge, on the one hand, and psychological motivation, on the other. In other words, the fact that a given individual knows God's commandments, acknowledges their validity, and wishes to fulfill them is no guarantee that the individual will in fact obey them in practice, because the behavioral patterns and reactions of a human being are not guided and directed by rational consciousness, but by powerful, irrational emotional drives. In light of this interpretation of the problem of Mussar, and in light of the theological framework described above, we are better able to understand Salanter's conception of the proper limits and subject matter of Mussar. Obviously, Mussar is not conceived here as an autonomous source of the norms of religious behavior; those are defined in halakhic literature. Therefore, Mussar has no positive value outside of the framework of observance of the mitzvot. Rather, its entire purpose is to create a connection between the normative demands of the halakhah and the individual's psychological capacity to carry them out in real life. The way to accomplish this task involves two stages, the first being the development of a psychological theory explaining the components and dynamics of the psychic mechanism, and second, the development of educational methods based upon this theory, through which one may gain disciplined control over one's psychic life, and thereby over one's behavior in general.

"Appetite" and the Evil Impulse

The point of departure for Salanter's Mussar system lies in his understanding of the drives motivating human beings to ethically negative behavior. The most frequent and important concepts in his discussions of this problem are "appetite" (*ta'avah*) and "the Evil Impulse" (*yezer ha-ra'*). The meaning attached to these terms by Salanter is based upon a psychological perspective, in which they are freed from the metaphysical burden imposed upon them by kabbalistic Mussar literature. Despite the fact that the terms *ta'avah* and *yezer ha-ra'* occasionally appear in Salanter's writings as synonyms, adequate ground exists for clearly distinguishing between them.

At the basis of the Evil Impulse lies the appetite which is identical with the natural inclination toward pleasure implanted in a person from birth:[18] "The Evil Impulse . . . strongly dominates man by the power of lust implanted within man. . . ."[19] By means of one's senses, a person experiences both painful and distressing experiences, and pleasurable and enjoyable ones. The appetite is the psychological drive to return to pleasurable experiences and to avoid painful ones. Even though *ta'avah* is a force implanted within a person from birth, it tends to become stronger over the course of the years, either through habit or under the influence of the environment.[20] What most characterizes *ta'avah* is its attraction to instant pleasures and its inability to weigh long-term consequences.[21]

To the best of our knowledge, Salanter's writings contain no statement categorically repudiating physical pleasures as such. He does not accept the polarization between matter and spirit found in those streams of Mussar literature influenced by neo-Platonic thought. While the latter advocate abstention from physical pleasures because the very fact of relating to them distances one from God, Salanter holds that the only criterion determining desirable religio-ethical behavior is the maximal fulfillment of the commandments of the halakhah. His rejection of *ta'avah* is therefore not based upon the fact that it drives a person to seek physical satisfactions, except insofar as this drive is in conflict with the commands of the halakhah[22]—a conflict that is in many cases unavoidable, because of the restrictions and limitations halakhah places upon one's physical pleasures.

At this stage of our discussion, we should take note of the peculiar way in which Rabbi Israel uses the concept *yezer ha-ra'*. The Evil Impulse is the consequence of the confrontation between the appetite and the normative demands of the halakhah; it is the intellectual embodiment of *ta'avah* within the human consciousness. The great power of the *ta'avah* motivates people to seek intellectual justification for the satisfaction of their appetites, even when these are in opposition to the halakhah. It is clear from this why the *yezer* requires tricks and deceptive tactics in order to carry out its plans. It should not be surprising, therefore, that at times the Evil Impulse adopts a learned mask within the souls of Torah students and makes use of arguments that are based, so to speak, upon halakhah.[23]

Salanter believes that the appetite exercises a profound influence upon all of humankind's activities, an influence that is extremely dangerous, because the world is filled with stimuli arousing people's appetites and bringing them into conflict with the halakhah. It follows from this that a person's life in this world is filled with difficult tests and ceaseless struggle:

> . . . Man's purpose in this world is the service of the Creator, blessed be He. . . . This goal of entering into the inner chamber is possible only after much labor and effort in subduing his Impulse and in hard work to withstand the tests of the vicissitudes of the world and the troubles of time, and all one's days one is in danger of being doomed, Heaven forfend, by the net of the Impulse which is spread before one's feet every day and every hour. . . .[24]

In his attempt to emphasize and to concretize the great danger entailed in the activity of the Evil Impulse, Rabbi Israel follows the earlier literary tradition depicting it in the image of a demonic personality. This personification is, however, no more than a rhetorical device. Fundamentally, Salanter understood the Evil Impulse as a force whose source dwells within the human soul, and not as the messenger of some external metaphysical persona.[25]

In light of what we have said thus far, it is not surprising that his evaluation of an individual's spiritual ability to act in an ethical manner is extremely pessimistic, since *ta'avah* is a force implanted within the human soul from birth; it is able to dominate even the intellectual powers of a person, as expressed in the tricks of the Evil Impulse; earthly life is filled with points of conflict between the stimuli of the appetite and the halakhah. It follows from this pessimistic evaluation that people's routine patterns of behavior, and certainly their spontaneous activities, are primarily guided by their appetites.

Yir'ah—The Fear of God

According to Salanter, the main tool capable of shattering the power of the appetite and its control over human actions is the "fear of God" (*yir'ah*), a concept that played a central role in Mussar literature throughout the generations. Generally speaking, a distinction was drawn between *yir'at ha-'onesh* (the fear of Divine punishment— that is, that type of fear based upon the principle of retribution) and *yir'at ha-rommemut* (the fear, or awe, of Divine transcendence, in which one is motivated to serve God by a positive spiritual relationship to the Creator).[26] It is widely believed in ethical literature that the "fear of Divine majesty" is a more sublime level than "fear of Divine punishment"; indeed, there were those who completely rejected fear of Divine punishment as a legitimate motivation for the service of God.[27] Even those authors who did not advocate such an extreme view, but recognized the legitimacy of fear of punishment, saw it as a relatively low level, appropriate only to those who are just beginning their path in Divine service, or to the multitude who are unable to serve God on a higher level.[28]

Salanter seemingly ignored the above-mentioned tendency, basing the struggle with appetite primarily upon the principle of "fear of Divine punishment." He did so because he believed that the only force capable of halting the appetite when one finds oneself in an actual situation of ethical temptation is the fear of anticipated punishment for sin. However, we still need to determine the psychological processes by means of which fear of punishment can withstand the appetites. In a typical passage Rabbi Israel writes:

> . . . The intellect would require man to break his lusts, for otherwise he is like an animal—who sees nothing at all but that thing which is sweet to his tongue, even though it ends in death—unlike man, who has an intellect. Is it possible for man to eat that which is sweet to the pallet and good to the sight when he knows that it contains a poisonous potion, from which he will certainly soon die? How can he exchange a small plea-

sure in exchange for his whole life? Just so, literally, how could
it occur to one to perform a sin, when we believe without doubt
that he shall certainly incur a great and bitter punishment, far
greater than the degree of pleasure derived from the deed. . . .[29]

Thus, the intellect arouses the fear of punishment to withstand and
restrain the appetite. This is accomplished first by the intellect recognizing the principle of Divine retribution and then (unlike the appetite,
which is a spontaneous drive demanding immediate satisfaction)
weighing the consequences likely to follow upon a given course of
action in the present. The success of the fear of punishment in the
struggle against the appetite is supported by an additional assumption
expressed in the above passage—namely, that the punishment to be
anticipated by a person for a given sin is greater, both in terms of quality
and quantity, than the pleasure derived from that same sinful act. This
statement would appear to be Salanter's own innovation. In any event,
it reflects his view that, in the final analysis, Divine retribution is
intended to serve as a factor mitigating against sin.[30]

In allocating a central role to the intellect in the process of ethical
education, Salanter was seemingly close to the view of philosophical
Mussar literature. However, while, for instance, Bahya ibn Paquda
holds that, as the intellect is the bearer of religious truths—namely, the
unity of God and His attribute of kindness—it may motivate people to
serve God on a higher level,[31] for Salanter there is a kind of "deval-
uation" of the intellect: the recognition by the intellect of religious truth
does not in itself motivate a person to serve God; the importance of the
intellect is expressed rather in its function as a pragmatic tool allowing
people to calculate their own personal benefits.

Salanter would doubtless agree with Bahya and other thinkers that
Divine service activated by "motivation of the intellect" or by "awe of
the Divine transcendence" is far superior to that motivated by fear of
punishment. However, he was convinced that these and similar motivations, sublime as they may be, are not sufficiently powerful to influence human behavior when one is overwhelmed by appetite. In light
of this awareness, Rabbi Israel came to the conclusion that one must
distinguish between the conscious motivations of one's service of God,
and the psychological motivations that directly influence one's actions.
"Fear of Divine punishment" may serve as a psychological motivation
for the service of God, but under no circumstance does Salanter see it
as a value motivation. This distinction[32]—that is, between motivations
for religious service operating on the conscious level and unconscious
psychological motivations—is one of Salanter's major innovations. It is

another indication of the manner in which Salanter moved the focus of Mussar from the theological to the psychological realm.

Mussar Study

We saw above that the intellect's capacity for anticipating the future is able, when necessary, to awaken the "fear of Divine retribution." But even when the intellect does fulfill this mission, there is no assurance that it will indeed be successful in halting the appetite, for experience indicates that, whenever intellectual consciousness collides with emotional drives, it is overcome by the latter.[33] Therefore, even *yir'at ha-'onesh*, fear of Divine punishment, so long as it remains merely an abstract idea, is not strong enough to withstand the appetite. Salanter noted this problem and the means of confronting it in the opening sentence of his *Iggeret ha-mussar*:

> Man is free in his imagination but bound by his intellect. His imagination leads him wildly in the direction of his heart's desire, fearing not the inevitable future, when God will hold him to account for all his deeds, and he will be chastised by severe judgments. . . . Woe to the imagination, this evil enemy. It is in our hands, in our power, to put it far away by turning an attentive ear to the intellect, to pay heed to the truth, to calculate the pleasure gained through transgression against its loss [that is, punishment incurred]. But what shall we do, as the imagination is an overflowing stream in which the intellect drowns, if we do not place it aboard a ship, that is, the excitement of the soul and the storm of the spirit.[34]

Essentially, Rabbi Israel uses the concept of imagination here in a derivative sense, as synonymous to what is generally referred to as appetite. However, while the concept "appetite" has a distinctly religious connotation, "imagination" is more neutral. The use of the term imagination hints at the nature of the psychological mechanism that motivates the appetite. The imagination stores the memory of sense impressions;[35] when a person encounters an incident that entails sensory pleasure, the imagination awakens the drive toward that same act. Thus, a "person is free in his imagination" in the sense that, so long as the imagination is the decisive factor in shaping our behavior, we may take for granted that we will act in a wild and undisciplined manner in order to satisfy our appetites. On the other hand, a person is "bound by his intellect," since the intellect, which realizes the principle of Divine retribution and anticipates the future, allows us to reflect upon and restrain our behavior.

The crux of the question of Mussar education is rooted in the fact that the imagination is an "overflowing stream" capable of inundating the intellect. Through that metaphor, Salanter expressed the axiom that the emotions are infinitely more powerful than reason in their influence upon human behavior. The solution to this problem is also alluded to at the end of the paragraph cited above: that is, the intellect boards "a ship, which is the excitement of the soul and the storm of the spirit." The resolution is therefore to be found in the transformation of *yir'ah* from an intellectual consciousness to an emotional drive, which is able to confront the appetite and thereby subdue it. Rabbi Israel sees this process as one of the central pillars of moral education:

> For Mussar and proper behavior cannot be sustained without great stratagems to harness the organs of the mind to this, until a deep impression is made in the heart, to give strength and power to the external organs, to realize the superior behavior, that the inferior physical appetites not halt it. . . .[36]

The point of departure of moral education therefore remains in the realm of reason, which provides people with critical standards against which to measure their own actions. However, that is not sufficient, as one ought to find a stratagem so that actions may be guided by rational understanding. Rabbi Israel sees in the practice of Mussar study such a stratagem.

Our discussion of the nature of Mussar study must be prefaced by the remark that Salanter distinguished between two different kinds of Mussar study. The first, known as intellectual study, consisted simply of the study of Mussar texts in the usually accepted manner. His innovation appeared in the second kind, known as Mussar study *be-hitpa'alut* (in a state of emotional excitement).[37] Our discussion focuses upon the latter type.

Unlike regular Mussar study, whose purpose is to expose the consciousness of the student to the principles and general rules that ought to guide his behavior, the aim of study *be-hitpa'alut* was to arouse the emotions of the student, cultivating in him intense feelings of fear of Divine retribution, feelings that will accompany him constantly and affect his actions. The aim is thus to transform the "fear of punishment" from an abstract theological principle, present on the conscious level, to a quality residing within the soul.[38]

This method of study is intended to accomplish its purpose through an experience of powerful emotional arousal. The ethical contents "studied" are not the subject of intellectual analysis, but are rather the focus of an intense emotional experience through which they are internalized in the soul. Salanter proposed various methods for stimulating this "excitement":[39] Mussar study *be-hitpa'alut* was performed aloud, the power of the voice, the special melody, and the rhythm all serving to arouse the emotions. Interestingly, the special melody, unlike the traditional one used for Talmud study, was characterized by sadness and broken-heartedness, mingled with groans and at times even with outbursts of tears.[40]

The psychological influence attributed by Rabbi Israel to vocal effects may be learned from his student, Rabbi Naphtali Amsterdam:

> I once heard from his mouth concerning the matter of Mussar study *be-hitpa'aluth* that it is a skill like that of music—that is, to awaken the inner powers of the soul to emerge from their potential. It is known that in the science of music and song, those engaged in this activity are required to perform certain motions with their hands—even lowly ones—in the book of notes which is before them, and no one laughs or makes fun of their lowly motions as it is needed for their activity. Similarly, in the study of Mussar, which is a skill intended to arouse the inner forces of the human soul so that the good may come into effect, which at times also demands an excitement of the soul, like the activities of melody and the like, in order to arouse fear. . . . Therefore . . . it will not seem strange in the eyes of the world that one need perform certain actions and excitation for Mussar study, and certainly they will not be mocked. . . .[41]

Thus, Mussar study "with excitement" involved making sounds and bodily motions that might arouse ridicule and mockery. Despite the many differences between them,[42] one cannot help being reminded of the ecstatic prayer of early Hasidism, whose strange movements and sounds were the target of criticism and ridicule. It seems that the act of Mussar study *be-hitpa'alut* was also at times an ecstatic experience.

Another characteristic of this form of Mussar study was repetition: The student would read a given sentence aloud from a Mussar work or a Rabbinic saying expressing some ethical idea, which would then be repeated over and over again for a considerable period of time.[43] We know from a number of sources that Rabbi Israel made extensive use of this device. Thus, Rabbi Naphtali Amsterdam relates that: "I saw with my own eyes in my youth that our master repeated the saying, 'Whoever departs from words of Torah is consumed by fire' over and over again, with a loud voice and burning lips, and with great excitement. . . ."[44] Finally, in addition to the raised voice, the special melody, and the repetition of words, Salanter recommended the arousal of excitement by means of parables. Each student would attempt to explain to himself the Mussar lessons in which he was involved by means of parables taken from his daily experience. These means of concretization were also intended to bring about the desired emotional state.[45]

While one searches in vain in Rabbi Israel's writings for directions concerning any particular Mussar book that ought to be made the focus of Mussar study *be-hitpa'alut*, he did recommend *Hovot ha-levavot*, whose author belonged to the philosophical stream, or *Mesillat yesharim*, rooted in a kabbalistic worldview. The important thing was not the specific ethical contents, but the emotional experience aroused through this system of learning. As for the ethical contents, Rabbi Israel is interested in a general idea expressed in many and varied Mussar works: "Mussar study calls upon man to remember his end, for he will not live forever in this lowly world, for we are but sojourners in this life; [therefore] it is incumbent upon us to engage in His service, that our reward may be paid in our true place."[46] The recognition of the trivial and transient nature of this world, and the idea that earthly life is an religio-ethical test whose purpose is to receive reward in the World to Come, is the positive content of the "fear of God." The purpose of Mussar study is the transformation of such *yir'ah* from an abstract intellectual consciousness to an inner emotional feeling.

One cannot discuss the study of Mussar "with excitement" without referring to the institution of the Mussar house, the two being closely related in Salanter's educational theory.[47] The Mussar house was originally established to serve as the framework for Mussar study *be-hitpa'alut*, owing to the inappropriateness for this purpose of the traditional *bet midrash* and to the advantages offered by a Mussar house for the process of Mussar study. The traditional *bet midrash* served as a place for the study of Torah by individuals and groups, and was dominated by the air of intellectual sobriety characteristic of talmudic study. Even though this study was also generally conducted aloud and to the accompaniment of a melody, the traditional Talmud melody, which was a melodic expression of its dialectical patterns of thought, differed greatly from the melancholic chant of Mussar study. Anyone trying to study Mussar in this manner within the walls of the traditional *bet midrash* would most likely be subjected to objections and ridicule, due to the peculiar sounds and motions that accompanied this study. Moreover, Mussar study *be-hitpa'alut* required the student to overcome deeper inhibitions, namely the self-revelation and psychological stripping required by this method. Thus, the Mussar house was intended to provide a place where one could engage in Mussar study *be-hitpa'alut* without fear or inhibition. The special atmosphere existing in the Mussar house, stemming from the fact that this place was used exclusively for Mussar study, would moreover facilitate the study of Mussar, while the power of the group gathered there at fixed times would further encourage and stimulate the *hitpa'alut* of each individual.

Despite the fact that the avowed purpose of study *be-hitpa'alut* was to arouse fear of punishment, there is no doubt that it yielded additional emotional and spiritual consequences. For example, the feelings of regret and broken-heartedness over sins, as well as the awakening of longing for ethical uplifting, created a feeling of purification and purgation in the heart of the student.[48] As far as we can tell, this feeling lay at the basis of the joy related by Rabbi Naphtali Amsterdam: "I sit at present in a special room, and for some two hours every day I study Mussar books . . . and when the ideas entered my heart fittingly, then I am comforted, for Mussar study *be-hitpa'alut* renews the heart and gives joy to the soul. . . ."[49]

There is no doubt that Rabbi Israel was not the first to discover the inherent effect of Mussar study *be-hitpa'alut*. We previously saw that the Vilna Gaon had criticized those who did not become excited in Mussar study, as their study does not yield any fruit. There may also have been an element of excitation in the method of study of Rabbi Zundel Salant, who influenced Rabbi Israel, as was noted. At the same time, Rabbi Israel seems to have been the one who developed Mussar study *be-hitpa'alut* as a specific technique. He did so both by perfecting the various means of arousing emotional excitation, and by the major weight that he gave to this technique in his teaching and his addresses to the public. The importance he attached to his innovation in this area is seen in the following testimony of Rabbi Naphtali Amsterdam:

> For this is a new matter, to study Mussar with excitation . . . and to set aside for it a special house called the Mussar House. Why, therefore, was this matter not brought out in the world by the great luminaries . . . such as the Gaon Rabbi Elijah and his disciple Rabbi Hayyim, of blessed memories, who enlightened the face of the world with the light of their Torah and *yir'ah*? . . . This question has been answered by our master, of blessed memory [that is, Salanter], speaking before his students in these words: "Are these not the words of the Talmud in Hullin 6 [*sic*—should read 7a] . . . 'they left room for our teacher to distinguish himself [through] it.' "[50]

"Worldly Wisdom"

In addition to the study of Mussar, intended to arouse the emotion of fear of God, Rabbi Israel prescribed a complementary means of achieving ethical perfection, which he referred to as "worldly wisdom" (*hokhmat ha-'olam*). This wisdom was deemed necessary because *yir'ah* in and of itself was regarded as being inadequate,[51] since it is very difficult to implant fear of God in the human heart, and even when *yir'ah* has found a place inside the human soul, there is no guarantee that it will succeed in overcoming the enormous power of the appetite in times of ethical trial. Therefore, one needs to strengthen *yir'ah* with worldly wisdom.

Rabbi Israel writes of the function of worldly wisdom as follows: "to foresee the consequences of actions, to take steps in advance before the evil days arrive, to prepare advice and stratagem as to how to conduct oneself and others, and to minimize the stimulus to sin and to ease the temptation until the fear of God becomes greater than the appetite."[52] In brief, worldly wisdom is based upon anticipation of developments, identification of the ethical trials that a person is likely to encounter in the future, and advance planning of future actions in order to avoid these trials. But anticipation of the future is not enough; it must be preceded by the demand for self-examination, in the course of which we discover our own weaknesses and faults. The main obstacle in the way of this examination is our tendency to deceive ourselves and to conceal our own sins. For this reason, penetrating self-criticism is required, to the point that we will be ashamed to deceive ourselves about our own shortcomings.[53]

In addition to individual examination of oneself, one's patterns of behavior, and one's real-life situation, with all its temptations and stimuli, worldly wisdom also demands a considerable degree of shrewdness and artfulness. In this respect, Salanter advises that one take a lesson from contemplation of the ways of the world—that is, the interpersonal relationships expressed in social reality.[54] Contemplation of this sort will reveal that, when society or the individuals within it uncover the weaknesses of a particular person and learn how to exploit it with shrewdness, they are able to manipulate as they wish. Rabbi Israel advises those who seek ethical perfection to act upon this lesson in respect to themselves.[55]

He believed that *yir'ah* and worldly wisdom complement one another: "One strengthens its neighbor: worldly wisdom lightens the burden, and fear of God assists it. We must fear and tremble before every evil deed and transgression. And from this we shall flee from the evil trap."[56] While worldly wisdom lightens the burden imposed upon *yir'ah*, *yir'ah* itself stimulates one to be wise and to think about worldly wisdom. This conception implies a certain expansion of the meaning of *yir'ah*. In its original sense, *yir'ah* is understood as fear of the wages of sin; this form of *yir'ah*, however, when joined by the awareness of the powerful danger inherent in *ta'avah* (lust, appetite), becomes transformed into fear of sin. Once such fear is rooted in the soul, one is fearful every step of the way lest one fall into sin and attempt to avoid ethical trials by means of worldly wisdom. Thus, the consciousness of fear of sin—that is, the deep inner conviction that a person is liable to stumble into sin at every step, and that the appetite and the Evil Impulse lie in wait in every corner—are strikingly expressed in the writings of Rabbi Israel.[57] The most sublime expression of fear of sin is seen by Salanter in the ability to uncover hidden sins and to refrain from them.[58] While ordinary sins are visible to the eye, and thus weigh upon the conscience of the sinner, hidden sins are not manifested directly, and it is therefore easy for a person to ignore their very existence. Herein lies the difficulty in dealing with them. It is nevertheless possible, according to Rabbi Israel, to overcome such a syndrome by combining the fear of punishment, which is acquired by the aid of Mussar study, with the power of penetrating self-observation and contemplation.

Salanter deliberately refrained from providing too many details of worldly wisdom, which is by its nature a strictly personal wisdom, and which we acquire through examination of our own life experiences.[59] Nevertheless, his writings included several points of advice and guidance for those engaged in this aspect of ethical self-correction. For example, he advises one to pursue modest, but attainable, goals, rather than grandiose ones whose realization seems more doubtful.[60] This recommendation is based, first of all, upon his pessimistic assessment of the power of the appetite, presumably joined by the fact that success in executing a relatively modest goal will encourage one to persist in one's efforts, while failure in executing a more far-reaching plan is liable to weaken one's resolve. Against the background of these and similar considerations lies one important basic fact: that Rabbi Israel did not see himself a thinker in the realm of ethics, but as an educator who devoted all his strength and talents to raise the ethical level of his contemporaries. He was therefore not interested in preaching high levels when the prospects for attainment were slim. Unlike earlier ethical writers, who presented far-reaching portraits of the desired as against the existing, Rabbi Israel stressed the desirable that was also possible.

8

The First Cell of the Mussar Movement in Vilna

THE MESSAGE implicit in the ideas that Salanter began to disseminate among the Jews of Vilna in the mid-1840s contained several components. The first of these was that the religio-ethical improvement of the Jew demanded an investment of time, attention, and spiritual energy far beyond that which most people were prepared to devote to it. In effect, Rabbi Israel challenged the widespread assumption that one fulfills one's obligations of Divine worship by devotion to Torah study and punctiliousness in the observance of the mitzvot, and that these two assure one's ethical level. Of course, in view of Salanter's understanding of the appetite and its influence over human behavior, such an assumption would seem groundless and even dangerous.

In order to exemplify the implausibility of this widespread attitude toward *yir'ah* and Mussar, Salanter used a parable closest to his audience's experience:

> How much thought does the merchant with wares engage in before concluding a [given] business deal, [to decide] whether to carry it out or to refrain from it. He will think it over within himself and consult with his friends . . . he will examine the details, seek out [possible] errors, until the matter is clear. . . . So in the study of our Holy Torah, each one on his own level will study and examine it, to uncover its hidden treasures, establish fresh insights and to analyze argumentation. Not so in matters of Mussar; the contemplation—the examination of all the ways and deeds of man, to guard against the tendencies of the will and the Impulse which disturb and obstruct everything good and superior—such is necessary and essential in order to acquire *yir'ah*. . . . In all these matters man's laziness is very great. He feels it burdensome to himself to turn to it even for a

short while, to the extent that he would consider it a waste of time.[1]

Rabbi Israel thus charges the public with an irresponsible and unbalanced approach toward Mussar. If commercial activity and the process of Torah study demand profound thought and reflection, balanced consideration of options, and effort, how much more are these required for the battle against the Evil Impulse!

The second major component of his message is implicit in the very system of ethical education, expressed in another homily, once again taken from the realm of commercial life:

> A person who is troubled will do badly wherever he turns, his business will do poorly, his power and his intellect will be confused, held back by his worries and confusion. . . . And if a person comes and says to him, "I see a light for you. If you do such and such a thing, according to the proper estimate, you will be able to profit a thousand thousand gold dinars" . . . he will summon all his powers of concentration until that matter becomes enrooted in his heart, in a proper and sustained manner. . . . So are we here today. . . . Our sins overwhelm us, each in his own way. We stand far away from the goal for which we were created, each on his own level. . . . And now we have a bright light beckoning to bring merit to the multitude, to strengthen weak hands through the study of Mussar. . . .[2]

While Rabbi Israel's evaluation of the psychological mechanism is characterized by melancholy pessimism, an optimistic tone in his remarks concerning Mussar study as a means of Mussar education stands out. His evaluation of the prospects of its influence, and the fact that this new technique had not yet been tried, at least not on a mass scale, filled him with great hope. That hope explains the pathos and sense of certainty that characterize his call for the dissemination and implementation of his system.

In practice, Salanter sought to make Mussar study a fixed institution in public life: "For this reason it is entirely proper to strengthen it in a fixed manner, by setting regular times for this every [day] between the afternoon and evening prayers. . . ."[3] The demand to fix times for the study of Mussar is directed toward the general public, in all its variety and levels:

> . . . . For this study of Mussar is not like other kinds of study. There is no other study which imposes its obligation upon all the people: women are exempt from Torah study; there is considerable latitude to exempt [from Torah study] those who en-

dure suffering or who are lacking in intellect or who are in acute distress, Heaven forbid; each one according to his particular situation may be exempt from this obligation. . . . But not so this study, which is an obligation that embraces every person without exception. For the battle encompasses every intelligent being, namely, the battle of the Evil Impulse with its cunning tactics. . . .[4]

While the demand for Mussar study applies in principle to all, whether *lomdim* or *ba'alei batim* (ordinary householders), the main thrust of Rabbi Israel's efforts at this stage was directed toward the public of *ba'alei batim*.

The task of transforming Mussar study into a fixed institution of public life was one that Salanter hoped to realize through a restricted circle of his close students. The five letters written by him in 1849, after he left Vilna for Kovna, were addressed to this group, presumably composed of those people who had become attached to him when he taught in the *bet midrash* of Zarzecze, and who had become his disciples, not only in halakhic areas, but also in matters of Mussar. The tone of the letters that Rabbi Israel sent to the members of the group, seemingly outstanding young scholars and learned *ba'alei batim*, seems to indicate that the relationships among them were quite intimate.[5] At the same time, one senses a tone of authority, appropriate to the relations between a leader and his followers. Their contents and their formulation imply that they were intended to stimulate the members of the circle to continue the activity begun while Rabbi Israel still resided among them. Since his move from Vilna was involuntary, and also presumably rather hasty, the letters were intended to prevent the cessation of activities as the result of his absence.

Salanter, seeing this group of close disciples as the core of a Mussar movement that he wished to establish in Vilna, demanded first of all that they themselves set aside regular times for the study of Mussar, with a special emphasis on peer pressure.

> . . . Each person shall strengthen his neighbor and encourage him to devise strategies, as the time is ripe for this, and should not be missed. If a person be absent or perhaps be antagonistic to this, Heaven forbid, it is then appropriate to pay careful attention to it, to seek advice and stratagem to bear with his foolishness, and to persuade him with soft words, each one according to his path and his intellect, and thereby the ethical mode will be established upon a firm foundation.[6]

Despite the fact that ethical education is by its very nature a personal matter, Rabbi Israel preached that Mussar study be specifically within a group, seeing that the social pressure that the group can impose upon each individual is a legitimate and powerful tool. At the same time, this pressure should be adjusted to the nature and character of the individual.

The very fact that the members of the group gathered on a regular basis for purposes of Mussar study was liable to be an influential example for the general public. However, Rabbi Israel demanded that the members of the group also devote conscious, direct efforts toward disseminating Mussar study to the broader public:

> For this you should devote a time set apart on the holy Sabbath, to gather together at a particular hour, to contemplate how to attract the [people of] quality, the great ones of the city, whom many will follow to study Mussar. Speak gentle and calm words, without joking or foolery. Evaluate the virtues of the person and his shortcomings, in what matters he may be admonished, and how he may be kept in check.[7]

The means recommended here by Rabbi Israel in the attempt toward personal persuasion are directed first and foremost toward "the quality, the great ones of the city." This refers to the more honorable and prominently related pedigreed among the *ba'alei batim*, the assumption being that, if these people are drawn toward Mussar study, many others will follow in their footsteps. In effect, Rabbi Salanter sought to transform Mussar study into something fashionable and into a source of social prestige, similar to that which Lithuanian Jews gave to the study of Torah. Thus, Salanter hoped that Mussar students would enjoy a social status similar to that of Torah students and that Mussar study would become the heritage of a broader public: "If God will make our path successful, there is no limit in the future to how much its value may grow."[8]

Salanter was well aware of the difficulties standing in the way of the realization of the task he had imposed upon his circle of students. Among other things, he feared that, in the course of their activity, a split or disagreement might come about among those members of the group who were left in Vilna without a leader. Therefore, he suggests to his students:

> Do not make a decision precipitously. Divide the work among all of you, for a short time and without burdensome labor. . . . So that, with a quiet mind and clear and considered thought, each one shall strengthen his fellow . . . with propriety and

> calmness, each one should guard the honor of his fellow; with
> peace and patience, to follow the majority, and without stub-
> bornness or controversy.[9]

No less of a danger awaited Salanter's program from the negative
reactions he was liable to arouse in the public. Moreover, those who
call for change and reform in religious life are prone to a feeling of
superiority toward the general public. Therefore, Rabbi Israel warned
his disciples:

> And with this, if we would be valiant men, we shall not hasten
> to get angry at our neighbor, [asking] why his mind is closed
> against understanding the nature of this study; we should tell
> ourselves that foolishness also grows within us in many mat-
> ters. . . . So let us accustom ourselves to the quality of patience
> and humility of spirit, so that we not exalt ourselves above
> others.[10]

Rabbi Israel saw the success of his program dependent upon the
proper division of labor, by which each member of the group finds
expression for his own particular talents:

> When we divide up the labor among the people, so that each
> one may hold sway in regard to his own special talent, one will
> chastise in practiced tongue, another will draw him close with
> a pleasing countenance; this one will strengthen him by the
> enthusiasm of his pure heart, and that one will restrain him
> with his righteous stratagems and requisite cleverness. . . . Thus
> . . . how easy it will be to establish everything with a minimum
> of effort and at minimal expense, to revive many souls and to
> sustain an entire world.[11]

Our only source of information concerning Salanter's attempt to
disseminate Mussar study in Vilna is this set of letters he sent to his
disciples. There is thus no accurate information about either the degree
of their response to Salanter's program of action or to its success. While
we may assume that his disciples did attempt to act according to their
master's orders, and that they attracted a number of people in the city
to the idea of Mussar study, they were not successful in winning over
large numbers of Vilna Jewry. Hints of difficulties and obstacles appear
in the letters themselves. Thus, for example, Rabbi Israel writes: "Be-
hold what my ears have heard, you are lax, are lax in this."[12] In another
letter, he alludes to the fact that the members of his circle had been
weakened by reactions of ridicule.[13] Another expression of his dissatisfaction is the following: "You, my friends, kindly inform me who are

those who walk faithfully and who are those who are lax."[14] The fact
that the circle of Rabbi Israel's disciples did not succeed in fulfilling
their master's hopes can also be inferred, it seems to me, from the
silence of contemporary sources. We may reasonably assume that, had
a broadly based movement of Mussar study developed in Vilna during
this period, it would have found an echo in the literature of the period.
Such echoes are nowhere to be found.

Rabbi Israel's directives that they should first try to win over the
distinguished people of the city to his ideas, as well as the attempt to
make Mussar study a source of social distinction, indicate that the
persuasive activities of Salanter's disciples were not primarily directed
toward the *lomdim* in the yeshivot and study houses. His intention was
to win over to his ideas the *ba'alei batim*,[15] whose economic situation
was relatively strong and who had studied in the yeshivot for a number
of years during their youth and early manhood. Thanks to their economic and intellectual background, this group formed the social and
economic backbone of Jewish society in Lithuania. The leadership of
the communal institutions was generally chosen from this group, and
their influence was clearly discernible among the masses. Salanter jus-
tifiably assumed that if the *ba'alei batim* could be won over to his
approach, its influence would spread throughout Jewish society.

There is much evidence from a later period to indicate that this was
indeed Salanter's intention. In a letter from 1860, Salanter again states
that "a person must have a single-minded concern, particularly one
burdened with business, to make it a fixed rule to go regularly to the
Mussar House. . . ."[16] The stories that he used to relate to his students
in praise of Rabbi Zundel of Salant were also intended to set him as an
example to be emulated by the *ba'alei batim*: "I have written at some
length in praise of this great man (a light of the world, in my estima-
tion), may God grant him length of days and years, that the householders may hear and walk in his ways."[17] Other explicit remarks are
cited in the name of Salanter by Rabbi Gershon Mendel Ziv:

> I can say what I heard from the mouth of our friend, and dear
> one, the crown of Israel, the rabbi and Gaon . . . Israel Salanter,
> of blessed memory; that when he established Mussar houses
> this was only for the householders who engage in business, and
> that he did not establish them at all for the students of Torah,
> for everyone who studies Torah is able to study works about
> *yir'ah* by himself, and not in a group. But the householders who
> engage in business should come every day at fixed times to
> study Mussar books and to perform an accounting of their
> souls. . . .[18]

In light of our discussion thus far, we may propose the following approximate reconstruction of the creation of the Mussar movement. Rabbi Israel Salanter laid the foundations for the new movement between 1845 and 1849. His activity during this period, which was concentrated in Vilna, was divided into three areas:

1. He crystallized and formulated the ideological foundations of his system, including a sufficient intellectual basis for his activity in the public realm.
2. He also devoted himself to preparing the tools that would assist him in spreading and applying his ideas, namely, the publication of Mussar books and the establishment of a special house for Mussar study.
3. During these same years, Rabbi Israel took the first step toward disseminating his ideas within the broader community through a series of sermons concerning *yir'ah* and Mussar, which he delivered in the study house in Zarzecze. These sermons, which stylistically still had a strongly learned tone, were intended to attract people to the subject of Mussar and thereby prepare the ground for more far-reaching activities.

A second step was the establishment of a circle of disciples intended to be the founding nucleus of the movement and the vehicles of its message to the broader public, particularly the *ba'alei batim* of Vilna. Even if the disciples' task was not fully realized, one may consider the members of that circle, as well as those few who were presumably affected by it, the first cell of the Mussar movement in Lithuania.

PART THREE

The Founding of the Mussar Movement: Historical Background

9
Rabbi Israel Salanter's Intellectual Sources

AT THE beginning of this work, I referred to the view that Rabbi Israel Salanter's Mussar system was closely associated with a series of figures, beginning with the Gaon, Elijah of Vilna, and continuing through Rabbi Hayyim of Volozhin and Rabbi Zundel of Salant—the latter being Rabbi Israel's own teacher. At this point in our discussion, having described Salanter's own activity and thought during his Vilna period, we can return to our initial question: Should we evaluate his lifework as the continuation of the thought of these figures? To formulate the question somewhat differently: To what extent, or in what sense, was the Mussar movement rooted in the typical outlook of Mitnaggedic society during the first half of the nineteenth century, which was both shaped and exemplified by these figures? A comparison of the thought of Salanter with that of his teachers reveals a dialectical relationship.

We have already seen something analogous, in our discussion of the similarities and differences between the Gaon of Vilna and Rabbi Hayyim of Volozhin. It is clear that, even in a highly traditional culture, the first rank of disciples will differ somewhat from their renowned teachers. It should not be surprising, therefore, that Salanter's relation to his own teachers was marked by a combination of continuity and change.

Continuity and Change in Salanter's Relation to His Predecessors

Rabbi Israel Salanter doubtless shared many of the basic assumptions of the Gaon, Rabbi Hayyim, and Rabbi Zundel, first and foremost, believing in the centrality of Torah study in the life of the

Jew, concurring that Torah study ought to be the principal focus of Divine service in everyday life. He likewise shared their consciousness as to the need to cultivate the fear of God alongside Torah study and their evaluation of the nature and strength of the Evil Impulse. Despite the striking difference in their respective understanding of the origin of the Impulse, Salanter shares his predecessors' assumption as to its power and deviousness. From this, there follows the common conclusion of the Gaon, Rabbi Hayyim, Rabbi Zundel, and Salanter that a person's life in the world consists of a series of difficult trials, requiring a constant struggle against the temptations of the *yezer*. The tendency toward self-criticism and fear of sin, which is also common to Rabbi Israel and his teachers, is likewise based upon this pessimistic evaluation.

The continuity between Rabbi Israel and his three forebears is similarly manifested in the means they advocated in the struggle against the Evil Impulse. As mentioned, the Gaon and Rabbi Zundel attached considerable importance to the study of Mussar works as a means of ethical improvement. Even Rabbi Hayyim, who had certain reservations regarding the involvement of *lomdim* in Mussar books, recommended this form of study to *ba'alei batim*, and in certain unusual cases to *lomdim* as well. Rabbi Hayyim likewise recommended that *lomdim* meditate upon certain Rabbinic sayings bearing ethical messages. His disciple, Rabbi Zundel, even developed a technique that involved the repetition of verses of salvation and trust, as well as short Rabbinic dicta. It follows that each of these exerted some degree of influence over the shaping of Mussar study according to Rabbi Israel Salanter's teaching.

One should also point out the similarity between Salanter and his teachers in the area of *tikkun ha-middot*—character improvement. As mentioned above, the Gaon attached great importance to character improvement within the framework of the effort toward ethical improvement. Following a widespread tendency within Mussar literature, the Gaon recommended that one should utilize the power inherent in habit as an instrument for *tikkun ha-middot*. *Tikkun ha-middot* does not appear as much in the writings of Rabbi Hayyim, no doubt for the same reason that lay behind his reservations with regard to the involvement of *lomdim* in Mussar works, but it again played a major role in the life of Rabbi Zundel. As we shall see below, *tikkun ha-middot* was to be central to Salanter's own teaching, and he himself recommended that the power of habit be harnessed toward this end. In this context, it is worth noting that the book *Heshbon ha-nefesh*, by Rabbi Menahem Mendel Lefin, reprinted at Salanter's initiative, was "discovered" prior to this time by Rabbi Zundel.[1] Indeed, it is not entirely impossible that Rabbi Zundel was the one who first drew the young Salanter's attention to the importance of this book. In any event, an additional sign of the continuity between the two is the fact that this unusual work, in which *tikkun ha-middot* plays so central a role, engaged both Salanter and Rabbi Zundel.

As mentioned, Rabbi Hayyim of Volozhin based the ethical education of his disciples upon an individual approach, in which each student was guided in accordance with his own personal qualities. In keeping with this approach, which was grounded in an awareness of the psychological aspect of the educational process, Rabbi Hayyim stated that one should not present the public with far-reaching, uncompromising demands in the area of religious service, because such demands are liable to weaken those who are unable fully to realize them. Instead, Rabbi Hayyim advocated that the reaching for religio-ethical perfection be understood as a graduated and complex process, in which individuals progress at their own pace and in accordance with their own individual talents. Certainly Rabbi Israel's approach to ethical education was likewise characterized by the individual approach, in which the greatest importance was given to the psychological characteristics and social circumstances of each individual.

In brief, Salanter's lifework exhibited continuity with the religio-cultural tendency embodied in the writings of the Gaon, given systematic formulation by Rabbi Hayyim, and again embodied in the person of Rabbi Zundel of Salant. Salanter's relation to this tendency may be explained in terms of the influence of these three and the fact that he belonged to the same sociocultural stream and was nourished by the same spiritual sources. Thus, for example, the work *Mesillat yesharim* by Rabbi Moses Hayyim Luzzatto was greatly esteemed by the Gaon, Rabbi Hayyim, and Rabbi Zundel, and greatly influenced Salanter as well.[2] However, in recognizing the continuity between Rabbi Israel and the Gaon, Rabbi Hayyim, and Rabbi Zundel, I do not mean to minimize the elements of innovation and change in his enterprise, which make both his Mussar system and movement new and distinct historical phenomena. One may observe certain points of change and innovation both in Salanter's public activity and in his theoretical teaching. On the social level, the very decision to make the subject of Mussar a focus of activity in the broader public was a turning point: the shift of the context of ethical education from the elitist circle of the *lomdim* to the broader framework of the *ba'alei batim* inevitably implied significant changes.

In the context of the worldview of the Gaon of Vilna, Rabbi Hayyim, and Rabbi Zundel, the problematic of Mussar was to a large extent focused upon the relationship between Torah and *yir'ah*: the proper balance of time and resources one should expend on the study of Torah and the cultivation of *yir'ah*; the nature of the relationship between Torah and *yir'ah*; and the interdependence of one upon the other. In the life and thought of the Gaon of Vilna, asceticism served as a kind of bridge between Torah and *yir'ah*. Asceticism assisted people to devote most of their time and energy to Torah study, at the same time serving as a kind of protective wall against the vanities of this world, with all the moral tests involved therein. Another characteristic expression of *yir'ah*, found both in the Gaon and Rabbi Hayyim and his disciples, was the cultivation of a vital and intense relation between study and practice. The problem of the relationship between Torah and *yir'ah*, in all of its manifold aspects, took on particular acuteness in the thought of Rabbi Hayyim of Volozhin, thanks to the confrontation with Hasidism. The attempt to systematize the appropriate balance between Torah and *yir'ah*, as well as the nature of interdependence between the two, lies at the center of his thought. In light of the Hasidic challenge, Rabbi Hayyim needed to pay special attention to the intention that accompanied study. He therefore devoted extensive discussion to the meaning of the concept of *Torah li-shemah*, the status of Torah study when not on the level of *li-shemah*, and the manner in which the ideal of *devekut* was to be integrated within the process of study.

These questions, which were of central concern to the Gaon and to Rabbi Hayyim, were of marginal interest in the thought of Salanter. Being more concerned with the ethical-religious character of society as a whole, he understood the problem of Mussar in close relation to practical life. In that context, *yir'ah* was understood as the ability to behave in an ethical manner within the framework of economic and social life. Indeed, one of the significant points of departure for Salanter's Mussar enterprise was his awareness of the tremendous gap between the patterns of behavior of his contemporaries in the economic and social realm, and the ethical norms inherent in the halakhah.[3]

While Rabbi Hayyim succeeded in formulating a response to the Hasidic challenge from the point of view of the *lomdim*, Rabbi Israel answered the needs of the *ba'alei batim* by changing the focus of Mussar education from the four walls of the study house to the center of practical life. The Mussar movement, like its predecessor, Hasidism, was also a voluntary religious movement, which issued a call for religio-ethical renewal on the part of the broader public.

In the theoretical realm, Salanter's innovation was expressed first and foremost in the fact that he removed himself from the conceptual world of the Kabbalah, not that he doubted the authenticity or sanctity

of Jewish esoteric teaching, not that he rejected study of some kabbalistic works, but that Kabbalah had no significant influence upon his
teaching,[4] while it did play a decisive role in the spiritual world of the
Gaon, of Rabbi Hayyim, and of Rabbi Zundel.[5]

This self-removal from the influence of the Kabbalah is one innovation; another, which perhaps more than anything else characterizes
Rabbi Israel's work from a theoretical point of view, is his transfer of
the problem of ethical education from the theological to the psychological plane. That development is significant in a number of respects.
First of all, it reflects a dwindling interest in the theosophical aspect of
religious life and an increased interest in its anthropological aspect.
Second, in the wake of this change, the normative understanding of
Mussar was replaced by an instrumental understanding. In addition,
the change implies the ability to absorb and to develop a new understanding of the *yezer ha-ra'*, in particular, and of the functioning of the
psyche, in general. Rabbi Israel, as mentioned above, explained the
factors motivating a person toward ethically negative behavior through
the concept of appetite, a potential he believed to be inherent in the
soul from birth. In this he severed himself from the kabbalistic tradition
to which the Gaon, Rabbi Hayyim, and Rabbi Zundel subscribed. Here
the Evil Impulse was understood in relation to the forces of the *Sitra
Ahra*. As opposed to this, Salanter developed a psychological theory
that may be described as naturalistic in the sense that it understood the
soul as an autonomous organism independent of the influences of
external metaphysical forces.

In his theory of moral education as well, based upon this new
understanding of the human soul, Rabbi Israel stands out in contrast
to the approach of his teachers. His main innovation in this area consists
neither in the refinement of previously existing methods that he found
among his predecessors nor in the development of new methods, but
in the imposition of the full weight of ethical education upon the
rational activity of human beings themselves. In the tradition to which
Salanter belonged, emphasis was placed upon the vital necessity of
Divine assistance for the success of a person's stand in the battle with
the Impulse. While Salanter does not deny this traditional motif, he
treats it as marginal, and instead makes human action the main basis
of ethical perfection.[6]

One of the changes that characterized Salanter's approach was the
increase in the relative importance of *yir'ah*. Of course, he did not
intend to reject or diminish the value of Torah study, for he was not
only himself a *lamdan* who spent most of his days in the study of Torah,
but he also took care to warn his students not to allow their involve-

ment with *yir'ah* to adversely affect the preferential value of Torah study. Nevertheless, it was inevitable that the thought and activity of Salanter would be interpreted as a demand to give added importance to *yir'ah* alongside Torah study. This relative increase in the value of *yir'ah* found expression in the demand that one fix times for the study of Mussar, in the statement that even those who are exempt from Torah study are obligated to study Mussar, in the establishment of a "Mussar house," and in the founding of a movement centered on the cultivation of religious and ethical values (*yir'ah u-Mussar*). The unavoidable result of that was a certain erosion in the status of Torah study. The relative increase in the status of *yir'ah* as opposed to Torah study was likewise a function of the difference between Rabbi Israel and his teachers in their understanding of the value of Torah study as a means of ethical perfection. Whereas the Gaon, Rabbi Hayyim, and Rabbi Zundel afforded that factor a most important role in the battle against the *yezer*, at least in respect to *lomdim*, whose main occupation was Torah study, in Salanter's thought one is struck by the tendency to downgrade its value in comparison with other means of ethical perfection.[7]

The effort to enhance the value of *yir'ah* in a society that respected learning predictably led to a certain degree of tension between the two values. That seems to be the meaning of a number of sayings attributed to Rabbi Israel in praise of *yir'ah*: "He once said that he felt that he had the strength to compose several volumes of Torah novellae, even of the caliber of the *Noda' be-yehudah* [highly regarded eighteenth-century responsa], but that he was unable to write even one page like the *Mesillat yesharim*."[8] Or, "It is easier to become expert in the entire Talmud than it is to correct a single stubborn character trait."[9] So long as Rabbi Israel's activity was centered upon disseminating the study of Mussar among the *ba'alei batim*, one does not sense so strongly the tension between his stress upon the value of *yir'ah* and the ideal of maximal devotion to Torah study. However, once his disciples and their disciples thereafter began to penetrate the world of the yeshivot with their Mussar message, the inevitable conflict took place. In the 1890s, the world of the yeshivot and the rabbis of Lithuania was split down the middle between supporters and negators of the Mussar movement.[10] It is instructive that both sides to this controversy based their positions upon the authority of Rabbi Hayyim of Volozhin. Mussar advocates represented him as one of the forebears of their movement, as the teacher of Rabbi Zundel, who stated that without *yir'ah* there is no value to Torah study. Its opponents, on the other hand, relied on Rabbi Hayyim's remarks opposing excessive devotion to the study of Mussar at the expense of halakhic studies.[11] Rabbi Israel, of course, had not intended to arouse such a controversy. Nevertheless, the seeds of the future controversy were already implicit in the principles that underlay his system.

To conclude our discussion, the view that Rabbi Israel received the major components of his system from his teachers is flawed by a certain naiveté and oversimplification. True, there are numerous expressions of continuity between Rabbi Israel and the Gaon, Rabbi Hayyim, and Rabbi Zundel, and there is no doubt that Rabbi Israel's shift toward acting more deeply in the realm of Mussar was rooted in a characteristic tendency of this trio of personalities.[12] Ideas and patterns of thought absorbed by Salanter from their teaching appear to have influenced his own thought and served as building blocks for his own system. Nevertheless, the tokens of innovation and change that we have seen in the Mussar system, not to mention the innovation implicit in the very founding of the Mussar movement, make Rabbi Israel's enterprise a new and original creation in its own right.

Salanter's Mussar Doctrine and Rabbi Menahem Mendel Lefin's *Sefer heshbon ha-nefesh*

While it is clear that Salanter knew thoroughly the Mussar literature of earlier generations and was impressed by it, one Mussar work may be singled out for its decisive influence upon the direction of Rabbi Israel's thought—namely, Menahem Mendel Lefin's *Sefer heshbon ha-nefesh*.

Rabbi Menahem Mendel Lefin of Satanow (1749–1826) was one of the outstanding pioneers of the Haskalah movement in Eastern Europe.[13] During his youth, he had devoted himself diligently to Torah studies, but his intellectual curiosity caused him to go beyond the narrow confines of rabbinic culture. While his earliest knowledge of philosophy and sciences was obtained from medieval Jewish literature, most of his secular education was acquired during the four years he spent in Berlin (1780–84). During this period, he acquired total fluency in German and French, and studied extensively in the fields of the natural sciences and philosophy. He likewise became friendly with a circle of Jewish Maskilim in Berlin, including Solomon Maimon and Moses Mendelssohn. Thus, together with the broadening of his general education, Lefin was influenced by the ideals and dominant spiritual trends of the European Enlightenment.

Upon returning to Poland, he was befriended by Prince Adam Czartoryski, who was to become his patron. In Warsaw in 1792, Lefin published a pamphlet in French containing a detailed proposal for the amelioration of the condition of the Jews in Poland. He may have been stimulated to write this essay, which was directed toward the Polish government, in the wake of his contacts with Czartoryski and the circles of the nobility. Even though Lefin's essay, generally speaking, expresses a typical program of the Haskalah, its position is that of a moderate who takes exception to manifestations of extremism even in the camp of the Maskilim; particularly striking in its originality is the strategy he proposes for the struggle against Hasidism.[14] After spending several years in those portions of Poland that were annexed to Russia, Lefin left for Galicia in 1808, and lived alternately in Brody and Tarnopol, two centers of Galician Haskalah, where he was a friend and teacher of several of the leading Maskilic figures of the period.

Lefin's literary output reflected his desire to disseminate knowledge and enlightenment within the Jewish public. In that spirit, he published in 1789 the book *Moda' le-binah*, consisting of seven "Epistles of Wisdom," which convey information in the realm of the natural sciences. In addition, at Mendelssohn's request, he translated into Hebrew a book by the Swiss doctor, Tissot, which gave practical instruction in the field of medicine; the translation was published under the title *Refu'at 'am* (Zolkiew, 1794) and enjoyed a wide circulation. Another literary enterprise of Lefin's was his translation of portions of the Bible into Yiddish. Unlike Mendelssohn, who translated the Bible into "pure" German, and the archaic and flowery language of the standard Yiddish translation used in the traditional *heder*, Lefin's translation is noted for its popular character.[15]

Sefer heshbon ha-nefesh, first published in Lvov in 1808, was to enjoy a number of further editions,[16] one of which—the 1844 Vilna edition—was published at Salanter's initiative. The influence of Lefin's book upon the later generations of the Mussar movement is attested to by its reprinting in 1937 by the Association of Slobodka Students in Lithuania.[17]

Heshbon ha-nefesh was written with the intention of benefiting the public, a point to which the formula given on the title page alludes:

> This book *Heshbon ha-nefesh* (lit., "accounting of the soul") is a wondrous device for the healing of character flaws by means of persistence in education for their correction through accounting and behavior which is easy and light, as well as for becoming expert in healing others and to render their education easy in the best way.

The heart of the book is the following device, referred to on the title page:[18] The one engaged in training himself is to prepare a list of thirteen attributes (*middot*) that he wishes to improve. He then prepares a brief maxim for each of these thirteen traits, each one of which is directed toward one of the traits requiring improvement. The student is then to divide the year into seasons, devoting a week to the improvement of each attribute. During that week, he is to use the appropriate Mussar maxim in order to focus his attention upon the attribute requiring improvement. At the end of the first thirteen weeks, the student returns to the beginning of the process. Thus, over the course of a year each attribute receives four weeks of attention. An important component of this device was a special notebook, containing charts referring to the calendar of the year and the list of attributes requiring improvement, in which the student was to record systematically the data pertaining to his progress in improving his *middot*. This list then constitutes a source of encouragement, allowing the student to focus more attention upon weak points.

Several of Lefin's biographers have noted the relationship between *Sefer heshbon ha-nefesh* and the writings of the American statesman and thinker, Benjamin Franklin.[19] Some go so far as to argue that *Heshbon ha-nefesh* is a translation or reworking of a book written by Franklin. Others, more precisely, state that the device for correcting one's character that lies at the center of Lefin's book is taken from a work by Franklin. Indeed, in his *Autobiography*, Franklin describes a device for improving one's character, which he developed in the course of his own efforts at character improvement. A superficial comparison reveals that the device suggested by Franklin in his memoirs indeed corresponds to that advocated by Lefin in his book.[20] While not all scholars are in complete agreement as to the precise source within Franklin's writings that influenced Lefin, the essential fact that Lefin was influenced toward this device by Franklin's writings seems established beyond a doubt.[21]

In any case, most of the authors who have observed Lefin's dependence upon Franklin have ignored a fact of great importance from the point of view of the present discussion: that in *Sefer heshbon ha-nefesh*, Lefin outlines in considerable detail a psychological theory that provides the theoretical basis for the educational device borrowed from Franklin. This psychological view reflects the major developments in psychological theory that took place in European thought at the end of the seventeenth and in the eighteenth centuries. Two who have noted this fact, albeit very briefly and in passing, are Israel Zinberg[22] and Raphael Mahler.[23] More recently, in a study by Hillel Levine,[24] *Heshbon ha-nefesh* has been subject to a detailed and profound analysis, which likewise takes note of Lefin's relationship to various tendencies in eighteenth-century European thought, including its psychology and epistemology. It would seem to me that the explanation for the new direction in

Salanter's thought is to be found in the psychological theories incorporated by Lefin in *Heshbon ha-nefesh*.

Several authors have indeed noted the relationship of Salanter's thought to Lefin's book, but have not analyzed its significance.[25] Some were content to mention the fact that Rabbi Israel initiated the reprinting of *Heshbon ha-nefesh*. Zinberg adds that his intention was to use Lefin's work as a "textbook for self-education." A. R. Malachi relates that Salanter "followed in the light of" *Sefer heshbon ha-nefesh*, but does not explain how this expresses itself. Klausner, relying upon the statement in A. B. Gotlober's book that there were circles of young men who practiced character improvement based upon *Sefer heshbon ha-nefesh*,[26] suggests that, in founding the Mussar movement, Salanter was influenced by these groups. There is, however, no support in the sources for that theory, no mention by Salanter himself or his disciples or close friends of the existence of such circles. Nissan Waksman has suggested an additional conjecture concerning Salanter's relationship to Lefin's work. In his opinion, the list of thirteen qualities that ought to be corrected, attributed to Rabbi Israel, may be based upon the thirteen qualities that Lefin enumerates in his book. Unfortunately, the attribution of the former list to Rabbi Israel is itself extremely doubtful.[27]

Menahem Glenn went further than anyone else in identifying the influence of *Sefer heshbon ha-nefesh* on Rabbi Israel, positing that Salanter used Lefin's approach for practical exercises in ethical improvement.[28] Unfortunately, this statement of Glenn's has no basis in fact, as no reference whatsoever is made to Salanter's alleged use of that same "device" either in his writings or in the numerous accounts of his words and deeds. Indeed, in a certain sense this "device" was opposed to Rabbi Israel's entire approach. Whereas Lefin assumed that it was possible to correct an imperfection of character by repeatedly subjecting oneself to ethical trial,[29] Salanter took exception to such deliberate self-exposure to dangerous situations.

Thus, even though Salanter's exposure to *Sefer heshbon ha-nefesh* has been widely known to a number of authors, the nature and significance of the connection was unclear to them. As stated above, Salanter's thought was decisively influenced by the psychological theories that Lefin incorporated in *Sefer heshbon ha-nefesh*. Since a detailed and exhaustive description of Lefin's theory of the mind is beyond the purview of the present study, we shall suffice here with a survey of a few ideas that particularly influenced Salanter.[30]

Following the accepted viewpoint of the ethical and philosophical literature of the Middle Ages, Lefin draws a distinction between the "animal soul" and the "intellective soul." However, his use of these terms is liable to be misleading, as Lefin went well beyond the conceptions of medieval psychology in his own understanding of the nature of the animal soul and the interaction between it and the intellective soul.[31] The animal soul is passive and totally lacking in any will of its own, and is only activated by the awakening of "a spirit of desire or of pain." In other words, what activates the animal soul is the emotional impulses of desire for a given object or, alternatively, repulsion and repugnance from it. These impulses are implanted in the animal soul from birth, or are acquired through habit. When a given urge is satisfied, the animal soul again sinks into the "sleep of dormancy," and is no longer able to move by its own power. Moreover, the animal soul is unable to anticipate or weigh future consequences of a given action in the present; consequently, it also lacks the power of choice. Therefore, when two opposing spirits of lust do encounter one another within it, it submits to the stronger of the two.

In light of this conception, Lefin explains our ability to rule our own soul and to shape its behavior as follows:

> Indeed, the person who has intelligence and shrewdness and controls his spirit is able to move at will his animal soul for his own good—that is, literally to awaken within it a spirit of lust and anguish. For example, to chase the birds away from the standing grain by ringing a bell, or tempting them with meat to catch them in a trap, or to bring about within it [that is, the animal soul] appetites and feelings trained by means of habit, as above. And one who is expert in the technique of training may make use of all kinds of powers of the animals, doing whatever he wills.[32]

This brief passage alludes to two characteristic themes in Lefin's attitude toward ethical training: (1) that the subject of ethical education (the factor that initiates and directs it) is always the intellective soul, while its object is the "animal soul"; the intellective soul is unable to influence a person's actions directly, and must therefore intervene in processes occurring within the animal soul; (2) the comparison of ethical education to the training of animals implies that people are able to dominate their animal soul if they know how to expose its weaknesses and to cleverly manipulate them toward their own will.

Lefin expounds several of the theoretical assumptions underlying the device of character correction in that part of the book entitled "Introduction to the Thirteen Chapters."[33] The situation of the animal soul during those periods in which it is not ruled by the lusts is designated by Lefin as "the stage of laziness." During this state, there takes place within the soul the "exchange of thoughts"—a random flow of thoughts without any particular direction, order, or purpose. The flow does not require any investment of psychic energy; indeed, the intellective soul is able to impose itself upon the exchange of thoughts and direct it by means of the power of the will. This refers to a psychological channeling bearing a clearly defined content and direction, whose source is in intellectual cognition. Such activity, however, demands great effort, and is therefore confined to a restricted period of time. Moreover, the "power of the spirit of appetite, before which the animal soul moves as a driven leaf . . ."[34] is far stronger than the power of the will. This is probably the case because the appetite is the power implanted within the animal soul. It follows that a great effort is required when the intellective soul wishes to overcome even the slightest appetite, as in such cases the power of the will must overcome the state of laziness of the animal soul, as well as defeating the appetite that acts freely within this soul. Lefin concludes from this that, were the appetites to operate uninterruptedly within the animal soul, the intellective soul would be totally unable to influence the animal soul. The ability to interfere in what is done in the animal soul and to influence it is rooted in the fact that the spirit of appetite only acts within it in a fragmentary and diffuse manner.

In light of the above-described relationship of powers, Lefin offers those who wish to overcome their appetites a simple device: to separate oneself from the cause of the lusts—that is, that external cause that stimulates and awakens the appetite to act within the animal soul. In this way the intellective soul, which is far-seeing, can overcome the lust while it is still weak or before it has become manifested to the animal soul. But such a device is insufficient, for it happens at times that one is suddenly exposed to a cause of lust. One then finds oneself in a trying situation in which the power of lust aroused is far greater than that of the power of the will. The solution is therefore to be found in the labor of education.

The following assumptions underlie the labor of education:

1. No feeling, even the slightest, is ever completely forgotten by the animal soul, but a certain residue thereof always remains within the memory.[35] These impressions eventually accumulate over the course of time into a psychological tendency not originally present in the soul. This law concerning the impressions left and accumulated in the soul explains the inherent power of habit.
2. Just as the feelings aroused in the animal soul as the result of chance external stimuli leave a certain impression and influence the animal soul through their cumulative effect, so does the intellective soul influence the animal soul by means of certain repeated feelings that it arouses within it. The habits initiated and directed

for that purpose by the intellect are referred to by Lefin as *hinukhim* (educational acts).

3. Not only do the emotions as such leave an impression upon the soul, but even those things that are imagined leave behind impressions, which are likewise accumulated and always remain within the person.[36] The ability of the intellective soul to act upon the animal soul may be more readily understood in light of this statement. Not only is it able to stimulate and to initiate real, concrete feelings, but even the image of the feeling leaves an impression upon the animal soul.

4. From everything that has been said above, it follows that, despite the relative weakness of the power of the will as against the appetites, the intellective soul is capable of decisively influencing what occurs within the animal soul by means of the accumulated impressions that it initiates and guides; "and the matter depends upon nothing more than continuous persistence . . ."

5. Two factors affecting the intensity of the impressions accumulated in the soul are (a) the period of time during which the feelings that leave behind their impression are repeated, and (b) the power of those impressions. The impression left by spiritual excitement is far more powerful than that left by calm and relaxed emotions, but this excitation entails an effort and expenditure that is likely to exhaust the powers of the intellective soul. Therefore, one must find the appropriate balance for one's personality between the amount of time and the intensity of effort invested in the labor of education. In light of what has been said above, Lefin understands the impact of the educational devices as follows:

> Because each particular trait, during the course of the week [devoted to it], awakens an extended anticipation on account of the longings of the soul, saying, "when will it come to me and I shall perform it," therefore, when temptation comes, it finds the soul prepared to be aroused with great intensity. The more the temptations are multiplied during this week, the more the impressions of the opposing power of the will are increased with great strength. Moreover, if there is a complete breathing space between one temptation and the next, a great force of opposition thereby becomes cumulative.[37]

The repeated experience of withstanding temptation with respect to a particular trait leads to an accumulation of impressions in the soul, which brings about the correction of that same trait. On the other hand, the assumption that self-educating individuals will succeed in repeatedly withstanding temptation is based upon the consideration that all of their effort and willpower will be concentrated upon the correction of that trait during the course of that same week, and that the intense desire to succeed in that goal will awaken powerful feelings of opposition to the appetite within the soul.

As I have said, I do not pretend in this survey to give a comprehensive presentation of the psychological teaching of Lefin. The object of this discussion is rather to explain the influence of *Sefer heshbon ha-nefesh* upon the thought of Rabbi Israel Salanter. However, before turning to examine the manner in which that influence was expressed, I must again note that the psychological outlook set forth by Lefin in this book reflects the impact of European thought of the late seventeenth and the eighteenth centuries.[38] One may point to a series of assumptions that are characteristic of the understanding of the psyche in eighteenth-century thought,[39] the impact of which is clearly discernible in *Sefer heshbon ha-nefesh*, including (1) the transfer of attention from the nature of the psyche to its character—that is, to its structure and to the laws governing its activities;[40] (2) a naturalistic understanding of the psyche as an autonomous entity, whose actions are determined in relation to the stimuli of the environment, rather than in relation to metaphysical forces;[41] (3) the sense-oriented outlook, which states that events in the psyche are grounded in sense experience;[42] (4) the assumption that experiences of pleasure and pain, together with the feelings of fear and hope that follow from these experiences, are the basis of psychological motivation;[43] (5) the physiological approach, which explains the impact upon the psyche of the external world in terms of the nervous system, which carries sense impressions to the brain;[44] (6) the mechanistic approach, which describes the conflict of forces within the psyche in terms of models borrowed from physics; and (7) attention to the psychology of animals, and the analogy from it to the realm of the human psyche.[45] As I have said, all of these concepts reflect the relation of Lefin to eighteenth-century European thought. To these points I would add the attitudes of activism and optimism that underly the device borrowed by Lefin from Franklin, which are also characteristic of the line of thought of the eighteenth-century European Enlightenment.

In what way, then, did the influence of *Sefer heshbon ha-nefesh* upon Rabbi Israel find expression? Despite the fact that Salanter does not use the concepts of animal soul and intellective soul, there is a striking similarity between himself and Lefin in their understanding of the relationship between the intellectual and emotional components within the psyche. There is a clear parallel between what Lefin describes as the animal soul and the realm of emotion in the soul as depicted in Salanter's writings. Both Lefin and Salanter identify the Evil Impulse with the appetite[46]—that is, the natural tendency within the soul to be attracted toward any experience that causes pleasure and to avoid any experience that causes pain. Both likewise agree that the appetite is, generally speaking, in a situation of dormancy, and that it awakens to act within the soul in response to its exposure to external stimuli. While Lefin depicted the animal soul as unable to evaluate the future consequences of an act in the present, and as therefore lacking in freedom of choice, Salanter, on the other hand, attributed these same characteristics to the appetite. In any event, they both believed that the actions that a person is driven to perform by the appetite for its immediate gratification are not subject to rational considerations. Moreover, so long as the intellect tries to bring about a confrontation between the rational judgment and the impulses of the appetite, the latter are likely to prevail. Thus, Salanter shares with Lefin not only the assessment of appetite as being superior in strength to the intellect, but also the mechanistic understanding of psychological processes: that is, the view that when opposing forces clash within the soul, the more powerful one overwhelms and imposes its will.

In light of the above shared assumptions, there is also a striking similarity between Salanter and Lefin regarding the nature of moral education. Interestingly, Lefin compared ethical education to the training of animals and Salanter quoted Lefin's remarks on this matter regarding character improvement.[47] But beyond any influence in this specific matter, the comparison of Mussar education to animal training reflects an overall view, accepted jointly by both Lefin and Rabbi Israel: that ethical education is a process initiated, directed, and controlled by the intellect. The latter, which is unable to overcome the appetite in a frontal battle, attempts to circumvent it while exploiting its weaknesses through intervention in the emotional life of the psyche, and by attempts to marshal and to awaken forces capable of defeating the appetite.

Lefin's educational device was based upon a theory pertaining to the accumulation of impressions left in the soul in the wake of every feeling or image. While Salanter does not make use of the specific device advised by Lefin, he does adopt the theory about the accumulation of impressions, basing his view as to the influence of Mussar study *be-hitpa'alut* upon it.[48] As noted, Lefin, too, observed the advantage of *hitpa'alut* with respect to the intensity of the impressions that it leaves in the soul. Indeed, the recognition that a person is capable of implanting the fear of punishment in his soul by means of Mussar study *be-hitpa'alut*, repeated at frequent intervals, and amplifying its power until it is capable of overwhelming the appetite, is based upon the theory about the accumulation of impressions and the mechanistic understanding of the soul. An additional idea of Lefin's, to which there are parallels in Salanter's thought, is the device of overcoming the appetite by removing oneself from the situation that caused it. This is based upon the assumption that the appetite is prompted to act within the soul when a person is exposed to a particular external stimulus. That appetite may therefore be overcome by a deliberate effort to avoid exposure to that stimulus. This idea underlies the system of action designated by Rabbi Israel by the term *hokhmat ha-'olam* (worldly wisdom).

One should also note an additional idea from Lefin's book that was to play an important role in Salanter's thought—namely, the recognition of the impact of unconscious psychic forces upon human behavior. Concerning this, Lefin writes:

> It is clear that a considerable number of the motions of the psyche are concealed in the hidden chambers of man's heart every day, one within another, so that he no longer knows or recognizes them. But the more deeply they are hidden, the more strongly do they act within the psyche upon the barrier of revealed ideas.[49]

In these remarks, we do not yet find the sharp distinction between conscious and subconscious that later appears in Salanter's thought.[50] As we shall see below, Salanter himself only used this distinction at a relatively late date. It will likewise become clear that he drew upon sources other than *Sefer heshbon ha-nefesh* in order to express the distinction between conscious and subconscious. It is nevertheless possible that Lefin's remarks paved the way for Salanter to become aware of the phenomenon of the subconscious. In any event, it seems clear that these comments augmented Salanter's awareness of the influence of irrational forces within the soul upon human behavior.

Evidently, Salanter was also influenced by the literary aspects of *Sefer heshbon ha-nefesh*: Just as one of the literary devices extensively used by Lefin was the parable that made use of examples from everyday life,[51] so homilies drawn from everyday experience likewise played an important role in the letters and sermons of Rabbi Israel. Salanter even recommended the parable as one of the means to be incorporated within the study of Mussar *be-hitpa'alut*, because of the power of the parable to concretize a moral point and to act upon the emotions.

Of course, the observation of Lefin's influence upon Salanter in no way detracts from the latter's stature as an original creator, for Salanter was not influenced by Lefin unqualifiedly. His originality is manifested both in the choice of ideas that he took from Lefin, and in the manner in which these were integrated within the framework of his own original thought. But despite these qualifications, one may still state that *Sefer heshbon ha-nefesh* had a decisive influence upon the contents and development of Salanter's doctrine, in part because it took place during the period when Salanter was taking his first steps as a thinker in the area of Mussar. There are thus three major characteristics of the Mussar system that may be ascribed to Lefin's influence: (1) the naturalistic understanding of the psyche; (2) the development of an educational system based upon an understanding of the causual relationship between disease and cure; and (3) the optimism implicit in the recognition that people are capable of improving their character traits and changing their nature through means of devices created by the intellect. This optimistic mood is clearly seen in the formulation in which Lefin presents his educational device as a promising discovery, which, with a little effort, may bring about wondrous results.[52] The advantages of Mussar study are presented by Salanter in the same optimistic vein,[53] but such optimism was characteristic of the eighteenth-century European Enlightenment, which believed it possible to correct the failings both of the individual and of society by means of reason. It should not be surprising, therefore, that the enlightened Jew Lefin shared this mood. What is surprising is that Salanter was fully prepared to accept such a line of thought—even if only within the limited area of Mussar education.

There is a certain irony in the fact that Menahem Mendel Lefin, one of the pioneers of the Eastern European Haskalah, so deeply influenced Rabbi Israel Salanter, one of the outstanding leaders of Orthodoxy in Russian Jewry. Was Salanter conscious of Lefin's identification as a Maskil? The latter in fact attempted to formulate his work in such a manner as to be acceptable to the traditional community in Eastern Europe, a fact that may have made it easier for Rabbi Israel to make use of his book. However, it is difficult to imagine that Salanter was unaware of the modernist tone of many of the innovations proposed in *Heshbon ha-nefesh*. It nevertheless seems likely that he was not fully aware of the extent of Lefin's activities and views as a Maskil. But even had he been aware of all these, it seems to me that he would not have refused to use *Sefer heshbon ha-nefesh*, just as at a later period he did not refrain from utilizing non-Jewish sources on these same subjects. In his own consciousness, these books merely supplied him with tools and means, while the goal they were intended to serve was that determined by the authority of the tradition. We may nevertheless speculate as to whether this is not one of those cases in which tools and means leave their impression upon contents and goals as well.

10

The Intensification of the Haskalah Movement in Russia and the Founding of the Mussar Movement

MANY authors who have dealt with the biography of Rabbi Israel Salanter have explained the founding of the Mussar movement as a response to the growth of the Haskalah movement in Russia.[1] However, that thesis remains to be adequately proven. It may be that those scholars who suggested the explanation did not trouble to verify it because it appeared to be so self-evident, since in a later period Rabbi Israel took a strong stand against the trends of the Haskalah. However, both the growth of the Haskalah movement in Russia and the formulation of the traditionalist response to it were slow and gradual processes. The question that presents itself to us here is thus whether already in the mid-1840s, when he established the basis for the Mussar movement, Salanter was alert to the threat inherent in the Haskalah. In order to answer this question, we must first address ourselves to other questions: What was the status of the Haskalah during the 1840s in Russia generally, and in Vilna in particular, and what relations existed between the circles of Maskilim and those of the traditionalist camp? I have elsewhere devoted a separate study to this subject;[2] here it will suffice to summarize those conclusions needed in the context of the present work.

The Change in the Status of the Haskalah During the 1840s

During the 1820s and 1830s, the handful of Jewish Maskilim in Russia constituted a marginal and uninfluential minority. Their weakness in the public arena stemmed both from their small number and from their geographical dispersion. Generally speaking, the supporters of Haskalah were a small and isolated group wherever they lived, being found in relatively large numbers in only a few communities, such as Vilna and Odessa.

Among the manifestations of the Haskalah's weakness during this period may be included the persecutions and attacks to which the Maskilim were subjected. The pressure of the environment not only limited the field of action of the Maskilim as individuals, but also deprived them of the daring and the ability to organize public activities. Thus, the efforts undertaken during the 1830s to publish a literary journal and to establish a society of Maskilim ended in failure.

It therefore ought not to be surprising if the Maskilim felt a sense of helplessness with regard to the possibility of influencing society in general. Indeed, not a few Maskilim limited themselves to the narrow confines of their own literary or scholarly activity, while those who continued to act on behalf of the revitalization of Jewish society tended to thrust the burden upon the government. These latter appealed to the ruling circles in letters calling upon them to impose the desired changes in Jewish life through the coercive power of the government. Underlying this appeal was the following line of reasoning: The Maskilim were convinced that the program of the Haskalah contained the key to the solution of the problems that troubled Russian Jewry, but in light of the reluctant and even negative response of that society, and the weakness and limited influence of the Maskilim themselves, they lost hope of making their view universally accepted by means of propaganda and education alone. However, following the example of the Jewish Maskilim in Central Europe, those in Russia also felt that the Russian regime fundamentally shared their high ideals and hopes. This image of the regime, which was widespread among the Russian Maskilim, was to a great extent heightened by the optimistic mood of rationalism and humanism of the eighteenth century, as well as by the model of enlightened absolutism in Central Europe. Unfortunately, this positive view reflected the abstract principles and longings of the Maskilim more than it did the harsh reality of Jewish life during the reign of Nicholai I.

The Maskilim's hopes were seemingly fulfilled when, at the beginning of the 1840s, Nicholai's regime began to take steps toward reforming the Jewish educational system. The education minister, Sergei Uvarov, had contact with enlightened Jews from Germany and was convinced that the Haskalah movement in Russia could be made into an instrument for the advancement of the goals of the government—that is, the abolition of Jewish separatism by means of cultural and, if possible, religious assimilation. The government tried to obfuscate this goal behind a facade of good intentions: that they wished to improve the status of the Jews who needed to acquire a general education.

The situation of the Maskilim began to change at the beginning of the 1840s, shortly after the governmental announcement concerning the establishment of committees to investigate various changes in the arrangements pertaining to the rabbinate and education. Seeing themselves as allies of the czar, the Maskilim were filled with self-confidence and began to assist the government enthusiastically in the realization of its program. Their new spirit was expressed in a call addressed to the authorities, formulated by the circle of Maskilim in Vilna. At the heart of this document was the plan to establish a nationwide communal organization to be headed by leaders who identified with the ideology of the Haskalah, which would concentrate in its hands far-reaching authority in the realms of religion, culture, education, and society, and would derive its power and sanction from the backing of the government. The program reflected the desire of a small minority to impose its will upon the overwhelming majority by means of governmental coercive power.

This improvement in the public situation of the Maskilim was expressed concretely when, in 1841, the Maskilim in Vilna finally succeeded in publishing a literary collection (entitled *Pirhei zafon*) and during that same year two "remodeled" schools were established in Vilna, based upon the educational program of the Haskalah. The Maskilim saw these new institutions as models for the schools that the government would, they hoped, establish in the future.

The ferment and struggle that surrounded the government's attempt to change the character of Jewish education were largely focused upon the two tours conducted by Max Lilienthal (1815–82) in the Pale of Settlement, during 1842–43.[3] As emissary of the education minister, Lilienthal was charged with the task of attempting to convince the communal leaders to "willingly" accept the government's suggestion, albeit from the outset this propaganda trip was accompanied by the threat that, were the Jews to fail to meet the government half-way, the latter would impose its will by force. In practice, Lilienthal's trips were a focal point for sharp struggles between the supporters and opponents of Haskalah, which elicited fierce emotions. At a certain stage, the enthusiasm in the camp of the Maskilim bordered upon messianic fervor, while among the camp of those loyal to the tradition there were many indications of uneasiness, accompanied by grave deliberations and uncertainties concerning the appropriate response to the governmental initiative. In the final analysis, the traditional leadership decided to cooperate with the government, largely at the initiative of Rabbi Yitzhak, the son of Rabbi Hayyim of Volozhin (d. 1849). Two main considerations evidently lay behind this decision, namely, the fear of governmental reprisals against the Jews in the event of refusal and the belief that, by their cooperation, the traditional leadership would be able to exert some influence on the running of these new schools, thereby minimizing the danger inherent in them. Indeed, the committee of rabbis established in St. Petersburg in the summer of 1843, in which both Rabbi Yitzhak of Volozhin and the Hasidic leader Rabbi Menahem Mendel Schneersohn of Lubavitch (1789–1866) participated, supported the governmental plan concerning the establishment of "remodeled" schools and rabbinic seminaries.

Despite the fact that the governmental initiative brought about no far-reaching change in Jewish education,[4] the struggle that took place around this issue had important consequences for the life of Russian Jewish society. In principle, the affair of Compulsory Enlightenment changed the balance of forces and pattern of relationships between the Maskilim and the traditional camp. I have discussed above the change that took place in the status of the Haskalah in the wake of governmental involvement: the strengthening of the Maskilim's self-confidence and daring, their organizational capability, and the radicalization of positions. One may add to this that the position of the Maskilim as a minority within the traditionalist majority also improved considerably. But society's reserved attitude toward the Maskilim not only did not improve, but became exacerbated, although in light of the alliance between the Maskilim and the government, the capability of the traditionalist majority to attack them was henceforth limited: The Maskilim were able to rely upon the government in the event of need and many Maskilim received teaching positions in the new government schools, thereby becoming free of economic dependence upon a society that was generally hostile toward them.

The inevitable consequence of the struggle between the Maskilim and their opponents was the widening of the gap between the opposing sides and the consolidation of two distinct camps even from a social point of view. One of the striking signs of this development was the establishment in the early 1840s of a separate *minyan* (prayer group) for the congregation of Maskilim in Vilna. The need for such a *minyan* was rooted, on the one hand, in the fact that the opponents of the Haskalah did not welcome the Maskilim in their synagogues because of the fact that the prayer houses also served as meeting places in which to organize for their public struggle; on the other hand, the separate *minyan* likewise served as a center of public activity for the Maskilim.

In 1847, the *minyan* of the Maskilim moved from the private home where it had been located into a permanent building, adopting several practices characteristic of the Reform synagogues in Western Europe in terms of its internal organization and external decorum, while simultaneously retaining the traditional liturgy without alteration.

In general, one may note three principal developments in the status and nature of the Haskalah movement in Russia in the wake of Compulsory Enlightenment: (1) the patronage and protection of the czarist regime and their own economic independence strengthened the ability of the Maskilim to withstand the pressures of the majority society; (2) the Maskilim themselves underwent a process of radicalization, expressed in the strengthening of their self-confidence and daring and the struggle for positions of influence; and (3) the crystallization of the Maskilic circle as a distinct, separate social group continued, and even received institutionalized expression in the establishment of a separate synagogue in Vilna.

We have thus far examined several expressions of the changes brought about by Compulsory Enlightenment, as these were expressed in the activity of the Maskilim, but no less profound were the traces left behind in the camp of the loyalists to the tradition. Admittedly, tension existed between them and the Maskilim even prior to the 1840s, but at that time the phenomenon of the Haskalah was understood as a marginal one of individuals who violated the accepted norms, and not as one that posed a significant threat to traditional Jewish society as a whole. Once the Haskalah became an ally of the regime of Nicholai or, if one prefers, an instrument in its hands, it was perceived as a dangerous factor. The events of the early '40s brought about a drastic change in the image of the Haskalah movement in the eyes of the traditionalists who were forced, for the first time in its history, to prepare themselves for a comprehensive struggle against the Maskilim.

The new image of the Haskalah was complex and many-sided. It was seen as a dangerous threat not only because it displayed the weak points in Jewish life to the government and assisted in imposing "reforms," but also because people became aware of the dangerous impact of the ideas and spirit of the Haskalah.

This sense of potential danger did not penetrate uniformly to all levels of society. It may be assumed that there was a greater degree of sensitivity to this issue among the circles of *ba'alei batim* with a Torah background, and even more so within the circles of the spiritual religious leadership. Likewise, we may reasonably assume that those who came into closer contact with the Maskilic circles more easily developed such an awareness. But what is more important is that, for the first time in the history of Russian Jewry, this consciousness became sufficiently deeply rooted so as to influence the picture of society in general. In effect, we find here what may be properly designated the beginnings of Orthodoxy in Russian Jewry: that is, a traditionalist society confronting processes and phenomena that threaten the authority of its tradition, and whose consciousness of these threats, as well as its attempts to deal with them, leave a deep impression upon its very being.

The awareness of the dangers inherent in Haskalah was primarily held by the educated class, while the hostility toward the Maskilim was widespread through all levels of the public. This hostility seems to have become ever stronger as new measures were added, connected in one way or another with the cooperation of the Maskilim with the regime. Not only were the leaders of the traditionalist camp forced to agree to the establishment of reformed schools, but a new tax, the candle tax, was imposed upon the Jews of Russia in order to finance them. And, as if this were not enough, shortly thereafter there came the Clothing Edict, the order to substitute what was known as "German dress" (a short jacket) for the traditional knee-length Jewish coat—causing much pain and bitterness on the Jewish street. The public was presumably aware of the influence exerted by the Maskilim toward the promulgation of such decrees. The feelings of hostility that became progressively strengthened as a result of these and other events doubtless sharpened the polarization of the two camps and widened the gap between them.

Israel Salanter went to live in Vilna in 1840 and was thus an immediate witness to all these developments, as Vilna was at the time the most important center for the Maskilim of Lithuania and one of the primary fronts in the struggle between the Maskilim and those loyal to the tradition. Salanter saw the growth in the activity of the Maskilim and the strengthening of their position from close up; he accompanied the struggle that took place around Lilienthal's mission; he was certainly influenced by the controversies entailed in this struggle, and closely followed the process of exacerbation of the relationships between the rival groups, to the point of separation into two rival camps. It therefore seems reasonable to assume that the Haskalah and the struggle against it were in Salanter's mind during the period in which he was beginning to lay the foundations of the Mussar movement. This theory relies upon the conjunction in time between Salanter's strengthening and buttressing of traditional values, and the fact that the traditional camp was at that time involved in a struggle with a government-sanctioned movement that was understood as a factor threatening the integrity of the tradition. To summarize, we may say that a reconstruction of the historical framework within which Salanter began to found the Mussar movement supports the theory that the struggle with the Haskalah was one of the factors influencing this activity.[5] But that conclusion is based upon circumstantial evidence only. One must still examine the activities and writings of Rabbi Israel from this period to determine whether they contain any clear confirmation of the theory associating the founding of the Mussar movement with the ascent of the Haskalah movement.

Salanter's Reaction to the Haskalah

Notwithstanding the paucity of biographical information pertaining to the period of Rabbi Israel's residence in Vilna, we do know of a number of incidents that shed light upon his attitude toward the Haskalah, two of which are associated with the visit of Moses Montefiore (1784–1885) to Vilna in 1846.[6]

Following the promulgation by the Russian government of a number of severe edicts concerning its Jewish citizens during the first half of the 1840s, Montefiore traveled to Russia in the hopes of ameliorating their plight. He met with the czar and with several governmental ministers in St. Petersburg, who confronted him with severe accusations against the Jews of Russia, including laziness, expressed in their refusal to engage in manual or agricultural labor. Moreover, they were accused of being ignorant fanatics, so that any concrete improvement in their legal status could only come about after their enlightenment.[7]

From St. Petersburg, Montefiore set off on a tour of the cities of the Pale of Settlement, of which Vilna was a major stop. It is difficult to describe the excitement and enthusiasm with which the Jews of Vilna anticipated this visit, which may only be understood in light of the tremendous pressure under which Russian Jewry found itself at this time and the prominence enjoyed by Montefiore for his role in the Damascus Blood Libel.[8] The Jews of Vilna, whose hearts were infused with new hope as the result of Montefiore's visit, overwhelmed him with demonstrations of honor and affection.[9]

Although the Maskilim and the traditionalists agreed to cease their struggle in order to appear before Montefiore as a united body on the occasion of his visit to Vilna,[10] the struggle did not cease, but merely took on a more restrained and covert character, in which both sides attempted to influence the distinguished visitor. So far as we can tell, the Maskilim gained the upper hand,[11] for, despite being a minority, the very fact of their Enlightenment gave them a number of advantages which were reflected in the management of the contacts with Montefiore. For example, the honor of organizing the reception for the distinguished guest was given to the wealthy maskil Nissan Rosenthal, who was thought of as an "organizer and statesman" by virtue of his connections with the regime.[12] A more important position of power was held by Rabbi Zvi Hirsch Katzenellenbogen, one of the leading Maskilim in Vilna, who served as a kind of personal advisor to Montefiore during his stay, and in effect determined which visitors could see him, informing his personal secretary in Latin who they were.[13] The advantage of the Maskilim was also reflected in the fact that all those who appealed to Montefiore with requests for aid required the assistance of scribes to formulate their requests in literary Hebrew.[14]

Jacob Lifschitz, relying upon traditions passed down to him from contemporaries of the event, relates that, despite the excitement surrounding Sir Montefiore's visit, there was also a group within the Orthodox camp who were saddened and embittered by his trip to Russia.[15] This uneasiness is explained by Lifschitz, as follows: "These were days of struggle between the orthodox and the free-thinkers, and when there appears an advocate of his people, a righteous man, who is nevertheless beardless, the free-thinkers may argue that it is possible to be a good Jew and yet be clean-shaven."[16] Such an explanation seems a bit anachronistic, since the issue of shaving did not engage the attention of the Maskilim and the "God-fearers" during the 1840s in Vilna. Nevertheless, these remarks do help us to understand the unease described by Lifschitz. The fact that Montefiore was clean-shaven was an external sign of his being a Westerner. The same was true of his secretary, Rabbi Dr. Louis Loewe (Eli'ezer) ha-Levi, who played the major active role in the contacts between Montefiore and the Jewish community. In terms of both their educational background and their way of life, Montefiore and Loewe tended to be more sympathetic toward the Haskalah tendencies. In light of this, it is not surprising that due to the claims of the government and the persuasive efforts of the Maskilim, Montefiore, through his secretary, took a pro-Maskilic stand.

A sermon delivered by Loewe in Montefiore's name, to the community leaders of Vilna, repeated the government's claims that the Jews refused to engage in labor and agriculture because of their laziness. In addition, Loewe spoke out in support of the study of Western culture and languages, citing the Damascus Blood Libel as an indication of the value of knowledge of languages,[17] since, according to him, it was lack of fluency in Arabic that was the cause of that melancholy affair and, by contrast, he indicated Montefiore was able to act on behalf of the Jews of Damascus thanks to his (Loewe's) knowledge of that language. In another sermon delivered by Loewe in the Vilna Synagogue on the Sabbath in the presence of Montefiore himself, various distinguished leaders, and a large crowd, he again spoke in praise of labor and enlightenment.[18] Moreover, in the course of their visits to a number of educational institutions in Vilna, including the Talmud Torah and yeshiva of Rabbi Meile, Loewe (in Montefiore's name) ordered the directors of those institutions to teach their students the language of the land.[19] The aforementioned discomfort among the opponents of the Haskalah was brought about by the fact that the representative of Montefiore, whom everyone knew and honored and upon whom they had pinned their hopes, supported the Haskalah position.[20]

There are two extant accounts of Salanter's reaction to Montefiore's visit in Vilna. The first of these is brought by Yaakov Lifschitz, based upon what he heard from Salanter himself:

> The Gaon . . . Rabbi Israel Salanter told me the following: "On one of the days of Sir Montefiore's stay in Vilna, I met the Gaon . . . Itzele [that is, Yitzhak] Volozhiner, of blessed memory, walking briskly and hurriedly to one of the gatherings. I stopped him and asked him with astonishment, 'Rabbi of Volozhin, where are you going and why are you hurrying so?' The intent of the question was sharply diplomatic, since the Gaon Rabbi Itzele was at the time practically a prince in Israel, the head of the sages of our people and of the community leaders throughout the province of Vilna. . . . It was therefore appropriate, by manner and proper behavior, that all of the meetings of the nobleman [that is, Montefiore] with the distinguished persons of both parties be held in the home of the Gaon . . . and thus his words would also have been taken more seriously. . . . The Gaon Rabbi Itzele immediately understood my question . . . and also answered me diplomatically, as follows: 'Does the evil-doer in Gehinnom know where they are taking him? So do I not know where they are leading me.' . . . The point is clear: because the Maskilim had the upper hand, they did not wish to honor a great Torah Gaon, even though his name was revered throughout Israel."[21]

Despite the stylized form of the conversation between Rabbi Salanter and Rabbi Yitzhak of Volozhin as presented by Lifschitz, it seems likely that the basic facts given here are as he heard them from Salanter; indeed, that Rabbi Israel remembered this incident, and saw fit to repeat it to Lifschitz many years later, is indicative of the importance he attached to it. We may infer from the story that Salanter was not at all happy with the influence of the Maskilim upon Montefiore's contacts and activities in Vilna. Salanter may have hoped to convince Rabbi Yitzhak not to cooperate with Montefiore at all, so long as he was under the influence of the Maskilim. However, the latter feared that any step of this sort would be interpreted as an affront to the honor of the guest, and thereby harmful to the interests of Russian Jewry. Salanter himself, on the other hand, was not afraid to argue directly with the representative and spokesman of the distinguished prince. This encounter is briefly described by the Maskilic author, Isaac Meir Dick:

> From there [Montefiore] traveled to the synagogue in Zarzecze, and he visited their study house, where he criticized the rabbi, the Gaon Rabbi Israel Salanter, through his interpreter, Loewe, for not knowing how to speak the Russian language. The rabbi berated the interpreter, Loewe, for a half-hour. The words of Loewe were more forceful than those of Rabbi Israel in that he mentioned the Damascus case, and he returned from there to his home, dissatisfied. . . .[22]

Despite the brevity of Dick's description, we may reconstruct the following picture: In the course of their visits to Torah institutions in Vilna, Montefiore and his secretary visited the *bet midrash* in Zarzecze, where Salanter's yeshiva was located. The very fact of their visiting this place indicates the great prestige that Rabbi Israel enjoyed as a scholar and as *rosh-yeshivah*. That may even be the reason why Loewe criticized him for being unable to speak the language of the country. One must remember that the argument that rabbis ought to learn the vernacular was a typical one of the Haskalah; the Maskilim repeatedly berated the rabbis that they were unable to properly fulfill their task without such knowledge.[23] Thus, in person with Salanter and in his sermons and visits to other educational institutions, Montefiore's spokesman articulated an argument commonly leveled by the Maskilim against the rabbis. But Salanter's response is rather surprising given that the leaders of all factions of the Vilna community spared no effort to honor and cater to the visiting dignitary. Nevertheless, despite the fact that Louis Loewe was viewed as one who spoke in the name of Montefiore, Rabbi Israel did not hesitate to answer him forcefully and at length: "The rabbi berated the interpreter, Loewe, for a half-hour. . . ." As far as we can tell from the descriptions of Montefiore's visit to Vilna, this was the only case of confrontation between the distinguished guest and a local personality.

There were no doubt others who had reservations regarding the positions expressed by Loewe in the name of the nobleman, but due to the dignity of the guest and the hopes that they pinned on him, they evidently preferred to maintain their silence. Rabbi Israel was the only one who dared to confront him in a direct and public manner. The

Maskilic author Dick understandably concludes the story with the victory of ha-Levi: "And the words of Loewe were more forceful than those of Rabbi Israel, in that he mentioned the Damascus case. . . ." As in the above-cited sermon, here too Loewe relied upon the Damascus affair as an indication of the importance of knowledge of the vernacular and, at least according to Dick, this argument was sufficient to decide the balance of the argument. For our purposes, the concluding sentence of the story is significant: "And he [Loewe] returned to his home dissatisfied. . . ." That ending is a clear indication that the conversation was not a polite one, such as those to which Montefiore and his entourage were accustomed in their travels in the city, but a sharp exchange of words.

It is not unlikely that, in the course of their debate, Loewe and Salanter moved from the subject of the teaching of Russian to other topical subjects of dispute. The demand that the rabbis themselves learn the vernacular symbolized a certain line of thought regarding the solution to the problem of Russian Jewry—namely, the Maskilic approach, supported by Loewe and opposed by Salanter. The fear that silence in the face of Loewe's words might be construed as assent, thereby strengthening the hands of the Maskilim, led Rabbi Israel to respond firmly where others preferred silence. In standing up to the spokesman of Montefiore, Salanter revealed himself as a personality of spiritual daring and moral force.

More clearly even than in the above encounter, or any other known case, Salanter's attitude toward the Haskalah was expressed in the affair of the rabbinical seminary. In 1848, two rabbinical seminaries were established at the initiative and with the patronage of the government, one in Vilna and the other in Zhitomir.[24] The establishment of these institutions was in a sense the culmination of the efforts by the regime to change the nature of Jewish society, since the government looked upon these institutions as the cradle of a new religio-cultural elite through which it could hasten the assimilation of the Jewish minority within the Christian population. For this reason, the administration of these seminaries, as well as the instruction of general subjects, was entrusted to Christians. The seminary in Vilna also included a dormitory, intended to separate the young students from the influence of the Jewish community.[25]

In the eyes of the Maskilim, these rabbinical seminaries were intended to foster that cultural and social transformation for which they longed and toward which they labored. Blaming the rabbis for a good deal of the misfortunes of Russian Jewry, the Maskilim argued that the traditional rabbis, who shut themselves away within the narrow confines of halakhah, and who lacked knowledge of the vernacular and other aspects of learning required by the "spirit of the times," were totally unfit to lead their flock in the desired direction or to represent them properly before the authorities. Therefore, rabbinical seminaries whose curriculum would combine Torah and secular wisdom were needed to train the new breed of rabbis who would be fit to lead the community.[26]

Those in the traditional camp saw the establishment of these rabbinic seminaries as an edict imposed upon them against their will and to their disadvantage. Even if some of them thought it desirable that candidates for the rabbinate acquire some knowledge of the vernacular and of general learning, they preferred their training to be left in the hands of the Jewish community, rather than being turned over to an institution under the aegis of the government, whose faculty included Maskilim and Christians.[27] Nevertheless, once the seminary had become an established fact, the leaders of the Vilna community sought some degree of influence and supervision over what went on there, asking to be included in the determination of the curriculum and to be consulted concerning the appointment of the Jewish instructors there. Only after this request was refused, and they despaired of influencing what went on within this institution, did the leaders of the Vilna community turn to another method of struggle: Several students at the seminary were kidnapped and turned over for military service.[28]

Prior to the opening of the rabbinical seminary in Vilna, Rabbi Israel was offered the position of teacher of Talmud.[29] He rejected the offer and, after the government authorities put pressure on him, he secretly left Vilna and escaped to Kovna.[30] The initiative to appoint him evidently originated in the circles of the Maskilim in Vilna: Aryeh Leon Mandelstamm, advisor to the minister of education on matters concerning Jewish enlightenment, recommended Salanter to Minister Uvarov, who approved the appointment.[31] It seems reasonable to assume that Mandelstamm acted in this manner in concert with the Maskilim in Vilna. The obvious question that arises is: Why was such a position offered to Salanter rather than to a Maskil? In point of fact, following Salanter's refusal, the instructorship in Talmud was turned over to Rabbi Zvi Hirsch Katzenellenbogen, who also served as overall supervisor of Jewish studies in the new institution.[32]

The appeal to Salanter seems to have been based upon the Maskilim's fears that the rabbinical seminary would encounter severe opposition from traditional circles. Were Salanter, who enjoyed prestige and prominence for his outstanding knowledge of Torah and for his piety, to agree to accept the position of Talmud instructor, it would greatly enhance the legitimacy of the institution.[33] Some speculated that the offer to Salanter was based upon the Maskilim's mistaken belief that he leaned slightly in their direction, being an unconventional personality.[34] There is no evidence to confirm that theory. Yet, it may be corroborated by the fact that, even at a later period, Rabbi Israel enjoyed a positive image in the eyes of a number of Haskalah authors.[35]

As to Salanter's motivations for rejecting the proposed offer, it is related that, when asked about it by the Vilna Maskil Dr. Trachtenberg, he replied that there is a difference between a rabbi and a physician. While the physician makes a greater effort on behalf of a wealthy person, the rabbi is required to make his greatest efforts specifically on behalf of the poor, as certain halakhic problems may be questions of life and death for the poor. The rabbi must therefore be expert in all branches of Torah, and also God-fearing. Salanter concluded that the graduates of the rabbinical seminary will not be blessed with all these qualities.[36] His suspicions in this case were based upon the character and structure of the rabbinical seminary per se. As an institution whose declared goal was to train rabbis, just as a university trains physicians, the rabbinical seminary is unable to imbue its graduates with the *yir'at shamayim* (fear of Heaven) that must accompany and guide them as authorities in rendering halakhic decisions. Those attributes can only be acquired by study of Torah for its own sake, as is done in traditional yeshivot.[37] Furthermore, Rabbi Israel seems to have sensed the danger inherent in the influence upon the seminary students of Christian teachers and Maskilim.[38]

In addition to his skepticism concerning the piety of the graduates of the rabbinical seminary, Salanter had serious doubts as to whether great Torah scholars were liable to emerge from it—first and foremost, because of the division of time between Torah studies and the other subjects of study. There was also a marked contrast between the approach to study advocated by him and that proposed by the Maskilim. The practical goal of the seminary, as well as the negative attitude held by the Maskilim toward *pilpul*, resulted in a curriculum that primarily emphasized the pragmatic aspect of halakhah—that is, the study of the Codes—rather than the theoretical side, as was the case in traditional yeshivot.[39] Salanter, by contrast, thought that it was only possible to train great Torah scholars by means of the traditional method of study.[40]

Testimony concerning the pressure brought to bear upon Salanter, and the motivations of his response, is cited in the name of one of his students from that same period:

> We sat before him in a semi-circle, while Rabbi Israel Salanter was sitting expounding [the halakhah] before us. . . . The door opened, and Rabbi H. Katzenellenbogen, and behind him Education Minister Uvarov, were waiting for [him].

> After he stood before the minister calmly and listened to the
> proposal of Katzenellenbogen, [namely] that the minister
> wished to promote him up to be director of the school for rabbis
> in Vilna, with a high salary, Rabbi Salanter in his wisdom slipped
> away from them, and no longer spoke with them, [either] for
> good or for ill.[41]

Was the visitor indeed Uvarov or another governmental functionary?
In either event, the presence of a governmental official obviously constituted a covert form of pressure or threat. It is not surprising that
Rabbi Israel preferred to avoid giving a clear response. On the other
hand, he did express his opinion to Rabbi Yitzhak of Volozhin. The
same student relates that:

> On a certain day Rabbi Yitzhak Volozhiner, of blessed memory,
> returned from Petersburg, and visited Rabbi Israel Salanter at
> Zarzecze, where we studied. . . . And they greeted one another,
> and went into a private room. . . . My soul greatly trembled and
> longed to hear the words of these sages, but they spoke quietly
> and I was unable to hear a word from the mouth of Rabbi Israel
> Salanter, until he said the following loudly and angrily: "Rabbi
> Yitzhak, leave this path! It is a time of apostasy, and we must
> allow ourselves to be killed, great and small alike, rather than
> violate [the law]. For the idea of the government is to assimilate
> our new generation among them." On Tuesday Rabbi Israel left
> for Kovna. . . .[42]

From the above account, it would appear that Rabbi Yitzhak attempted to persuade Salanter to accept the office of teacher at the
rabbinical seminary, which the latter staunchly refused. Rabbi Yitzhak,
no less than Rabbi Israel, was presumably sufficiently clearheaded to
understand the nature of Nicholai's regime. The argument apparently
revolved around the question of the extent of concrete danger inherent
in the rabbinical seminary, and the best way to stop it. Rabbi Yitzhak
thought it desirable that Salanter accept the position that had been
offered him, so that those loyal to the tradition might have some degree
of influence and supervision over what was done in the seminary,
despite the fact that Rabbi Israel's presence on the faculty would accord
the institution the stamp of legitimacy. Salanter, on the other hand,
held that there was no basis whatsoever for cooperation with the
Haskalah, and that the rabbinical seminary was "off limits" to anyone
loyal to the tradition.

It seems that the difference between the positions of Salanter and
of Rabbi Yitzhak Volozhiner derived from tactical considerations alone.
It is likely that the difference between them in the tactical realm

stemmed, at least in part, from a more fundamental difference—namely, their respective evaluations of the Haskalah, the extent to which it was seen negatively, and the dangers to be anticipated in connection with it. On this question, Salanter appears to have held an unequivocal stance, which rejected the approach of the Haskalah and firmly objected to the new institution that embodied these tendencies. By his stand, Rabbi Israel differed, not only from Rabbi Yitzhak Volozhiner, but also from the leadership of the Vilna community, which wished to be included in the supervision of the new seminary. From a personal standpoint, Salanter was again shown as an individual of strong moral fiber, who preferred what he understood as the collective welfare above his own personal good. In this case, he not only refused a highly paid governmental position, but exposed himself to the not-inconsiderable dangers entailed in rejecting the appeal of the government; he ultimately had to go into exile in another city in order to escape their pressure.

Even though the incident of the rabbinical seminary took place in 1848, Rabbi Israel's attitude toward the Haskalah seems to have been formed already at the beginning of the decade. Hence, the stand that he took in this case is an additional confirmation of the thesis that, in founding the Mussar movement, Rabbi Israel was sensitive to and aware of the dangers inherent in Haskalah.

IN THE sermons given during the years 1845–46—at least in those that are extant—Salanter does not engage in direct and explicit polemics against the Haskalah. They nevertheless seem to contain some echoes of the new reality in which the impact of the Haskalah threatened traditional values. An example of this is the following passage:

> . . . If so, we find a difficulty in the statement in *Avot*, "It is good to [combine] Torah with worldly affairs (*derekh erez*)."[43] This seems to make no sense, for [it makes] worldly affairs the main thing, and Torah secondary. . . . For the word "good" is not at all applicable to worldly affairs, as there is no ultimate benefit in worldly affairs [per se], and it would be better were it possible [to live] without such . . . any involvement in the world being only out of necessity, for it is impossible to serve the Creator when one is ill or hungry. . . . Hence, if [the term] "good" is not at all applicable to worldly affairs, one ought not to begin with the words, "good are worldly affairs . . . ," as they are [in fact] very bad. How can they become good? by means of Torah (which sweetens its bitterness). . . . Therefore, a person should not forbear from [studying] Torah, [thinking that] he will pos-

> sibly or certainly need to leave his studies and engage in worldly affairs. For the labor of Torah is unlike the labor [invested in] other matters, in which the effort is nothing more than a prelude to the goal, the entire purpose being to arrive at the final end, otherwise, it is as if it [the effort] is all for nothing. Not so the Torah; for the exertion [in studying Torah] is an end in itself, and each and every day that one studies becomes the great goal. . . .[44]

The Maskilim made extensive use of the remarks of the Sages in praise of *derekh erez*, some of them interpreting this concept as referring to knowledge of sciences and languages, as well as to the acquisition of good character and manners.[45] It likewise served those Maskilim who wished to enhance the prestige of manual labor and agricultural work. The demand of the Maskilim for productivity and for the incorporation of occupational training within the framework of Jewish education was accompanied by the effort to argue that even the authoritative sources of Judaism ascribe a positive value to involvement in *derekh erez*.[46] Moreover, the Haskalah program stated that most youths ought by right to prepare themselves to engage in some occupation, while only a small minority, who would serve in some Torah office as their profession, ought to devote themselves to Torah studies on a high level. This understanding of Torah study in purely functional terms was sharply opposed to the valuational approach of *Torah li-shemah* as accepted in traditional society. The above-cited remarks of Rabbi Salanter would therefore seem to be directed against this Maskilic tendency. First of all, he denied any independent value to involvement in *derekh erez*: Such involvement is only a necessary means for the sake of subsistence. The study of Torah, by contrast, is not a means toward an end, but an end in itself. Therefore, Salanter continues with the demand that "the father may not refrain from teaching his son Torah, even if afterwards he will not continue his studies."[47]

Further on, Salanter poses an additional demand to the fathers:

> But for the father, there is another important matter; he must gird his loins with strength to teach his son Torah. . . . For it is known what is written in Ezekiel (3:17–19), "Son of Man, I have appointed you as a watchman to the house of Israel, etc. . . . When I say to the wicked etc. . . . and you did not warn him . . . that wicked man shall die in his iniquity, but his blood I will require at your hand. . . . But if you warn the wicked . . . you have delivered your life. . . ." Thus, we find that a person is required to chastise his fellow-man even though it is possible that it may not help. It is known that, so long as a child is small, it is easy to guide him in the proper [character] traits, to direct him toward the fear of God and to break his evil impulse, but

> once he becomes old in his evil traits this is not the case. We
> conclude [from this] that when the father has guided his son
> on the right path . . . even if afterwards [the son] does not listen
> to him once he leaves his domain, he has saved his own life,
> because he educated him as far as was within his power. . . .[48]

The father's obligation to teach his son Torah is among the most
important precepts. In this sermon, Rabbi Israel develops the idea that
there is an additional obligation incumbent upon the father: to be
diligent about the education of his sons while they are still small, so
that they not stray from the proper path. Salanter warns the fathers
that, if they do not do everything within their power to prevent a
deviation of this sort, they will be held culpable for their son's behavior.
These remarks would seem to imply a reality in which there are sons
who abandon their father's path. Salanter, then, sounds the alarm about
the educational responsibility of the fathers in connection with this
phenomenon.

A decisive proof for the direct connection between Rabbi Israel's
attempt to disseminate the study of Mussar in public and the attacks
upon the status of the tradition by the Haskalah movement appears in
a letter written by Salanter himself. I have refrained from relying on
the letter hitherto because I do not know when it was written. However,
in light of our discussion thus far, we may use it as supplementary
evidence. The letter in question was addressed by Rabbi Israel to his
disciple and friend, Rabbi Elijah Levinsohn of Cartinga. In it, he asks
the latter to act on behalf of the dissemination of Mussar study and its
transformation into an accepted public norm. Among other things, he
writes:

> . . . [concerning] the matter of Mussar study—to strengthen it
> with immovable nails, to strengthen weak hands [so as] to give
> advice [to] the simple and unintelligent to bring them towards
> the way of life, and to give them strength to wage the battle
> that is a mitzvah, the battle of the Lord. Particularly in these
> times, when the everyday habit [that is, of observance of Torah
> and mitzvot] grows weaker from day to day and from hour to
> hour, where can one find Torah and Divine service? And who
> shall put a stop to it [this fall] and reinvigorate [Torah study]
> seeing that it has fallen so drastically from the status which it
> formerly held. . . . If we are silent and thereby sin, who knows
> whether we will not be required to give an accounting for our
> failure to seek out the collective good by strengthening the
> Divine service. And what can they, the flock, do? The battle
> surrounds them from every side and corner, [even] if they have
> the strength of stones and their flesh is bronze, how can they

not be tempted by the foolish [counsel] of these people who sin against their own souls to deflect them from God and His service. [Unless] those who have been given by God a greater share of wisdom and understanding than their brethren . . . spread their understanding and extend wings in whose shade those weak of mind and understanding may take shelter, to build a rampart and to construct an embankment, in order to strengthen the Torah like a fortified city. . . .[49]

This letter clearly reflects Salanter's great fear in the face of the challenge to the hegemony of the tradition among his contemporaries. He describes activity to fortify the fear of God among his contemporaries by establishing circles of Mussar students, whose activity would be concentrated around Mussar houses, thereby immunizing them against the dangerous influences of those who sought to deflect them from the Torah—that is, the Maskilim. As mentioned, the date of this letter is unknown. However, as its subject is the dissemination of Mussar study in public, which Salanter began at the end of the 1840s and the beginning of the '50s, it may be ascribed to that period.

In light both of the transformation that took place in the status of the Haskalah and its relationship with the traditional camp in the course of the 1840s, as well as what we have seen concerning Rabbi Israel's attitude toward the Haskalah during this period, it follows that in laying the foundations of the Mussar movement, Rabbi Salanter was, in part, reacting to the threat that the Haskalah posed to the values and forms of the tradition. It seemingly became clear to Salanter that the traditional community was no longer able to guarantee the commitment of its adherents to the values of the tradition. This inability stemmed both from the involvement of the regime in the internal affairs of the Jewish community and its decision to cut down the authority of the community to the point of abolition, as well as to the fact that the traditional community had begun to lose its homogeneous spiritual-religious character. This development was particularly striking in Vilna, where a circle of Maskilim presented each individual with an ideological and social alternative to the traditional way. Rabbi Israel hoped that, in light of these circumstances, a voluntary movement that would both assure and deepen the piety of each individual who joined it might serve as a serious response to the threat inherent in the Haskalah. By this means, responsibility for the integrity of the tradition would pass from communal institutions, which were becoming progressively weaker, to the shoulders of those who felt a strong loyalty to the tradition as individuals, and who would further benefit from the encouragement and stimulus of the *esprit de corps* of the new movement.

11

The Social Background and Its Influence Upon the Founding of the Mussar Movement

ANOTHER important factor that will help us to understand the aims and motivations of Rabbi Israel Salanter in establishing the Mussar movement is the social and economic distress[1] that afflicted the Jews of Russia during the reign of Nicholai I.[2] This distress was rooted in the fact that no new sources of income became available to the Jews despite their appreciable natural increase. On the contrary, in addition to those regulations that were intended to reduce the Jews' religious and national uniqueness, such as forced conscription into the army and the Compulsory Enlightenment, the government restricted the permitted sources of livelihood, causing widespread impoverishment. While the alleged aim of these regulations was to protect local farmers against exploitation by the village Jews, the regime in fact undertook a cruel policy of expulsion, which uprooted thousands of Jewish families from their place of residence, leaving them with neither a source of income nor a roof over their heads.

The situation of the urban Jews was not much better. Their own natural increase, coupled with their displacement from the villages, led to an enormous increase in the number of Jewish artisans living in the cities, far beyond the needs of the population. The result was a situation of severe competition and meager incomes. Commerce also failed to provide an adequate livelihood, save for a small minority. The prohibition against moving to the commercial centers in the interior of Russia, various restrictions placed upon commerce even within the Pale of Settlement, the large number of those occupied in commerce, and the intensification of competition among them—all these reduced the income available from this source. A further aggravation of the economic situation of those who lived in the cities and towns came about in 1845, in the form of the order prohibiting the manufacture of liquor;

this regulation eliminated the livelihood of some two thousand people in Vilna alone.

The manifestations of impoverishment among the Jewish masses of Vilna were particularly severe. Max Lilienthal, who visited Vilna in the early 1840s, related that there were at that time about two thousand cobblers and tailors in the city who, due to their large number, barely eked out a living. There were also many laborers in Vilna in that period who engaged in the simplest and most backbreaking kinds of work. According to Lilienthal's impressions, some two-thirds of the Jews of the city were constantly running about in the streets attempting to eke out some form of meager livelihood.[3] An additional wave of expellees from the villages arrived in Vilna in 1845. This development, together with the prohibition against the manufacture of liquor issued that same year, exacerbated the economic distress among the Jews of the city.[4]

This economic distress was predictably accompanied by social tension. Despite the fact that the policy of edicts and restrictions affected the Jewish population as a whole, there seems no doubt that the bulk of the suffering was borne by the masses, whose economic situation was most tenuous and vulnerable to begin with. Social tensions were also heightened by the fact that the dominant control over communal institutions was concentrated in the hands of the economic elite, who on occasion exploited this fact to its own advantage, provoking the masses to complain to the authorities of oppression and economic exploitation by the community leaders.[5] The system of taxation, which was expanded during this period, likewise entailed a social injustice: The indirect tax, called *korobka*, which was imposed upon the consumption of various items, particularly meat, made the burden of taxation upon the poorer people even heavier.[6]

Most of all, social injustice was reflected in the way the laws about military conscription were executed.[7] The regime introduced conscription into the army as a means of religious and national assimilation of the Jews, sparing no effort to get those drafted to change their religion. In the eyes of their families, the conscription or kidnapping of a son for army service was tantamount to his being lost forever. The communal leadership, which bore responsibility for meeting the quota of draftees, was faced with an extremely serious ethical dilemma. According to the governmental regulations, each community had to prepare a list of potential conscripts, to be headed by the families with the largest number of children. By this criterion, the well-to-do families would tend to head the list. However, by relying upon a clause that allowed the inclusion of those who did not pay taxes, vagrants, and violaters of community discipline, the communal leadership was able to ignore this principle, and imposed the full burden of conscription upon the shoulders of the masses. Thus, the weakest elements in society, such as the orphans and the homeless, were the first to be drafted.[8] The cruelty and injustice of this system reached their peak when children and youths were snatched from the bosoms of their helpless mothers to be delivered into military service.[9]

The reaction of the masses to the edict of conscription was generally a passive one,[10] expressed in folk songs characterizing the community leadership as agents of the wicked government. There were also some isolated cases of active rebellion, in which the infuriated masses attacked the community house and freed the draftees who were held there, and we know of isolated incidents in which such outbursts were led by a rabbi or other Torah personality.[11] However, generally speaking the rabbis and learned elite sanctioned this unjust policy—if not by active collaboration, at least by their implied consent through silence.[12] The members of the Torah elite sought first of all to save themselves, their families, and their own students, from the evil decree,[13] an objective that was achieved as the communal leaders agreed not to draft Torah students into the army. This is indicative of an additional factor that typified the social gap in Lithuanian Jewry: In this society, which accorded the highest religious value to Torah learning, there was a considerable overlap between those who were poorest and those who were unlearned in Torah. Thus, the masses further suffered from being looked upon with contempt and being perceived as worthless from the religious-spiritual viewpoint.

As said above, the economic distress of the Jews living in the Pale of Settlement worsened toward the middle of the 1840s due to the new expulsion from the villages and the prohibition against producing liquor—both edicts issued in 1845.[14] To these were added two additional measures. In 1844, a candle tax had been imposed upon the Jews of Russia, intended to finance the maintenance of government schools for Jewish children. More serious was the imposition of classification in 1846, by which all of the Jews of the Pale were divided by the government into several "types" based upon their degree of utility to the state economy. Those unpropertied masses who were not registered in one of the guilds were to be included in the category of the "unprofitable," destined by the government for a number of cruel decrees, such as an appreciable increase in army conscription, thus intensifying anxiety and panic among the impoverished masses.

Rabbi Israel Salanter took the first steps toward the establishment of the Mussar movement during the very same years in which the impoverishment of the Jews of Russia assumed such serious dimensions. The question that arises is whether any significance ought to be attributed to this coincidence. In answering this question, we must attempt to determine whether Salanter's words and deeds constituted a response, direct or indirect, to the manifestations of distress described above. We shall begin by attempting to define Salanter's attitude toward the role of economic activity in human life.

The Gaon of Vilna, Rabbi Hayyim of Volozhin, and Rabbi Zundel were all identified with a religio-ethical outlook that denied the value of this world, a fatalistic approach, based upon the quality of *bitahon* (trust). According to this approach, there is no reason to overemphasize concrete, worldly efforts in order to earn a livlihood, since a person's fortunes are in any event dependent upon Divine will. In contrast with this line of thought, one is struck by the more ambivalent character of Rabbi Israel's position. In principle, Salanter followed in the footsteps of his teachers in expressing strong reservations about the value of this world;[15] however, once the question of how one ought to behave was raised in practice, not only did he not preach asceticism or restriction of one's economic involvements, but he even found religious justification for them within the framework of values mentioned above. This stance is expressed in the manner in which he resolves the contradiction between the view of Nahmanides and that of the author of *Hovot ha-levavot* as to the meaning of *bitahon*:

> There are two kinds of trust: the trust of *Hovot Ha-Levavot*, and the trust of Nahmanides. According to *Hovot Ha-Levavot*, one ought to trust in the Holy One, blessed be He, specifically by making an effort, for it is forbidden to rely upon miracles. . . . But according to Nahmanides, trust means to cast one's burden upon God alone . . . and according to him, no effort is required even in matters of earning a livelihood, but only [that one] trust in God. Both of these [views] seem to me to be the words of the living God, for we have found a dispute among the Sages concerning this very same matter, [Berakhot 35b]: [following the words of Rabbi Ishmael] one should combine the study of them [the words of the Torah] with a worldly occupation. . . . But Rabbi Simeon bar Yohai dissents. Note the distinction [regarding this matter] drawn in *Nefesh Ha-Hayyim* (1:5) between the multitude and the [unusual] individuals. For our Sages specifically said, "Many acted as Rabbi Simeon bar Yohai and did not succeed"—"many," specifically. We thus find that unique individuals certainly ought to have trust [as defined by] Nahmanides . . . while the words of *Hovot Ha-Levavot* are intended for the generality of people. . . .[16]

Salanter's proposed solution is thus based upon Rabbi Hayyim of Volozhin's interpretation of the talmudic passage cited from Berakhot. However, a more careful examination of Rabbi Hayyim's remarks, compared with Salanter's, will reveal that they tended toward diverging conclusions, even if based upon the identical interpretation within the talmudic controversy. Rabbi Hayyim's interpretation of the tannaitic controversy and of the conclusion derived by the Talmud is as follows:

> . . . Rabbi Ishmael alluded in his holy language . . . that even during that brief period of time in which one is engaged in earning a livelihood, for one's minimum and necessary needs in order to sustain oneself; even then, one's thoughts should only be concerned with matters of Torah. . . . For it is certainly nearly impossible for the multitude constantly to devote themselves to the study of Torah alone, and not to turn to matters of livelihood for even a brief while. . . . But it is certainly incumbent upon an individual who is able to engage only in Torah and Divine service all his days not to separate himself for even a brief period from the Torah and [Divine] service in order to engage in livelihood, heaven forbid, which is the opinion of Rabbi Simeon b. Yohai.[17]

Rabbi Hayyim of Volozhin was afraid that the words of the Talmud—"many acted as Rabbi Ishmael and succeeded; as Rabbi Simeon bar Yohai, and did not succeed"—would be interpreted as implying that the halakhic norm was the opinion expressed by Rabbi Ishmael rather than by Rabbi Simeon bar Yohai. In fact, Rabbi Hayyim's ideal, according to which he educated his disciples, was specifically that expressed by Rabbi Simeon; Rabbi Hayyim emphasized that Rabbi Ishmael's path was legitimate only for the multitude. Rabbi Hayyim held that the preferable path is one of exclusive dedication to Torah study and separation from worldly involvements, and that deviation from that path is only permitted out of necessity.

On the basis of the same talmudic saying, Rabbi Israel Salanter tends toward a different conclusion. Underlying his remarks is the desire to span the gap between the radical understanding of *bitahon* as found in Nahmanides, and embodied in Rabbi Simeon bar Yohai, and between the economic reality of his day, in which it was difficult to make ends meet even with considerable effort. Relying upon the distinction between the individual and the multitude, his intention was to justify the path suitable for the multitude. The path of Rabbi Simeon ben Yohai and the interpretation of *bitahon* given by Nahmanides, of course, represented positive values for Salanter as well; however, their application is limited to unique individuals alone. The masses, who are in this case the majority of the people, are allowed to engage in efforts to earn a living without in any way implying the negation of the value of *bitahon*.

The idea that one is required to engage in effort toward earning a living, while remaining loyal to the principle of *bitahon*, is more clearly expressed in a letter that Salanter sent to one of his close associates who had gone to visit the Land of Israel:

> He should see fit to speed his journey home from the Holy Land in peace, so that he be sure, in accordance with commercial usage, not to lose his business or his position. And even though it is a great mitzvah to tarry in the Holy Land, one nevertheless ought not thereby to jeopardize one's livelihood and thereby bring about, Heaven forbid, unhappy consequences, whether between man and his fellow, etc. This does not contradict the attribute of trust.[18]

The affirmation of making an effort in relation to earning a livelihood emanates not just from a practical, clear-sighted evaluation of the economic reality of the period, but also from an ethical argument: namely, that the weakening of one's economic basis brings about an ethical deterioration in the realm of interpersonal relationships. One finds an instructive expression of Salanter's unconventional stance concerning economic activity in a letter to his disciple, Rabbi Elijah Levinsohn of Cartinga, from 1850.[19] In this letter, Rabbi Israel severely criticizes the social convention that treats physical labor and those who engage in it with contempt. He rejects the widespread tendency to see commerce as the preferred means of earning a living, for three reasons: (1) this branch of the economy is unable to provide a livelihood for the masses who engage in it; (2) involvement in commerce, under conditions of sharp competition, encourages deceitfulness and cheating; and (3) commerce demands such great psychic and mental effort on the part of those who engage in it that it leaves them no energy to engage in Torah. Rabbi Salanter seemed to have had in mind specifically the Torah-oriented householder, whose youth was spent studying in a yeshiva. He advises the members of this social stratum to educate their sons to engage in some form of skilled labor that, in his opinion, will enable them both to earn an honest living and to devote themselves seriously to Torah study. Further on in his letter, Rabbi Israel asks Rabbi Elijah Cartinga to assist a certain Jew who is "an outstanding scholar in Talmud, Rashi and Tosafot" to acquire a trade by which he may earn a living. Salanter expresses the hope that this individual will serve as an example to others who will follow in his path.

This approach differed from the conventional wisdom of society

during that period generally, and that accepted among the *ba'alei batim*
in particular. In effect, it is a call for revolution in the manner in which
society relates toward various areas of economic activity. Salanter
sought to make physical labor, which was generallly associated with
the masses and the ignorant, into an acceptable, respected source of
livelihood for one who was an outstanding talmudic scholar. Moreover,
Salanter's critique of commerce partly coincided with that of the Maskilim. The Haskalah's demand for the productivization of Jewish economic activity and the inclusion of vocational training within the system of Jewish education also argued that commerce, and particularly
petty commerce, is an inadequate source of income and entails exploitation and deceit. Salanter was evidently aware of the similarity and
took pains to stress the points of disagreement between himself and
the position of the Maskilim: While the latter demanded the implementation of vocational training already in the early stages of education,
Salanter insists that it must be preceded by the acquisition of the basic
fundaments of Torah study, and that vocational training be postponed
to a later stage. His consideration was not only ideological, but also
pedagogical:

> . . . . So long as the son can find his way in the study of Talmud,
> one ought not to assist him [to learn] a trade, for the study of
> craft has no fixed time, and may be acquired in maturity just as
> in youth (as will be attested by expert craftsmen). But this is
> not true of the study of Talmud, which is the basis of our lives
> and protects our souls; its foundation can only be laid in the
> days of childhood; let us not move from it.[20]

The change in Salanter's attitude toward economic activity compared with that of his teachers was not accompanied by any declared
change in values toward the earthly reality. Unlike German neo-Orthodoxy, Rabbi Israel's position did not grant independent value to worldliness. One is nevertheless struck by the innovation in his approach
toward the question of how one earns a living, a change arguably
brought about by his awareness of and sensitivity toward the economic
and social distress that troubled many of his contemporaries, and his
realistic evaluation of the connection between economic pressures and
ethical decline in the area of interpersonal relationships.

A clear, albeit indirect, expression of Salanter's sensitivity toward
this matter appears in the sermons delivered from 1845 to 1856 and
published in the volume *Even yisra'el*. One of the initial steps taken by
Salanter toward the dissemination of his approach among the public,
these sermons had a distinctly learned style. While most of each sermon

is devoted to a series of scholastic difficulties and their solutions, the ethical consequences included therein only appear as an afterthought. However, it is instructive that their ethical lessons focused upon the social realm, with the preacher on occasion interrupting the formal exposition of the sermon to present the practical ethical consequence to be learned from a paranthetical remark. It seems reasonable to assume that these deviations from the regular progress of the sermon, as well as their concrete formulation, reflect the importance attached to this subject by Salanter. We shall now examine several excerpts that exemplify this phenomenon. The first deals with the commandments pertaining to charity and hospitality.[21] Salanter begins the discussion with a typical homiletic question:

> . . . . Why does it state regarding the order to prepare bread for the angels who visited our Father Abraham, "Ready quickly three measures of fine flour" [Gen. 18:6], while concerning the meat it says, "And Abraham ran to the herd . . . and he gave it to the lad. . . ." [v. 7], but he did not command him to [prepare it] quickly as he did concerning the bread?

Salanter's answer to this question is based upon the following distinction:

> There are two kinds of mitzvot involved in feeding the hungry. One relates to a poor person, even one from his own city, who has nothing of his own; [in such a case] it is a mitzvah to provide him with food and drink. This [act] is subsumed under the commandment of charity (*zedakah*), and it relates only to poor people. The second mitzvah relates even to a very wealthy person, who possesses much of his own; if he is a traveller, passing through a strange land, it is a great mitzvah to take him into one's home, and to feed him and give him to drink according to his ability. This [mitzvah] is called hospitality (*hakhnasat orhim*). . . .

On the basis of this distinction, Rabbi Salanter arrives at a conclusion of halakhic significance: "One who receives a poor guest into his home fulfills two mitzvot at one and the same time—[that of] *zedakah* and *gemilut hasadim* [act of lovingkindness]." Thereafter, he goes on to argue, even though the mitzvah of hospitality applies to both rich and poor, the host is required to behave toward each one in a different manner:

> [In the case of] the poor man, the host is required to hasten as much as possible in order to provide him with something to eat immediately, without any delay or preparation whatsoever, for

> perhaps [the guest] has not eaten for several days, and [otherwise] it would be as if he were shedding blood. . . . [But] this is not the case with a wealthy guest. It is not [a sign of] honor to hurriedly feed him immediately, for he would be treating him like a poor and starving person. It is fitting for him to perform many preparations, and to slaughter [animals] and to prepare them in accordance with the honor befitting him. . . .

The question then arises: How ought a host to behave when he does not know whether his guest is rich or poor? Salanter replies:

> We must initially assume that there may be some danger and threat to life, and give him something to eat immediately upon his arrival. . . . But after he is no longer in danger, one should prepare delicacies, and postpone the meal for quite a while as is appropriate for an important person, for perhaps he is a great man. . . .

Here is the answer to Salanter's question, raised at the beginning of the sermon concerning the manner in which Abraham behaved toward his guests—namely, that he initially made haste to prepare bread for them to eat, while he did not order the servant to hasten in the preparation of the meat. Salanter concludes: "We find that in the case of the poor guest we fulfill both [mitzvot], charity and hospitality at once (for even after he has fed him to his full and there is no longer a mitzvah of *zedakah*, he still fulfills the commandment of hospitality in respect of the other food that he prepares for him)."

There are two ethical lessons to be derived from the passage presented here: (1) that those who take a poor guest into their home may not delay feeding that guest; (2) that it is preferable to receive a poor guest into one's home rather than a wealthy one (the poor guest provides the opportunity of fulfilling not one but two mitzvot). What is unique about this passage is the halakhic form of discussion—the application of the concepts of "danger to life" and "shedding blood" to one who delays serving food to a poor guest, and the conclusion that one who takes a poor guest into his home fulfills two mitzvot simultaneously. These ethical lessons are thus not presented as an appeal to humanitarian sentiments, but as statements bearing halakhic force and validity.

The concept that a given act is considered as one mitzvah if performed on behalf of a wealthy person, while the same act is considered as two mitzvot when performed for a poor person, is applied by Salanter to the giving of loans as well. One who loans money to an established person fulfills only the mitzvah of *gemilut hasadim*—that is, that of performing an act of kindness to another Jew—while one who loans money to a poor person simultaneously fulfills the commandments of *gemilut hasadim* and *zedakah*.[22] (While the Torah prohibits taking interest, it does attach monetary value to the fact that the lender's capital is not working on his behalf while on loan, and the value of this monetary loss may be assessed in terms of the accepted market rate of interest. Thus, in the case of a loan to a poor person, the monetary loss sustained by the lender may be considered as a kind of charitable gift. On the other hand, in providing a loan to a wealthy person, for whom the mitzvah of *zedakah* is not applicable, one only performs the mitzvah of *gemilut hasadim*.)[23] Salanter later notes that the rule by which a loan ought to be given to a poor person before a wealthy one only applies when the poor and rich person appeal to the donor simultaneously with their request; one who has money available to loan and is approached by a wealthy person may not refuse such a person on the grounds that a poor person may later come along. He derives from this the conclusion that:

> One who has money available with which to perform an act of *gemilut hasadim* and is approached by a poor person who is in straits, certainly [enjoys] a great "find," for he may thereby perform two mitzvot at once. For had he previously been approached by a wealthy man, he would have been required to loan him the money, and would have nothing left with which to perform *gemilut hasadim* for a poor person. But once the poor person came to him, he earns the mitzvah of *zedakah*.[24]

Rabbi Israel's social sensitivity went beyond the economic realm. He was well aware of the spiritual impoverishment of the masses, as a consequence of the interrelationship between the valuation of Torah study and social class. Mitnaggedic society highly prized learning and mocked ignorance; as learning was generally the prerogative of the relatively prosperous class of the *ba'alei batim*, while ignorance was identified with the masses, the socioeconomic differences within society assumed a spiritual and religious dimension. Salanter was confronted with a complex problem in attempting to encourage the masses and to uplift their spirits: How could one overcome the prevailing way of thinking that held ignorance in contempt, without simultaneously undermining the value of Torah study? Salanter overcame this difficulty by drawing a distinction between two different criteria pertaining to accomplishment within Torah study:

> There is a great distinction between all [other] wisdoms and labors and our holy Torah. For ... if one worked at some wisdom or labor all one's life and did not attain it, it is [as if]

he did nothing . . . which is not the case in our holy Torah, in which the main thing is . . . the exertion with integrity towards knowledge of the Torah in depth; and if one labors with integrity, even if one did not achieve anything, it is nevertheless also considered as if one had attained the goal.[25]

In light of this distinction, Salanter examines a Rabbinic saying in Sanhedrin 99b:

Rabbi Eleazar said: Every person is born [in order] to labor, as is said, "For man is born to labor" (Job 5:7). I do not know if [this means] he was created for the labor of his mouth, or for manual labor. When it says, "for his mouth compels him" (Prov. 16:26), we know that he was created for the labor of his mouth. . . .

Salanter offers this interpretation of Rabbi Eleazar's words:

One does not understand at all [what is meant by]: "I do not know whether he is created for labor of the mouth or for manual labor." For who does not know that the main [purpose of] the creation of the world was the Torah, and certainly that this is the purpose of all human beings. How then can it occur to anyone that he is created for manual labor? . . . He [that is, Rabbi Eleazar] therefore said . . . "for his mouth compels him"— means that he was created for the labor of his mouth, [that is,] every person is at least required to fix appointed times for the study of Torah, so that even one of coarse intellect and strong limbs, who is suited for [physical] labor, may not exempt himself from this. . . . For the [intention of] the commandment of the Creator is not that one attain complete knowledge, "for it is not incumbent upon you to complete the labor" (Avot 2:16), but only that the labor be [carried out] faithfully and with great integrity. So that even if one knows nothing, he is a perfectly righteous man, and more beloved of the Holy One, blessed be He, than one who has comprehended a great deal of the Torah through his intellect without effort, due to the great clarity and speed of his intellect. For [such a one] will not be quickly admitted to the Garden of Eden, but to the contrary, he will inherit Gehinnom because of the slightness of his effort. And concerning this the sages said at the end of Chapter 5 of Avot . . . "in accordance with the effort is the reward."[26]

As opposed to the commonly accepted approach that measures the study of Torah first and foremost by the criterion of achievement, Rabbi Salanter presents the very act of laboring in Torah, even if not accompanied by intellectual attainments, as a value and a standard of measurement. In effect, he does not wish to negate the value of knowledge of Torah, but to qualify it. Knowledge is no longer the exclusive or primary criterion; rather, the knowledge that a person acquires by studying Torah must be measured against the student's own talents and the degree of effort invested therein. This relativistic approach applied to the study of Torah, while characteristic of Salanter's mode of thought, represented a striking departure from the prevailing view. Once again, Rabbi Salanter is revealed as one who does not shrink from developing and expressing unconventional positions. Within the context of Lithuanian Jewry, which was fond of the saying, "An ignorant man cannot be pious,"[27] and which related to Torah geniuses with sacred awe, Rabbi Israel declared that even an *am ha-arez* could be considered as "a perfect *zaddik*"—provided that he labor to study Torah in accordance with his own ability!

We have thus far traced the manifestations of social sensitivity in Rabbi Israel Salanter as expressed in the sermons published in *Sefer even yisra'el*. However, as these sermons express but one dimension of his overall activity, it is not surprising that the picture derived from them is fragmentary and incomplete. Our knowledge is supplemented by the many stories that have been preserved concerning Salanter's behavior and practices. A considerable degree of reliability may be accorded these stories, which circulated among his disciples and their disciples in turn, not only because many of them are recorded in the name of his contemporaries who were his intimates, but primarily because of their unique flavor. The "glories" related of Rabbi Israel differ in content, style, and overall tendency from the conventional frameworks for such hagiographic legends, reflecting new and unconventional norms and criteria of behavior. Of course, one or another account may be inexact, suffer from exaggeration, or be a retelling of a motif found in another, earlier story, but one who studies these stories with a sensitive and critical eye will find many authentic characteristics of Rabbi Israel Salanter.[28]

These stories, which are very numerous, are of particular interest in terms of the present discussion. Salanter is portrayed therein as a personality whose entire behavior and range of activities were motivated by a love of his fellow human being of rare intensity, by a unique sensitivity to the suffering of the unfortunate, and by a profound involvement in the destiny of society generally. However, as his concepts took form within the strict boundaries of the halakhah, he did not perceive this unique pattern of behavior as a spontaneous demonstration of love of humanity, but simply as what was required of him by law. Such an understanding sufficed to make his behavior an example to be followed by others.

In a number of these stories, Salanter appears as demanding ex-aggerated care both of himself and of others in anything related to causing damage or pain to the other. For example, it is related that Salanter once walked in the streets of the city with another rabbi, a renowned Torah genius. The latter held his cane under his armpit with its end sticking out. Rabbi Israel warned him that this behavior made him guilty of "having his thorns protrude into the public domain," for which one is held liable under the law of "a pit which causes dam-age."[29] For the same reason, Salanter criticized those of his students who leaned their study-stands forward at an angle into the study hall as creating an "obstacle within public property."[30] The meticulous care that Rabbi Salanter took not to cause pain to others is indicated by the following story. One year, the second day of Rosh Hashanah happened to fall on a Friday. It is customary in such a case to abbreviate the recitation of *piyyutim* (medieval liturgical poems) in order to allow adequate time both for the festival meal and for preparations for the Sabbath. When Rabbi Israel was asked which *piyyutim* they might skip, he answered: "One may omit all of the *piyyutim*, even *U-netaneh tokef* [the dramatic highpoint of the service that describes the fear and trem-bling felt in anticipation of Divine Judgment], but for Heaven's sake, do not skip the *piyyutim* in Mussaf between *Malkhuyot*, *Zikhronot* and *Shofarot*, so that the cantor can rest for a few moments."[31]

His combination of acute sensitivity to the rights and well-being of others, coupled with his profound conviction that all of a Jew's actions must be guided by the halakhah, led Salanter to utilize new and un-conventional criteria in his interpretation and application of the laws of damages, as his close disciple, Rabbi Simhah Zissel Ziv, testifies:

> Our master, of blessed memory, introduced many new laws in both civil law and in the laws of damages, which seemed strange in the eyes of many people. There were likewise great *geonim* in that generation who saw this and were also astonished at his wondrous innovations, which no one had heard [of] until now.[32]

Rabbi Israel's son relates that his father once went to participate in a wedding celebration. Upon realizing that he'd stayed to a late hour, he did not return home but remained there to sleep, lest he awaken his neighbors by knocking on the door of his house, thereby stealing from them some of their sleep.[33] The severity with which he interpreted the prohibition against stealing may be further inferred from the fol-lowing story. One winter day, Rabbi Salanter went for a walk to an inn, accompanied by Rabbi Yaakov Meir. When they arrived at the inn,

Rabbi Meir hastened to open the door, so that Salanter might enter first. The latter quickly shut the door and asked his companion: "Does an uncertain performative mitzvah override the sure violation of a negative mitzvah?" Upon seeing the latter's incomprehension, Rabbi Israel explained: "There is an uncertainty here as to who is required to honor whom, which pertains to the performative commandment, 'You shall show deference to the elder' [Lev. 19:32]. On the other hand, when one is holding a door open, the heat goes out of the inn without the permission of the host, so one is certainly violating the prohibition, 'thou shalt not steal' [Ex. 20:13], which cannot be cancelled even by a sure performative mitzvah."[34]

Alongside his extraordinary concern not to offend other people, one is impressed by Salanter's constant efforts to benefit others. He was particularly meticulous concerning the mitzvah of hospitality (*hakhnasat orhim*). His son relates that he would himself interrupt whatever else he was doing in order to attend to a guest. Salanter made particular efforts to relate to each guest in accordance with his "quality." His son relates on this point: "I heard it told several times in his name that he would say of one person that it would be an insult to ask him to eat, while regarding another he would say that he was very needy. . . . He always said that, until he knew the nature of a given guest, the most difficult thing was [to know] how to receive him, whether to say Torah before him or in some other way."[35] From this, we may perhaps conclude that the ethical teachings found in his sermons were not merely abstract concepts about which it was nice to talk, but fundamental laws that he himself took pains to fulfill.

On one occasion, Salanter was seen standing and conversing at great length with an acquaintance "concerning worldly matters, and with a laughing countenance." This seemed strange to his students, as it was his practice both to avoid "unnecessary speech" and to caution others about refraining from idle words. In reply to the questioning of one of his students about his behavior, Rabbi Salanter explained: "This man was feeling very bitter, and it was a great act of kindness to cheer his sad soul and to make him forget his worries and sadness. How could I cheer his soul? By engaging upon a discourse concerning matters of *yir'ah* and Mussar? [No!] Only by pleasant talk about worldly matters."[36] The story reflects a striking feature of Salanter's behavior: whenever there was a conflict between a person's tendency to act piously toward the Creator and between doing kindness to a neighbor, Salanter chose the latter option, even though it vitiated the former.[37]

Rabbi Israel found it necessary to warn his disciples that a mood of fear of God may at times cause a person to behave in an inappropriate way toward a fellow human being. To exemplify this phenomenon, he related a certain incident that had occurred to him, which Rabbi Isaac Blazer describes:

> Once, on the eve of Yom Kippur, while going to the Study House to recite the Evening Prayer, he [Salanter] met a certain person who was one of the great God-fearers. Fear and awe of judgment were visible upon his face, and tears upon his cheeks. Our teacher [Salanter] asked him for some information which he needed. And this God-fearer, because of his great anxiety and fear, did not answer him at all. Our master said as follows: "After I passed by that person, I thought to myself, 'How am I guilty and responsible that you are a God-fearer and that you tremble and quiver concerning the Day of Judgment? What has that to do with me? Are you not required to answer my question calmly and pleasantly, as this is one of the ways of doing good and of performing kindness.' "[38]

Rabbi Salanter took care not to be excessively strict about the commandments between people and God in those cases where one would bring about a transgression in the interpersonal realm ("commandments between man and his fellow"). He once traveled to the health spas in Germany together with a certain rabbi. While that rabbi had equipped himself from the start with an adequate supply of bread for the entire journey, Rabbi Israel did not hesitate to buy fresh rolls along the way. To the surprise of his companion, who wondered why he did not refrain from eating gentile bread, Rabbi Israel replied that the expense of the journey to the resort had been provided him by a friend, who stipulated that he refrain from any extra stringencies that might affect his health. Were he to refrain from eating gentile bread, he would be fulfilling an extra stringency, but violating the prohibition against theft and deception.[39]

The following remarks attributed to Salanter poke fun at the widespread tendency to perform acts of piety in the ritual area without a corresponding effort in the realm of interpersonal relationships: "I am astounded by those people who wish to benefit their fellow by standing outside of the synagogues calling out, 'Kedushah! Kedushah! [thus calling them to prayer]—Please come in. . . .' Why do they not also stand at the gates of their home when a rich and bountiful meal is spread on their table and cry out, 'A feast! A feast! Please come in. . . .' "[40]

Many of the exant stories about Rabbi Israel Salanter depict him as graced with exceptional sensitivity toward the lot of poor people, widows, orphans and other unfortunates. But even in relation to these, he acted in ways that went beyond the usual solutions, as the following account of Rabbi Isaac Blazer illustrates:

> I once saw a certain poor person with no means of livelihood come to him in great distress. He poured out [the tale of] his bitterness and misfortune, and said that his only recourse would be to go about to the various towns and preach in the communities, except that he was unable to do so, not being gifted in the art of sermonizing. . . . He therefore sought a kindness and favor from our Master, that he would teach him some sermon [that he could preach]. And our master did not withhold this from him . . . but taught him a certain sermon, and repeated it over with him two or three times.[41]

On another occasion, Rabbi Israel encountered an orphan boy wandering about and not going to school. When he asked the charity wardens why they did not see to defraying the costs of that orphan's studies, they evaded the question with various excuses. Rabbi Israel responded to them with the cry: "One may sell Torah scrolls in order to pay the cost of study! . . ."[42]

Once, while still living in Salant, Rabbi Israel was pressed for time during the days preceding Passover and was unable personally to supervise the baking of the matzot, as was his usual practice. When those close to him, who had assumed this task in his place, asked for directions concerning those things over which they ought to take especial care (matzoh preparation is exacting and must be completed within eighteen minutes), he answered: "The only thing which I ask of you . . . [is] to be exceedingly careful that you not cause anguish to Zippah the kneader through excessive strictness, when it seems to you that she does not knead the dough fast enough. Do not forget that she is a widow, and it is forbidden to cause anguish to a widow. . . ."[43] It is likewise told that Rabbi Israel was strict both with himself and others not to be overly generous in one's use of water for the ritual washing of hands, bearing in mind the effort of the servants who had to carry the water.[44]

The sense of awareness and responsibility that characterized Salanter's attitude to public matters were sharply expressed in the relief activities that he initiated and directed when the cholera epidemic struck Vilna in 1848, claiming many lives. The epidemic, of course, frightened people, and all worried for themselves and their own families. It might be anticipated that Salanter, as a *rosh-yeshivah* and one given to ethical exhortations, would work hard at that time to offer aid and spiritual encouragement. He indeed worked to calm people, and encouraged others to aid the sick.[45] However, he was not content just with this, but himself headed the relief activities.[46]

Salanter headed a special committee recruiting some seventy young Torah students, whom he charged with the ongoing care of those who were ill. In order to enlist these young men, Rabbi Israel had to overcome the fears of their parents lest they themselves become infected with the disease. He therefore personally obligated himself in the presence of the parents to return their sons well and whole. Among other things, Salanter took pains to bring to the public's awareness the idea that one must meticulously implement the instructions of the physicians, and that these carry the authority of a commandment of the Torah.

His attitude during the epidemic may be inferred from a letter that he wrote several years later, when the cholera epidemic again struck Russia:

> Now that this disease is abroad in the land—Heaven deliver us, here also—this is the teaching for man, and the way of common sense: not to fear it at all, for what is man's life in all its aspects, for who knows if one's path is proper? One must also heed the instructions of the physicians, in light of whose words we shall walk, even by law [that is, of the Torah], and to establish the life of this world for good and for betterment. For experience has taught us that in days past, when the disease spread greatly, that whoever took upon himself the burden of the doctor's orders in his diet, etc. . . . was free of the signs of the disease—may Heaven protect us. And . . . one is not to worry and to complain about the precious soul which has been relieved of its suffering in this life of vanity, in order to go on the straightforward path to its haven. . . .[47]

Salanter's attitude to this disease combines two seemingly contradictory aspects. On the one hand, there is a call not to fear the plague or to be excessively despondent over those who have died, because life in this world is of small value. While this might be interpreted as a sign of fatalistic indifference, Rabbi Israel simultaneously demands that one heed the orders of doctors, as is required both by common sense and by experience. Thus, he issues a call to activism based upon rational considerations, the goal being to preserve "this vain life." It is instructive to see how in this dual system of values in a critical situation the humanistic element was the dominant one. Not only are his remarks concerning the slight value of the life of this world not intended to minimize the obligation to make all possible efforts to preserve life, but they are aimed at fostering that same goal by calming people and preventing hysteria. One might add that, from Rabbi Israel's viewpoint, the stand he took was identical to that required by the halakhah. The commandment to preserve life was interpreted in this context as conveying obligatory religious force to the orders of the physicians.

The strength of courage and decisiveness that characterized Salanter's personality were revealed in relation to the question of treatment of the sick on the Sabbath. Permission to violate the Sabbath in order to save life is well known. Nevertheless, there is a widespread psychological resistance toward doing so even when permitted, which is at times combined with doubts concerning its applicability to one or another specific case. Salanter was forceful in insisting that all those labors required for the care of the sick be performed on the Sabbath specifically by Jews, and not by Gentiles. He was therefore in the habit of personally going to visit the sick on the Sabbath, because he suspected that those caring for them might be negligent in their duties, and he attributed great importance to the permissibility of violating the Sabbath in order to take care of the sick. We learn this from the following incident: The grandson of Rabbi Joseph Halfan, one of the "elders and God-fearers" of Vilna, once fell ill at the beginning of the Sabbath. After the youth recovered, Rabbi Joseph Halfan came to Rabbi Israel to thank him, but added that in his opinion the young Torah students who were taking care of the sick were violating the Sabbath excessively. Upon hearing this latter comment, Rabbi Israel answered angrily: "You *prostak* [i.e., ignoramus]! Are you going to tell me what is permitted and what is forbidden? I have taken sixty or seventy young Torah students to care for the ill constantly, and I promised their fathers that I would return them whole, and whole I will return them, God willing. . . . You do that! Have you done such a thing?"[48] These sharp remarks seem to be motivated, not by Salanter's zeal for his own honor, but to bolster his authority, as if to say: That same authority that took upon itself the responsibility for the well-being of these young men is that which allowed them to violate the Sabbath.

The incident concerning the permission granted by Salanter to eat on Yom Kippur of 1848, when the cholera epidemic was still at its height, gained wide currency. There are two versions of this incident. According to one version, Rabbi Salanter posted notices in all the synagogues on the Eve of Yom Kippur:

> . . . not to fast on this holy and awesome day, to cut short the [recitation of] *piyyutim*, and to walk about outside in the city during the cool of the day. And the next day, following the Morning Service, he took in his hand some baked goods, ascended the *bema*, recited the blessing . . . and ate in the presence

of the entire congregation, so that the people might see and act likewise. One of the worshippers, among the distinguished people [of the town], rose up upon seeing this, excited by zeal for the sanctity of Yom Kippur, and shouted: "Do we not have rabbis and [righteous teachers] who know the laws of *Pikuah Nefesh* [laws regarding the saving of life]? They did not allow [eating] in public as he has done!" And the entire assembly was greatly agitated.[49]

This version has been accepted by most authors, and has even been subject to a literary reworking.[50] However, a more moderate version is cited by Ya'akov Mark in the name of Rabbi Shimon Starshun, who was present at the time. According to this version, Salanter issued a ruling on the Eve of Yom Kippur, in coordination with the *morei-zedek* (halakhic authorities) of Vilna, that due to the plague one was not to extend the recitation of *piyyutim*, but to cut short the service and to be outside in the fresh air as much as possible. In addition, in the side rooms adjoining each synagogue there were to be prepared pieces of sponge cake, cut to less than the minimum size,[51] so that one could eat when necessary. Following the Morning Service of Yom Kippur, Rabbi Israel stood up and announced that whoever felt weak could go into the side room and taste some food even without asking the advice of a doctor.[52]

Mark's version seems to me a more faithful reflection of the incident, both because of the source upon which it is based, and because it attributes to Salanter more balanced and careful behavior, which would seem more in keeping with his image. The more dramatic version, in which Salanter stood up, recited the blessing, and ate in the presence of the entire congregation, is evidently a hagiographic embellishment of the original story.

It does not diminish the significance of Rabbi Salanter's role on this occasion to prefer the more moderate version. One must remember that he held no official position in Vilna as an halakhic teacher, so if despite this he saw fit to take the initiative, it may be explained in terms of his fear that the official teachers of halakhah would be reluctant to permit that which was needed, thereby causing danger to life.

Another source describing this incident, which supports the authenticity of the more moderate account, appears in the memoirs of Salanter's son, Rabbi Isaac Lipkin:

During the time of the sickness—may it not happen to us—when Yom Kippur arrived, he permitted the eating of less than the [forbidden] quantity for food, etc., as is known; and he decided this only on the night before Yom Kippur. And it is

> known that he declared publicly on Yom Kippur that he took
> upon himself [responsibility for] all of Israel, and that the *morei-*
> *zedek* should take upon themselves [responsibility for] one [in-
> dividual] to whom, Heaven forbid, some harm might come. And
> he added [as another mitigating factor] in support of leniency
> the desecration of the Divine Name which would come about
> from the Gentiles, that they not say that this illness came upon
> them because of the Jewish religion, heaven forfend. . . .[53]

In this testimony too, Rabbi Israel appears as the decisive figure in
granting permission to eat to a public that was hesitant and fearful to
make use of this permission. The fact that he took upon himself the
responsibility for all of Israel, while he asked the *morei-zedek* to take
responsibility for only one person each, reflects their own reluctance to
grant this permission, and perhaps also a certain tension between himself and them. It is instructive that Rabbi Israel, who was usually very
modest, saw fit to use such seemingly arrogant language in this case.
He had reacted in a similar manner in his conversation with Rabbi
Joseph Halfan, when the latter complained against the violation of
Sabbath by those dealing with the sick. These two incidents indicate
that this was a deliberate and calculated pattern of reaction. In light of
the serious circumstances, and of what seemed to him a failure on the
part of the established halakhic leadership, Salanter saw fit to stress his
own personal authority to insure that the lenient ruling he taught be
accepted by the public, thereby preventing danger to life.

The testimonies about Salanter's activities relate, of course, to different periods in his life: Some pertain to the period during which he
lived in Vilna or that in Salant, which preceded it, while others have
been passed down without any definite indication of time or place, or
are clearly identified with later periods in his life. However, within the
context of our attempt to determine his motivations in founding the
Mussar movement, it seems legitimate to rely even upon those stories
and testimonies that pertain to later periods. In terms of our present
discussion, we are not interested in one or another specific deed, but
with the totality as reflecting habits, patterns of behavior, character
traits, values, and emotional stances—in brief, Salanter's total personality.

To complete this stage of our discussion, let us return to the question I posed at its beginning: Is there any significance to the conjunction
in time between the economic and social troubles that beset the Jews
of Russia in the 1840s, and the laying of the foundations for the Mussar
movement by Rabbi Israel Salanter during those same years? In light
of his sensitivity to and involvement with others, coupled with his sense

of responsibility toward society—especially the weaker sectors—the answer appears to be "yes." Distinct confirmation of this evaluation may be found in what Salanter wrote years later in his "Mussar Epistle" (*Iggeret ha-mussar*).[54] In pointing out what seemed to him to be the moral weaknesses of his generation, Rabbi Israel argued that the generation was blemished in the societal realm. He moreover protested against the severe gap between the meticulousness with which they observed the mitzvot between people and God and the serious neglect of the mitzvot between people and their fellows. Thus, Salanter's Mussar message of personal ethical improvement and his proposal of a new method for religio-ethical change, based upon a systematic and naturalistic approach to the psyche, is now joined by an additional element: the demand to correct ethical injustice in the societal realm.

It should therefore not be surprising that Salanter wished to found a movement specifically of *ba'alei batim*, because the true religio-ethical test in the societal realm is not found in the study houses and yeshivot, but in the marketplace. By the power of his sermons, by the comments and warnings that he uttered to his students and to those who were close to him, as well as by the example of his own personal behavior, Rabbi Israel Salanter wished to inculcate a new criterion among his contemporaries concerning the relationships among people. In a certain sense, his aim in establishing the Mussar movement may be seen as an attempt to provide a traditional answer to the problems that the Haskalah movement raised for public discussion, and which it wished to solve by radical change in the economic activity of the Jews, by providing them with general and vocational education, guiding young Jews toward crafts and agriculture, and, of course, bringing about a change in their legal status.[55] Salanter, who did not accept the radical solutions proposed by the Maskilim, suggested instead a path that drew upon the immanent sources of Judaism itself. While he did not attempt to alter the objective circumstances from which the difficulties of his generation stemmed, he hoped that by imposing proper ethical norms in the life of society, it would be possible to relieve somewhat the weight of this distress and blunt its sharpness.

TO SUMMARIZE our discussion concerning the establishment of the Mussar movement, one may state that Salanter's activity was shaped by the convergence of a number of factors.

Salanter's concentration upon the ethical realm per se, and his pursuit of the consummate and efficient means of ethical education, may be understood as the outcome of a particular tendency, rooted within the spiritual tradition of Mitnaggedic Jewry, to cultivate the "fear of God" alongside the study of Torah. This tendency was embodied in the personality and heritage of the Gaon of Vilna; it guided the educational program of the yeshiva of Volozhin; and it left a direct impression upon Rabbi Israel through the personality of Rabbi Zundel of Salant. At the same time, we have found that both in his educational theory and in the tendencies that guided his societal activity, Rabbi Israel departed markedly from those models that characterized his predecessors. The movement he created may therefore best be described as a substream within Mitnaggedic society.

That which was original in Salanter's activity may perhaps be explained as the result of his unique personality and of the particular circumstances of his times. That is, Salanter developed an appropriate response to the problems of his generation in the founding of the Mussar movement. We have seen that he was well aware of the threat inherent in the Haskalah movement. Moreover, unlike certain other leaders in the traditional camp who thought that there was room for a certain degree of cooperation with the Maskilim, already in the 1840s Rabbi Israel took a vigorous stand that negated any form of cooperation with that movement. In light of the chronological proximity between the strengthening of the Haskalah and the commencement of Salanter's activity in the field of Mussar, as well as the disclosures of his stand regarding the Haskalah, it seems probable that in founding the Mussar movement he had in mind the implicit threat posed toward the tradition by the Haskalah. The establishment of the Mussar movement, a voluntary movement that raised the banner of ethical and religious renewal, must therefore be seen as one of the earliest and most important expressions of a traditional society that had become aware of the dangers confronting its values and forms, and which organized itself to take action in their defense.

PART FOUR
Kovna, 1849–57

12

The Growth of the Mussar Movement in Lithuania During the 1850s

IN THE autumn of 1848, wishing to escape pressure from the government to teach at the rabbinical seminary, Rabbi Israel Salanter fled from Vilna to Kovna.[1] His activities on behalf of the dissemination of Mussar study among the Jews of Vilna were cut short at their height due to this unanticipated departure. Salanter had originally hoped that his efforts would continue to develop despite his absence, a hope expressed in the letters he sent to the circle of his intimate disciples during the year 1848–49, in which he asked them to continue their activities among the ba'alei batim of the city.[2] This hope, as far as can be determined, was dashed. Echoes of this disappointment are evident from the text of the letters themselves.[3] If we add to this the information found in the extant sources from the period, in which there is no indication of any continued growth of the Mussar movement in Vilna, we may assume that the movement gradually weakened following his departure; in any event, it was certainly not able to expand beyond its narrow limits to reach a broader public.

After his precipitous move, Salanter found himself both without a source of income and without any framework through which to spread his views among the public. But he quickly secured a position that provided for both of these needs. Rabbi Isaac Blazer tells that, when Salanter settled in Kovna, "the distinguished members of the community appointed him to be overseer of the affairs of the city, for which he received a salary." He then continues, "However, in the middle of his term he left this position."[4] Rabbi Blazer neither explains the nature of this position, the like of which is not found in any other Jewish community in Russia during that period, nor why Rabbi Israel prematurely terminated the position. In Rabbi Naphtali Amsterdam's version of the events, Rabbi Israel "was appointed as the (official) preacher (*maggid mesharim*) of the city. . . ."[5]

There is yet a third account, which may help to clarify the first two. In the introduction to *Sefer shevil ha-zahav*, by Rabbi Mordecai Eliasberg, the author's son describes his father's life. Among other things, he writes:

> During that period the Rabbinical Seminary was opened in Vilna and, at the request of the Minister, the position of Talmud instructor was assigned to the *Ga'on* and *Zaddik*, Rabbi Israel Salanter. . . . But as he did not wish, in his righteousness, to take part in the building of such a house, he uprooted his residence from Vilna to Kovna. And when he came to Kovna he visited my father, master and teacher of blessed memory, and told him of the reason for his move, and my father . . . consulted with his brother-in-law, Rabbi Ya'akov Meir Margaliot, of blessed memory, and they drew up a document granting a salary from the treasury of the community to that said *Ga'on*, that he would oversee matters pertaining to the fear of God. And thus was it done and completed.[6]

What was the nature of this office of "overseer of matters pertaining to the fear of God"? Why not an ordinary "righteous preacher," as was customary? It may be that, because of his outstanding reputation, it was decided not to limit Salanter's position to that of "righteous preacher," but to expand it in terms of its weight and extent of authority. That Rabbi Israel found a suitable framework in this new office for spreading his ideas among the broader public is confirmed by the testimony of Rabbi Naphtali Amsterdam: ". . . for then all of his effort was devoted with wisdom to implant within the hearts of the people the obligation to study Mussar, and towards this end he delivered a sermon every Sabbath including Mussar, with a lengthy *pilpul*, until he astonished all those who heard him. . . ."[7]

The Spread of the Mussar Doctrine in Kovna

Upon leaving the office of preacher,[8] evidently at the beginning of the 1850s, Salanter began to spread his teachings among a circle of students who gathered around him in the *kloiz* (prayer house) of Rabbi Zvi Nevyozer. Simultaneously, he continued his efforts among the *ba'alei batim*, whether in Kovna itself or in other communities. There is no direct evidence as to the kind of materials Rabbi Israel disseminated among the *ba'alei batim* of Kovna, although judging from his letters to other communities it is clear that he remained loyal to the approach of making Mussar study fashionable. Toward that end, he felt the need to win over the prestigious and well-to-do members of the community, in whose footsteps many others would presumably follow. He likewise wished Mussar study to be considered as a personal quality that would win for its devotees greatness and honor. Thus, while originally studying Mussar "not for its own sake," the Mussar students would eventually reach the level of acting "for its sake."[9]

Salanter likewise attempted to convince the *ba'alei batim* that the occasional devotion of small amounts of time to the study of Mussar is a relatively easy task even for one who is preoccupied with a business, whereas the results of such study would be far-reaching and profound.[10] Something of this mercantile approach, which seeks to convince the customers that they will receive something of value in return for their relatively small investment, likewise appears in the instructions that Salanter gave those engaged in the spread of Mussar study in one of the communities: "Now yield and do not insist upon the price, go easy on the details, for those who pursue it are few and weak, lest you discourage them; bolster those who falter. . . ."[11]

Salanter's tendency to use persuasive means of this type reflects his awareness that there were not many takers for the message he wished to spread. But more than anything else, this tendency indicates Salanter's stance as a leader and educator whose primary concern was the desire to influence society. Unlike the classical Mussar authors, who were very interested in the analysis of the various stages upon the ladder of religious ascent, which stands upon the ground and whose summit reaches heaven, Rabbi Israel was concerned with placing that same ladder at the feet of his contemporaries. To this end, he was prepared to move its lowest rungs down a bit. Nevertheless, the compromise that Salanter was willing to make in the level of his demands during the initial stages was only a "descent for the purpose of ascent." Being convinced of the great persuasive power inherent in the study of Mussar, he thought that whoever would begin to ascend the ladder of *yir'ah*, even for reasons not altogether pure, would in the end continue that ascent.

Salanter saw the establishment of Mussar houses as a vital means of dissemination of Mussar among the public. This is reflected in the letters he wrote about the study of Mussar and the frequenting of the Mussar house as two acts that are by their very nature interdependent.[12] The valuation of the Mussar house as the natural framework for the study of Mussar may also be seen from the demand that this house remain open through all hours of the day and night, so that whoever feels the impulse to engage in Mussar study may do so at any time, free of any obstacle. Salanter likewise suggested that the Mussar house be situated close to the *bet midrash*, so that the *ba'alei batim*, who devote their free hours on the Sabbath to the study of Talmud, may easily go to the Mussar house as well.[13]

It seems clear that Rabbi Israel's efforts in Kovna indeed bore fruit, as several of the *ba'alei batim* of this community began to fix regular times for the study of Mussar, and a Mussar house was even established there.[14] Moreover, those who gathered around the banner of Mussar included some of the well-to-do and prestigious men of the community.[15] Though we have no numerical information, it would appear that in terms of numbers, and even more so in terms of social standing, there was a recognizable group, and certainly not an inconsiderable one. Otherwise, it would be difficult to understand why Salanter's activity in Kovna aroused such energetic and vociferous opposition, the opponents' criticism being focused upon the sectarian and separatist character of the movement. Indeed, one would expect a distinctive group of this sort, which separates and distinguishes itself from the public, to elicit such a critique. On the other hand, the very arousal of controversy itself constitutes an argument against the separatism of the Mussar advocates, and is testimony to the fact that not all, or even most, of the inhabitants of Kovna were captivated by the Mussar message.

Although we are unable to venture an exact estimate of the extent of the growth of the Mussar movement in Kovna during the 1850s, it was sufficiently widespread that this community became a center of the Mussar movement even after Rabbi Israel left it. It is no accident that Salanter's disciples, and their disciples in turn, who attempted to introduce the teaching of Mussar into the yeshivot, made Kovna one of the foci of their activity. This activity required the support and backing of the class of the *ba'alei batim*, which was available to them in Kovna. Even in 1897, when the Jewish communities of Russia were in an uproar over the outbreak of the controversy surrounding the Mussar yeshivot, and when a number of leading rabbis addressed severe criticism against these yeshivot in various periodicals, the Mussar yeshivot enjoyed backing among the *ba'alei batim* of Kovna.[16]

All signs point to the impact of Mussar teaching as having been far greater in Kovna than it had been in Vilna, perhaps because Rabbi Israel's activities in Vilna were cut short after only a few years, while he had nine years in Kovna and could build on his earlier experience. Another explanation for his greater success in Kovna may have to do with its being a relatively new community. During the eighteenth century, the residence of Jews in Kovna, apart from a small number who lived in two streets especially set aside for this purpose, was proscribed. The attempts of Jews to find their way into the city despite this prohibition encountered fierce opposition from the Christian townsfolk. Only after the annexation of the area to Russia did the czar, in 1798, permit Jews to live in Kovna and confirm their right to engage in trade. But even this permission was partial, and only gradually, with the help of bribery, did the Jews expand the borders of their settlement in this city.[17] It then became a mecca to Jewish settlers due to its economic opportunities, as a major trade center located upon waterways that traversed Prussia, and upon the royal highway that passed between the capital of St. Petersburg and Warsaw.[18] Thus, the community of Kovna, known to us from the second half of the nineteenth century as an important Jewish center, in fact sprung up only during the first half of that century. It therefore seems likely that, as a relatively young community without an ancient, well-established local tradition, Kovna was more open to new and unconventional ideas.[19]

Mussar Houses and Study Groups of Artisans in the Lithuanian Communities

As I have already mentioned, Salanter was not content with spreading his ideas among the inhabitants of Kovna, but attempted to reach other communities of Lithuania. This was accomplished by means of disciples and close associates, each one of whom he activated in his particular place of residence. A typical example can be seen in the letter he wrote at the end of the 1840s or the beginning of the '50s to his disciple and friend, Rabbi Elijah Levinsohn of Cartinga, in which he calls upon him to disseminate the study of Mussar.[20] Of particular interest is its postscript:

> I send greetings to my dear friend, the great light, *harif u-baki*, our teacher Rabbi Gershon Mendel—may he have a long life— the rabbi of Plongian. It is no small matter for a rabbi and *moreh zedek* in his city to enlighten and awaken others toward the study of Mussar, with burning lips and a straightforward heart. . . .[21]

It is significant that he not only contacts his disciple here but also attempts to harness communal rabbis in the dissemination of Mussar study. While one must not conclude from this that Rabbi Israel similarly addressed all the rabbis of Lithuania—such an appeal was presumably restricted to those rabbis with whom he had close relations—it indicates that the separatist character that the Mussar movement took on in the eyes of its opponents did not stem from the intentions of its founder and originator.

Another disciple who acted on behalf of the spread of Mussar study under Salanter's inspiration was none other than the *gevir* (wealthy man) Kalonymus Ze'ev Wissotzky. In an autobiographical essay, Wissotzky relates that he went to Kovna in 1854 in order to learn Torah and Mussar from Salanter. During that period Wissotzky was a young householder who engaged in trade and devoted part of his time to Torah study. The decision to go to Kovna followed a successful deal in which he made several hundred rubles. Concerning his activities in his home city of Zager following his return from Kovna, Wissotzky relates that:

> I then took counsel to establish a *Hayyei Adam* society [focused on the laws of daily life, Sabbath, and Festivals] whose purpose would be to teach the artisans of the city. . . . And I began to teach them *Hayyei Adam* every Sabbath, neither hastily nor in a rushed manner. And I began to teach them Mussar from it. I explained each section to them carefully and in clear language. . . . The artisans' . . . thirst for learning was not quenched on the Sabbaths alone, but they began to gather during the weekdays in the evening hours, and I hired a special house for them, to which they came every day after finishing their work, and from the time of the Afternoon Prayer until the Evening Prayer [about one hour] they listened to words of Torah and Mussar. For in addition to the book *Hayyei Adam*, we also read to them works of Mussar which guide the heart of man toward every good and desirable attribute in the eyes of God and man. . . . I also set aside a small house in my courtyard for those special people who took it upon themselves to study Mussar works every afternoon. . . .[22]

Wissotzky's narrative draws a clear distinction between artisans, who gather together in order to study *Hayyei adam* as well as Mussar books, and those whom he calls "special people" (*ba'alei-segulah*), who gather daily between *Minhah* and *Ma'ariv* (Evening Prayer) in order to study Mussar works. It is clear that these special people were *ba'alei batim*, who differed from the artisans not only in terms of wealth and social status, but also through their Torah education. The gap between the level of knowledge characteristic of workmen and that typical of *ba'alei batim* required a difference both in terms of the contents and manner of study. The underlying assumption of Wissotzky's activity among the artisans was that they required strengthening and a firmer basis for their knowledge of halakhah and custom, being unable to study even a popular work such as *Hayyei adam* by themselves, but needing a teacher to read it and explain it to them, passage by passage. For these circles of artisans the study of Mussar was intended merely as an addition, and even here the teacher read and explained the text to them. The model of Mussar study with *hitpa'alut*, on the other hand, was more suitable to the *ba'alei batim*, for even though this kind of study was intended to arouse emotional excitement, the point of departure was the ability of the individual to read and understand the plain meaning in Mussar works, which was beyond the competence of the masses.

Certainly there is no doubt that Wissotzky was influenced by Salanter in his decision to set aside a room in his courtyard as a Mussar house.[23] I would argue similarly that Salanter's teaching prompted his activity among the laborers, for the attentiveness of a successful and Torah-learned merchant to the spiritual and religious cultivation of the masses reflects a social sensitivity that we have already seen in Rabbi Salanter.

There is further evidence of individuals close to Rabbi Israel who acted in a similar manner among the artisans. In a book containing sketches of various Vilna personalities from the beginning of the twentieth century, we find a description of a figure who is identified by the author with the title "rabbi of the workers":

> In his youth he studied for a brief time under the Gaon, Rabbi Israel Salanter, of blessed memory, from whom he received the idea of founding "worker's confraternities," and he was devoted to this [idea] with all his heart and soul. He established workers' societies in several Jewish communities, but he preferred to make his [own] home in Vilna. . . . The rabbi was graced with special power of attracting his worker-disciples, who came tired and exhausted every evening to hear his lessons in *Hayyei Adam*, which he recited before them in a melody so pleasant, and with such great enthusiasm. . . .[24]

We do not know who this "rabbi of the workers" was, but from what is said here, it would appear that his activity among the workers spread over the last decades of the nineteenth century and into the beginning of the twentieth. In any event, this is a case in which the initiative for establishing study circles for working people is specifically connected with the name of Rabbi Salanter.

We know of another individual who was active in establishing study circles among artisans who may also be described, to a certain extent, as a disciple of Salanter. I refer to Rabbi Moshe Yitzhak ben Noah Darshan, better known as the "Kelmer Maggid."[25] The Kelmer

Maggid was a well-known figure throughout the communities of Lithuania during the latter half of the nineteenth century. The synagogues in which he preached were filled to capacity, and his visit to a given community for the Sabbath was a major event for its inhabitants. His fame and influence derived, not only from his talents as a preacher, but to a great extent from his honesty and integrity. He was prepared to criticize and to chastise even stubborn *gevirim* (wealthy men), for which he was more than once persecuted. The focus of his sermons was the demand for proper behavior in the interpersonal realm, particularly in economic life. At the same time, the Kelmer Maggid was among the stubborn opponents of the Haskalah movement. He mocked and ridiculed the Maskilim of the period in his sermons, and they responded through letters of satire and mockery about him published in their periodicals.[26]

We do not know much concerning the relationship between the Kelmer Maggid and Rabbi Salanter, but from the biographical sketch based upon information given by his son, the following picture emerges: About 1849, when he was twenty-one years old and already enjoyed a reputation as a talented preacher, the Maggid spent a brief period in the circle of Rabbi Israel. The latter was impressed both by his talents and the purity of his motivations, and encouraged him to continue to preach the fear of God in the Jewish communities.[27]

Rabbi Yaakov Mazeh writes in his memoirs of the method the Kelmer Maggid used among the artisans of Mohilev, a Jewish city he visited periodically:

> He first conducted a mustering of his "army"—that is, the manual workers, whose master and teacher he was in the full sense of the word. . . . He also established a separate house of prayer for them, which he named Workers of Righteousness. And he accustomed them to read Jewish books on the Sabbaths and holidays, [such as] *Hayyei Adam* and *Hokhmat Adam* in Yiddish translation, as well as Mussar works, that they might know what the Lord their God requires of them. And he demanded of his disciples that they be expert in *Hovot Ha-Levavot* [see above, chapter 2], *Messilat Yesharim* [the most widely studied Mussar work, by eighteenth century Italian Kabbalist Rabbi Moses Hayyim Luzzatto] and *Menorat Ha-Maor* [the major work of Rabbi Isaac Aboab, late fourteenth century Spanish scholar]. . . .[28]

We find a common pattern of activity among three individuals who had a disciple relationship with Rabbi Israel Salanter, each one of whom acted to establish study circles intended for artisans. It would therefore seem reasonable to associate this mode of activity with Salanter's influence. Confirmation of this appears in an account given by Salanter's grandson, Rabbi David Sidarski:

> Rabbi Israel was particularly concerned for the welfare of the poor people and the laborers and simple people, to ameliorate their spiritual condition and raise them from their lowly condition. During the years 1868–69 he attempted, with the help of his friends and disciples, to establish special Study Houses for working people in all of the cities of Lithuania, where they might gather every evening for prayer. And their own teacher would be there to study with them selected chapters from the Talmud, *Shulhan 'Arukh, Sefer Hayyei Adam,* and the like, between *Minhah* and *Ma'ariv;* and every Sabbath he would preach to them words of Mussar or on matters pertaining to the [particular] day.[29]

Although these remarks relate to the end of the 1860s, they appear to reflect a tendency typical of Rabbi Israel even earlier; seemingly both Wissotzky's and the Kelmer Maggid's activities among the workers were associated with Salanter's influence. It is possible that, apart from those names known to us, there were other people who were active during the 1850s according to the same model.

At this point in our discussion, we should note the existence of a certain direct item of evidence connecting Salanter with the study circles of artisans—namely, the letter written by Rabbi Israel himself in 1874. He relates there:

> I remember a method established by one person in Vilna nearly twenty years [ago]:[30] to study *Hayyei 'Adam* for a brief period every day with those who engage in manual labor, to study with them easily and to explain to them, at the start, each word by itself, and afterwards each sentence together, and immediately thereafter those hearing it repeat it several times before their teachers. When I first saw this I stood astonished and amazed at seeing the workers learning ... constantly ... [repeating] before their teachers what he had said and explained ... [and afterwards] this method spread. ...[31]

From these fragmentary comments we can prove only that Salanter was very impressed by the sight of the study circles of workmen that he had encountered in Vilna.[32] However, after we combine this letter with what we have already explained above, the course of events may be reconstructed as follows: Around 1854, Rabbi Israel had encountered a study circle of laborers in Vilna, was particularly impressed by the method of instruction that had been developed by the teacher of this group, and decided to spread it to other communities in Lithuania. About the same time, Rabbi Ze'ev Kalonymus Wissotzky came under Salanter's influence and guidance, and began to establish study groups for laborers in his own town.

At this point, I must warn against confusing the Mussar house with the study circles of laborers, even if the workers engaged in Mussar study. We have already observed the distinction between these two institutions in terms of the nature of the activity that took place therein, deriving from the gap between the level of erudition of the *ba'alei batim* and that of the laborers. One might add to this that, while the study confraternity had been a well-known and established institution for a long time, the Mussar house was a new institution especially created to suit the form of Mussar study advocated by Rabbi Israel. Therefore, while the attendance of a certain individual at a Mussar house was rightly seen as an expression of conscious identification with the Mussar movement, the same was not true of those laborers who gathered for the purpose of study, even of Mussar works.

In light of our exposition thus far, we may conclude that, while Rabbi Israel's primary efforts were focused upon the establishment of Mussar houses and the dissemination of Mussar study in his own unique way—an activity that by its very nature was directed toward the class of *ba'alei batim*—he also wished to be active among the masses by encouraging his students and close followers to establish study circles for laborers. In practice, this activity occurred within the framework of a traditional and accepted institution. For that reason, the study circles of the laborers should not be seen as an organic part of the Mussar movement, but as an epiphenomenon.

I noted above the relation of the Kelmer Maggid to Rabbi Israel in terms of his activity among the laborers. However, his biographer also points out a more direct connection between him and the spread of the Mussar movement:

> In 1853 he was chosen as preacher (*maggid mesharim*) in New Zager, and he spread his Mussar teaching both among the members of the Mussar association founded there by Rabbi Israel Salanter (among whom was numbered the rabbi of outstanding piety . . . Rabbi Kalonymus Ze'ev Wissotzky, may he live) . . . and for about five years he served in Zager as preacher. . . .[33]

This provides additional evidence of the fact that a circle of Mussar adherents was established in Zager in the 1850s. Wissotzky was also part of this circle, and over the course of time made a "house" available to them in his courtyard. The growth of the Mussar circle in Zager may be explained not only in terms of its relative proximity to Kovna, but on the basis of its having been Salanter's birthplace. He presumably made use of his special connections with the members of this community in order to disseminate his ideas. Thus, during the years 1853–58, while the Kelmer Maggid served as communal preacher in Zager, he was also active within the circle of Mussar devotees in this city. This activity, which evidently found expression in the delivery of special sermons to those who gathered in the Mussar house, was not demanded by his position as *maggid mesharim* per se, and is therefore indicative of his closeness to Salanter and his movement.

Another question arises in light of this conclusion: Ought one perhaps see the extensive preaching activity of the Kelmer Maggid as itself a manifestation of the Mussar movement? Rabbi Dov Katz implies that this is indeed the case by the very fact that he includes a detailed discussion of the image and activity of the Kelmer Maggid within the frame of his book, which is devoted to the personalities and methods of the movement.[34] Katz adds to this a number of additional statements, which leave no doubt as to the relation of the Kelmer Maggid to Rabbi Israel Salanter: for example, that the Maggid encountered various difficulties at the beginning of his career as a preacher—though profound, he did not find a path to the hearts of his listeners—and that while seeking new ways to reach the public, he heard of the approach of the Mussar movement and traveled to Kovna to learn the system from Salanter himself. The latter sensed both his profound piety and his personal gifts for influencing others, and charged him with the task of spreading the Mussar idea and establishing Mussar houses. After conveying to him the fundaments both of his ethical ideas and of his didactic techniques, Rabbi Israel sent him on his way and, in Katz's words, he (the Maggid) acquitted himself nobly of his charge.[35]

This description is not only factually inexact, but is also faulty in that it confuses and obscures concepts. I have already alluded to the fact that the Kelmer Maggid spent too brief a period of time in the presence of Rabbi Israel Salanter to be considered one of his genuine disciples, nor is it reasonable to attribute his success as a preacher to what he received from Salanter. His biographers note that he was already an outstandingly talented preacher from an early age, before going to Salanter, and so we derive the opposite picture: Salanter encouraged him to act in this area because he was impressed by the Maggid's talent as a preacher. Moreover, comparison of the printed sermons of the Kelmer Maggid[36] with those of Rabbi Salanter reveals little similarity between them, either in terms of style or structure. Nor does the Kelmer Maggid quote either the writings or letters of Salanter in his book, while he does cite extensively from *Nefesh ha-hayyim* by Rabbi Hayyim of Volozhin.

It is true that the Kelmer Maggid did devote a good part of his sermons to the commandments between people and their fellows,[37] and he likewise stressed the importance of the fear of punishment.[38] While it is not impossible that the Maggid was in fact influenced by Rabbi Israel regarding these matters, there is nevertheless a considerable difference between acknowledging the existence of similar or identical motifs in the preaching of these two individuals, or even suggesting that this similarity is rooted to a certain extent in the influence of Salanter, and drawing the conclusion that the public activity of the Kelmer Maggid is to be treated as a chapter in the history of the Mussar movement. Dov Katz's error seems to be based, more than anything else, upon the tendency to include every and any phenomenon in which Mussar or the fear of God plays a role under the rubric of the Mussar movement. The proper limits of the Mussar movement are in fact determined in terms of the relationship to the doctrine of Mussar study and character improvement as taught by Salanter, and which he wished to spread. Had we found in the center of the Kelmer Maggid's sermons exhortations to correct one's *middot* delivered in the spirit of Rabbi Israel's system, it would be right to assume that he acted to disseminate the message of the movement. But neither the accounts of nor the texts of his sermons give any support to such a conclusion.[39] We may therefore decide that, while the Maggid did in fact come under the influence of Salanter at a given stage of his public activity, his overall activity as a preacher stands in its own right, and should not be included within the context of the Mussar movement.

I have elaborated at some length upon the relationship of the Kelmer Maggid to the Mussar movement because the conclusion to be drawn from this discussion holds true as well with regard to other cases concerning individuals of undisputed stature, but of doubtful connection to the Mussar movement, whom Dov Katz has "drafted" to the ranks of the movement. Thus, there is no justification for including Rabbi Israel Meir ha-Kohen (the *Hafetz Hayyim*) and his literary output under the rubric of the Mussar movement.[40] Dov Katz is admittedly aware of the fact that the spiritual development of the *Hafetz Hayyim* was not based upon the influence of Salanter and his teaching, but nevertheless employs various arguments in order to justify his inclusion within the Mussar movement.[41] In my opinion, these claims constitute another example of obscuring the distinction between what is typical and unique to the teaching of Salanter, and other phenomena that bear some connection to Mussar and *yir'ah*.

Most of the authors who have dealt with the life of Salanter observed that he enjoyed greater success during the period of his activity in Kovna than he did in Vilna; there are even some who argue that the Mussar movement attained the height of its flowering in Kovna.[42] However, these authors have been satisfied with making general observations and have not attempted to determine the actual growth or extent of the movement during the period under discussion. The only author who relates to the question is Dov Katz. He states that:

> Rabbi Israel also operated in the surrounding towns ... he established Mussar houses in many places, around which there gathered the important local people. It was his plan to establish five hundred Mussar houses throughout the cities of Russia, in order to create an all-encompassing Mussar movement, and he acted in this direction.[43]

After describing Salanter's activities toward the establishment of study circles for the masses, Katz concludes:

> Rabbi Israel lived in Kovna for some nine years, acting in his unique way on behalf of the dissemination of *yir'ah* and Mussar. His activity was successful, the Mussar movement growing and spreading among the people to encompass extensive circles.[44]

Elsewhere, Katz relates that the Kelmer Maggid alone "established dozens of Mussar houses in the cities of Israel."[45] One would presume from these remarks that the Mussar movement expanded during the course of the 1850s to include scores of Mussar houses, around which thousands of people presumably gathered. That estimate seems to me greatly exaggerated.

Though we are unable to find any exact information in the known contemporary sources pertaining to the number of *ba'alei batim* who adhered to the teaching of Rabbi Salanter, if we can determine the number of Mussar houses that existed at that time, we shall at least have a rough criterion for estimating the actual extent of the spread of the movement. We shall begin by examining the claim made by Dov Katz, according to which the Kelmer Maggid established dozens of Mussar houses. On this point, he relies upon an article published in *Allgemeine Zeitung des Judentums* from 1861 by Judah Leib Gordon, an outstanding Haskalah poet and satirist of the religious leadership.[46] Yet anyone reading this article will search in vain for any confirmation of

Katz's statement. Gordon lists there a number of phenomena that he describes as obstacles toward the spread of Haskalah in Russia, among which he includes the preaching of the Kelmer Maggid and the establishment of Mussar houses. However, not only does Gordon fail to attribute to the Maggid the establishment of "dozens of Mussar houses," he does not even credit him with the establishment of one such institution.[47] In fact, Gordon does not speak about the establishment of tens of Mussar houses generally, but of *the establishment of Mussar houses in a number of important communities*, including that in the capital city of the district of Courland, namely, Mitava. It should be noted that Gordon's article was written in a pessimistic mood, with the definite intent of emphasizing the degree to which the Jews of Russia were still enshrouded in darkness. That being so, and since, as we have seen, he interprets the establishment of Mussar houses as an obstacle in the way of the Haskalah, it seems reasonable to assume that if in fact many Mussar houses existed during that period, Gordon would have mentioned the fact.

We know of two additional testimonies that confirm the impression derived from Gordon's article. One appears in the article by Rabbi Hayyim Zvi Hirsch Broide, written within the framework of the polemic surrounding the Mussar movement in the 1890s. Rav Broide tells what he heard from his own teacher, Rabbi Abraham Shmuel of Rosein, who was among Salanter's opponents at the time of the first controversy in the 1850s. Among other things, he writes: ". . . at that time the doctrine was not widespread, only a bit there and a bit here. . . ."[48] The second testimony appears in a publication connected with the polemic of the 1890s. In a letter signed by a number of rabbis who vehemently attacked the Mussar adherents of their own day, the authors portray Salanter's public campaign on behalf of his teaching, arguing that "Mussar houses were established in only about five communities, and even they were closed over the course of time due to public opinion. . . ."[49] While it is true that these rabbis did have an interest in emphasizing the limited dimensions of the spread of the movement, it is nevertheless difficult to imagine that they would attempt to distort facts that were known to at least a portion of their contemporaries. The number five cited by the authors of this letter roughly corresponds to the number of cities in which we specifically know there to have been Mussar houses—namely, Kovna, Vilna, Zager, Mitava, Rosein,[50] and apparently also Plongian.[51] Thus, during the course of the 1850s, Rabbi Salanter and his colleagues succeeded in establishing Mussar houses in a total of only five or six communities; in any event, their number certainly did not exceed ten. If we assume that a few dozen *ba'alei batim* gathered around each Mussar house, then during this stage the entire movement did not encompass more than a few hundred heads of households.

EARLIER, we observed the role that the Haskalah movement played in the establishment of the Mussar movement. At this stage of our discussion, we need to determine whether that factor also found expression during the period of Salanter's activity in Kovna. One author argues that Rabbi Israel's very decision to live in Kovna was the result of his intention to establish "a fortress which would protect against the destructive spirit of Western European culture."[52] Another author relates that it was the wealthy *gevir* Rabbi Hirsch Nevyozer who, "as an extreme Orthodox zealot, invited the Gaon Rabbi Israel Salanter from Vilna to Kovna (about 1844)[53] in order to spread Torah and Mussar there, as a remedy and cure against the Haskalah, which was spread in Kovna and its environs at that time by the author A. Mapu and his circle."[54] The reliability of this story seems doubtful, as Rabbi Israel had already moved to Kovna in 1848/49, while the *kloiz* of Rabbi Hirsch Nevyozer was established only in 1851. Nevertheless, this story reflects a fact that is significant for our discussion: that Kovna was one of the foci of the spread of the Haskalah movement during that period.

Active in the Haskalah movement in Kovna during the 1850s was the Hebrew author Abraham Mapu (1808–67). Among other things, he served as a teacher in the government school for Jewish children, to which he attempted to attract the children of the prominent families of the city.[55] But more than anything else, Mapu influenced his contemporaries by means of his novels. The first of these, *'Ahavat zion (The Love of Zion)*, was published in 1853, while his book *'Ayit zavu'a (The Hypocritical Vulture)* was published in 1857. There are those who explain the profound impact of *'Ahavat zion* upon its readers by the fact that Mapu portrayed a reality that, in terms of its beauty, richness, and freedom, was diametrically opposed to all that typified the impoverished life of the Jews in Russia. Despite that difference, his readers felt a connection with the heroes of his novel and its scenery, because of their "biblical" milieu. In this first novel, Mapu expressed his critique of Jewish life not through an appeal to reason, as was customary among Haskalah authors, but indirectly, through an appeal to the emotions.[56] In *'Ayit zavu'a*, on the other hand, Mapu attacked the way of life practiced in the Jewish communities of Lithuania directly and very sharply. In terms of our present discussion, it is extremely significant that two of the negative figures satirized and ridiculed in *'Ayit zavu'a* were based upon real people: in the image of Rabbi Gediel, Mapu seemed to allude to Rabbi Israel Salanter, while that of Rabbi Zaddok corresponds to Rabbi Elijah Levinsohn of Cartinga,[57] the colleague and disciple of Salanter who assisted him in the establishment of Mussar houses and other public activities. Moreover, in an 1857 letter, Mapu explicitly identifies the Mussar movement as an enemy of Haskalah:

> . . . . The private schools[58] continue in their customary way: there is no reference to Bible, and the Hebrew language is cast aside. . . . And who is Rabbi Elinka Cartinger?[59]. . . . The very image and shape of Rabbi Zaddok! For I knew the beginnings of his path and way—he will now praise Rabbi Israel,[60] so that Israel may say that he is a man of great deeds. . . . I was in Rosein and I did not recognize the place, for it is entirely changed; there are six study houses there as well as a Mussar house. And this is the spirit of the day of the new generation: [one goes] either to the university or to Torah, to marriage and to Mussar houses. There is no middle way for the people. . . .[61]

Mapu describes a process of radical polarization within Lithuanian Jewry: on the one hand, those who went to the universities, which entailed complete alienation and separation from the tradition; on the other hand, those who went to Mussar houses, which expressed opposition to the Haskalah. Mapu is pained that in a city such as Rosein, where there had previously been a circle of Maskilim,[62] Haskalah was displaced by Mussar houses.

We also learn from the above-quoted 1861 article by J. L. Gordon that the Mussar movement of the 1850s was understood by the Maskilim as bearing an explicitly Orthodox tendency. Gordon notably lists the Mussar houses among the obstacles in the way of Haskalah; he moreover describes the establishment of Mussar houses as an offensive initiated by the Orthodox strategy, and argues that opposition among the inhabitants of Mitava, the capital of Courland, against the learned and enlightened rabbi who served there, originated in the Mussar house.[63] As one of the militant fighters on behalf of the Haskalah movement, Gordon was aware of and sensitive to what was being done in the camp of his opponents. It therefore seems likely that his arguments reflect an authentic reality, in which Mussar houses and those who patronized them stood out as the spokespersons of an anti-Maskilic tendency.

In light of the remarks of Mapu and Gordon, one is struck by the fact that the cities in which the Mussar houses were established in the 1850s were generally those in which the Haskalah had succeeded in gaining a stronghold.[64] Perhaps that is because Salanter devoted particular effort to establishing Mussar houses in those places in which the influence of the Haskalah was prominent, or it may be that it was specifically in those cities that one found *ba'alei batim* who were attracted to the Mussar doctrine because it offered them a form of spiritual and social activity within the confines of the tradition that was a kind of alternative to the attractive power of the Haskalah. Support for the latter theory may be found in the memoirs of the Ba'al Makhshoves (Israel Elyashev) concerning the period of his study in the Talmud-Torah of a major disciple of Rabbi Salanter in Gerobin.[65] Among other things, Ba'al Makhshoves (the pseudonym of the founder of modern Yiddish literary criticism) relates how his own father became a Mussar devotee, so that he sent him to that Talmud-Torah. His father, Rabbi Simhah Zalkind Eliashev, was a native of the city of Zager, a town particularly prone to the influence of the Haskalah due to its proximity to Prussia. Thus, Rabbi Simhah learned in his youth how to read German, became an accomplished Hebrew stylist, and also learned bookkeeping. Because of his Haskalah tendencies, he had planned to enter the rabbinic seminary in Vilna. On his way there, he passed through Kovna, where he met Rabbi Yaakov Karpas, one of the close followers of Rabbi Salanter and a militant fighter against Haskalah. Under the influence of Rabbi Yaakov, in whose home he occasionally met Rabbi Israel Salanter, Rabbi Simhah became a Mussar adherent. The transformation in the course of his father's life is depicted by Ba'al Makhshoves as follows:

> While it may sound strange on the face of it, one may nevertheless say that the Mussar movement included the aspiration to unite Haskalah with the fear of heaven. The fact that a Mussar devotee paid more attention to the imagination and to knowledge of the heart rather than to the mind—that in itself has in it something of the spirit of the new age.[66]

Ba'al Makhshoves adds that the process undergone by his father was characteristic of that type of householder who was drawn toward the Haskalah, but at the same time committed to the tradition.

To summarize our discussion, we may state that the tendency toward opposition to the Haskalah movement, which was already inherent in Salanter's activity during the period in which he lived in Vilna, received a more open and explicit character over the course of the 1850s. Together with the spread of the Haskalah in the cities of Lithuania, Mussar houses were established in those communities, which were identified by the Maskilim as foci of opposition to the Haskalah. The confrontation with the Haskalah was not necessarily expressed via direct encounter with the Maskilim of the period; essentially, the Mussar movement provided its adherents with a focus of spiritual and social support that enabled them to continue to adhere to the tradition in the wake of contemporary crosscurrents.

The Beginning of Opposition to the Mussar Movement

Opposition to the Mussar movement began to emerge during the first years of Rabbi Israel's activity in Kovna;[67] at first it was a reaction to his attempts to disseminate his ideas and then it grew as these ideas strengthened their hold among the public. The opposition to Salanter's activity was headed by Rabbi Leib Shapira, the rabbi of Kovna from 1849 to 1854,[68] who was supported by a number of prominent rabbis and scholars of that generation.[69] Among those who joined Rabbi Shapira in the struggle against Salanter's teaching was Rabbi Mordecai Eliasberg, who had originally assisted Rabbi Israel in attaining his office in Kovna.[70] The rallying of the rabbi of Kovna and rabbis of other communities reflected their concern for the religious integrity of the public within the bounds of their responsibility. At the same time, the fact that it was specifically rabbis and scholars who led the opposition to the Mussar doctrine suggests the threat posed by this doctrine to the worldview of the *lomdim* in Lithuania. We may understand something of the significance attached to this struggle by the opponents of Mussar teaching from an anecdote about Rabbi Yeshayah of Salant: Near his death, this rabbi said that, even if he had no other merits, he was guaranteed a share in the world to come because of his struggle against the Mussar movement.[71]

It seems clear from the extant sources that the opposition to the Mussar movement was primarily expressed in a propaganda war, with sermons by Salanter in which he attempted to influence his listeners in the spirit of his system and then counter-sermons by rabbis of the opposition.[72] In any event, we do not hear of the use of such means as excommunication. But we should not conclude from this that there was no social pressure applied to Rabbi Israel and his followers. It seems likely that the prestige of Rabbi Israel as an outstanding figure both in Torah learning and in piety exerted a moderating influence on his opposition, as may be seen in the following remarks attributed to Mordecai Gimpel Yaffe, one of the leading rabbis of that generation:

> He was asked why it was that, as long as Rabbi Israel stood at the head of the Mussar devotees, he [Rabbi Yaffe] said nothing against this doctrine, while now that others have taken his place,

he speaks out against them. Either way [it is illogical]: if this doctrine is itself reprehensible, why did he not protest against Rabbi Israel, for in a situation of profanation of the [Divine] Name one does not show honor [even to] a rabbi. The Gaon answered him: it is true, my brother, that the teaching itself is deserving of refutation. But Rabbi Israel is a wholly righteous person, and as "The Holy One, blessed be He, does not bring about mishap through the righteous" [Gittin 7a], we were therefore certain that the counsel of Rabbi Israel would not stand and would not be. And if the Holy One, blessed be He, Himself negates it, why should we battle against it? But now that they who stand at its head are no longer righteous people . . . one must take care lest some mishap really comes about through them. . . .[73]

One of the main arguments raised against the Mussar movement during the '50s is expressed in a clever saying attributed to Rabbi Leib Shapira. In the Hallel prayer it states: "House of Israel praise the Lord, House of Aaron praise the Lord . . ." (Ps. 135:19ff.), while further on it says, "those who fear the Lord, praise the Lord," and it does not say, as it did earlier, "*The House* of those who fear the Lord." It follows from this that fear of God is a matter for every individual in Israel, and not for a separate sect, which even has special study houses of its own![74] This argument seems to be complemented in certain remarks also cited in the name of Rabbi Leib Shapira: "Fixed study of Mussar books is a great thing, and very much to be desired; but to gather groups around this matter is very dangerous, lest it lead to disturbances within Israel, heaven forbid. . . ."[75] It is clear that this opposition was not directed against Salanter's demand for the study of Mussar per se, but rather against the fact that *yir'ah* as a value had become a focus around which a new social grouping developed. Their opposition was not directed against this social separatism as such, but rather against the fact that this new separatist grouping was based upon the cultivation of a religious value that was properly the inheritance of all Jews. The very establishment of special study houses and societies that championed the value of ethics and the fear of God implied a certain protest or criticism of society in general, as if it did not appreciate these values.

It was only natural in this traditional Mitnaggedic society, based upon homogeneity and uniformity in the realm of religious values and the service of God, that the Mussar adherents who grouped around Rabbi Salanter should have been understood as being haughty and as having pretensions to a "higher level" of religious life. We learn that such an opinion did in fact exist among the public from a letter by Salanter in which he attempts to refute the accusation:

> . . . for the public has fallen into the error of thinking that studying Mussar in a special house set apart for this purpose is some sort of "level" or [special act] of piety. So that when they see a person going to a Mussar house, they look at him as if he has been arrogant to hold himself on a special level, and they pay close attention to his behavior, [how can] such a person do thus and such. . . .[76]

In addition to the aforementioned motivation of the opposition, Salanter's teaching was also deemed dangerous because it involved a certain transformation of values: namely, the decline in the status of Torah study in light of the emphasis upon *yir'ah*. According to the approach that was widely accepted among scholarly circles in Lithuania, as formulated and explicated by Rabbi Hayyim of Volozhin, it was seen as axiomatic that the very act of studying Torah fills those who study it with *yir'ah* and holiness, and thereby protects them from the Evil Impulse. Salanter taught that this was insufficient, and that one should take additional and special means in order to assure one's ethical perfection. Moreover, Salanter's teaching concerning the means of ethical education demanded new criteria for evaluating a person's level in the Divine service. Thus, even if he did not initially intend to challenge or affect the centrality of Torah study, his teaching necessarily brought about a serious change in its status.

From the limited relevant sources available to us concerning the polemics of the 1850s, we have no evidence that the opponents of Mussar mentioned the threat to the status of Torah study, but this issue was at the center of the polemic in the 1890s. At that later stage, the Mussar movement had penetrated into the yeshivot, where the tension between the value of Torah study, as understood among the circles of Lithuanian *lomdim*, and of *yir'ah*, as interpreted by the Mussar movement, became far more real. However, it seems likely that the threat to the centrality of Torah study played a role in the disputes of the 1850s as well. In the final analysis, the value of Torah study was shared by the society as a whole, and particularly among the class of the *ba'alei batim*, most of whom had studied in yeshivot in their youth. This assumption seems to be confirmed by the fact that in *Iggeret ha-mussar*, which reflects his concerns and struggles during that decade, Salanter argues with the prevailing forces concerning the significance of Torah study in respect of perfection of the student.[77]

Our discussion of the opposition to the Mussar movement would be incomplete without mentioning the opposition of Lithuanian Jewry to Hasidism. The historical memory of the struggle against this separatist sect, which in a relatively short period of time was transformed into a mass movement, also seems to have influenced the opposition to the Mussar movement. In light of the bitter experience of the struggle with Hasidism, it was only natural that the Lithuanian rabbis should have been sensitive to and suspicious of this new sect in the first stages of its growth. Indeed, a disciple of Rabbi Abraham Samuel of Rosein, one of the outstanding opponents of Mussar teaching in the 1850s, heard him say that "the Hasidim of Zamot[78] will cause more evil and destruction to us in days to come than did the Hasidim of Galicia, and we will suffer much because of them."[79]

Despite the profound difference between Hasidism and the Mussar movement in terms of contents and religious mentality, there is nevertheless a strong resemblance between them in terms of the social dynamic brought about by their establishment. In each case, we are speaking of a group that claimed to act in the name of values accepted by all, but that brought about significant change of these values through the manner of their interpretation and execution. In both cases, the separatism of the group was interpreted by society as casting aspersions against the existing order of things; perceived as posing a threat to authority by proposing new criteria for measuring an individual's religious level,[80] the innovators were accused of arrogance and hypocrisy.[81] Finally, in both Hasidism and in the Mussar movement, the new forms of religious service are accompanied by striking externalities, which by their very strangeness epitomize the departure from the accepted norm. It is well known that the opponents of Hasidism frequently attacked the manifestations of ecstasy characteristic of Hasidic prayer,[82] which made it the object of ridicule on the part of the surrounding society; and the Baal Shem Tov (in several sayings attributed to him) comes to the defense of Hasidic prayer against its critics.[83] The study of Mussar *be-hitpa'alut* was likewise accompanied by strange gestures that aroused the ridicule of the environment, and Salanter similarly came to the defense of his followers against their critics.[84]

In concluding this discussion, one should call attention to the fact that two of the outstanding opponents of the Mussar doctrine held a somewhat positive attitude toward the Haskalah—namely, Rabbi Leib Shapira and Rabbi Mordecai Eliasberg. While neither of them identified with the worldview of the Haskalah movement as a whole, they evidently belonged to that small group of Lithuanian rabbis who wished to combine Torah and secular learning in a manner that would not affect the underpinnings of the tradition. Rabbi Leib Shapira was a leading disciple of Rabbi Manasseh of Ilyeh.[85] He was familiar with a number of secular subjects, and his moderate stance toward the Haskalah was expressed in his refusal to make common cause with a group of rabbis who wished to remove Rabbi Hayyim Wasserzug from office because he had been shown to tend toward Haskalah.[86] As for Rabbi Mordecai Eliasberg, he supported finding a way to combine the tradition with Haskalah and the national revival; his views on this matter were articulated in his book, *Shevil ha-zahav* (*The Golden Mean*). I do not mean to say that the question of the attitude toward Haskalah was explicitly included in the polemic against the Mussar movement of the 1850s. Nevertheless, it seems to me that there is more than mere symbolism in the fact that these personalities, who stood at the head of the opposition to the Mussar movement—which firmly rejected the Haskalah—held quite a different stand on this matter, in their more favorable attitude toward Haskalah.

At this stage of our discussion, we ought to return to the question of why Rabbi Israel Salanter left the office that the community of Kovna had granted to him. We remember that his resignation took place in the middle of the period agreed upon, and as such is rather surprising. The office not only provided him with an income, but also served Salanter as an important tool for the spread of his ideas. The chronological proximity between Rabbi Israel's leaving of this office and the beginning of the polemic against his doctrine prompts the conjecture that, in fact, it was this controversy that forced him to abandon the position of preacher, or at least prompted him to do so. As noted above, among the opponents of the new ideas that he wished to disseminate were such influential figures as Rabbi Mordecai Eliasberg, thanks to whose intervention Salanter originally received the job,[87] and Rabbi Leib Shapira, whose agreement, as rabbi of the community, was clearly required for this office to be granted to Rabbi Israel. It is not surprising that those who originally supported Salanter became the opponents of his approach. When he first came to Kovna, he was preceded by an irreproachable reputation as a giant in Torah and in piety, and as one who took pains to cultivate the fear of God among the public. Over the course of time, as they became acquainted with the specific contents of his teaching, and particularly after his sermons began to make their mark upon the public, the opposition began to mature and take shape. It seems reasonable to assume that, once the nature of his teaching and its social implications were understood, Salanter's opponents, and especially those who supported him at the beginning, demanded that he cease using the office of preacher in Kovna as a platform from which to spread his ideas.

Whether any direct and explicit pressure was applied to him, and whether he was pushed because of the public revelations of the dispute, Rabbi Israel was forced to retire from this office in order to continue working for the dissemination of his ideas without fearing the criticism of the leaders of the community. From that point on, the focus of his activity moved to the Nevyozer *kloiz*, his income being supplied by some of his wealthier supporters. Steinschneider, followed by other authors, writes that Rabbi Salanter was supported by the wealthy Rabbi Zvi Hirsch Nevyozer.[88] This support was evidently considered as payment for the lessons that he began to give in the *kloiz*. It would nevertheless seem that this support did not cover all his needs. According to reliable evidence, from the time of his resignation from the position of *maggid*, he also received support from his close disciple and friend, Rabbi Elijah Levinsohn of Cartinga.[89] Rabbi Salanter related to the fact that he was supported by benefactors with some bitterness, to which he occasionally gave overt expression.[90] However, he made his peace with this means of earning a living, because it was the only way in which he could devote himself to the dissemination of his ideas in public without being subject to those limitations that would have come with fulfilling some official task. Both his consistent refusal to accept any rabbinic office and his resignation from the position of *maggid* in Kovna would appear to have been intended to enable him to act outside of the institutionalized frameworks of society, and on occasion even in confrontation with them.

13

Salanter's Thought in the 1850s: The "Mussar Epistle"

RABBI Israel Salanter's thinking from the period of his sojourn in Kovna is expressed in *Iggeret ha-mussar*—the "Mussar Epistle." This document was first published as an appendix to the 1858 Koenigsberg edition of *Tomer devorah*, the seminal work of kabbalistic Mussar written in the sixteenth century by Moses Cordovero.[1] The first work ever written by Rabbi Salanter for publication, *Iggeret ha-mussar* may have been executed while he was still living in Kovna, as it was published only one year after he left. But even if it was actually written while its author was already residing in Prussia, there is no doubt that the ideas expressed therein crystallized during the Kovna period, as the social reality it both reflects and attempts to confront is characteristic of Lithuanian Jewry. In terms of its contents, *Iggeret ha-mussar* is directed toward the public of *ba'alei batim*. By publishing this epistle, Salanter signified his intention of continuing his activity for disseminating Mussar ideology within Lithuanian Jewry despite his move to Prussia.

Several of the principal ideas found in his thought from the Vilna period are repeated by Salanter in the "Mussar Epistle" but, alongside these, he develops several new ideas. The line of demarcation between old and new may be seen in the distinction he draws between two categories of sins, which in fact does not relate to the sins per se, but to the motivation for their performance. Thus, we are talking about a distinction between two kinds of motives that drive a person to sin.

The first kind of sin is described by Salanter as deriving from "the widespread appetite to love that is momentarily pleasant without anticipating the consequences, even though its end be bitter."[2] "Appetite" here denotes an emotional drive implanted in a person's soul, motivating that person to immediate satisfactions. One of its characteristic features is the inability to foresee consequences—that is, the inevitable punishment for a sinful act. Appetite in this sense refers to the psychic force inherent in the Evil Impulse, which causes people to stumble in sins insofar as the pleasures that they desire conflict with the command of the halakhah.

People can overcome the influence of the appetite by means of *yir'ah*—the fear of God—or, to be more precise, the fear of Divine retribution. In Salanter's teaching, belief in the principle of Divine recompense is the main motivation behind a person's service of God. However, experience reveals that this faith is unable to motivate human behavior so long as it remains on the level of abstract cognition.[3] Actualization of the power inherent therein depends upon its transformation from abstract cognition to a concrete sense of fear, which may be accomplished by the study of Mussar: "This is all the labor of man in His service, may He be praised: by means of Mussar works and Rabbinic aggadot, to think upon and contemplate the fear of God and the punishment he metes out, until he will almost hear with his ears and see with his eyes the great punishment, in both quality and quantity, present before his eyes. . . . "[4] So far, Salanter essentially reiterates ideas that have already been explained above.

The second motivation for committing sins is described by Salanter in what seems to be puzzlement over the failure of his efforts to spread the study of Mussar within the broader public:

> Indeed, great is the evil of man on the earth [Gen. 6:5]. There is no one who seeks righteousness or who exercises intelligence in the fear of God, to set fixed times for the labor of *yir'ah*; to tap the waters of understanding from that faith which is concealed and hidden in the depths of the heart, to extend it and sustain it, to give it strength and power, to give it authority to rule over the limbs, that they not break out of their domain, but perform as they should. This is the second type, the like of which we have not seen in worldly affairs. For there is no man facing trouble who does not take time to think of plans [by which] he may be saved from them. This being so, its cause is not the appetite, this sin is remarkable . . . that [a person] does not take it to heart to contemplate the fear of God and the reproof of His punishment. Such sins cannot belong to the first kind, as the appetite is an inadequate cause for them; they come only from the impure spirit which embraces man to make him sin.[5]

A close reading of the above passage reveals that Salanter is no longer satisfied here, as he was in his writings from the 1840s,[6] with a generalized, undifferentiated criticism of the widespread tendency of people to ignore matters of *yir'ah* and Mussar. This criticism clearly reflects his disappointment in the limited spread of his teaching, given that he began to disseminate the doctrine of Mussar in the hopes of its becoming a widespread cultural vogue, which would catalyze extensive change in the life of Lithuanian Jewry. The optimism characteristic of his activity at that time was based upon his evaluation that the system of ethical education that he taught would be efficacious, and therefore a reliable cure for the ailments of the generation. But the years of strenuous labor invested by Salanter to convey his teaching to the public did not yield the desired results: Only a small minority followed Mussar teaching, while the majority of Lithuanian Jewry remained indifferent to it, and opponents were not lacking. From Rabbi Israel's point of view, this response was both puzzling and extraordinary. How could people not wish to save their souls from sins and the punishments that they bring in their wake? The appetite seems an inadequate explanation for such a reaction. There must therefore be an additional force acting within the human soul, apart from the appetite, which prevents people from acknowledging the need for Mussar study as a means of ethical perfection; this power is the "impure spirit which embraces man to make him sin."

Awareness of the existence of this "impure spirit" is an innovation in Salanter's writings. In the understanding of the human psyche expressed in his sermons and letters from the 1840s, he only speaks of the appetite, while the impure spirit is not mentioned at all. Now Salanter notes that, in addition to the appetite, which constitutes a function of the psyche whose action is subject to rational explanation, and which may even be predicted in advance, the impure spirit that operates within a human being's soul is a metaphysical power the forms of whose activity are not dictated by the laws governing the psychic mechanism.

Salanter presents his recognition of the power of the impure spirit, in addition to that of the appetite, as a compromise between two approaches that had until then been understood as mutually exclusive:

> We find in this the explanation of the dispute between the [different] approaches concerning the nature of the Good Impulse and the Evil Impulse. One approach is the known one, [which claims] that the Evil Impulse is the power of impurity in man causing him to sin, while the Good Impulse is the power of holiness within man bringing him towards the good. This approach is that of most of the major authors. The second approach is that [which holds that] the Evil Impulse is the power

of appetite within man, which turns toward every thing that is
momentarily pleasing. . . . And the Good Impulse is the upright
intellect which anticipates and sees the consequences of actions,
it is the fear [and] awe of God—may His Name be praised—and
of His harsh judgments.[7]

The compromise between these two approaches—that adopted by
the majority of major authors, and that originally advocated by Rabbi
Israel Salanter—finds expression in the recognition that both are correct
and that one does not exclude the other. This conclusion is based upon
arguments taken from Salanter's own reflection upon the nature of the
sins to which people are prone. Experience shows that different individuals tend to err through different sins, a phenomenon that may only
be explained by recognizing the influence of the appetite, which, because it is a power of the psyche, is inherent within the particular
makeup of each individual. But experience likewise indicates the existence of sins that cannot be explained through the concept of appetite
alone: "Do we not see with our eyes people performing grave sins to
which they are not strongly driven by their appetites, or to which at
times their appetite is even opposed: such as the person who greatly
desires and longs for imagined honor, while his soul abhors the honor
of a *mitzvah,* and the like." Such phenomena can only be explained by
means of the influence of the spirit of impurity.[8]

How is one to explain the fact that Salanter first mentions the
existence of the spirit of impurity in *Iggeret ha-mussar*? Does this represent a significant transformation in his understanding of the Evil
Impulse? It is difficult to answer that question with certainty. It may
indeed be the case that, when Salanter adopted the naturalistic understanding of the Evil Impulse, he abandoned its traditional understanding, whereas he now reached the conclusion that both approaches are
equally valid. However, it seems more likely that Salanter never denied
the validity of the traditional approach, but that it simply became less
important in light of his adoption of the newer approach. So long as
Salanter's writings and sermons from the 1840s were only known
within his own small, immediate circle, he did not bother to mention
the traditional approach. However, in *Iggeret ha-mussar*, which was
intended for a broader public, he felt it necessary to resolve the tension
between the two approaches and to maintain both simultaneously. In
any event, his explicit acknowledgment of the approach of "the majority of the great authors" did not change his understanding of ethical
education, which, as we shall see below, continued to be based upon
the naturalistic interpretation of the Evil Impulse.

In light of his recognition of appetite, on the one hand, and the

spirit of impurity, on the other, Salanter drew a distinction between
two aspects of the struggle with the Evil Impulse. The former is the
physical aspect, also referred to as the natural aspect, while the latter
is the spiritual aspect. The significance of these concepts, as well as
their interrelationship, is clarified by the metaphor used to describe
them. Salanter metaphorically describes ethical education in terms of
the healing of a sickness of the soul, compared in turn to a sickness of
the body. Essentially, a person who strives to maintain sound health
wishes to preserve the soul within the body. Nevertheless, all of the
person's efforts are directed toward the physical aspect, as there is no
way by which one can act directly upon one's soul in order to sustain
it within one's body. The same is true regarding one's ethical perfection:
"The principal device is to sustain the Good Impulse according to both
methods—namely, the power of holiness and that of truthful intellect
. . . while rejecting the Evil Impulse, which is the power of impurity
and of the appetite, depends upon the physical aspect, [namely,] to
feed him good food, which is meditation upon fear of God and
Mussar. . . ."[9]

The influence of the physical aspect upon the soul is understood
by the intellect.[10] That understanding is based both upon knowledge
of the psychic mechanism and upon the individual's self-examination,
aimed at identifying one's own weak points. This way is a natural one
in the sense that it is based upon pinpointing the relationship between
cause and effect, and that it seeks to prevent the effect—that is, the
sins—by controlling the causes.[11] On the other hand, it is typical of the
spiritual aspect that "the intellect and the senses of man are unable to
recognize their cause,"[12] and since the action of the latter is not even
understood by the intellect, it cannot use it in an intelligent and controlled way, taking into account the specific ethical condition of each
individual.

The spiritual aspect is expressed in practice in the study of Torah.
This is based upon the Rabbinic dictum that "Torah, while one studies
it, protects one" (Sotah 21a). Salanter writes the following with regard
to the nature of this study: "It does not matter in what words of Torah
one engages, it protects one from sin; [even] if one studies matters
concerning an ox which gored a cow and the like, it will protect one
from engaging in malicious speech, even though they have no bearing
upon that subject. The spirituality of the Torah will itself protect one."[13]
Elsewhere, Salanter includes prayer in the spiritual aspect; this refers
to prayer in which a person beseeches God for protection from the Evil
Impulse—namely, the spirit of impurity—and to be infused with a spirit
of holiness.[14]

In the above passage, we see the superior status that Salanter gives to the physical aspect over and above the spiritual. Further along in that discussion, he reasserts that preference, accompanying it with a detailed argument:

> If one looks with a penetrating eye, one will notice that our devices for healing the Evil Impulse are centered upon the physical aspect alone. . . . For the latter [kind of] healing, which is the spiritual aspect, comes about of itself, and is therefore called an incidental healing. For the commandment to study Torah is a positive commandment in its own right, whose definition depends upon what is given in the laws of Torah study. . . . There is no practical consequence in respect of how it is to be practiced, whether [a person's] Evil Impulse overwhelms him much or little. . . . But when one properly fulfills the commandment of Torah study, spiritual healing is automatically brought down upon one's Impulse, however this may be. [On the other hand,] the physical aspect is [that of] contemplation of the fear of God, and the study of halakhah[15] is his self-healing, for man needs to behave in [these matters] as he does in matters of healing the bodily ills. Just as the [manner of] healing the sicknesses of the body, in quantity and quality, depends upon the character of the sickness, so does the cure of the sicknesses of the soul depend upon the nature of the sickness. So long as his urge attacks him, he must increase contemplation of *yir'ah* and study of halakhah, as said above. And if a person does not make use of physical [ways of] healing, so also the spiritual [means], namely, the study of Torah, will not so much give its strength [against] the spiritual Evil Impulse. . . . [16]

Salanter gives a more marginal status to the spiritual aspect for two reasons. First, the very obligation to engage in Torah study, as well as the extent of that obligation, is totally unrelated to the ethical condition of a given individual, so that the spirit of holiness with which a person is infused by study is no more than a side result of the performance of the mitzvah of Torah study.[17] Second, the fact that the intellect does not understand the effect of the spiritual aspect upon the soul eliminates the possibility of establishing a causal connection between the ethical condition of a particular individual and the extent and means of use of Torah study for its correction. The opposite is true regarding the physical aspect, which is from the start exclusively intended to cause the ethical correction of a person. Because it is based upon the cognition of the soul in general, and upon the relationship to the situation of each individual soul in particular, this facilitates its verification and regulation in each and every case. It follows from this that one's primary effort must be guided in this direction. Rabbi Israel's activistic approach is thus reflected in these arguments; he seeks to place the main burden of ethical change upon human activity, while minimizing the weight of Divine assistance.

The distinction drawn by Salanter between the physical aspect and the spiritual, granting greater weight to the former rather than to the latter, implies a certain polemic against the dominant view accepted among the Lithuanian *lomdim*. According to that view, which was given prominent formulation in the teaching of Rabbi Hayyim of Volozhin, the Evil Impulse is identified with the spirit of impurity, the most effective way of doing battle with which is through the study of Torah. Salanter's polemical tendency is expressed in the manner in which he interprets the Rabbinic dictum: "The Holy One blessed be He created the Evil Impulse, and He created the Torah as its antidote" (Bava Batra 16a). Thus, the Sages wish to teach us that the Torah is an "antidote" to the Evil Impulse, particularly when used in an enlightened way as a means of ethical education. While this saying is generally understood as comprising the commonly accepted view, Salanter argues that "the antidote of Torah lies in the *yir'ah* which flows from it . . . this is a physical aspect, tangible to eyes of flesh [and blood]. . . ."[18]

As noted above, Salanter admits the existence and influence of the spirit of impurity, and also recognizes the power inherent in the study of Torah as a means of protection against the Impulse. However, because of the distinction drawn between appetite and spirit of impurity, and between the physical aspect and the spiritual, Salanter argues that the dominant view concerning the nature of the Impulse and the means of struggle against it are based upon a partial perception of the ethical problematics involved, so that this approach is unable to propose an adequate method of ethical correction.

The new concepts introduced by Salanter in *Iggeret ha-mussar* broaden his perspective concerning the problem of ethical education and accord it a more complex character. But their main significance lies in their repeated confirmation, albeit from a different perspective, of the legitimacy of Salanter's system as earlier known. Indeed, one finds an interesting development in *Iggeret ha-mussar* with regard to the purpose of ethical education. If thus far Salanter's discussions have concentrated upon the methods of halting and restraining the appetite, from here on he emphasizes the possibility and need to uproot it from the soul—that is, to uproot the natural urge toward sin and to replace it with a natural inclination to perform the mitzvah. The goal is thus nothing less than a transformation of human nature. That purpose is indeed mentioned in one of the sermons from the 1840s, in which Salanter advises each individual to set himself "limits" with regard to matters in which he is likely to falter—"until he becomes so accustomed [to it] that he no longer longs at all for that thing."[19] But while these matters occupied a marginal place in these sermons, and they are not even mentioned in his letters to his disciples from 1849, in *Iggeret ha-mussar* Salanter returns to this subject with great elaboration and detail and, as we shall see below, even proposes a new educational technique for attaining them.

Salanter bases the possibility that changing human nature might be made a goal of ethical education upon his observation of the patterns of religious behavior found among his contemporaries:

> Nearly all of our brethren, the children of Israel, will not eat without [ritually] washing their hands, even if they are very hungry and in great distress. But they easily violate the serious [prohibition regarding] malicious speech, even without much appetite for it. . . . And in our region, thank God, the prohibitions against [eating] various sorts of non-kosher meat and the like are rooted in the Jewish soul, to the extent that no one needs to conquer his nature or his appetite in order to avoid them, for they are disgusting to him. It would not occur to [even] one of the merchants of kosher meat to refrain from asking a *moreh-zedek* should he happen to find any thing which might present a possibility of *terefah* in one of the inner organs, even though at times it might entail substantial [financial] loss. The fear of heaven is upon him in his nature and in his habits. . . . [20]

These examples illustrate that it is possible for people to acquire patterns of behavior that run contrary to the appetite—that is, the natural impulses of the soul implanted in them from birth. By nature, human beings do not tolerate pangs of hunger or of monetary loss; nevertheless, these Jews are prepared to go hungry or to lose money in order to avoid eating without washing their hands or to incur sin with respect to non-kosher meat. Salanter finds the explanation for this behavior in the change in human nature brought about by habit.

From the point of view of ethical education, the significance of habit is found in the theory of the accumulation of impressions. This theory, which is taken by Salanter from Rabbi Menahem Mendel Lefin's *Sefer heshbon ha-nefesh*,[21] constitutes the background for his discussion in several places,[22] and also appears between the lines of *Iggeret ha-mussar*. Every act performed by a person, and even every feeling, leaves its impression upon that person's soul. The impressions accumulated as a result of the repetition of the same action—that is, habit—as well as those impressions accumulated as a result of the repetition of the same emotions, add up to a quantitative mass capable of bringing about genuine change within the psyche. In the initial stage, the impressions accumulated as a result of positive habits can create a sufficiently strong impulse within the soul to halt the negative drives (namely, the appetite) implanted in the soul. At a certain quantitative point, the mass of positive impressions accumulated are liable to uproot the appetite from the soul and to implant in its stead psychological tendencies of a positive force.

This theory, even if not explicitly mentioned in *Iggeret ha-mussar*, explains how, according to Salanter, the habit of observance of particular mitzvot operated within the psyches of Lithuanian Jews to the extent that they uprooted their appetites with regard to those particular mitzvot. The theory also seems to underly the new path recommended by Salanter as an effective means of altering human nature:

> The highest [level] and the principal method of utilizing the healing of the Torah for the ailments of the Impulse is to study the laws concerning that [particular] sin, intensely and with deep reflection, in all aspects and implications of the halakhah. . . . For the change in [one's] nature may only come about as a result of study and great habituation; therefore, the primary foundation and proper basis by which to prepare oneself to be protected from sin and to perform the mitzvot is only by extensive study in that halakhah pertaining to this sin or commandment. . . . For this study leaves a strong impression in the soul, so that the sin becomes removed from him by nature.[23]

What is referred to here is the study of those specific laws regarding which the particular individual tends to fail. Further along in his discussion, Salanter explains that he is referring to the study of the Talmud with *poskim* (halakhic decisors);[24] the emphasis is thus laid upon the understanding of the practical halakhah. The kind of study suggested here does not entail any innovation in terms of methodology, but follows the well-known model of Torah study known in those days as *limmud le-ma'aseh* (practical study—that is, practical application). What is new here is the educational significance attached to this form of study by Salanter and the function assigned to it.

From what we have seen above, it clearly follows that the aim of practical study is not restricted to the halakhic information acquired by the student. From the point of view of ethical education, the study of halakhah is meant to effect a change in the person's character in that same area in which he was most prone to fail. Salanter does not elaborate upon how practical study influences the soul, but is content with the statement that "this study leaves a strong impression upon the soul, so that sin is remote from it by nature." He furthermore warns that the influence of halakhic study upon one's soul is acquired slowly and by degree. As far as we can tell, Rabbi Israel thought that the careful, precise study of halakhot (that is, individual laws) leaves an impression upon the soul similar to the effect of acts or emotions repeated over and over again. Even though study is not an action in itself, it creates the image of the act in the consciousness of the student. The study of halakhot also has emotional significance, as the student relates to those laws discussed as obligatory norms that must be fulfilled.

It should be noted that the practical study recommended by Salanter in *Iggeret ha-mussar* is not intended for those who are preparing themselves for rabbinic office, but for *ba'alei batim*, who, generally speaking, have sufficient background in Torah studies to be able to study Talmud and *poskim* by themselves. The following passage clearly indicates the element in society to which his remarks are addressed:

> Indeed, if a person will apply his heart and soul to study in depth those halakhot pertinent to money matters—each one [studying] the *gemara* and *poskim* according to his ability—and particularly if the focus is upon the characteristics of what is forbidden and permitted, so that he may know how to avoid [the sin of] theft. . . . How great is its [that is, the study's] power firmly to implant it within his soul, until questions pertaining to *'Orah Hayyim* [that is, everyday life] and those pertaining to monetary matters will be the same [that is, equally compelling] to him.[25]

Salanter was thus clearly referring to *ba'alei batim* who dealt with business matters in their everyday life. Indeed, we know from elsewhere that he attempted to introduce *limmud le-ma'aseh* among the circles of *ba'alei batim*. This is implied in one of his letters, in which he writes: "My dear friend, how astonished I was at the lacunae in your letter to me. You told me nothing about practical study, concerning which I troubled you greatly [to know] how it is among you. And you know that my heart is concerned with this matter, to implement this much-needed thing, [namely,] practice-oriented study, within the hearts of those who fear God."[26]

One ought to mention that, among the positive qualities of Rabbi Zundel Salant described by Rabbi Israel, was the fact that "his main fixed study stressed that which he needed for practice."[27] In this context, *limmud le-ma'aseh* is seen as indicative of Rabbi Zundel's piety, his concentration upon the practical aspects of halakhah indicating his intention to fulfill the mitzvot of the Torah to the maximum extent.

What was a sign of piety in the case of Rabbi Zundel now becomes an important means of ethical education. It is not inconceivable that the personal example of Rabbi Zundel, which so impressed Rabbi Israel in his youth, influenced the new use to which he put *limmud le-ma'aseh*. But it would appear that Salanter primarily discovered the idea of practical study as a tool of ethical education in light of the lessons he learned from his own activity among Lithuanian Jewry. These Jews, who so cherished the study of Torah, did not reveal overly great enthusiasm for the message of Mussar study, since the latter was not considered a form of Torah study at all. Indeed, it will be remembered that there were even those who saw excessive devotion to the study of Mussar as a kind of neglect of Torah (*bittul Torah*). *Limmud le-ma'aseh*, on the other hand, was considered "real" Torah study, through which one fulfilled the commandment of Torah study according to all opinions, while at the same time functioning as an instrument of ethical education. These Lithuanian *ba'alei batim*, who were used to setting fixed times for Torah study, were now presented with a relatively easy task: They were expected to alter the center of gravity of their studies from the widespread pattern of studying Talmud with commentaries, to that of studying Talmud with Codes, the principal effort being directed toward clarifying the practical aspect of the halakhah in those specific areas in which the student was prone to fail.

But even if our assumption is correct that Salanter, in proposing *limmud le-ma'aseh* as a form of ethical education, sought a form of study that would be close to the hearts of Lithuanian Jewry, one must not think that he ceased to engage in preaching on behalf of Mussar study. Both at the beginning and end of *Iggeret ha-mussar*, Salanter repeatedly emphasizes the importance of Mussar study as a means of ethical improvement. Mussar study *be-hitpa'alut*, intended to arouse the feeling of fear of sin in order to break one's appetite, was the purpose cited for Mussar study by Salanter at the beginning of the *Iggeret ha-mussar*. Toward the end of the letter, he adds a new emphasis to his argument on behalf of Mussar study: While the Evil Impulse attempts to prevent people from recognizing their sins, thereby making it impossible for them to progress along the path of ethical improvement, the study of Mussar, because of the *yir'ah* that it inspires in the soul, motivates people to critical self-examination and to the pursuit of ethical improvement.[28]

At this point, one ought to clarify Salanter's understanding of the relationship between a person's ability to engage in critical self-examination and *yir'ah*. In *Iggeret ha-mussar*, Salanter decries the fact that the learned element within the Jewish public—that is, the *ba'alei batim* and the *lomdim*—do not correctly perceive their own ethical and religious situation. Because they compare themselves with the common people, who are visibly culpable of religious transgressions, they tend to see themselves in a positive light. However, they are in fact themselves frequently guilty of sins in the areas of business morality, malicious speech, and the neglect of Torah study. In explaining this phenomenon, and the means by which one might possibly be able to overcome it, Salanter writes:

> We stumble in great and mighty sins, being like blind men, due to the darkness of our hearts, and we do not see their seriousness (compared with the sins of the multitude). But if we make use of binoculars (which enlarge things, which due to our weak vision seem to be small, such as the stars, which are of greater size than the earth itself, but which look like small points, and by means of the binoculars seem somewhat larger, whereas in truth there is nothing comparable to them in size; so is this thing), that is correct thinking, according to the faithful Torah, we find them to be exceedingly more serious in their quality.[29]

The fact that the learned public is unaware of the sins in which it habitually stumbles is interpreted by Salanter as a blindness that stems from darkness of heart. He refers to the situation of self-deception caused by the domination of the power of judgment by the appetite. This blindness may be overcome by means of the fear of God, which functions like a magnifying lens, exposing those things hidden to the eye. It follows that the sense of fear of punishment, apart from being a force that brakes the appetite at times of ethical test, constitutes a positive instrument of self-criticism by freeing the intellect from the grasp of the appetite.

Relying upon the Rabbinic dictum that "whoever is greater than his fellow, his Impulse is [likewise] greater" (Sukkah 52a), Salanter states that each person's self-examination ought by rights to correspond to his individual level.[30] These remarks contain an unarticulated assumption characteristic of Rabbi Israel's system in general. We occasionally find in Mussar works a hierarchy of levels (*madregot*); the higher one ascends upon them, the higher the religio-ethical level upon which one finds oneself—that is, among other things, the further away from sin. In Salanter's system, ascent on the scale of *yir'ah* and Mussar is accompanied by stricter self-criticism. To be a *Tzaddik*, therefore, does not mean to be free of sins but, on the contrary, that one is aware of hidden sins that the majority of people would not consider to be sins at all. This element of doubt and self-criticism is not weakened in Salanter's teaching even when he posits change of one's nature and correction of one's character as possible goals of ethical education. This is evidently so due to his pessimistic reading of the nature of the human psyche and the power of the appetite implanted therein from its creation.

14

Theory and Practice in the Cultivation of Scholars and Rabbis

AROUND 1851, Rabbi Israel Salanter left his position as *maggid* and began to teach in the *kloiz* of Rabbi Zvi Hirsch Nevyozer,[1] which remained the center of his activity in Kovna until his departure in 1857. At this time, the *kloiz*, a small building set aside for the purpose of Torah study, was a popular and widespread institution in Lithuanian communities. As a rule, it served as a place of study and occasionally prayer for young Torah scholars and youths who were able to study independently. At times, the young *lomdim* had their needs taken care of within the framework of the *kloiz*. But unlike those *kloizn* where study was generally unorganized and independent and whose main attraction was the financial aid or free meals that they offered to their students, the prominence of the Nevyozer *kloiz* derived from the great personality who stood at its head. Thus, despite its being new and without any tradition of its own, this *kloiz* became an important center of Torah study by virtue of Salanter's reputation.

The Nevyozer *Kloiz*

The special quality of the Nevyozer *kloiz* was also ex- pressed in the high level of its students. We find contemporary testimonies using such phrases as "outstanding scholars" and "prodigies in Torah" to suggest the talent and industry of its students.[2] This is confirmed by the tasks that graduates of the *kloiz* filled in later life in the rabbinate and the dissemination of Torah. Among the students of Salanter from this period were such outstanding personalities as Rabbi Eliezer Gordon, who was to become the head of the religious court in Kelm and Telz, and who for many years headed the famous Telzer yeshiva; Rabbi Isaac Blazer, who served as rabbi and head of the religious court of Petersburg and was active in disseminating Mussar teaching among the yeshivot; Rabbi Jacob Joseph Harif, a noted preacher and *moreh-zedek* in Vilna who subsequently served as Chief Rabbi of New York City; Rabbi Yeruham Leib Perlman, better known as "the Minsker Gadol"; and others.[3]

From the fragmentary evidence available to us, it would appear that some of the students in the Nevyozer *kloiz* were young *lomdim* who continued to devote themselves to Torah after their marriage.[4] In light of the early marriages customary at the time, we may assume that the average age of the students was between fifteen and twenty years of age. The students of the *kloiz* also included boys who had not yet married. Salanter evidently gave a regular class (*shi'ur*) to the youngest students several times a week,[5] while the framework of study of the young men was presumably more independent. The exact number of students in the *kloiz* is not known, but from a number of sources it would appear that it was a relatively large one in terms of those days, and may have amounted to several dozen.[6]

Rabbi Yaakov Lifschitz relates the following concerning the innovations introduced by Rabbi Israel in the method of support of *kloiz* students:

> It had been the custom that each yeshivah student went to eat on his "day" at the home of a householder, and thus went about begging all week. This custom, which degraded the respect for the yeshivah student, was abolished by our teacher. . . . Instead, he arranged that those *ba'alei batim* who wished to do so sent their meal to the *kloiz* for this particular young man. He also set aside a special residence for them to stay in, rather than in the Bet Midrash itself, which was reserved exclusively for study. The honor of the students of Torah was thereby elevated, and it was thereafter done likewise in many communities of Lithuania and Zamot.[7]

Although Lifschitz did not live in Kovna during the 1850s and his remarks are therefore not the direct testimony of a contemporary in time and place, they reflect what he knew by hearsay. Nevertheless, the regulations that Lifschitz attributes to Rabbi Salanter are in keeping with his great sensitivity to human dignity, and are also confirmed by other sources.[8] Further on, Lifschitz adds that the status of Torah students improved throughout Lithuania as a result of Salanter's influence, until wealthy *ba'alei batim* sought Torah prodigies as husbands for their daughters, whom they then supported generously. However great Salanter's contribution to uplifting the standing of Torah study may have been, it is still impossible to see him as the exclusive, or even as the principal, factor in such a widespread sociocultural phenomenon. But even if we acknowledge that Lifschitz's language is exaggerated, his words still contain an important truth. The impact of Salanter's activity was such that, in the popular mind, he was associated with the improvement that came about in the status of Torah study throughout Lithuania during the latter half of the nineteenth century. As for Kovna itself, it seems clear that Rabbi Salanter's activity placed it on the map as a major center of Torah in Lithuania.

A number of authors claim that the aim of Salanter's activity in the Nevyozer *kloiz* was to prepare young Torah scholars who studied there to fill rabbinic offices. For example, Rosenfeld writes that:

> He gathered a suitable number of young men at the Bet Midrash of Nevyozer. . . . These young men prepared themselves to become rabbis, and Rabbi Israel saw in them the true rabbis, a shield against the false rabbis being trained in Vilna. . . . This too was an innovation in Israel—that people should prepare themselves *ab initio* to be rabbis, for learned and God-fearing Jews study Torah for its own sake—for the sake of the Torah, and not for any ulterior purpose. Rabbi Israel came and taught that study of Torah for its own sake means to study in order to become a rabbi.[9]

Was Rabbi Salanter's *bet midrash* indeed created in order to train future rabbis? And if that was in fact its purpose, how was such an aim expressed in the program of study practiced there? Neither Rosenfeld nor the others who argue as he does addresses this question.

The error of those authors who describe the Nevyozer *kloiz* as a kind of *bet midrash* for the training of rabbis lies in retroprojecting from a later period to an earlier one. In the late 1870s and early '80s, Salanter was indeed active in creating frameworks to assist young men studying to become rabbis. In the context of this activity, in 1877 he helped to found in Kovna *Kollel Ha-Perushim*,[10] a Kovna institution meant to meet the needs of young men studying to become rabbis and of their families. The extent to which some historians fail to distinguish between the earlier and later periods in this matter may be seen in the description by Menahem Glenn. Glenn writes about Salanter's activity in *Kollel Ha-Perushim* as if this institution already existed in the Kovna of the 1850s and was under Salanter's direct supervision,[11] although it wasn't established for another twenty years, when Salanter had long since been residing in Prussia.

Salanter's Approach to the Truth of Torah and to *Pilpul*

The basic difficulty confronting anyone attempting to understand Salanter's approach to the guidance of youths in study and the preparation of young men for rabbinic tasks is the fact that he did not leave a systematic, explicit teaching on this subject. His survivng comments on these matters are fragmentary and scattered, and at times even seem to contradict one another. In order to overcome this difficulty, one must examine his various remarks in their respective contexts and in relation to the group to which they were addressed. As a point of departure, we will analyze a passage from Rabbi Israel's introduction to the periodical *Tevunah*,[12] which he published during the years 1861–62. In this passage, Salanter develops a methodological discussion on the question of the proper means of arriving at the ''truth'' of the Torah.[13]

Salanter begins by rejecting the axiom that a superior means of discovering the truth is study that uses the method of *pashtut* (straightforward or simple interpretation). By this concept, he seems to have meant the explanation that first occurs to one on the basis of the straightforward reading of the text being studied, without engaging in careful, exact analysis of its language or analogy to other sources elsewhere in the Talmud. He argues that *pashtut* is only one of the methods of proof, and not always the correct one. In many cases, both in the talmudic text and in the Tosafot, one encounters serious difficulties forcing one to reject the explanation based upon *pashtut*. Thus, for example, the *'okimtot* in the Talmud—that is, those tannaitic statements that, on the surface, are of unlimited application, but that are restricted by the amoraim to a specific, limited context—are a prime example of the fact that the Talmud itself does not always interpret tannaitic statements in a straightforward manner.

After qualifying the superiority of learning by the method of *pashtut*, Salanter adds the argument that ''nor is the truth supported by the short *hiddush* [novellum].'' We sometimes encounter a brief explanation in which the logical connections among the various components do not stand up to criticism. On the other hand, there may be a lengthy and complex interpretation, all of whose elements logically combine in a sustained, coherent manner, albeit Salanter admits that such interpretations require more careful examination because, as its component parts are numerous, once one of them is invalidated the whole no longer holds together. Finally, he rejects the assumption that the student's desire will in itself somehow provide assistance in arriving at the truth. Nor should one rely entirely upon Divine assistance to achieve one's goal—"for it is not in heaven" (Deut. 30:12, as used in Bava Metzia 59b). Against all these options, Rabbi Israel proposes two fundaments which, in his opinion, are a necessary and prior condition for achieving truth in Torah study: the student's ability and his purity of thought.

The first of these elements is defined by Salanter by the term *yekholet* (ability)—that is, comprehensive knowledge of the literature and intellectual acuity. His innovation lies in pointing to these two categories, which have generally been used as criteria for greatness in Torah, as "the natural causes which lead to the effect, which is, the knowledge of the truth." That is, there is a rational, causal relation between these two factors and the discovery of the truth. In order to clarify a given halakhah, one first requires expertise in the halakhic literature that is the clarification of the subject at hand. In addition, one requires logical acuity, which operates within the boundaries of common sense. This is needed in order to construct logical models, structures for relating one element to another until one arrives at the correct conclusions.

But that is inadequate. A further condition for arriving at the truth of Torah is purity of thought on the part of the student:

> Purity: this refers to what is called by the scholars scientific cognition, and what the sages of Mussar call the thrusting off of corporeality—that is, that the intellect is isolated, without any connection with the other powers of the soul which lie within man; for without this, the powers of the soul tend to act as barriers between him and knowledge of the truth. . . .

Thus, purity is a psychic state in which intellectual judgment stands alone, free of any emotional tendencies. As the clarification or interpretation of the halakhah is an intellectual process whose goal is the discovery of the objective truth inherent within the Torah, a person's feelings, which by their nature reflect subjective, personal tendencies, may not be involved in or influence this process.

Salanter would seem to have adopted here the concept of scientific objectivity, one of the basic concepts of the humanities as they developed during the nineteenth century, which he attempts to apply to the realm of Torah study. In doing so, Salanter "Judaizes" this concept by calling it "purity of thought"—a term borrowed from Jewish ethical literature.[14] Moreover, by means of a psychological interpretation of scientific objectivity, Rabbi Israel connects it with his own ethical doctrine, the restraining of emotional impulses being one of the fundaments of Salanter's doctrine.

We have seen above that Salanter's viewpoint concerning the fundaments upon which truth in Torah study is to be established is presented in contrast with a competing viewpoint, which assumes that it is possible to achieve this lofty goal by using the methods of simplicity and brevity, as well as by the very desire to achieve the truth. The source of this view and the identity of its advocates has thus far not been clarified. Both the answer to this question and a number of other instructive points concerning the ideal way to develop Torah scholars are found in another passage from the editor's introduction to *Tevunah*, which proposes a reevaluation of the role of *pilpul* in Torah study:

[handwritten note: Cursiv]

> There is one thing which the Mussar masters[15] did not allow in the community of Israel—namely, *pilpul*.[16] In my opinion, the opposite is the case, for *pilpul* is a great and strong element in the quest for truth, and it is nearly impossible to achieve truth without it. This is so for two reasons: first, that profound and straightforward reason is the primary element (second only to the element of the extent of one's erudition) in [pursuit of the] goal of truth; the obligation and necessity to expand it and sharpen it and to straighten it (each person according to his measure) is nearly impossible [when] examination of the truth is limited from all sides. Therefore, by means of deliberating on *pilpul* of Torah, which each person may expand as he wills . . . a person's reason becomes straightened and sharpened. When this is accompanied by great erudition, it comes within his reach to achieve the truth (according to his level). Second, it is known to me from the experience of my youth that when I was captivated by the study of Mussar and its laws, I made up my mind to force my Impulse (which longed to exhibit my *pilpul* to my contemporaries) to completely abandon the way of *pilpul*, and to seek the truth alone . . . which then imagined it to be simplicity, brevity and the desire to seek it. While I followed this view, I saw with a penetrating eye that my wish to display my mental power overleaped the bounds of truth, and deceived my mind to bend the truth towards my own desire, so that truth could be determined at will. I then said [that is, realized] that it would be better for me to permit it [that is, *pilpul*] without any aspersions, and I saw fit to use *pilpul* (just as the Sages permitted acuity), so that my mind might be free of the captivity of the Impulse.

In this view, not only is the path of *pilpul* not invalid, it even performs a necessary function in the training of scholars, enabling them, in the final analysis, to reach the truth of Torah. Salanter bases this surprising conclusion upon two arguments: the first relates to the method of study, and the second is based upon his intuitive understanding of the psyche of the student.

We have seen above that one means of arriving at the truth of Torah is speculative ability, built upon logical acuity by which the student is able to create complex halakhic constructions. Since the student who wishes to remain faithful to the literal truth of the text is left with extremely limited room to speculate, Salanter argues that the acquisition and refinement of this acuity is impossible except through study with *pilpul*.

The second justification for *pilpul* offered by Salanter relates to the psychological aspect of Torah study. Salanter posited the purity of the student's thought as one of the conditions for the discovery of the truth. He now argues that *pilpul* is almost essential in order for the student to achieve purity of thought. From his own experience, he concluded that it is very difficult for students to restrain their desire to exhibit their reasoning and acuity in Torah study to others. That being the case, total abstention from *pilpul*, accompanied by a deliberate effort to adhere to the literal truth alone, is in the final analysis liable to lead to self-deception. The students' intense desire to demonstrate mental sharpness may dominate their powers of reasoning and cause them to bend the truth toward their own will. Deliberate and controlled permission to engage in *pilpul* may therefore serve as a safety valve against this danger; the students find an outlet for the wish to show off their acuity, without harming the purity of their thought when they come to learn the truth of Torah. Moreover, the urge to exhibit one's brilliance is thereby guided toward a constructive and legitimate channnel; even the talmudic sages permitted one "to use *pilpul* . . . to sharpen one's mind."[17]

Having understood the arguments advanced by Salanter on behalf of *pilpul*,[18] let us return to a question that has meanwhile been left unresolved: What was the rival viewpoint concerning the proper path toward the truth of Torah, to which the mature Rabbi Israel took exception? In his youthful avoidance of *pilpul* and pursuit of "simplicity, brevity and the desire to seek the truth," was he adhering to a view of his own creation, or did he receive it from someone else? And if he received it from others, what was the source of this view and who upheld it?

The most likely conjecture is that the change that took place in Salanter's approach to study during his youth—namely, the attempt to avoid *pilpul* and to study in order to understand the truth of Torah alone—was rooted in the influence of the Gaon of Vilna and his disciples.[19] During the 1820s and '30s, the period during which Rabbi Israel crystallized his path as a Torah student, the influence of the

Volozhin yeshiva over the world of Lithuanian scholarship became increasingly powerful. Under the inspiration of Rabbi Hayyim of Volozhin, the yeshiva adopted the position of the Gaon in regard to *pilpul.*[20]

In formulating his own point of view concerning the proper way of study, Rabbi Israel saw himself in confrontation with the view to which he had adhered during his youth, under the influence of the school of the Gaon; yet in the final analysis, the Gaon's influence is reflected in the very quest for the path of discovering the truth of Torah. Moreover, like the Gaon, Salanter stressed the importance of extensive knowledge as a necessary prerequisite for properly interpreting the talmudic text. Nevertheless, the methodological approach developed by Rabbi Israel does take exception to the approach advocated by the Gaon and his followers. While the latter totally rejected the value of *pilpul*, Rabbi Israel accepted it as a didactic instrument—so long as it was used in a conscious and controlled way. Moreover, against the view that holds that the pursuit of truth requires one to refrain from clever interpretations and demands spiritual commitment to the truth, Rabbi Salanter proposes purity in the thought of the student. There is thus no longer any reason to be suspicious of or to reject mental acuity; on the contrary, it may even play an important role in clarifying the halakhah. As for the danger of excessive acuity—namely, that it may distract one from the truth in pursuit of honor and fame—this may be overcome by purity of thought. Such an original use of this concept could only be the creation of a unique person like Rabbi Israel Salanter, in whose personality the ethical thinker was combined with an outstanding talmudic scholar.

But even if our theory is correct—namely, that Salanter's understanding of the path toward the discovery of the truth of Torah was formulated in conscious confrontation with the viewpoint he himself had held during his youth under the influence of the school of the Gaon—the actual target against which Rabbi Israel's polemical arrows were addressed at the time he wrote his introduction to *Tevunah* was the Haskalah. Among those who adopted the reservations of the Gaon and his students with regard to *pilpul* were the spokesmen for the Haskalah, who proceeded to incorporate it within a systematic critique of traditional society. It is clear that the basic axioms and values underlying the Maskilic critique of *pilpul* profoundly differed from the Gaon's critique. That fact notwithstanding, the Haskalah spokesmen did not hesitate to cite that great figure.[21] Indeed, by the time that Salanter wrote his introduction to *Tevunah*, the role of *pilpul* had ceased to be a bone of contention between differing factions of the *lomdim*;

rather, the war against *pilpul* had become one of the symbols of the Haskalah.

Confirmation of that "war" appears in Salanter's homiletic interpretation of a talmudic saying in Sotah 22a: " 'My son, fear the Lord and the king, and meddle not with them that are given to change (*shonim*)' [Prov. 24:21]. Rabbi Yitzhak said, this refers to those who repeat (*shonim*) *halakhot*." Regarding this saying, Salanter wrote: " . . . also regarding the fear of God, this is the teaching of the true path. . . . Its basis is ability and purity, and then they will assist him from heaven. And with the *shonim*—i.e., those who repeat *halakhot* without Talmud—do not involve yourself."[22] Salanter draws a connection between study based upon ability and purity, which he describes by the title "the true path," and the fear of God. By contrast, the path that engages in study of halakhot without Talmud is presented as the polar opposite of "the true path" and of the fear of God. What is the nature of this method of study and where was it practiced? Salanter seems to have directed these remarks against the educational approach typical of the rabbinical seminaries, which stressed the study of *poskim* while neglecting the intense effort demanded in learning the talmudic source. It is doubtful whether he intended to attack the government-sponsored rabbinical seminaries of Vilna and Zhitomir of the 1840s, since their graduates had long failed to acquire a status of authority within traditional Jewry.[23] However, it may be that at that time Salanter had in mind the recently established rabbinical seminary in Breslau, reports of which were published in the Hebrew press.[24]

We may sum up by stating that Salanter's methodological discussion in the introduction to *Tevunah* reflects an educational approach concerning the desired method of cultivating talmudic scholars. The approach was shaped on the basis of Salanter's experience as a scholar and *rosh-yeshivah*, and was a kind of response to the tendencies of the Haskalah, as expressed in the rabbinical seminary. We may assume that the same approach also underlay Rabbi Israel's activity in the Nevyozer *kloiz*.

How Should Rabbis Be Trained?

The introduction to *Tevunah* did not refer explicitly to the question of the training of rabbis. Rabbi Israel's views on this issue were expressed in a fragmentary manner at the end of the 1870s and at the beginning of the '80s in the context of his involvement in the establishment of the *Kollel Ha-Perushim* in Kovna and the struggle against the renewed attempt to open a rabbinical seminary in Russia.[25]

Yet despite the fact that his later remarks were formulated in response to these events, the general principles inherent therein seem to me to suit the worldview expressed in the introduction to *Tevunah* and to complement it.

The qualifications expected by Salanter of one who wished to serve in the rabbinate may be inferred from the following remarks: ". . . And the highest level of Torah study is to know how to issue legal rulings in Israel properly and in accordance with the halakhah, based on the Talmud and *poskim* and without needing to search in the rulings of the *Aharonim*[26] [mainly sixteenth century commentaries] . . . .[27] These words imply a polemical barb against a certain alternative way of arriving at halakhic rulings. In fact, in one of the letters in which he explained his opposition to the establishment of a rabbinical seminary in Russia,[28] Salanter argued that the graduates of the rabbinical seminaries of Central and Western Europe are unable to arrive at halakhic rulings on the basis of the Talmud, relying entirely upon the *Shulhan 'arukh*, because these institutions do not give their students the requisite ability to learn in order to rule on the basis of the Talmud. This is presumably so because the practical character and structure of these institutions must of necessity bring about an excessive emphasis on study of the Codes literature at the expense of a more profound study of the Talmud and its commentaries, while ability and greatness in Torah study can only be developed through concentrated study of the Talmud, as is done in the framework of traditional institutions.

In two other letters relating to the rabbinical seminary,[29] Salanter argues that these institutions are deficient in that they fail to transmit to their students a sense of deep spiritual commitment toward the truth of Torah. This commitment, which insures that the *posek* (rabbinic decisor) will not distort his decision on the basis of extraneous factors, can only be acquired by years of study of *Torah li-shemah*—that is, not in order to earn the title of rabbi. Rabbinical seminaries, which are by their very nature intended to prepare their students for rabbinic office, are unable to convey this necessary quality.

A detailed description of the qualifications required of one who would serve as a rabbi, which both completes and further confirms the above, appears in the testimony of Rabbi Naphtali Amsterdam:

> [These are] the holy sayings which I received from my teacher, the righteous one . . . Rabbi Israel Salanter, may he live long and blessed years, as follows: [*lomdim* who are would-be rabbis] must be learned in all the words of the tannaim and amoraim, in the Babylonian Talmud, etc., and in the earlier and later *poskim*; [they must possess] acuity and clear intellect; and must

also have implanted and acquired in their souls the good qualities listed for a sage; and they need to have served the great
and known scholars (*talmidei hakhamim*) of their generation. . . . [30]

We thus know that Rabbi Salanter presented anyone seeking to
prepare for rabbinic office with three essential conditions: (1) to acquire
extensive knowledge both of the tractates of the Talmud and of the
classical medieval *poskim*, because an halakhic ruling may not be based
upon the later *poskim* alone; (2) the development of ability in study—
that is, the intellectual ability to draw an analogy between one law and
another and to derive one thing from another; and (3) the cultivation
of ethical qualities that guarantee loyalty to the truth of the Torah. One
is struck here by the correspondence between these three demands and
the fundaments enumerated by Rabbi Israel in the introduction to
Tevunah as prerequisites for uncovering the truth of Torah, prompting
speculation that, even though his remarks in the introduction to *Tevunah* were formulated in general terms, without any specific reference
to the training of rabbis, he nevertheless had this subject in mind as
well. This theory is supported by the fact that there is a certain polemical
note against the rabbinical seminaries found in the introduction to
Tevunah. If our theory is correct, the approach toward the training of
rabbis that appears explicitly in Rabbi Israel's later expressions of opinion, and that also lay behind his remarks in the introduction to *Tevunah*,
likewise guided his educational activity in the Nevyozer *kloiz*.

Salanter's approach to the training of rabbis may be summarized
in a formula that contains an element of paradox: The preferred way
to train young students to acquire those elements needed for them to
become halakhic authorities is to educate them specifically in the framework that is not intended to train rabbis—neither in terms of its declared
purpose nor in terms of the structure of the studies practiced therein.
It follows from this that the descriptions, both of Rosenfeld and of other
authors, according to which Salanter ran a kind of institution for training rabbis in the Nevyozer *kloiz*, does not fit his approach to this issue
at all. On the contrary, we may assume that in this *kloiz* they studied
Torah for its own sake—that is, not for the sake of the rabbinate—with
the emphasis being placed upon acquiring expertise in Talmud, and
not upon the study of *poskim*.

How then did Rabbi Israel perceive the transition from *Torah li-
shemah* in the pure sense to study directed toward teaching halakhah?
With all the importance of knowledge of Talmud, one who wishes to
serve in a rabbinic office nevertheless needs to know and understand
the literature of the Codes. The following remark of Rabbi Isaac Blazer

provides a hint of an answer to this question. "Generally speaking, he held that the matter of the teaching of halakhah (i.e., the rabbinate) in our generation is the living basis of the law of Torah. . . . And in particular he guided his best students to pay attention to become competent in their studies as to how to rule on halakhic matters, to be prepared when occasion demanded."[31] This testimony does not refer in any way to an institutional framework whose main concern was the training of rabbis, but to the directing and guiding of individual students to concentrate upon the literature of the *poskim* in order to become qualified for the rabbinate.

We may therefore summarize by saying that Salanter distinguished between two stages in the cultivation and education of young *lomdim*. The earlier and more protracted of the two is that of study for its own sake—that is, Torah study that both in terms of its declared purpose and its contents and style is not specifically intended to prepare rabbis. This stage is not limited to future rabbis, as the commandment of Torah study applies to every Jew. During this stage, which begins in the years of youth and young adulthood, one must first acquire wide erudition in the talmudic literature, as knowledge attained during one's youth is not lost even with the passing of time. Together with the acquisition of erudition, and in a gradual manner suitable to the age and intellectual maturity of the student, one begins to cultivate certain intellectual tools in the young person; one may make use of *pilpul* toward this end. Together with acquisition of erudition and the development of the ability to study, the young students must also engage in character improvement. Only after these young adults have devoted years to studying *Torah li-shemah*, after they have acquired erudition and acuity, and after they have made efforts to perfect their character, are they ready to move on to the second stage, intended for those meant to engage in the teaching of halakhah. At this stage, the students must acquire extensive knowledge of the literature of the *poskim*, both classical and later, must serve scholars who engage in ruling of halakhah, and must learn how to activate their theoretical knowledge with the aim of interpreting and applying the halakhah in practice. There is no special framework needed for this stage, as by then each student is able to study independently or with a partner.

Guidance of the *Lomdim*

While no direct evidence is extant concerning the study arrangements practiced in the Nevyozer *kloiz*, an indication of Salanter's path among the students of the *kloiz* is included in several letters written at the beginning of the 1860s, containing personal advice and guidance relating to Torah study and ethical education. These letters were addressed to Salanter's nephew, a young man studying independently, and to his disciple, Rabbi Isaac Blazer, who was preparing for the rabbinate. The letters thus reflect Rabbi Israel's way of directing the guidance of each of the aforementioned stages.

Salanter's four letters to his nephew,[32] Aryeh Leib ben Yedidyah Lipkin, constitute only a part of an extensive correspondence in the course of which the young man sought the guidance of his famous uncle. The latter qualified his readiness to answer Aryeh Leib's questions with the caveat that "it is difficult to fix general rules pertaining to the appropriate way to study, which must of necessity vary from one individual to another in accordance with their personal characteristics."[33] For this reason, he confined himself to general instructions and did not go into detail, and while following his individualistic approach, it seems likely that he gave more personalized and detailed advice to his students at the Nevyozer *kloiz*, whose personalities and talents he knew from close up, than he was able to offer to his nephew.

In all of the letters to his nephew, Salanter stresses the importance of acquiring broad erudition of the sources: ". . . for the acquisition of erudition is the pivot around which everything else revolves, other than your fear [of God] and your behavior."[34] This is so because the period of youth, during which the student is not yet subject to the distractions and responsibilities of adult life and enjoys free use of his time, is the most suitable one for this goal, and "If not now, when?" [Avot 1:14]. Salanter therefore instructs Aryeh Leib to give the highest priority to study oriented toward the acquisition of erudition, "and at this time the acquisition of fear of God and of [mental] acumen are secondary compared to this great thing. . . . "[35] Salanter writes the following concerning the nature of study whose goal is the acquisition of erudition: "Study without excessive preciseness, even if at times the meaning (*peshat*) is not clear, [and] simply repeat [the passage being studied] several times to remember the basic elements; and perhaps it is best to [study] simply the *gemara* [talmudic text] with Rashi's commentary."[36] In order to assure the continuous flow of one's study, it is preferable that one temporarily forgo excessively fine distinctions in the *peshat* of the *gemara*, as well as the complex scholastic difficulties and solutions of the Tosafists. In this kind of study the emphasis is on quantity and repetition. In order to increase the amount of erudition acquired, Rabbi Israel recommends that young Aryeh Leib set himself a certain quantitative goal every few months. In addition, he repeatedly asks his nephew to inform him explicitly of what he has accomplished, the method of encouraging a student by requesting ongoing reports being typical of Rabbi Salanter. It seems likely that he acted similarly with his students in the *kloiz*.

In addition to study for the purpose of acquiring broad erudition, Salanter told Aryeh Leib to set aside time for two other lessons: to be devoted to "*gemara* with Tosafot, understanding the *peshat* exactly," and to be devoted to "close study of some subject (it does not matter if it is a book of responsa), or in the same tractate in which you are studying *gemara* with Tosafot. . . . "[37] It is clear that in both of these lessons the emphasis is upon greater depth in the material studied, and that they are intended to develop the intellectual tools of the young scholar. In the former case, the goal is accomplished by close attention to the straightforward sense of the *gemara*—to understand the progress of the back-and-forth argumentation on the page of Talmud, in all its details and niceties, without leaving even a trace of uncertainty or unclarity. This is combined with systematic study of the Tosafot, the nature of which is to broaden and deepen the terms of discussion through comparison of the subject at hand with similar matters, or similar-appearing matters, from other tractates. Understanding of the difficulties raised by the Tosafists and the solutions developed by them is bound to cultivate analytic ability in the young students by means of which they will be able to ask questions and propose solutions on their own.

In that form of study known as *'iyyun* (study in depth), the qualitative element becomes the decisive one. Here the student may go beyond the confines of the immediate page being studied to grapple with the overall subject extended over several tractates. One of the possible directions of study *be-'iyyun* may then be to attempt to interpret all of the material pertaining to the subject in terms of an overall view. Nor does Salanter reject the possibility of studying a volume of responsa as the subject matter of study *be-'iyyun*. In this case, the young scholars follow the reasoning of the *posek* in deriving their legal decision from the sources, and thereby begin to cultivate their own ability to rule on halakhic matters. It must be emphasized that, by its very nature, study *be-'iyyun* constitutes a framework in which there is relatively extensive play for the students' independent creative powers. It follows that the character and direction of study *be-'iyyun* will differ from one student to another in accordance with the student's available tools and personal inclinations. Another piece of advice that Salanter gives to his nephew is the following: " *'Iyyun* should be performed in moderation, each day a little bit, and at times [you may] do more depending upon circumstance." Thus, Salanter does not insist upon stubborn adherence to a rigid schedule of study. Even though the proportion of *'iyyun* ought to be relatively small, it may be increased at times, when the heart of the student is drawn toward it. One should also mention that, in addition to the directives he gave Aryeh Leib concerning study arrangements, Salanter advised him concerning the acquisition of *yir'ah*; this area is discussed below.

As previously suggested, the letters Salanter sent in the early 1860s to his disciple Isaac Blazer may be seen as an example of the guidance to those preparing for rabbinic office.[38] As in the case of the letters to his young nephew, Salanter incorporated advice and instructions both regarding his program of study and concerning the area of Mussar. With regard to the method and contents of study, the basic message of these three letters is identical with what is stated explicitly in his later writings, in the account of Rabbi Naphtali Amsterdam, and in what we have found alluded to in the introduction to *Tevunah*: namely, that the tools required by one who wishes to be qualified to issue halakhic rulings include comprehensive erudition of the Talmud and the Codes literature, intellectual acuity, and those ethical qualities that insure the purity of halakhic considerations against the interference of the inclinations. To this is added the need to serve talmudic scholars.

Salanter was not content with offering guidance to those of his disciples who inclined toward the rabbinic office at their own initiative, but he also made efforts to convince those students whom he considered suitable to follow this path. This is indicated in the following testimony of Rabbi Blazer:

> He never in his life took upon himself the yoke of the rabbinate.
> . . . However, he did not advocate this path [that is, his own]
> to his students, for in general he believed that the institution of
> the rabbinate is the living foundation of the law of Torah in our
> generation. . . . He particularly guided his best students to pay
> heed that they concentrate in their studies upon [acquiring the
> skills relating to] halakhah [the issuing of decisions, particular
> to the office of rabbi], so that they might be ready when [an]
> occasion presents itself. Some of his best disciples, who imagined
> that they would have the strength to overcome all obstacles and
> difficulties and to sanctify their lives to be holy to God without
> taking upon themselves the yoke of the rabbinate, asked him
> for his views and his advice, [namely,] whether it is [considered]
> *Torah li-shemah* for one to learn those subjects [required for] the
> rabbinate. Our master and teacher of blessed memory answered
> them that, "There is no greater [*Torah*] *li-shemah* than that, and
> you have been mistaken by imagining . . . that you shall be able
> to withstand the trial. When the hour presses upon you, Heaven
> forbid, due to the need to earn a livelihood for the members of

your household, all your calculations will come to nought. And then, not only will necessity force you to take upon yourselves the yoke of the rabbinate, but you will not yet be whole and perfected [that is, adequately prepared for it]. . . . We [therefore] find that the purpose of study is not [to enter] the rabbinate, but that . . . one's study for the goal of the rabbinate may be *li-shemah*, so that when the time comes and necessity forces itself upon one, he will not Heaven forbid lead the public astray [that is, through lack of erudition]. . . . And there is no greater *li-shemah* than this.[39]

On the basis of this description, it would appear that Salanter's disciples were reluctant to study toward the goal of the rabbinate, because they adhered to the value of *Torah li-shemah* in the sense of study that was not directed toward earning a livelihood, an ideal embodied in Rabbi Salanter himself. Yet in his response to his students Salanter raised a pragmatic consideration: As the circumstances of life would force his students to accept rabbinic office even against their will, it is preferable that they be qualified for it and capable of issuing halakhic rulings without erring. In effect, in the traditional talmudic manner, Rabbi Israel answers the difficulty of his students with a subtle dialectical distinction: By studying *poskim* at this time, they are not specifically preparing for the office of rabbinate, but they will be thrust into such offices in any event; the study of *poskim* is only intended to prevent them from erring in rendering halakhic decisions, and is as such *Torah li-shemah*. One may assume that the above reason—namely, the exigencies of earning a livelihood—was not Salanter's only motivation in directing his best students to the rabbinate. One may imagine that he also hoped that his students, whose merits and talents he knew well, would be active within and on behalf of the community. However, he did not wish to put forward the sense of a public calling or responsibility as a value competing with the study of Torah "for its own sake," because of the great value that he attributed to such Torah study. This was Salanter's approach during the 1850s, when he headed the *kloiz* in Kovna. However, over the course of the years and changes in circumstances, he was to coin the formula that "at this time" study for the purpose of rabbinate is in itself study *li-shemah*.

15
Mussar Education in the Nevyozer *Kloiz*

THE UNIQUENESS of the Nevyozer *kloiz* in comparison with other Torah institutions of the period lay in its combination of Mussar education with Torah study, which Salanter saw as a necessary condition of the quest for wholeness in the Divine service. Moreover, as we have already observed, he thought that the ethical level of scholars had a direct effect upon the quality of their functioning as halakhic authorities. We may assume that Salanter's activity in the *kloiz* had a public aim in addition to his wish to raise a generation of God-fearing talmudic scholars: Namely, he hoped to train spiritual leaders who could influence the wider public in the spirit of Mussar doctrine. Indeed, several of the students at the *kloiz* later emerged as leaders of the Mussar movement.

One may distinguish two complementary channels in Salanter's Mussar activity in the *kloiz*: The first consisted of activity carried out within a group framework—that is, in the presence of all or a portion of the student body; the other was expressed in the individual guidance that Salanter gave to various students. At the center of the collective activity stood his sermons, described by Rabbi Isaac Blazer:

> In addition to preaching in public before the congregation, he
> would specifically preach before his students. These sermons
> were not based upon the expounding of [biblical] verses and
> the harmonization of *midrashim*, but upon matters which he
> conceived and thought of in his own heart: profound elucida-
> tions of the ways of service of God, may He be blessed, and
> [concerning] retribution and the ways of the traits [of the human
> soul]. And when he would preach for a number of hours, he
> would at times embody some thought in the idiom of the Bible
> or some Rabbinic dictum. The power of his speech was awe-

some, and in nearly all his sermons, he never failed to mention [the motif of Divine] recompense and punishment.[1]

It therefore becomes clear that the tendency toward intellectual acuity, expressed in the application of the forms of halakhic deliberation to aggadic material, either disappeared or was greatly reduced in importance in Salanter's sermons to his students. The change is understandable, because the learned nature of his earlier sermons, which were intended to attract *ba'alei batim* and to enhance Salanter's authority in their eyes, was no longer needed when preaching to the *lomdim* in the *kloiz*. It should therefore not be surprising if there was a greater tendency toward direct, explicit ethical exhortation in these sermons.

Rabbi Blazer relates that Salanter's sermons generally continued for a number of hours,[2] illuminating the point that their purpose was not to develop fresh interpretations of Torah, but rather to instill in the audience certain moods and feelings. The length of these sermons evidently stemmed from Rabbi Israel's assumption that, through repetition and use of appropriate rhetorical techniques, one could elicit change in the souls of those listening. One means Salanter believed effective was the use of homilies and metaphors taken from everyday life, thus concretizing abstract ideas and converting them into a motivating force within the human soul. Another rhetorical device advocated by Salanter in connection with ethical education was the reliance upon a style containing some elements of song and poetry. While such a style would be totally out of place in the context of an halakhic discussion, in which the intellectual judgment must be safeguarded against the influence of emotional impulses, in respect of character improvement "the opposite is the case, for it is almost impossible to represent and to explain them without thinking about the way of [poetry], whose basic aim is to awaken the powers of the soul which depend upon it."[3]

Rabbi Blazer tells us that Salanter's sermons included "profound investigations into the ways of Divine service." This evidently refers to Rabbi Israel's reflections upon the human soul, the Evil Impulse, its manifestations and tactics, and the various means of struggle with the appetite and on behalf of the correction of one's character. An additional subject included by Salanter in his sermons is indicated in the following testimony of Rabbi Naphtali Amsterdam:

> Throughout the summer he preached to us every Sabbath morning. . . . The essence of his words of Mussar to us was that a person must labor during the years he is studying—that is, during his youth . . . in order to learn the Torah of truth, that

is, without any tendency whatsoever towards his own will. For
without this, when a person attains [a position of] halakhic
authority, there is no end of evil and obstacles, and this is indeed
a grave matter and one of great principle, upon which all the
attributes [of the person's character] depend.[4]

One of the major goals of character education was the acquisition of
the psychological ability to learn "the Torah of truth"—that is, that
form of study in which objective, rational judgment is protected against
the subjective, emotional tendency.

While Salanter usually preached to his students once a week,[5]
during the month of Ellul (an intense, solemn period preceding the
beginning of the new year) and the Ten Days of Repentance he
preached almost daily, concentrating upon the motif of repentance.[6]
One subject that appeared in nearly all his sermons was the theme of
reward and punishment. His investigations into Divine Providence were
in no way motivated by theosophic curiosity, but were entirely intended
to transform the abstract awareness of the principle of reward and
punishment into a force motivating the human psyche and human
behavior. Thus, he presumably repeated the argument that the mag-
nitude of punishment that awaited a person as the result of a given act
of transgression is greater than the pleasure involved in performing that
same transgression. Salanter likewise repeated those discussions that
argued that the degree of recompense and punishment is determined
by the amount of psychological effort invested by the person in performing a mitzvah and in refraining from sin. This relativistic-individ-
ualistic understanding of reward and punishment is likewise intended
to make fear of punishment an effective factor in every case in which
the individual confronts an ethical test.

An additional example of an idea intended to stimulate the fear of
punishment, and instructive as to the contents of Salanter's sermons,
appears in one of the letters he wrote to his students:

> That person whom we cannot call "I," this "I" is the subject
> who speaks, who thinks, who desires, who struggles to attain
> his desires. It is he who is hidden in the physical matter of the
> body so that, when its powers are negated, that is, when it dies,
> this "I" still has vitality and strength—abstracted from the ma-
> terial world, namely, the connection of the soul, which is the
> "I," with matter, which is the body—in such a manner that this
> "I" is ready for pain and pleasure, for good and evil, for terrible
> and awesome suffering, or for marvelous pleasure beyond com-
> parison, far higher than the pain and pleasure of which this "I"
> is capable in this world, while connected with the body.[7]

Underlying these words is the suspicion that people may be uncon-
cerned about the reward and punishment awaiting them in the next
world, thinking that the pleasure and suffering familiar to us in our
earthly existence only apply to the earthly "I" composed of body and
soul. Salanter argues, to the contrary, the "I" is capable of feeling pain
and pleasure at a far higher level when it is separated from the body
than in its earthly life.

Through these sermons, Salanter hoped to implant in his disciples
a mood of self-dissatisfaction, severe self-criticism, and ceaseless striving
for ethical and spiritual improvement. Rabbi Simhah Zissel Ziv remarks
in the name of Rabbi Israel Salanter:

> It is certainly understood that a man is not considered as a
> human being if he lives a life of ease and does not labor in fear,
> for this is the whole duty of man. . . . But so long as a person
> is living a life of tranquility in the service of Creator, he ought
> to know that he has surely shaken off and is empty of the service
> of God, may He be blessed . . . for it is impossible that a person
> not daily encounter circumstances in which his desire and [the
> command] of the Torah conflict with one another. . . . [8]

Ease, spiritual tranquility, self-satisfaction, and the pursuit of pleasure
are incompatible with the service of God. By the very nature of the
human soul, and by the nature of the world in which we live, it is
impossible that there not occur severe conflicts in one's life between
personal appetite and the command of the Torah. Thus, tranquility and
self-satisfaction are only possible for one who progressively sinks into
the depths of sin without being aware of it.

On the basis of various testimonies of Salanter's students, we may
conclude that his sermons had a fixed structure. The first part, delivered
calmly, was devoted to various explanations and theoretical discussions
of the ways of Divine service. The turning point occurred about the
middle of the sermon, when the theoretical speculations were supplanted by words of reproof and spiritual awakening, with Salanter
becoming increasingly excited and the atmosphere more and more
tense; the tension reached its peak with an emotional outpouring of all
those present.

Let us attempt, on the basis of Isaac Blazer's description, to follow
the structure of Salanter's sermons:

> When we were privileged to stand before him here in the holy
> community [that is, Kovna] . . . there was a long period during
> which our teacher, of blessed memory, isolated himself all week
> long in self-abstention and seclusion in the nearby town of
> Aleksot, across the River Neimen, and would only come to his

home here in the city on the holy Sabbath. Then some of his
closest disciples would go to him once a week to his place of
seclusion, a full *minyan* of ten. When he had recited the Afternoon Prayer, our master wrapped himself in a *tallit*, and began
to preach to us concerning the fear of God, may He be blessed,
as he was wont to do, and at times he would preach for several
hours. In the middle of the sermon he would begin to say words
of reproof and spiritual awakening with great excitement, until
our hearts melted, and he would weep a great deal. He would
repeatedly arouse us to prepare ourselves to beseech mercy from
Him [God], may He be blessed, concerning spiritual matters.
Then, in the middle of the "awakening," he would recite a verse
in praise of God, and then some verse imploring mercy, such as
"Return us to You O God [and we shall return, renew our days
as of old"—Lam. 5:21] or "A pure heart [create in me O God,
and a new spirit renew within me"—Ps. 51:12], etc. And we
prayed together with him in public concerning the spiritual Evil
Impulse, to remove the heart of stone from our flesh and to
purify our hearts to serve Him in truth.[9]

We do not have any additional information regarding Salanter's
period of seclusion and self-abstention in the Kovna suburb of Aleksot.
This withdrawal from society was evidently intended to serve as an
appropriate framework for a concentrated effort at self-perfection and
ethical improvement. As an educator, Rabbi Israel did not see himself
as one who had already attained the ideal ethical level, which he now
wished to convey to his students. On the contrary: the demand he
addressed to his students for lack of complacency and self-criticism was
one of the roots of Salanter's own psychological being. Therefore, when
he moved to the stage of reproof and rebuke in his sermons, he included
himself together with all the others present. This was the secret of the
emotional force that characterized his sermons, and from this flowed
their power to sweep along and overwhelm all those present. The
authentic nature of the emotional arousal achieved by Salanter in the
course of his sermons may be seen by the fact that he was careful to
restrict them to his students alone.[10] Evidently, he thought it inappropriate for a talmudic scholar and leader to reach this degree of psychological exposure and self-revelation in front of the broader public.

In the second half of a sermon Rabbi Israel moved on to "words
of reproof and awakening," including the enumeration of specific matters in which his students were prone to stumble.[11] He infused his
listeners with a mood of fear of God, not only by the contents of these
words, but by the way in which he raised his voice, the use of a special
melody, outbursts of tears, and the like, so that one of his students
reports that "the fear of God was tangible to the senses. . . . "[12] The

accumulated tension both reached its peak and found release when, following his words of arousal, Rabbi Israel chanted loudly and in a doleful voice and with a heartbreaking melody, such verses as "Return us to You, O God, and we shall return, renew our days as of old," which his listeners repeated after him in a loud voice. This prayerful reciting and repeating of verses provided an outlet for the tempest that simmered in the hearts of those present, offering an outlet for feelings of purification and cleansing, as it gave expression to the longing of those present for ethical perfection.

As stated above, Salanter's Mussar educational activities were also expressed by providing personal guidance and advice. Rabbi Blazer's testimony about this is instructive: "Among his finest students whom he knew to be vessels capable and fit to receive his influence, he gave of his very being, devoting time to speak with them and teaching them the way of God and of desirable attributes, and to teach them to exercise prudence in the Torah and in the pure fear of God."[13] It is thus clear that the process of guidance was not divided equally among all his students in the *kloiz*; it seems reasonable to assume that the degree of personal guidance was determined, not only by the considerations of the teacher, but also by the degree of interest and persistence exhibited by the students. Presumably some students were particularly attracted by the subject of ethical perfection and turned to Salanter frequently to seek his advice in their personal striving for ethical improvement. Thus, particularly close relations were forged between Salanter and these students, as implied in Rabbi Blazer's above-cited description, of those who went to hear Rabbi Israel's sermons in Aleksot, referred to as "those students who were particularly close to him."

One of the subjects that lay in the center of the personal guidance given by Salanter to his students was that of *tikkun ha-middot* (correction of personality traits).[14] As explained below, Salanter held that *tikkun ha-middot* is particularly suited to the period of a person's youth, since the young psyche is more amenable to influences that can shape it and those who do not yet bear the yoke of earning a livelihood can more easily marshal the leisure and psychic energy necessary for *tikkun ha-middot*. In addition, Salanter thought that *tikkun ha-middot* is especially needed by those youths who study all day in the *bet midrash*, as there is a greater danger, in light of their intellectual ability, that their negative traits may come to dominate their intellect, which they will use as a vehicle for justifying evil ways. Moreover, as we have already seen above, *tikkun ha-middot* had a special importance for those who were to serve as rabbis in the future. Purity of thought—that is, the grounding of halakhic judgment upon purely intellectual considerations protected against emotional tendencies—also falls under the rubric of *tikkun ha-middot*.

The guidance Salanter gave to his students in this matter bore an individual stamp because "each person, and particularly every great person, is a world unto himself according to his powers, the powers of his intellect, the character of his *middot* and of his impressionability, the state of his affairs, etc."[15] For this reason, Salanter took care not to suggest fixed and rigid patterns of ethical correction to his students. When his student Isaac Blazer wrote to him, requesting detailed instructions in the area of ethical perfection, Rabbi Israel replied: "There is no established path for Mussar for a great person like yourself . . . and it would almost be a loss to do so, Heaven forbid."[16] Each person must find the way toward ethical perfection and the education of the *middot* on the basis of personal life experience. While it is possible in the realm of healing of the body, for example, to draw conclusions from the body of one person and apply them to another, this is not the case in healing of the soul—that is, ethical improvement.[17] Therefore, the fixing of rigid guidelines is of greater danger than it is a blessing. Further on in that same letter, Salanter suggests that he postpone the discussion of those questions that trouble him until they can meet and discuss them face to face. He evidently thought that, within the framework of a conversation, he could assist his student to formulate the solutions required in light of his own life experience and his particular circumstances at that time.

Among the methods adopted by Salanter's students in their attempts at ethical perfection, an important place was occupied by Mussar study *be-hitpa'alut*. In terms of the nature and aim of this activity, there was no difference between what Salanter taught his own students and what he taught the *ba'alei batim*, but there was a difference in terms of the framework within which this study took place. While Salanter attempted to institutionalize the Mussar study of the *ba'alei batim* by fixing the time, between *Minhah* and *Ma'ariv*, and by fixing the place, the Mussar house, there is testimony that this framework was not for *lomdim*:

> . . . . when our master and teacher Rabbi Israel Salanter set up Mussar houses, he did so for the *ba'alei batim* who engage in business and trade, but he did not establish this at all for those who study Torah, for each of the *lomdim* is able to study [Mussar books] by himself, and need not do so in a group. . . . [18]

This testimony of Rabbi Gershon Mendel Ziv, a close friend of Salanter,[19] was published during the stormy controversy of the 1890s surrounding the Mussar yeshivot, and indicates that Rabbi Gershon intended to draw a distinction between the practice of the Mussar yeshivot, which established a fixed and rigid framework of daily Mussar study, and the practice of Salanter, who intended fixed Mussar study groups specifically for *ba'alei batim*.

Though Salanter evidently thought that fixed study in a group, which serves as a means of stimulus and encouragement, was specifically needed by *ba'alei batim*, full-time Torah students who spent most hours of the day in the "tent of Torah" would find no particular difficulty in setting aside a brief period for Mussar study. Seemingly there were no fixed hours in the Nevyozer *kloiz* during which all of the students engaged in Mussar study; this study was of an individual character, and each one engaged in it at the time and to the extent that he found proper.

Salanter was conscious of the danger that time devoted to Mussar study was liable to impinge upon the realm of Torah study proper, and he therefore warned his students, "[D]o not cut into the study of Talmud and *poskim* because of the Mussar study, save during the Ten Days of Repentance. . . . "[20] We may conjecture that Rabbi Israel advised his students to fix a limited amount of time to Mussar study, while the rest of the day was to be devoted to Torah study.

Further light is shed upon Mussar education in the Nevyozer *kloiz* in a biographical sketch of one of Salanter's disciples, Rabbi Yeruham Yehudah Leib Perlman, later known as the Minsker Gadol (the great one from Minsk). The biographer records as follows concerning his practice during the 1850s: ". . . and he devoted himself to the Torah day and night, and subjected himself to privation and fasts. He fasted nearly all week long, and at night did not sleep on a mattress and pillow. He never slept [more than] three hours, but got up and strengthened himself like a lion for his assiduous [study], studying aloud and with a pleasant voice. . . . "[21] It is not likely that Salanter instructed his students to subject their bodies to mortification; on the contrary, in several places we find that he warned them to take care of their health. Rabbi Yeruham's self-imposed ascetic regime would rather seem to be an anomaly within the framework of the *kloiz*. Nevertheless, these self-afflictions do reflect the spiritual tension and the mood of seeking ethical perfection that characterized the *kloiz*.

The drive toward ethical perfection, which left its mark upon the atmosphere in the *kloiz*, was likewise expressed in the discussions of *yir'ah* and Mussar conducted by the young students among themselves. There was no set framework for these exchanges, which took place in a spontaneous manner among friends. During the course of these conversations, the students exchanged personal experiences in acquiring *yir'ah* and *tikkun ha-middot*, and stimulated one another to make further efforts in these areas.[22] Salanter himself claimed that it was desirable to have a friend to assist one in the process of ethical education, to play the role of critic and admonisher, because the ability to uncover the weak points in one's own behavior is limited. Salanter also held that the group has the power, and it is indeed one of its functions, to serve as a stimulus for the ethical perfection of each individual therein, not only by means of social pressure, which stimulates the individual to act in accordance with the norms of the group, but also by means of personal contacts, in the course of which all members of the group, by virtue of their own particular traits, endeavor to influence the deviant individuals.[23] It therefore should not be surprising that discussion of matters of Mussar was part of the atmosphere among Salanter's disciples.

We learn of the profound impact of Salanter's personal inspiration as a moving factor toward ethical perfection, as well as the function fulfilled in this respect by the circle formed in the Nevyozer *kloiz*, from the letters of a number of his disciples. I refer to Rabbi Isaac Blazer, Rabbi Simhah Zissel Ziv, and Rabbi Naphtali Amsterdam, who were among his closest disciples during the '50s and were later to become leading figures in the Mussar movement. In letters written by these three to one another, some from the 1860s and others from later periods, they repeatedly complained about the spiritual isolation they felt as a result of their distance from their teacher and the break-up of their circle. Thus, for example, in a letter to Rabbi Isaac Blazer, Rabbi Zissel wrote: "[S]ince the time we left the city of Kovna there is no one with whom to [confer] for advice and counsel and knowledge. Our teacher, long may he live, is far away from us; of friends who might listen, this one is there and this one is there; and who knows if . . . we have not, Heaven forbid, lost the way. . . . "[24] Rabbi Amsterdam writes in a similar vein: "[F]or because a person is alone and separated from his friends as we are, there descends upon him a torpor of matter and of the Impulse . . . and he becomes oblivious of his duty, but each time he sees or hears from his good friend it awakens him from his deep slumber."[25]

It would be a mistake to interpret these and similar remarks merely as expressions of nostalgia for the human surroundings in which the authors spent their youth. These letters reflect the intense spiritual effort demanded of these students, who wished to continue to advance in the path of ethical education shown them by their teacher after they had left his environment and were dispersed in different places. This effort was required, both by the very nature of ethical perfection according to Rabbi Israel's teaching, and because this path was conceived to be anomalous within the world of Lithuanian scholars. For this reason, the students attempted to continue the sense of social communion based upon their common relation to Salanter's teaching, even if only by exchanging letters. Through these letters, they continued their conversations on the subjects of Mussar and *yir'ah*, which had previously played such an important role in the atmosphere of the *kloiz*. They likewise attempted to be in one another's presence for a few weeks every year in order to engage in self-improvement.[26]

Salanter's educational activity in the Nevyozer *kloiz* was of great importance for the continued growth of the Mussar movement. This *kloiz* served as a training ground for those disciples who adhered to the Mussar doctrine and were to act in the future toward its penetration into the world of the yeshivot. Moreover, in a certain sense the *kloiz* in the 1850s was a kind of archetype of the Mussar yeshivot that were to come into existence at a later date. The Mussar sermon as shaped by Salanter during his activity in the *kloiz*, Mussar study with *hitpa'alut*, and the informal discussions on matters of Mussar were all characteristics of the later Mussar yeshivot, although those things that had a fresh and spontaneous character in the Nevyozer *kloiz* underwent a process of institutionalization, to become fixed and rigid forms in the later Mussar yeshivot.

PART FIVE

The Period of Wanderings, 1857–83

16
Salanter in the Jewish Communities of Western Europe

IN 1857, Rabbi Israel Salanter left Lithuania for Prussia. From then until the end of his life, he lived for varying periods of time in a number of different cities in Germany and, at the beginning of the 1880s, resided in Paris for two years. Throughout this time, he periodically returned to Lithuania, primarily Vilna and Kovna, his visits there lasting for several weeks or even months.

What motivated Salanter to leave Lithuania, where he had been active for so many years and where he enjoyed public recognition and considerable influence? What inspired him to leave his family, his students, and his friends, and wander to a strange land whose language and customs were unfamiliar?

Rabbi Israel originally traveled to Germany for medical reasons. He suffered from depression, and friends advised him to go to consult with the doctors in Halberstadt. While there Salanter stayed at the home of the wealthy Emil Hirsch, who attempted to hasten his recovery. After spending about half a year in Halberstadt, Salanter decided not to return to Lithuania, but to remain there in order to devote himself to activities on behalf of the Jewish communities in Germany.[1] To the surprise elicited by this decision, he responded with the following homily:

> When the horses begin to gallop wildly . . . down the hill, it is totally impossible to stop them in the middle of the mountain . . . but only after the horses have gone all the way downhill can they be stopped and calmed down. The same is true of the direction of communities. . . . In the great cities of Russia, the communities are galloping down the mountain, and are now in the middle of the descent, so it is impossible to bring about any order in them. But the communities abroad have already

reached the bottom of the hill, so that it is now possible to halt them and to put them in place.[2]

His remarks concerning the difficulty of halting horses galloping down the slope may reflect a certain disappointment or frustration as to the limited extent of the spread of the Mussar movement. During the years that Salanter actively pursued that goal, he had hoped that it would be possible to halt the tendencies that threatened the tradition. The gap between his expectations in this regard and their realization in life may have been one of the factors that influenced his decision to leave Lithuania. In any event, what primarily attracted him and motivated him to live in Germany seems to have been the challenge to reconstruct the values and forms of tradition in those communities.

From 1858 to 1860, Rabbi Israel lived in Koenigsberg. The Jewish community in this city had been engaged for some time in a fierce struggle between supporters of religious reform and its opponents. The Orthodox camp was headed by the rabbi of the community, Jacob Zvi Mecklenburg,[3] alongside whom Salanter worked, devoting most of his energy to the organization of informal educational activities. His main concern was the Jewish students who studied at the local university, to whom he devoted special lectures in Bible and Talmud.[4] These lessons were presumably totally different from the lectures that Salanter had given to the yeshiva students in Lithuania, as here he was teaching young people who were intellectually alert and possessed a broad general education, but in many cases lacked even an elementary background in Judaism. The attempt to fill in the gaps in their Jewish education, and particularly to implant in them a sense of commitment to a religiously observant way of life, would appear to have required techniques of education with which he had had no previous experience.

In 1860, Salanter moved from Koenigsberg to Memel. He was to reside in this city for a longer period of time than in any other place within the borders of Germany. This may perhaps be explained in light of the fact that many of the Jews of Memel were emigrants from Poland and Russia.[5] Their migration to Memel came about due to its geographic proximity to Lithuania as well as to the economic possibilities available there. Upon being uprooted from the communities of their origin and settling within Prussia, the Jews of Memel were exposed to the same processes and tendencies that had eroded the tradition in other Jewish communities of Germany.[6] With wide opportunities for activity, Salanter attempted to develop frameworks of traditional community life based upon the Lithuanian model; however, as the community in Memel was relatively new and lacking in traditions, he took upon himself the challenge of creating these practically from scratch, attracting a considerable community of admirers in the process.[7]

Salanter found a variety of avenues for activity in Memel,[8] some directed to the community as a whole, others directed toward specific groups and individuals within it. Every Friday evening, he gave a sermon in the main *bet midrash* of the city concerning the Torah section of the week. Though the interpretation of the scriptural reading gave him a framework and justification for engaging in words of reproof and Mussar, he could not give the same kind of Mussar talks in Memel that he had been used to deliver in Lithuania in earlier years, as he now needed to react to such phenomena as the desecration of the Sabbath[9] and other manifestations of public abandonment of the mitzvot. Salanter's custom of preaching in public continued for many years, and when his powers began to wane due to old age, so that he could no longer preach every Sabbath, he made an effort to continue to speak in public during the month of Ellul and on the Days of Awe.

Salanter devoted considerable effort to spreading the study of Torah among the Jews of Memel. In 1860 he founded a *hevrah shas* (fraternity for Talmud study) there, which continued to function for many years.[10] He likewise initiated and organized Torah lessons for the youth and paid special attention to the young *lomdim* who studied in the *bet midrash*, establishing a personal relationship with them and guiding them both in methods of learning and in character improvement,[11] in addition to seeing to their material needs. At Salanter's initiative, a special room was added to the new building of the *bet midrash*, dedicated in 1875, to serve as sleeping accommodations for the *lomdim*. The fact that Rabbi Isaiah Wohlgemuth was appointed rabbi of the community of Polish and Russian émigrés in this city thanks to Salanter's initiative and efforts is an indication of his authority and mode of operation among the Jews of Memel.

Rabbi Salanter continued to be active in Memel over a period of nineteen years, until 1879. During this period, he occasionally visited various other cities in Germany, including Berlin, Frankfurt, Hamburg, Halberstadt, and Koenigsberg.[12] These visits usually lasted for several weeks, and at times even longer. In 1873, Salanter spent an entire year in Berlin.[13] During the course of his visits to these cities, Rabbi Israel would stay in the homes of his friends and admirers, who also assisted him in his activity with the overall community. There is no detailed information extant concerning his activity in the various cities of Germany, but we may draw an analogy from what we know about his activity in Koenigsberg and Memel. Rabbi Naphtali Ehrmann, who was very close to Salanter during the year he spent in Berlin, relates that he was a focus of attention and source of inspiration to the Eastern European Jews there, many of whom came to his house in order to be received by him personally. Seen as the outstanding representative of the world of Lithuanian scholarship, Salanter used his influence among the Jews of Germany in order to combat their preconceived notions about the Jews of Eastern Europe.[14]

In light of the fact that Salanter lived and worked among the Jews of Germany for such a long period of time, one may ask whether, and to what extent, he adjusted himself to the new surroundings, and to what extent he might have been influenced thereby. Shortly after going to live in Memel, at the beginning of the 1860s, Salanter attempted to acquire Prussian citizenship. He even tried to learn a "useful" profession—the manufacture of ink—in addition to devoting himself to learning the German language and its grammar. As far as we know, he never acquired complete mastery of this language, but he was nevertheless accustomed to reading the daily newspapers and Jewish periodicals.[15]

Salanter's newly acquired knowledge of the German language assisted him in the study of scientific works. He was primarily interested in those sciences that were potentially useful in understanding various passages in the Talmud and even communicated with a number of scientists on this subject. He was interested as well in the scientific literature in the field of psychology,[16] and, at the end of the 1870s, was concerned with questions of the laws regarding ritual purification of women, and turned to expert gynecologists in order to learn the medical aspects of this topic.[17] But his interest in science had an additional motivation. During the period he resided in Berlin, he made efforts to acquire a knowledge of chemistry, and even met a number of times with a professor of chemistry from the University of Berlin, in order to demonstrate to the Russian Jewish chemistry students in Berlin that there was no contradiction between the study of this science and meticulous observance of the mitzvot and Torah study.[18]

Salanter's tendency to develop skills and activities appropriate to the circumstances of time and place was expressed in his program regarding the teaching of Talmud among the Jews of Germany.[19] His concern was how to interest enlightened youth, who had never received a traditional education, in the study of Talmud. Salanter originally toyed with the idea of composing a lexicon of talmudic Aramaic, and to this end consulted some scholars who lived in Memel, but after a period of time, he conceived of a more far-reaching plan: the composition of a new commentary to the entire Talmud.[20] He thought in terms of a commentary in Hebrew, which would explain the course of reasoning of the talmudic argumentation in such a manner that even novice students could study on their own. Because of the enormous scope of this project, Salanter wished to mobilize the help of about one hundred outstanding talmudic scholars, each one of whom would agree to write the commentary on approximately thirty folio pages. Like its predecessors, this daring project never came to fruition, perhaps because he was unable to find enough scholars willing to participate in the project or because he was unsuccessful in raising the necessary funding.[21]

The difficulties that Salanter encountered in attempting to attract educated youth in Germany to the study of Talmud were not limited to curricula. They were preceded by the question of these students' very interest in studying Talmud, as the process of striking roots in German culture generally entailed a stance of alienation toward the values and contents of the Jewish tradition. In attempting to enhance respect for the Talmud among German Jewish youth, Salanter proposed incorporating its study within the curricula of gymnasia and universities. He assumed that recognition of the importance of the Talmud by the general educational system would likewise elicit a positive attitude toward it on the part of Jewish youth. Like the methods of operating adopted by Salanter during the earlier periods, this program too was based upon the assumption that it is both permitted and even desirable to utilize social pressure and considerations of prestige as a stimulus to bringing people closer to mitzvot. Salanter proposed this idea to his closest friends, and negotiated with various personalities regarding its realization. However, he did not succeed in putting it into practice. In a certain sense this proposal was particularly daring, as the suggestion to incorporate the teaching of Talmud within the curriculum of general educational institutions involved a deviation from an explicit halakhah—namely, that one is forbidden to teach Torah to non-Jews. Salanter, who was obviously aware of that prohibition, told his acquaintances that he had studied the problem and found sufficient justification for leniency in this particular case.

We can now return to the question of whether the prolonged stay in Germany influenced Rabbi Israel's path, and if so, in what ways. We find that his attempts to adjust to the new surroundings—the pursuit of Prussian citizenship and the study of the German language—were quite superficial. No substantial change took place either in his overall cultural orientation or in his way of life, and even the interest expressed by Salanter in the natural sciences is not to be attributed to the influence of German Jewry, for a certain limited involvement in sciences, as ancillary to the study of Torah, was an accepted phenomenon among certain circles within the learned elite of Lithuania.[22] Salanter expressed cultural openness insofar as he worked on his German language facility and his knowledge of sciences, but acted within the framework of a model anchored in the traditional experience of Lithuanian Jewry. The change in his activity was restricted to the tactical sphere—to the adoption of new methods of operation appropriate to the conditions of the time and place. Even that tendency had already been characteristic of Rabbi Salanter when he lived in Lithuania, but it was sharpened and energized by virtue of the circumstances in which he worked in Germany. Apart from the various plans concerning the teaching of Talmud, one must mention in this context a project that Salanter did succeed in carrying out, to which we have already referred briefly. At the beginning of the 1860s, he published a Torah periodical, *Tevunah*, in Memel and Koenigsberg. In initiating and editing this periodical, Salanter adopted a literary form typical of the Central European *Wissenschaft des Judentums* (Science of Judaism), which he put to use for the aim of Torah study in its traditional format.[23] (See below, chapter 17, for further discussion of *Tevunah*.)

One of the criteria by which we may determine whether a substantial change occurred in Salanter's positions during the time of his stay in Germany may be seen in his attitude toward the neo-Orthodox trend. During this period, he came to know two central figures in the leadership of neo-Orthodoxy: Rabbi Samson Raphael Hirsch, generally considered the founder of neo-Orthodoxy, and Rabbi Azriel Hildesheimer, founder of the Berlin rabbinical seminary, which combined strict Orthodoxy with the scientific study of Jewish sources. Hildesheimer, with whom Salanter struck up a personal relationship during the year in Berlin, was deeply involved in relief activities on behalf of Russian Jewry. Salanter attended some Torah classes given by Hildesheimer,[24] evidently out of curiosity concerning his method of teaching Torah to German Jews. Salanter's connections to Hirsch were weaker, and were manifested primarily in correspondence between the two. There is nevertheless evidence of a meeting between them, which took place during a visit of Hirsch to Berlin, at which Rabbi Naphtali Ehrmann, who was Salanter's constant companion throughout this period, was also present.

Ehrmann relates that the conversation between the two revolved around the question of the condition of the Jews in Russia.[25] Salanter said that he had thought of publishing some books in Russian, for those members of the younger generation who had been educated in the Russian language and were estranged from their ancestral heritage, but that there were no authors among the pious Jews in Russia who were capable of writing in Russian. Hirsch responded that suitable works in

German might be translated into Russian and that such a translation could be performed even by a non-Jew who was competent in the two languages. Ehrmann goes on to relate that, after this conversation, Salanter decided to read Hirsch's famous book, *Nineteen Letters*,[26] and labored over the reading of the book for some time, as his knowledge of German was quite limited. Finally, Salanter expressed the opinion that this book was deserving of translation, not only into Russian, but also into Hebrew.

The above-mentioned conversation between Hirsch and Salanter would seem symbolically to express both the nature as well as the limits of their closeness. So long as they spoke about the willingness to adopt new tools to convey the Jewish heritage to their contemporaries, the two found a common language. However, there was a profound gap between them with regard to the contents of this tradition. Though Salanter praised the activities of Rabbis Hirsch and Hildesheimer, he added a caveat to these praises: So long as we are speaking of Germany, the doctrine of *Torah 'im derekh eretz* (Torah with worldliness—the synthesis of strict Orthodox piety with involvement in Western culture and society) is both permissible and effective, but under no circumstance does it have a place in Russia. This is so, not only because what was appropriate and effective for the unique circumstances of Germany was neither appropriate nor effective in the circumstances of Russian Jewry, but also because the traditional Jewish way of life as practiced by Russian Jews was preferable for him per se.[27] Thus, Rabbi Israel's positive stance toward the doctrine of *Torah 'im derekh eretz* must be interpreted as recognition of its tactical superiority only within the borders of Germany. In actuality, Salanter was far removed from the view that worldliness is a value in and of itself, as claimed by Rabbi Hirsch and his followers.

During the years he lived in Germany, Salanter did not hold any official office and belonged to no official organization. His tendency to operate outside of established frameworks and patterns, already noticeable in Lithuania, would seem to have been even more strongly expressed in Germany. Perhaps this was the case because in the German communities the damage already exceeded what remained intact, thus leaving greater room for individual initiative.

In lieu of those tools and means available to communal bodies and organizations, Rabbi Salanter made use of individuals among the circle of his admirers and friends, including both prosperous *ba'alei batim* who supported him and his projects with their wealth and social prestige, as well as close disciples who acted in his name and under his inspiration. The latter included Rabbi Dr. Naphtali Ehrmann, who stayed in close proximity to Salanter throughout the year that the latter lived in Berlin.[28] During that year, Salanter guided young Ehrmann in his Torah studies, encouraging him to prepare himself for the rabbinate, and after Salanter returned to live in Memel, he continued to maintain contact with his disciple by letter. Examination of the correspondence between the two enables us to observe in part the way Salanter activated his students.

Young Ehrmann's willingness to offer himself to Rabbi Israel's service appears in the introduction to one of his letters:

> How greatly I rejoiced upon the arrival last Sabbath Eve of a letter from the honorable Torah scholar, and I saw from it that his noble soul still remembers his servant who is ready to serve him at any time and in any matter, insofar as my short hand [that is, limited abilities] may reach.[29]

These flowery expressions are not to be viewed as mere lip service, as they were used in the context of a reply to a letter in which Salanter imposed a specific mission (a family matter) upon Ehrmann. It is clear from the exchange of letters between the two that Rabbi Ehrmann made efforts to fulfill Salanter's request. In another letter, Ehrmann reports that he had translated Salanter's response to an article that had appeared in the *Monatsschrift*,[30] and that he had sent the translated reply to the periodical *Der Israelit*. From yet another letter, we learn of a mission in which Rabbi Israel asked Ehrmann to give greetings to three young men who had been his students in Memel, "and with apologies; please inform me of their good behavior."[31] It would appear that Salanter tried to follow the course of the development of his students, and in this case Ehrmann served him as a contact and source of information.

In one of his letters to Salanter, Ehrmann tells of a new project he has launched in the place where he lives:

> Because I knew that you would be happy about this, I will not refrain from telling you that I have made here, at the place of my residence, a society called *Kiyyum Emunah* [maintaining the faith], in which there are fifty youths. . . . And every evening I study with them *Hayyei Adam* and the Pentateuch with [the commentary of] Rashi, and every Sabbath I deliver a sermon to them, and many of them are like the young man _____ from Berlin, who constantly increases in fear of God and Torah, as I saw when I was in Berlin for several days last month. . . . [32]

Though not explicitly stated, it would appear that Rabbi Ehrmann's project was begun under the inspiration and influence of Rabbi Salanter,[33] who himself was devoted to the establishment of study groups intended for youths who had not received a traditional upbringing. His close disciple now follows in his footsteps, and tells him about it in order to give him satisfaction. As for the young man from Berlin, "who constantly increases in fear of God and in Torah," it follows that Rabbi Ehrmann began activities there in order to bring young people close to the study of Torah, presumably also under Salanter's inspiration and guidance.

A different aspect of the cooperation between Rabbi Ehrmann and Salanter involves the affair of mixed dancing. The main features of this incident are described in an introduction to a halakhic discussion by Salanter concerning mixed dancing:

> When I was young . . . in a certain community in . . . Germany . . . our brethren were divided into two camps: the God-fearers and the free-thinkers. Before they split, the young people of the Orthodox (pious) and the free-thinkers used to gather together to eat and drink and to sing. . . . But after the Orthodox separated from the free-thinkers, there ceased among the former the voice of joy and fellowship, and this was very painful to the children of the Orthodox, who were no longer able to spend their days and nights in feasts of fellowship. . . . Therefore their pious fathers thought wisely (or rather, foolishly) to find an efficient means by which to banish the sadness of their children, to arrange gatherings and parties of friendship and fellowship once a week for them alone. . . . This ordinance seemed to me to be a sin for its own sake, to bring close the Evil Impulse with one's right hand after pushing him away a little bit with the left, and I kept silent in order to learn how it would turn out in the end. Indeed, what I feared came about: after they ate and drank, they got up to play singing and dancing, young men and women [together]. . . . And when I saw what was going on, I remembered the halakhah, and I told the owner of the house that the young people dancing in his house were violating a prohibition of the Torah. This householder was very angered by my words, in that he had thought, to the contrary, that he had done a mitzvah in giving his house to the dancers, so that they not gather together with the free-thinking and assimilated youth and not come to eat non-kosher food and the like. He wrote to a certain *talmid-hakham* among his relatives to ask whether the matter was truly as I had stated, and that scholar responded that what I had stated was an error on my part, and he permitted the matter via a lengthy argumentation, using fallacious arguments and proofs. Then I presented the matter before our master, the *Ga'on*, Teacher of all the communities of the Exile, Rabbi Israel Salanter, of blessed memory, who resided in Memel at the time, and this was his reply to me. . . . [34]

In his responsum, Salanter explains the various halakhic aspects of mixed dancing, and finally comes to the conclusion that it is to be prohibited. The introductory sketch quoted above, which was printed without the name of its author, is doubtless the work of Rabbi Ehrmann.[35] This clearly follows from his letter to Salanter, in which he describes how he presented this responsum before the two sides in the matter of mixed dancing.[36] The incident took place in the community of Carlsruhe, where young Rabbi Ehrmann lived[37] and devoted himself to Torah. Once the young scholar joined in battle against a social phenomenon that, in his opinion, involved a transgression, and having encountered someone who sought to permit it on halakhic grounds, he relied upon the learning and the halakhic authority of Rabbi Israel Salanter.

Rabbi Salanter's approach of employing his students in order to carry out the projects he had initiated was dramatically expressed in an announcement that he published in 1879 in the pages of *Ha-levanon*:[38]

A REQUEST

As my thoughts ramble over the days to come, at the time of my old age—for I have reached, thank God, "the days of our years" [that is, seventy years; cf. Ps. 90:7]—I said that I will turn to my honorable students and acquaintances—may they be blessed by my request—that they forgive me [for troubling them] to write me their address, clearly, so that perhaps I will succeed in explaining to them my concern and my intentions.

Israel from Salant

We do not know what tasks Rabbi Israel wished to impose upon his disciples, nor whether they responded to this call. In any event, reading between the lines of this announcement, one can imagine the elderly Rabbi Israel in a mood of self-evaluation, in anticipation of his approaching end. His mind was presumably set upon all those plans and projects that he had not succeeded in realizing. However, he does not see his own approaching death as a full stop: he asks his students to do what he did not succeed in doing himself.

In the 1870s, Salanter's illness grew worse and age began to show its signs upon him. Yaakov Mark, who knew him personally during those years, tells that:

At times he was subject to such depression that he could not bear the presence of other people. During such a state, which at times continued for several weeks, he would pray by himself and go about deep in thought, while holding his hand to his forehead. His close friends did not let him out of their sight, and followed him at a distance.[39]

Our information concerning Salanter's illness during this time is extremely scanty, as the accounts of his students and friends do not dwell upon this side of his personality. Salanter's own letters written during those years contain clear indications of exhaustion caused by failing health. For example, in 1874 he writes: "[B]ecause of the state of my health, I am almost unable to write abroad . . . ,"[40] while in a letter from 1877, he complains that: "because of the state of my health, my words are incoherent. . . . "[41] It is difficult to say whether these expressions relate to his depression, or whether they refer to a physical weakness that overcame him as the result of old age. In a later letter, from 1881, Salanter explicitly refers to an emotional disorder that oppresses him,[42] while in a letter from 1879, he explicitly points toward limitations due to old age. This letter is addressed to a scholar who had sent him some of his Torah *hiddushim* (novellae) for his opinion. Salanter apologizes, "for my comprehension is laborious, and particularly in my old age,"[43] so that he is forced to pass the things on to others for examination. Yaakov Mark tells the following about the manifestations of old age in Rabbi Israel Salanter:

> In his old age, it frequently happened that during the sermon he was sunk in thought, and at the same time he was as-it-were entirely alight with a holy fire, and his head was supported in his two hands, and he would stand silently for a long time. The congregation stood and waited with respect and in silence until he would arouse [himself] and complete the sermon. He would often descend from the pulpit and not finish it. It happened once in Memel that one of the important communal leaders named Leibzik Troub, who was very close to Rabbi Israel, died suddenly. In honor of the deceased, they brought his bier into the Great Bet Midrash, of which the deceased had been one of the founders. Rabbi Israel went up to the podium to recite a eulogy. He opened with the words: "For man does not know his time, as fishes are enmeshed in a fatal net" [Eccl. 9:12], and immediately sank deeply into thought, repeating the same verse some fifty times in his penetrating and tragic voice, until the audience had wearied itself with great weeping. Suddenly Rabbi Israel bestirred himself, ordered them to remove the bier, and did not say another word.[44]

The worsening of his sickness and the symptoms of aging would seem to have weighed upon Rabbi Israel's public activity and limited it. That may be the explanation, albeit only a partial one, for his lack of success in bringing to fruition several of the projects that he conceived at that time. In any event, the sickness and manifestations of old age did not daunt Rabbi Israel from taking upon himself new challenges.

In the winter of 1880, when he was already seventy years old, he went to Paris, where he worked for some two years among the Jews who had emigrated there from Poland and Russia.[45]

There are those who see the attempt to realize his plans for the publication of a new commentary of the Talmud and for the introduction of the teaching of the Talmud in gymnasia and universities as one of the goals of Salanter's trip to Paris.[46] While it is difficult to determine how much truth there is in this version,[47] it is clear that at most it was only of secondary importance, since the main purpose of the trip was to take care of the matters of the community of Polish and Russian émigrés in Paris.

Salanter was invited to Paris by Dr. Judah Sternheim, a close friend with whom he had stayed in Berlin and in whose home he lived during his stay in Paris. Sternheim had moved from Berlin to Paris several years earlier, where he began to devote himself to the affairs of the Jewish community, helping to establish educational frameworks of a traditional orientation.[48] Why did Dr. Sternheim find it necessary to trouble the seventy-year-old Salanter to come to Paris? The correspondent of *Ha-maggid* in Paris writes as follows:

> This esteemed person [Sternheim], contemplating the Jews of Poland and Russia who had lived there many years without guide or shepherd, was troubled about his brethren lest they become lost in a pathless wasteland, and decided to act on behalf of God and His faith, and girded his strength to arouse the great eagle from its nest—namely, the great *Ga'on* and sublime *Zaddik*, our teacher Rabbi Israel Salanter, may he long live—to come here so that he may oversee the activities of that congregation, and that this stumbling block be under his control.[49]

It follows from these remarks that Rabbi Israel was originally invited to Paris to himself serve as "shepherd" of the community of Polish and Russian émigrés in that city. If that was in fact Dr. Sternheim's intention, it quickly became clear to him that Salanter was not ready to take upon himself this office for a long period. Another explanation of Salanter's invitation to Paris appears in Yaakov Mark's description: There had been a prolonged and bitter controversy within the Polish and Russian émigré community in Paris, and Salanter was invited in order to make peace between the rival camps.[50] There is in fact no contradiction between the two explanations: the settling of the controversy and the arrangement of the subject of leadership are two sides of the same coin.

Our information concerning Salanter's activities and routine during the two years in Paris is very scanty, though we know that he saw as his main task the location of a suitable rabbi for the Polish and Russian communities. We learn of the importance he attached to this goal, as of the difficulties that it entailed, from one of his own letters:

> I have now been uprooted here for a year and a half, and I am unable . . . to discharge myself, for the community will be left like a person on Passover eve who has everything in front of him save for an olive's size quantity of matzah. It is difficult for me to find a rabbi who will be suitable here. . . . [51]

In addition to the personal suitability of the candidate, one also obviously had to secure his agreement. Indeed, when Rabbi Israel proposed this office to his student and friend Rabbi Hillel Salanter, the latter refused to accept it.[52] An additional difficulty involved finding the necessary funds for a permanent rabbi. While Dr. Sternheim attempted to raise a certain sum of money for this purpose, it was evidently insufficient.[53] We may also assume that, even before Salanter began the search for an appropriate candidate for the rabbinate, he needed to act to assure that his authority would be accepted by the community, or at least the majority of its members. To that end, he maintained contact with influential personalities in the community. Moreover, we know that he was accustomed to preaching publicly,[54] and these sermons doubtless served as a means of enhancing his influence upon the community.

After two years of effort Salanter finally succeeded in the person of Rabbi Joshua Heshel Lewin (1818–83), a relation of Rabbi Hayyim of Volozhin and one of the outstanding figures in the world of Lithuanian learning.[55] The fact that Rabbi Joshua was a person who combined Torah with secular learning and culture may have influenced Salanter to see him as the suitable figure. In any event, in the wake of Rabbi Lewin's affirmative decision, Salanter felt that his mission in Paris was completed and he was free to return to Germany.

Yaakov Mark relates in the name of Salanter's friends that he regretted his journey to Paris from the very beginning, and even more so because of his distress over failing to place his close disciple, Rabbi Hillel Salanter, upon the seat of the rabbinate there.[56] Salanter's disappointment would seem to have stemmed from the fact that Rabbi Joshua Heshel Lewin's appointment was a makeshift solution, intended for only a brief period. Rabbi Joshua initially came to Paris for medical reasons, and even when he agreed to accept the rabbinic leadership of the community, he limited himself to just a few years, as he intended to immigrate to the Land of Israel to spend his last years there.[57]

Another explanation of Salanter's unease may lie in the fact that the controversy within the Paris community did not completely cease even after he completed his mission there, as we learn from several sketches published in 1882 in the journal *Ha-maggid*. Following a report from Paris describing Rabbi Salanter's activity and the appointment of Rabbi Joshua Heshel Lewin,[58] a reaction was published from a pseudonymous "Ben Ish Naomi," who argued that at the head of "the community of Russia and Poland . . . stands Rabbi Judah Lubetzky. . . ."[59] In a marginal note to this sketch, the editor of *Ha-maggid* expressed astonishment as to how these remarks could be squared with the report that Rabbi Joshua Heshel Lewin had been appointed by Salanter to this selfsame position. Several weeks later in a brief *Ha-maggid* report under the heading "On Behalf of Truth and Justice," the editor cites "reliable sources" that claim Rabbi Lewin had never been appointed, but that Rabbi Lubetzky had been named rabbi of the émigré community through the efforts of Salanter in 1881; that Salanter's agreement with Rabbi Lewin was only that the latter be permitted to preach in the synagogues of that community; and that prior to leaving Paris, Salanter had warned the members of the Russo-Polish community to respect Rabbi Lubetzky.[60] It is not difficult to assume that these so-called reliable sources were the supporters of Lubetzky, who had been Lewin's rival for the rabbinic post.

These remarks did not remain unanswered. In a detailed article signed by Zalman Berran, "president of the Great Bet Midrash of the Russian-Polish community," published a few weeks later,[61] the version of the "reliable sources" was contraverted. On the basis of Berran's account, supported by letters from Salanter, which he made available to the editors of *Ha-maggid* for examination, we may reconstruct the course of events as follows: The community of Russian and Polish émigrés in Paris was divided between those who worshiped in the "Great Bet Midrash" and the "Small Bet Midrash." The latter supported Rabbi Lubetzky's claim to be considered as rabbi of their community, while the former vigorously opposed that. When Rabbi Israel arrived in Paris, the two rival camps agreed to accept his leadership and to place the choice of rabbi in his hands. Salanter opposed Lubetzky's appointment as rabbi of the community, but did not oppose his acting as *maggid* (preacher) in the "Small Bet Midrash," where most of his following was concentrated. When Salanter failed to find an appropriate rabbi for the community, he temporarily turned the leadership over to Rabbi Joshua Heshel Lewin. So far as we can tell, this was not an official appointment, due to its temporary nature. Before leaving Paris, Rabbi Israel asked Rabbi Lewin to appoint a suitable successor before migrating to the Land of Israel. As soon as Salanter left Paris, the worshipers in the "Small Bet Midrash" denied Rabbi Lewin's appointment and declared Rabbi Lubetzky as rabbi of the community.

It is no wonder that after two years of intense activity, Rabbi Salanter felt a sense of dissatisfaction regarding his mission. But the fact that Salanter's activity in Paris was not crowned with success, at least not to the extent that he had hoped, does not diminish the credit he deserves for his efforts. Not only did the attempt to make peace within the Russian-Polish community and to find a suitable rabbi for it entail considerable hardship, but his prolonged stay in Paris was a difficult experience for the elderly and sick Rabbi Israel. These difficulties are explicitly mentioned in a number of his letters from that period,[62] and they highlight the patience and dedication to the task at hand that Salanter manifested during those years.

Rabbi Israel returned to Germany in the summer of 1882. He spent the last months of his life in Koenigsberg, where he was invited to fill the vacancy created by the death of their rabbi, the noted biblical exegete Rabbi Meir Loeb ben Jehiel Michael Malbim (1809–79).[63] The city in which Salanter had first begun his activities on behalf of the Jewish communities of Germany thus became the final station in his life. In the one account extant of Salanter's final time in Koenigsberg, Michael Oriaszon, one of the founding members of the *Hibbat zion* movement in Vilna, relates in his memoirs that he happened to be in Koenigsberg,[64] and came across Jewish students with traditional religious backgrounds whom it would be worthwhile converting to Hovevei Zion. He went to Rabbi Israel Salanter to seek his assistance in finding a way of influencing these youths. Salanter suggested that Oriaszon organize Talmud classes for those students and, indeed, Oriaszon succeeded in organizing a group of students who met several times a week to study Talmud. Salanter himself gave one of these lessons every week. As far as we know, Rabbi Israel was not among the supporters of *Hibbat zion*;[65] nevertheless, he was prepared to cooperate with Oriaszon and to use his connections with the students to draw them closer to Torah study.

Rabbi Israel Salanter died in Koenigsberg on the twenty-eighth of Shevat, 5643 (February 5, 1883) at the age of seventy-three.

17

Strengthening Orthodox Society in Russia

ALTHOUGH Rabbi Israel Salanter lived outside the borders of Russia during most of the time after 1857, he continued to follow closely the developments taking place there and continued to be involved in leading and guiding the Jewish community in Russia. He generally acted through his students and close associates, with whom he maintained an active correspondence. Some of these, who lived permanently in St. Petersburg, acted as his agents in the royal city.[1] In addition, Salanter periodically visited Vilna and Kovna and took part in discussions and activities pertaining to major public issues of the day.[2] In brief, not only did Salanter continue to be a leader of Orthodox Jewry in Russia, he remained one of its leading spokesmen in the struggle against the Haskalah.

Changes in Russian Jewry During the Reign of Alexander II

To understand the conditions of Russian Jewish life during the 1860s and '70s, we need to briefly survey the vast sweep of historic change in Russia that began with the coronation of Alexander II in 1856. The first years of the reign of Czar Alexander II were notable for great reforms:[3] the liberation of the serfs, the establishment of institutions of self-rule, and reforms in the judicial system, the military, and educational fields, all of which brought about a new spirit across the length and breadth of Russia. The sense of dejection caused by the oppressive rule of Nicholai I was replaced by a deep feeling of hope and belief in the future, a feeling that did not bypass the Jews.[4]

Upon his coronation in 1856, Alexander issued an order abolishing the institution of the cantonists—the edict that had terrorized the Jews of Russia during the reign of Nicholai. The liberal policy toward the Jews was principally expressed by the abolition of the limitations of the Pale of Settlement in respect of certain groups within the overall Jewish population. In 1859, those merchants who belonged to the first guild of merchants were permitted to reside and to engage in trade throughout Russia. In 1861, the same privileges were granted to those holding degrees from institutions of higher learning; they were also permitted to hold office in government service. In 1865, Jews were allowed to serve as physicians in the army, and two years later Jewish doctors were also allowed to practice in the civilian sector. In 1865, the right of residence and of economic activity in all regions of Russia was granted to artisans as well, and in 1867 to demobilized soldiers. These concessions were all based upon the same principle of classification that was adopted by the regime of Nicholai I in the 1840s, only now, instead of punishing the "unproductive" groups, Alexander chose to give special privileges to those groups he saw as productive. By this means, he wished to foster the process of assimilation among the Jews of Russia, and in so doing to exploit their economic and cultural potential to develop his own empire.

The willingness of the Russian government to utilize the wealth and enterprise of the Jews for the sake of its own economic advancement led to the emergence of a new socioeconomic stratum within the Jewish population. Russia's defeat in the Crimean War exposed the backwardness of this empire, and moved the government to act forcefully in accelerating economic development on the basis of the capitalist model then practiced in the West. Within the framework of this effort, wealthy and enterprising Jews filled an important role in the construction of railways, the development of industry and mining, and in international trade in grain and timber. There thus began to develop a new class of wealthy Jews whose outstanding members lived in St. Petersburg and Moscow. Thanks to their economic power and close ties with the ruling circles, these wealthy Jews became the leading class of Russian Jewry.

Despite the limited and specific character of the concessions granted by Alexander II to the Jews, this czar was seen by many as bringing a message of salvation to all of Russia's Jews. The abolition of the edict of the cantonists had particular importance for the weaker classes, while all Jews welcomed the cessation of the special means used until then to encourage conversion to Christianity. Primarily, however, the Jews of Russia judged Alexander's regime by extrapolating from the few liberal measures already taken to those that they anticipated in the future. Many Jews, and certainly the Maskilim, interpreted his liberal policies as tending toward the complete emancipation of Russian Jewry. This interpretation was based, apart from their own wishful thinking, upon the assumption that Russia had decided to follow the path established some time before by the countries of Central and Western Europe. Their optimism regarding the regime's intentions was strengthened by the remarks of certain individuals within the ruling circle, who proposed extending the rights of the Jews or even equalizing them with those of the Christian population. Those who sought signs of a rosy future awaiting the Jews of Russia also found grounds for hope in the somewhat positive tone toward the Jews adopted by the liberal Russian press.

The changes in the legal status of Russian Jews, and the new economic possibilities that this opened for them, breathed renewed energy into the Haskalah movement.[5] The old claim that the legal status of the Jews would be improved as a result of the acquisition of general education and productivization was now confirmed by the government's policy. Not surprisingly, the demand of the Maskilim for a reform of Jewish society was strengthened, but in many cases the response to this demand now stemmed from pragmatic considerations. Many families who wished to assure the economic future of their children sent them to general educational institutions, resulting in a considerable growth in the number of Jewish students in the Russian gymnasia and universities during the 1860s and '70s.[6] In many cases, parents hoped that study at these institutions would not affect their children's attachment to Jewish heritage, and attempts were even made to exempt the Jewish students from the requirement of writing on Sabbaths and Jewish festivals. However, generally speaking, the Jewish students were forced to adjust themselves to their new environment, even if it was at the price of observance of religious law. The tendency of parents to send their children to Russian gymnasia was strengthened in the wake of the draft law of 1874, which imposed the same obligation of conscription upon Jews as on the general population. Far-reaching concessions were granted to those who were educated, most significantly that military service of graduates of gymnasia was reduced from four years to one year. For that reason, even pious families chose to give their sons a general education.

The flow of young Jews to the Russian gymnasia and universities, as well as the needs of the new socioeconomic elite, accelerated the process of Russification among Russian Jews. This process found expression in the adoption of Russian as the spoken language and in their close adherence to the dominant tendencies within Russian society and culture. A new class of Russian Jewish intelligentsia thus began to emerge, which was different in character from the Maskilim of the old generation. While those who belonged to this new intelligentsia had received a formal education and were involved in Russian language and literature, the older Maskilim were auto-didacts, whose secular education bore the stamp of German language and culture. But a more profound difference lay in their respective relationship to the Jewish heritage. The Maskilim of the old generation had by and large received a traditional Jewish religious education, and continued to be loyal to the fundamentals of Judaism and its observances. Despite their criticism of the traditional Jewish milieu and their demands for reform, they did not wish to undermine its foundations. In principle, they wished to combine Torah with *Wissenschaft*, Judaism with humanism. On the other hand, most of the members of the new Jewish intelligentsia were entirely estranged from Jewish tradition. There were those among them who wished to exchange their Jewish identity for Russian national identity; others adhered to cosmopolitan worldviews. Many members of this class joined the radical political and social movements that began to spring up as the result of disappointment with the regime of Alexander. Either way, this class, which was radically different from the old Haskalah, had no common language with the Orthodox public.

Alongside the emergence of the Russo-Jewish intelligentsia, a change began to take place among the circles of Maskilim who continued to create in the Hebrew language and who saw themselves as the heirs of the Haskalah movement of the previous generation. In these circles, too, a new generation emerged, which was influenced by the radical mood then prevalent among the Russian intelligentsia. Within the Jewish context, these tendencies were expressed in sharper and more radical criticism of the traditional milieu.[7] While the Maskilim of the previous generation expressed their reservations concerning customs that were not, strictly speaking, required by Jewish law, the authors of the 1860s and '70s demanded changes in the halakhah itself. These writers declared outright war against certain components of the traditional world, their harshest criticism being directed against the rabbis, portrayed by the militant Haskalah writers as heartless fanatics who were meticulous over "the tittle of a *yod*," while ignoring the needs of the Jewish masses. This literary attack on the rabbinic elite was led by such figures as Moses Leib Lilienblum, Judah Leib Gordon, and Alexander Zederbaum, editor of *Ha-meliz*—the first Hebrew weekly in Russia.

Thus, during the reign of Alexander II, Orthodox leadership was confronted with new challenges, the likes of which it had never before known. In addition, during the course of the 1860s, the liberal tendency that had characterized the early days of Alexander's reign was replaced by a reactionary policy, which became stronger during the '70s. Severe anti-Jewish positions were again manifested within Russian public opinion—in government circles, in the liberal educated class, and in various radical circles.[8] But these facts, with all the despair and disillusionment they caused to the Jews of Russia in general and to the circles of the intelligentsia and the Maskilim in particular, were insufficient to turn the clock backwards. The strengthening of the various schools of Haskalah among the Jews of Russia was an established fact. Moreover, the legal benefits granted to those possessing a general education, and the economic opportunities that this opened for them, continued to encourage young Jews to flock to the Russian gymnasia and universities. Despite their constant growth, the circles of the intelligentsia and the Haskalah encompassed no more than a very narrow segment of Russian Jewry as a whole, yet its influence upon communal life increased out of all proportion to its numerical weight. As we said above, the new socioeconomic elite assumed a position of leadership by virtue of its close connections with the regime. Further, from the point of view of Orthodox society, Haskalah authors enjoyed in the Hebrew press a platform for the dissemination of their ideas—whether in a restrained and moderate fashion or in a sharper and more strident tone.[9] The Hebrew periodicals thus became an important instrument for spreading the idea of the Haskalah among the class of *ba'alei batim* within the Orthodox public, and because of their intellectual curiosity and ferment, the young *lomdim* were natural candidates to be swept up by that influence. The literature of the period abounds in portrayals of *yeshivah-bokhurim* who secretly read "outside books,"[10] and it would seem that this reflects a real phenomenon.

Indeed, the tension and struggle between the Haskalah, which was becoming stronger and more extreme, and the Orthodox public, which was pushed into defensive postures, were central features of Russian Jewish life in the 1860s and '70s.[11] One of the major manifestations of this struggle was the literary battle waged in the pages of the Hebrew press.[12] In the wake of the constant attacks by Haskalah authors, some Orthodox leaders answered the Maskilim with their own weapons: In the 1870s the periodical *Ha-levanon*, which was then published in Paris, became the organ of the Orthodox in their polemic against the Haskalah.[13] Another current of Orthodox response to the challenges of that period was manifested in the thought of such figures as Rabbi Yehiel Michael Pines[14] and Rabbi Isaac Jacob Reines.[15] Each argued that, in light of the new circumstances, Orthodox society needed to undergo an ideological and institutional readjustment of its structures. (Both were exponents of religious Zionism—Pines a leader of the *yishuv* in Eretz-Yisrael, Reines a founder of the Mizrachi movement in 1902.) Among other things, they recommended the reforming of traditional education by the introduction of a controlled combination of general knowledge with Torah study.

As mentioned above, though Rabbi Israel Salanter lived outside Russia during these years, he maintaned his leadership role in the Orthodox community through correspondence, students and associates, and periodic visits. Salanter himself did not participate in the polemic on the pages of the Hebrew press, but he nevertheless thought it desirable that the position of the Orthodox camp receive appropriate expression. He therefore initiated and funded the publication of a leaflet entitled *Ma'oz ha-talmud*, which was intended as an answer to Lilienblum's call for halakhic reform.[16] But what most characterized Salanter's response to the growing threat of the Haskalah was not polemics or struggle over positions of power, but the attempt to fortify the heritage, to help it withstand the challenge by cultivating new and effective tools suited to the circumstances and needs of the time. Salanter's efforts primarily concentrated upon strengthening the Torah elite, in addition to continuing his activities among the devotees of the Mussar doctrine.

Tevunah—The First Torah Periodical in Eastern Europe

The periodical *Tevunah*, published in Memel and in Koenigsberg during the year 1861, was initiated, published, and edited by Rabbi Israel Salanter. In all, twelve issues of *Tevunah* were published, one per week over the course of three months.[17] In the main, its pages were devoted to Torah studies, organized in three sections: responsa, analyses, and talmudic novellae and commentaries. To these was added a fourth section, devoted to articles by Salanter in the area of Mussar.

Apart from Salanter, whose writings also appeared in the halakhic sections, eighteen authors contributed to *Tevunah*, including several outstanding figures in the Torah world of the time. Twelve of the contributors lived in the Russian empire, mainly in Lithuania; of the other six, two were from Prussia, two from Galicia (Austria-Hungary), and two were Lithuanian émigrés in Jerusalem. Thus, most of the authors whose Torah novellae were published in the pages of *Tevunah* were raised and educated in the study houses and yeshivot of Lithuania.

Among the Galician rabbis who contributed to *Tevunah* were Rabbi Joseph Saul Nathanson (1810–75)[18] and Rabbi Shlomo Kluger (1785–

1869).[19] The former served as rabbi of Lemberg and was considered one of the leading *poskim* of the day; many of his halakhic responsa appeared in his major work, *Sho'el u-meshiv*, which was printed in six volumes. Rabbi Shlomo Kluger lived in Brody and enjoyed the reputation of an important and productive author in all areas of Torah studies. Many of his books were printed during his lifetime, and many after his death. These two figures were likewise involved in the public affairs of Galician Jewry and were prominent in the struggle against Haskalah.

Among the Lithuanian rabbis whose writings were published in *Tevunah* were Rabbi Yitzhak Elhanan Spector (1817–96),[20] who served at the time as rabbi of Novehardok. Over the course of time, while serving as rabbi of Kovna, he was to achieve a unique status and authority as a sort of chief rabbi of all of Russian Jewry. We also find in the pages of *Tevunah* Torah novellae by Rabbi Alexander Moses Lapidot (1819–1906),[21] rabbi of Rosein, and of Rabbi Mordecai Gimpel Jaffe (1820–92), rabbi of Ruzhany.[22] These two were among the outstanding personalities of the Lithuanian rabbinate, who were later to be noted for their activity on behalf of *Hibbat Zion*. Another prominent Lithuanian rabbi to participate in *Tevunah* was Rabbi Joseph Baer Soloveichik (1820–92),[23] who at the time served as a senior Talmud lecturer in the Volozhin yeshiva. Rabbi Joseph Baer, a descendant of Rabbi Hayyim of Volozhin, impressed his contemporaries by his method of study. He was to later leave the yeshiva, following a confrontation with Rabbi Naphtali Zvi Yehudah Berlin of Volozhin (the *Natziv*, 1817–93) concerning the leadership of the yeshiva, and serve as rabbi of Slotzk and Brisk.

Two other outstanding personalities whose Torah novellae were published in *Tevunah* were Rabbi Eliezer Moses ha-Levi Horowitz (1818–90), who served as rabbi of Pinsk,[24] and Rabbi Shmuel Avigdor (1806–66), who served as rabbi in Karlin.[25] Both men were considered "Torah giants" (*gedolim*) in their generation. Rabbi Shmuel Salant and Rabbi Meir Auerbach, both of Lithuania, who were to become central figures in the Ashkenazic community in Jerusalem upon their immigration to the Land of Israel, likewise contributed to *Tevunah*.[26]

In brief, it would appear that the editor of *Tevunah* was not guilty of overstatement when he added to the cover of the periodical the subtitle, "A Collection of Torah Novellae by the Sages and Giants of Israel." Indeed, many of the authors who participated in this periodical, both those mentioned here and others whose names I have omitted,[27] were considered in their day as Torah giants and as holding central positions in the rabbinic world.

The proposition that *Tevunah* was a periodical rooted in the milieu of Eastern European Jewry is based both upon the background of its founder and editor and the identity of the majority of its contributors. On the basis of its contents and nature, it is clear that *Tevunah* was intended for a public of *lomdim* whose main occupation was Torah, youths who studied in the yeshiva and *bet midrash*, and *ba'alei batim* with a learned background, mainly concentrated within the borders of the Russian Empire, and particularly within the Jewish communities of Lithuania. The fact that *Tevunah* was printed within the borders of Prussia, albeit near the Lithuanian border, does not contradict this. Nor was *Tevunah* either the first or the only periodical aimed at Russian Jewry to be printed in Prussia, being preceded in this respect by *Hamaggid*.[28]

During the first few weeks of the publication of *Tevunah*, Salanter printed a notice to his readers on the cover of one of the first issues, expressing the hope that the publication would appear regularly: "It is my intention to publish, God willing, fifty issues a year . . . whoever wishes to honor me with his Torah novellae will kindly send them to my address: Israel Lipkin, in the city of Memel, in the state of Prussia."

Only a few weeks later Salanter had to inform his readers that he was unable to follow his original plan. In a notice attached to one of the later issues, he wrote:

> With God's help I will shortly have published up to twelve issues, and I am afterwards forced to wait until I shall know, God willing, the number of subscribers who wish [to receive] them. For the expense is very great, and if I see that God's work is successful in my hand and those who support me are numerous, then with God's help and salvation I will renew strength to distribute their fellows over the face of the earth, with greater beauty than [I have] until now.

It would seem that the income from the sale of the issues of *Tevunah* during the first weeks of its publication did not meet his expectations; moreover, printing expenses were greater than he had initially foreseen.[29] Rabbi Israel was thus forced to suspend publication of *Tevunah* due to lack of funds, but at the time he hoped that the halt would only be temporary, and that he would thereafter be able to increase the number of subscribers by distributing those issues that had already been printed, so that he might once again be able to print the magazine.

In a later notice to his readers, Salanter repeated his earlier explanation for the interruption in the publication of the journal, but with an important addition: He makes clear that his files are still filled with

Torah articles that have not yet been published. This fact, along with the Torah novellae that were published in the twelve issues, allow us to credit the editor with an important accomplishment—namely, his success in persuading such a prominent group of rabbis to publish their novellae on the pages of a weekly Torah publication, an unprecedented phenomenon in the world of Eastern European Jewry.

A later comment of Rabbi Israel Salanter pertaining to the subject of *Tevunah*, the last one to come down to us, is included in a letter to Rabbi Joshua Heshel Lewin, dated 21 Sivan 5622 (June 1862), about half a year following the cessation of publication of the journal. He wrote there that *Tevunah* had become "a matter bottled up" within him and that the obstacles in the way of its resumption "weaken all the forces of my body."[30] In these few, sparse sentences, one senses a mood wavering between hope and disappointment. On the one hand, it appears that Salanter continued to contemplate renewed publication and even attached great importance to it; on the other hand, in speaking about the difficulties preventing the realization of his plan, one hears a note of resignation to at least temporary termination of this project. It may be that Salanter found some small consolation in the fact that Rabbi Lewin was engaged in preparations for the publication of a Torah journal in Volozhin, and Salanter in fact promises, if Rabbi Lewin's plan is realized: "I will . . . be ready to help him according to the matter and my situation, etc."[31] In the final analysis, other than the original twelve issues, Salanter did not publish even one more. Thus, both in terms of quantitative scope and the period of time during which it was published, *Tevunah* was no more than a brief, passing episode.

The initial sum that enabled Salanter to begin publishing *Tevunah* was evidently given to him by his friends in Memel and Koenigsberg, the two communities in which he had been active since leaving Lithuania for Prussia in 1857, though Salanter's intention was to base the funding of the periodical upon revenue from subscriptions. Why did he not succeed in attracting a sufficient number of subscribers? It may be that lack of experience and of appropriate organizational means brought about the failure of its distribution. However, it seems to me that there was a deeper reason for it: The public from which he expected to find subscribers was not attracted to this strange innovation of a weekly periodical devoted mainly to Torah *hiddushim* (novellae), because it presumably preferred to continue to study Torah through the known and accepted literary channels that had been used for centuries.

What motivated Rabbi Israel Salanter to publish a weekly devoted primarily to *hiddushei Torah*, with the addition of sermons devoted to Mussar matters? Dov Katz's explanation—namely, that Salanter hoped to disseminate his Mussar ideas by means of *Tevunah*, and that their inclusion within the framework of Torah novellae by prominent scholars was no more than a device intended to attract the reading public—is unconvincing.[32] Of course, Salanter wished to disseminate his Mussar teachings to the wide public, but it seems doubtful that he would go to the extent of exploiting *hiddushei Torah* as a means of achieving such an end. Indeed, in the introduction to the first issue, Salanter himself enumerates the goals he had in mind when he launched this periodical.

Salanter explains the general purpose of his project as follows: ". . . to raise up the honor of the Torah and to expand its borders so that it not be isolated, each one in his own home, as in the saying of the rabbis (Makkot 10a), 'Whoever loves to study before the multitude reaps a harvest.' "[33] Salanter thus relies upon the traditional outlook, rooted in rabbinic teaching, in which study with others is preferable to solitary study. By means of the publication of a widely distributed Torah periodical, one could substantially expand the circle of those participating in the study process, thereby increasing the benefits to be derived. Following this general explanation, Salanter enumerates three areas in which the contribution of *Tevunah* to raising the prestige of Torah is expressed:

1. The dissemination of Torah novellae to the broad public: Thus far, Torah scholars who wished to bring their novellae to the attention of the public had been forced to publish them in book form. Now those who had novellae or articles that they wanted to share with others, and could not afford to publish in a book, would be able to do so.

2. The exposure of *hiddushei Torah* to critical review: Those who are reluctant to publish their *hiddushim* in book form because of the fear that people may find contradictions between them and the rulings of the earlier *poskim* may publish them in this periodical. Once they have been read by the public and no criticism is leveled against them, their author will realize that they are essentially sound; in fact, greater force and certainty is given to whatever is not refuted by the many readers. Thus, the quantitative advantage of the number of readers becomes an advantage of qualitative significance.

3. "Seeking the Torah of truth" is the third and paramount item enumerated by Salanter in his list of reasons for publishing this journal: Salanter develops here a methodological discussion concerning the means of clarifying the truth of Torah, a discussion that has importance in principle beyond the justification for publishing

Tevunah. For that reason, it was integrated into the chapter dealing with Salanter's approach to the cultivation of *talmidei hakhamim* and the training of rabbis.[34] As will be remembered, Salanter proposed an innovative methodological basis for study of Torah in the traditional manner, arguing that it is specifically by this means that one can be assured of uncovering the truth of Torah. Salanter was reacting here to a rival approach to Torah study, expressed by the approach of the Haskalah and realized in the rabbinical seminaries. In the wake of this discussion, Rabbi Salanter went on to state that the publication of *Tevunah* was likely to contribute to the discovery of the truth of Torah, thanks to the discussion conducted on its pages among scholars noted for their expertise and intellectual acumen.

While I earlier expressed reservations about Dov Katz's theory that Salanter's primary aim in publishing *Tevunah* was to spread his Mussar ideas, there is nevertheless no doubt that Salanter ascribed profound importance to the department of *derushim*, in which he published his studies on questions of ethical perfection. It seems to me that the intention of the editor of *Tevunah* may be defined more accurately by saying that he found special interest in the inclusion of such studies within the same framework as *hiddushei Torah*. This literary combination symbolizes that demand that is the very essence of Salanter's Mussar teaching—namely, that one ought to devote special effort to ethical improvement alongside devotion to Torah study. As mentioned above, Salanter directed this demand not only to *ba'alei batim* engaged in business, but to full-time scholars as well.

In addition to this general principle, Salanter observed a more concrete connection between the sermons included in *Tevunah* and an important segment of his intended readership:

> I find strength in my soul to explain further a precious matter brought about by the combination of things in this book which are [usually] separate, to set aright character traits and to make the youth who is sharp of mind used to them . . . while he is still in the springtime of life and has not yet encountered the transformations of time and their troubles. . . . For it is difficult for a person to relearn to accommodate himself to them; only in the days of one's youth, before one is buffeted by the billows of time, can one learn and regulate his traits. . . .[35]

The attempt to reshape those characteristics present in a person's psyche that dictate patterns of behavior and modes of reaction stands at the center of the Mussar articles printed in *Tevunah*. It would appear that the editor of *Tevunah* had in mind especially the public of young people engaged in study in *yeshivot* and *batei midrash*, whom he wished to influence through means of a balanced combination of Torah and *yir'ah*. It makes sense that Salanter's efforts to publish a Torah periodical directed primarily toward the circle of *lomdim* within the borders of the Russian Empire should be understood in terms of the transformations that came about in Jewish life in Russia during that period. In the wake of the strengthening of the Haskalah and the growing threat to the tradition, Salanter wished to provide the *lomdim*, who were the representatives of Torah within Russian Jewry, with a new tool that would contribute to their unity and strengthen their hearts.

But one may still wonder why Salanter required the format of a weekly periodical. Was this his own original idea, or was he influenced by his predecessors, two of whom he knew about and under whose inspiration he evidently acted? In one precedent, dating back to 1847, Rabbi Joshua Heshel Lewin turned to a number of outstanding figures in the rabbinic world with the request that they participate in a Torah periodical that he intended to publish.[36] Among those he approached was Rabbi Israel Salanter, who blessed Rabbi Lewin's initiative and promised his support.[37]

In a discussion elsewhere of Rabbi Joshua Heshel Lewin's initiative, I tried to point out its connection with the struggle taking place in Russia in the 1840s between the camp of the Haskalah and that of the traditionalists.[38] According to this view, Rabbi Lewin's project ought to be understood as a reaction of Orthodox Jewry to the strengthening of the Haskalah. In this respect, there is a certain resemblance and continuity between Lewin's efforts at the end of the '40s and the beginning of the '50s, and that of Salanter at the beginning of the '60s. In fact, Lewin's attempts to publish a Torah periodical did not bear fruit until many years later, and even then with an extremely limited scope. (One solitary issue of *Peleitat sofrim* was published in Volozhin in 1863—that is, after *Tevunah* had ceased to appear.) It nevertheless seems reasonable to assume that Salanter had Lewin's initiative in mind when he launched the publication of *Tevunah*.

Another Torah periodical that preceded and influenced Salanter's project was *Shomer zion ha-ne'eman*, published in Altona under the editorship of Rabbi Jacob Ettlinger (1798–1871), one of the early leaders of German neo-Orthodoxy. This periodical, which was published bi-weekly from summer 1846 until winter 1856, was strongly marked by the stamp of Orthodoxy: Its major interest was the struggle against the Reform movement, in all its varied manifestations. This fact was reflected, among other things, by the heading that appeared at the top of each issue—"to lift up the horn of the Torah and of duty and to remove stumbling blocks from the path of faith"—and in the section entitled "Meshalim u-melizot" ("Homilies and Letters"), a direct and explicit polemic against reform. That Salanter knew of this periodical and was influenced by it is indicated by the fact that he adopted the same format. In brief, Salanter knew of the attempt to strengthen the walls of the tradition by means of a Torah periodical, and it would appear that, in part, he acted under the inspiration of this precedent when he began the publication of *Tevunah.*

Finally, in the years preceding the publication of *Tevunah,* a number of Hebrew weeklies, intended primarily for Russian Jews, began to appear, including *Ha-maggid,* which began publication in Lyck in 1856; *Ha-karmel,* Vilna, 1860; and *Ha-meliz,* Odessa, 1860. The emergence of these periodicals, reflecting the strengthening of Haskalah tendencies, presumably impressed Salanter, and may also have been among the factors that motivated him to publish *Tevunah.*[39]

In summary, *Tevunah* may perhaps be characterized as one of the outstanding expressions of the process of consolidation of Orthodoxy in Russian Jewry. From its very contents and character as well as from the methodological discussion that the editor included in the introduction to the first issue, we learn that this periodical was meant as a response to the growing threat to the tradition, and was aimed at the public of *lomdim* in an attempt to strengthen the learned elite, and bolster the staying power of traditional society in general. Salanter's discussion of the preferred means of study may be understood as an attempt to present the circles of *lomdim* with a methodological program that would provide a new and original justification for the traditional way of study, in light of the criticism directed against it from without, and represents the adaptation of a literary form that had already been used years earlier by the *Wissenschaft des Judentums* school. Indeed, the willingness to absorb and adopt modern forms in defense of the tradition was one of the characteristic features of Salanter's public activity generally. However, in the matter of *Tevunah,* as in other matters, Salanter was ahead of the public in whose name and on whose behalf he labored, because the public of *lomdim* in Russia in the beginning of the 1860s was not yet ready to support a Torah periodical.[40]

Kollel Ha-Perushim in Kovna

Kollel Ha-Perushim was established in Kovna in the late 1870s, and in the context of its time, it was a completely innovative Torah institution. Its purpose was to assist young men who were preparing themselves to serve in the rabbinate by providing financial support for them and their families.

Dov Katz attributes to Rabbi Salanter the founding of *Kollel Ha-Perushim*:[41] The institution itself was made possible by a large financial contribution entrusted to Rabbi Israel, and he was the one who decided "after extensive counsel and with the agreement of the contributor . . . to establish a special *bet midrash* for Torah for young men with this money."[42] However, examination of the sources pertaining to this matter indicates that Katz's version requires qualification and amplification.

Of the sources known to us, each of which gives its own version of the founding of *Kollel Ha-Perushim*, three are particularly important.[43] They are in agreement concerning the financial contribution that facilitated the establishment of the *kollel*, obtained through Eliezer Ya'akov Haves, from the city of Yanishok in northern Lithuania. A friend of Haves's brother—a wealthy Berlin bachelor named Ovadiah Lachman—agreed to contribute a sum of about 10,000 rubles, the annual dividends of which would serve to support the Torah students. Haves's brother, Yosef Hayyim, also agreed to provide an additional sum of 100 rubles a year.[44] At this point the three versions of the *kollel*'s founding diverge.

In an article devoted to a description of the history and character of *Kollel Ha-Perushim*, Moshe Reines states that his father, Rabbi Yitzhak Ya'akov Reines, was the first one to originate the idea of a "special house of study for young men who were intending to become rabbis in Israel and whose poverty would be a stumbling block to them. . . ."[45] Rabbi Reines first presented his program to the public in 1872. Following the positive response elicited by this proposal, he approached several leading rabbis for their support. Two who responded favorably to the proposal were Rabbi Naphtali Zvi Yehudah Berlin, known as the *Natziv*, who was the head of the Volozhin yeshiva at the time, and Rabbi Alexander Moshe Lapidot, the rabbi of Rosein.

Reines goes on to relate that, following the receipt of the grant from Lachman, a split arose between his father and the *Natziv* and some other people who were active in the matter of the *kollel*: "Several of those who had made efforts [on its behalf], when they saw that 'a source was opened for money,' began to act improperly, their aim being to turn things around in such a way that the true founders would be forced to withdraw from it. . . ."[46] The author does not identify who these people were and what means they used, but suffices with references to letters cited in the footnotes.[47] Examination of these letters, all of which were written by the *Natziv* of Volozhin, indicates that Rabbi Reines was indeed the originator of the idea of founding this *kollel*. Moreover, Rabbi Reines proposed that the new institution be a kind of branch of the Volozhin yeshiva and that the *Natziv* stand at its head.

Despite various reservations, the latter was prepared to accept this task, and even proposed that a prominent rabbinic personality be appointed to serve together with him in the running of the *kollel*.

Two letters from the winter of 1876—one addressed to Rabbi Lapidot and the other to Rabbi Reines—hint at the nature of the controversy, as a result of which Rabbis Reines and Berlin withdrew from involvement in the *kollel*. It appears from these letters that Rabbi Lapidot and others had proposed as head of the *kollel* Rabbi "H"H" (referring to Rabbi Hayyim Hillel Fried of Volozhin, who was from the "family of the Rav" there).[48] He had even served as a teacher in the Volozhin yeshiva for a brief period, but was forced to give it up as the result of illness. It was against that background that a dispute broke out between Rabbi Hayyim Hillel and his family, and the *Natziv*. Berlin began to lecture at the yeshiva on those days of the week that had until then been the prerogative of Rabbi Fried, while the latter and his family thought that the privilege of giving those lectures ought to be granted to one of the members of their family.[49] The suggestion that Rabbi Hayyim Hillel be appointed as head of the *kollel* was intended to compensate him for the loss of his position in the Volozhin yeshiva.[50] The *Natziv*'s response to this proposal was qualified. In practice, Rabbi Berlin feared that, were the administration of the *kollel* to be given to Rabbi Hayyim Hillel Fried, the members of his family would be liable to carry out their plan to transfer the income of the Volozhin yeshiva to the new yeshiva bearing his name.[51]

What motivated Rabbi Lapidot and the others to suggest that Rabbi Hayyim Hillel Fried be appointed director of the *kollel*? Did they act in innocence, or was this a device intended to displace the *Natziv* and Rabbi Reines? Although I cannot answer that question, it is clear that the confrontation over the leadership of the *kollel* resulted in a split between Rabbis Reines and Berlin, on the one hand, and Rabbi Lapidot, Rabbi Haves, and the contributor, on the other.

Moshe Reines, upon whose account I have thus far relied, knows nothing about what happened to the *kollel* after his father withdrew, so we now turn to Yaakov Lifschitz, who lived in Kovna during this period and was among the close assistants of Rabbi Yitzhak Elhanan Spector, to learn of the beginnings of Rabbi Israel Salanter's involvement in the subject of the *kollel*. Upon his return from Berlin to Lithuania, bearing the news of the contribution promised by Lachman, Rabbi Haves stopped in Memel to consult with Salanter, who was living there at the time. According to this version,[52] the idea of establishing a *kollel* grew out of discussions in which Salanter played an active role, but this statement does not stand up to critical examination. Rabbi Lapidot, under whose guidance Haves acted,[53] participated in the earlier stage of the initiative to establish a *kollel*. Moreover, it is difficult to imagine that Lachman would have been prepared to accept such an extensive financial commitment without its purpose being clear to him. It therefore seems more likely that the consultation in which Salanter participated was not intended to determine the purpose for which the money was to be used, but how to carry out the plan of the *kollel*, for which purpose the money had originally been given. The idea of involving Salanter in the matter of the *kollel* evidently originated in Rabbi Lapidot, who was among his admirers and close friends.[54] It may also be that the philanthropist and his advisers were interested in Salanter's participation because he had become a well-known figure in Orthodox circles in Germany. In any event, from this point on Rabbi Israel was a senior partner in the activity involving the establishment of the *kollel* and its direction.

Lifschitz describes the course of events that brought about the location of the *kollel* in Kovna as follows: Rabbi Lapidot asked Rabbi Yitzhak Elhanan Spector, considered the outstanding figure among the rabbis of the Russian communities at the time,[55] to serve as head of the *kollel*. Lifschitz assumed that the new institution's chances of success would grow immeasurably were it to be headed by such a prominent rabbinic personality, but because of his numerous concerns, Rabbi Spector was reluctant to accept. He finally agreed to head the *kollel* provided the practical work of guiding it be carried out by his son, Zvi Hirsch, who at the time was engaged in business. Thus, *Kollel Ha-Perushim* was established in Kovna in the summer of 1877, numbering ten young men. Rabbi Zvi Hirsch, whose business started to decline, was soon forced to withdraw from the leadership of the *kollel*, and his place was filled by Rabbi Abraham Shenkar, one of Salanter's students. Lifschitz adds that he was given to understand that Shenkar exploited this position in order to attract to the *kollel* students who tended toward the Mussar doctrine.[56] Nevertheless, Spector supported Shenkar's continued service as director of the *kollel* on account of his talents and devotion. Dov Katz mentions another figure who participated in the direction of the *kollel* alongside Rabbi Abraham Shenkar: Rabbi Nathan Zvi Finkel (1849–1927), a relative of Haves.[57] It is thus clear that, in the early stages of its existence, *Kollel Ha-Perushim* in Kovna was headed by close associates of Rabbi Israel Salanter. This fact was no coincidence, as Salanter had a definite approach to the training of rabbis, and it seems reasonable to assume that he had an interest in seeing that the practical direction of the *kollel* be given over to his own students.

We know of Salanter's involvement in the attempt to broaden the financial basis of the *kollel* from a number of sources. There is an extant letter sent by Salanter in the spring of 1879 from Memel to "the honorable, great and respected ones of the holy community of Kovna."[58] In this letter, Salanter explains the importance and urgency of supporting young men preparing themselves to serve in the rabbinate through contributions to the *kollel*. In another letter,[59] evidently intended for the less prosperous classes of Kovna Jewry, Salanter advises every family to volunteer to supply at least one meal a week to the young men, the *perushim*. Unlike the older custom of "eating days" (taking meals) at the tables of *ba'alei batim*, Salanter proposed that food be brought to the *bet midrash* in order to safeguard the dignity of the students. He stresses that the advantage of giving contributions in this way is rooted in its more popular nature. Many people do not have enough money to make sizable contributions, but nearly all can offer at least a portion of the food prepared for their own table one or two days a week to the young men who devote themselves to the life of Torah.[60] Moreover, the more meals contributed, the greater the amount of money the young men were able to save from their financial stipend to send back to their families.

Salanter's letters to the Jews of Kovna reflect only a small portion of far more extensive and varied activity. One of the peaks of this activity may be seen in his participation in the book *Sefer 'ez-peri*, published in Vilna in 1881. The heart of this book consisted of two articles "concerning the strengthening of those who study our Holy Torah"—one by Salanter and the other by Rabbi Yitzhak Elhanan Spector. To these were added an unsigned appeal; a preface by the publisher—evidently Rabbi Nathan Zvi Finkel;[61] an introduction by Rabbi Israel Meir Ha-Kohen (the *Hafetz Hayyim*); and an opening and concluding note by Rabbi Alexander Moshe Lapidot. The structure of *Sefer 'ez-peri*, in which Salanter is given equal status to that of Rabbi Spector, is indicative both of the great respect accorded to Salanter among the Jews of Lithuania, and of his position as one of the leading activists on behalf of the *kollel*. But while Rabbi Spector's relationship to the *kollel* was expressed in the fact that he was willing to give it his patronage, Rabbi Israel was involved in decisions concerning its actual management.[62]

The urgent need to develop these new frameworks for supporting *lomdim* who were preparing for the rabbinate was ascribed by Salanter to the changes that had taken place in the status of Torah study among the Jews of Russia:

> For these days are not like the olden days . . . for the sources of sustenance from which the students of Torah have drawn have become shallow and dried up in our day. For in past days, the young man completed his course of studies, and was already able to rule in halakhah and to judge, before he found a place

in which to serve as rabbi; and even those who had not completed their set course of study to be a rabbi were assured of being able to proceed to its completion. For it was easy to make a living and to meet their needs, because the honor of the Torah was great in those days. Wealthy *ba'alei batim* who had sons in whom they saw signs of talent . . . spent much money on them and hired [young men] such as these as teachers for them; they received much money for their teaching, while the labor and time were little. From this they received a source for their support, and the rest of the time they gave over to their Torah studies. But it is not so in our day, when secular studies are widespread among our sons in an exaggerated way, and the honor of the Torah has declined, and the longing to study Torah has decreased both among the fathers and among the sons . . . and from whence shall help come for the remnants, who sit before God and study Torah day and night? If they do not find a source of income for their support . . . will not those who seek the Torah and study it decrease, and then there will be shaken, Heaven forbid, the first pillar upon which the world itself stands. . . .[63]

The diminution of those sources of income that had hitherto supplied the needs of these rabbinical students stemmed from the fact that many young people had turned to institutions of general learning, a tendency that grew during the 1860s and '70s. We ought to note once again that this phenomenon was not limited to those circles that tended outright toward the path of Haskalah. As Salanter suggests, even among those "fathers to whom the path of Torah and *yir'ah* is precious," there were many who saw fit to send their children to general institutions of learning, due to the advantages involved in attending them. From the point of view of Salanter, this phenomenon had disastrous consequences; not only did the number of young people devoting themselves to Torah studies decrease, but the sources of income for those who chose this path also shrank. Salanter's appeal to the public was therefore a call to save the traditional institution of the rabbinate in light of the dangers threatening its continued existence.

A new chapter in the history of the *Kollel Ha-Perushim* was opened in 1880, following the departure from Kovna of Rabbi Zvi Hirsch Spector, its first director. The direction of the institution had already been given over to Rabbi Abraham Shenkar, as mentioned. But now, once the connection between Rabbi Zvi Hirsch and the *kollel* had been severed, the need to appoint a new director grew more urgent. To that end, Zvi Hirsch's father, Rabbi Spector, called a special meeting of rabbis, in which there participated Rabbi Moshe Alexander Lapidot, Rabbi

Isaac Blazer, and Rabbi Eliyahu Eliezer Grodzinski, who was Salanter's son-in-law.[64] It was decided at this meeting to charge Rabbi Blazer, one of Salanter's closest disciples, with the responsibility for the coffers of the *kollel*.[65] In addition, two distinguished figures from the Kovna community were appointed as supervisors of the financial arrangements of the institution. The two, Eliyahu Markel and Baruch Broida, were among "the senior Mussar [practitioners] in Kovna."[66] In light of the influence that Salanter exerted over matters of the *kollel* generally, and in light of the personal composition of the meeting at which Rabbi Blazer was appointed,[67] it seems virtually certain that he was consulted on this matter. Blazer, having left his position in St. Petersburg to settle in Kovna, was seen by Salanter as an appropriate candidate for directing the *kollel* in the spirit of the Mussar movement.

During those years in which Rabbi Blazer served as head of the *kollel* (1880 to ca. 1891),[68] the scope of its activities increased considerably. In addition to the revenues from the fund set up by Lachman, substantial amounts of money were raised by emissaries who made the rounds of the communities of Russia and Prussia.[69] During this period, the number of young men supported by the *kollel* increased, reaching approximately 120. In addition, several groups of young men outside of Kovna were supported by *kollel* funds.

Along with the growth in the income and scope of activity of the *kollel*, a significant development took place in its character. Under Rabbi Blazer's inspiration, the influence of Mussar teaching became augmented among the students in the *kollel*, even though there was no official change in the definition of the aims and purpose of the institution. Further, the activities in the spirit of Mussar teaching took place outside the walls of the study houses in which the young men learned Torah. Nevertheless, the involvement of young men in this activity both broadened and deepened. Every Sabbath afternoon at dusk, Rabbi Blazer preached at his home on matters of Mussar. Many among those who heard his sermons were students supported by the *kollel* funds. The number of those students who were in the habit of regularly visiting the two Mussar houses then existing in Kovna likewise grew.

Shmuel Rosenfeld, one of the Haskalah authors who took part in the Mussar controversy of the 1890s, attributes this development to pressures that the new administration exerted upon the students.[70] According to him, Rabbis Blazer and Yehoshua Zadikovitz, the treasurer of the *kollel* from whom the students received their stipends, tended to favor those students who followed the Mussar approach. The inevitable result of this pressure, according to Rosenfeld, was the tendency toward hypocrisy among the young men: ". . . There were many who made a show of being Mussar devotees but whose heart was not in it, and when they came to the Mussar house they learned it with their mouths only. . . ."[71] We possess no evidence to confirm or refute Rosenfeld's account, though it seems likely that, even if no direct pressure was brought to bear on the students, the very fact that the *kollel* was directed by figures identified with the Mussar movement constituted indirect pressure. However, Rosenfeld, who was hostile to the Mussar movement, ignores the possibility that many of the students at the *kollel* may have adopted the Mussar teaching as the result of inner conviction. In the final analysis, it seems impossible to explain the great strides made by the Mussar movement within the yeshiva world at the end of the nineteenth century on the basis of pressure and financial allurements only.

That the *Kollel Ha-Perushim* under the leadership of Rabbi Isaac Blazer was considered by its contemporaries as a bastion of the Mussar movement may be inferred from the fact that it was the target of severe attacks by Mussar's opponents. The *kollel* was principally attacked by the Haskalah authors;[72] in directing their attacks against the leaders of the *kollel*—who were identified with the Mussar movement—the Maskilim revealed their awareness that this movement had become a leading force in the struggle of Orthodox society against the Haskalah.[73]

The Struggle Against the Establishment of a Rabbinical Seminary

During the summer of 1882, Rabbi Israel Salanter again found himself at the center of public activity concerning the institution of the rabbinate in Russia, this time in response to an initiative of the Jewish plutocrats in St. Petersburg to reestablish the rabbinical seminary in Russia. In attempting to understand this initiative, we must study the debates about the rabbinate that occupied the Russian Jewish public throughout the 1870s and '80s.[74]

Underlying the public discussion was the recognition that the rabbinical seminaries established by the czarist regime at the end of the 1840s[75] had fallen short of the hopes placed in them. Such awareness, already held by some of the Maskilim in the middle of the 1850s,[76] became more and more widespread in the '60s.[77] According to the vision of the Maskilim, these seminaries were meant to create a new type of religious leadership, which would combine Torah with *Wissenschaft* and disseminate the message of the Enlightenment among the broader public by virtue of its spiritual authority.[78] But since the decisive majority of the communities recognized neither the moral nor the halakhic authority of the graduates of these rabbinical seminaries, they were only able to serve as "official rabbis"—those appointed by the regime whose function was generally restricted to the conducting of the registry of births, marriages, and deaths. The Jewish communities of Russia continued to choose rabbis of the traditional type, even though these rabbis no longer operated within the framework of the law.[79]

Shortly after its establishment in 1863, the Society for the Promotion of Culture Among the Jews of Russia[80] placed the question of the rabbinate on its agenda, and asked various individuals, both of the Maskilic circles and from the Orthodox camp, to express their opinion on this matter. At the end of 1866, it summarized the responses that had been sent, and concluded that the graduates of the seminaries neither fulfilled the expectations of the Maskilim nor stood up to the criteria of the Orthodox, because of the low level of their accomplishments both in the realm of general culture and in that of Jewish learning. The Society for the Promotion of Culture therefore decided to turn to the government with the request that the Christian directors of the rabbinical seminaries be replaced by Jews—individuals with a high level of general education who would also be able to enjoy the trust of the Orthodox public. In addition, the directors of the Society offered financial support to talented young people who wished to go to study at the rabbinical seminary in Breslau. Indeed, during the second half of the 1860s and during the '70s, the Society supported a number of young Russian Jews who studied in Breslau.[81]

The Maskilim questioned how a generation of rabbis could be cultivated who would simultaneously have a store of broad general culture and also enjoy the recognition of the Orthodox public. The attempt to solve this problem by encouraging suitable candidates to study in Breslau was only an interim solution, as long as it was impossible to improve the existing institutions in Russia or establish others in their place. This solution nevertheless reflects the opinion, widespread among the Maskilim in Russia, that the seminary in Breslau run by Rabbi Zecharias Frankel (whose school is sometimes seen as a forerunner to the Conservative movement in the United States) was a successful example of the combination of Torah and *Wissenschaft*.[82] As for the Orthodox spokesmen questioned by the Society for the Promotion of Culture,[83] they complained that their status was harmed by their being placed outside of the law and by the granting of the rabbinic title to the government rabbis.[84] Moreover, since they were not recognized by the government, it was difficult for the communities to pay them their salaries, and in order to do so, they were forced to resort to various evasive and humiliating devices. Thus, all of the rabbis who participated in the discussion stressed the need for official government recognition of the traditional rabbis, proposing two different tactics toward the realization of this goal: (1) maintaining both the traditional rabbis and the official rabbis as recognized authorities—but with a clear distinction between their realms of jurisdiction; and (2) uniting all of the privileges and functions of the rabbinate in one individual—the traditional rabbi, who must then acquire a certain degree of general education. This latter plan proposed that Orthodox institutions for the training of rabbis be established in Russia, with emphasis upon Torah, and secondarily, on general studies. While Rabbi Mordecai Gimpel Jaffe and others supported the proposal for pragmatic reasons, Rabbi Yehiel Michael Pines held that, in this age, rabbis need general education for its own sake.

The public debate over the rabbinate renewed in 1878 when the government announced its intention to convene a congress of rabbis. In Maskilic circles it was thought that this would occasion the establishment of a new institution for training rabbis. After the hopes of the Maskilim were disappointed, the editor of *Ha-meliz*, Alexander Zederbaum, proposed to the Society for the Promotion of Culture that it take the initiative in establishing a rabbinic seminary on its own, and they agreed to discuss his proposal. Meanwhile, in the Orthodox camp some argued that the training of rabbis was in no way a concern of the Society for the Promotion of Culture, and that there was no need for a new institution for training rabbis; the problem would be solved once the government would once again recognize the authority of the traditional rabbis. Several of them admitted that rabbis now needed some general education and that it would be worthwhile to offer financial assistance to rabbinical students in order to enable them to acquire the necessary education privately.[85]

The Society's reaction to the Orthodox critique was articulated by its secretary, Abraham Eliyahu Harkabi, in an article published in *Halevanon* in the spring of 1880.[86] Harkabi argued that, in most of the large communities, there existed sharp polarization between a minority of enlightened intelligentsia and an Orthodox majority. Each of these two sects needed rabbis with qualifications appropriate to their respective character and needs. The Society for the Promotion of Culture saw itself as charged with the responsibility of training rabbis for the "sect of the Maskilim." At the same time, the Society would be willing to aid the Orthodox public as well by providing general education for its rabbis, so that they might enjoy recognition by the government.

The 1881 pogroms in the south of Russia not only failed to discourage the Society in its new initiative, but even lent a greater urgency to the solution of the problem of the rabbinate. The spokesmen of the Orthodox public expressed their astonishment that the Jewish nobility in St. Petersburg found no other matter with which to concern themselves at such a time of trouble. However, from the point of view of the Society's wealthy leaders, it seemed particularly logical to hasten the establishment of a rabbinical seminary in such circumstances, believing that the Jews of Russia must attempt to appease the government, so that it would become their ally and protect them. This tendency was strengthened by the contacts of some Jewish personalities with the Interior Minister Ignatyev, who "suggested" that the Jews of Russia concentrate upon the "correction" of various faults in their way of life. Among other things, he noted the need to abolish the Jews' cultural separatism and isolation.[87] In 1882, when young Baron David Guenzburg (1857–1910) addressed the governmental inspector of education posted in Vilna, to present him with the program for the founding of a rabbinical seminary,[88] it would seem that he acted in light of considerations that favored the establishment of such an institution, as expressed in the public debate of the 1860s and '70s. But in the wake of the pogroms, these considerations now took on a new sense of urgency.

Rabbi Israel Salanter learned of the intentions of the Society for the Promotion of Culture to establish a rabbinic seminary from Baron Guenzburg himself, as he relates in 1882:

> . . . . Two years ago when I was in Paris, His Honor Baron Guenzburg spoke with me about the creation of a *Rabbiner-Schule*, and I answered him at length that it was neither worthwhile nor acceptable, and that good is peace, etc. . . .[89]

Presumably, Guenzburg presented his proposal to Salanter in the hope of receiving his support. Rabbi Salanter's active opposition to Guenzburg's initiative was conducted on two fronts: an attempt to unite the Orthodox leadership in opposition and an attempt to undermine this initiative in practice.

We learn of Rabbi Salanter's efforts to influence the position of Orthodox leadership from two of his letters, the first written in Paris in July 1881,[90] addressed to his son-in-law, Rabbi Eliyahu Eliezer Grodzinski, who was among the active figures in the Orthodox leadership.[91] In that letter, he writes that the weakness in the character of the rabbinical seminaries does not lie in the combination of general education with Torah studies per se, but in the inability of these institutions to impress their students with the sense of ethical responsibility required of a rabbi/halakhic authority. Ruling on halakhic matters is not merely a function of intellectual acuity and expertise, but must also be based upon conscientious loyalty to the truth of Torah. We can only rely upon the fact that one who has spent many years studying *Torah li-shemah*— that is, for the sake of the mitzvah of studying Torah and not to prepare for the rabbinate as a profession—has acquired a sense of personal responsibility to the truth of Torah through this study. The rabbinical seminaries, intended to prepare people to serve in rabbinic office, are clearly unable to convey this quality to their students. Rabbi Israel bases this judgment upon historical experience: the tendency of rabbis in Central and Western Europe to be lenient in their halakhic rulings.

This letter was more or less a copy of an earlier one sent to Rabbi Yitzhak Elhanan Spector, who seemingly had turned to Rabbi Salanter requesting his views on the matter. The immediate reason for this consultation among the top Orthodox leaders was probably the gathering of community representatives planned to be held in St. Petersburg at the initiative of Baron Guenzburg, a meeting scheduled for the end of the summer of 1881. It seems likely that at this stage the Orthodox leaders were already aware of the program being proposed by the Society for the Promotion of Culture for the establishment of a rabbinical seminary,[92] and that they even assumed that the subject was liable to appear on the agenda of the meeting called by Guenzburg. They therefore met among themselves earlier in order to consolidate an agreed position.

Salanter's letter to his son-in-law leads one to think that the latter favored the establishment of a rabbinical seminary, as the official status of the traditional rabbinate would thereby be assured, a position shared by a number of rabbis who participated in the public discussion about the rabbinate. Therefore, Salanter made efforts to convince his son-in-law to join the camp of those who rejected this idea. That conjecture is confirmed by a letter to Rabbi Yaakov Lifschitz, dated January 1883:

> My son-in-law wrote to me (as I myself wrote him) that he tends towards that view out of necessity, but he negates his opinion before mine [, which is] the view of the Torah. This suggests that he does not really negate his own opinion, and that he is a cool-headed person.[93]

Thus, Rabbi Eliyahu Eliezer Grodzinski continued to support the initiative to establish a rabbinical seminary, justifying it "out of necessity." While he was prepared to suppress his own opinion before that of his father-in-law, who was both older and more knowledgable than he in Torah, Salanter inferred from this formal argument that in principle he did not accept his opinion. Therefore, further on in this letter, he asked Lifschitz to travel to Vilna and, in concert with Rabbi Yitzhak

Isaak Ha-Levi Rabinowitz,[94] to convince Grodzinski to join the opponents of this plan. Moreover, should Lifschitz and Rabbi Yitzhak Rabinowitz find it necessary, Salanter was prepared to ask his close friend
Rabbi Elijah Levinsohn of Cartinga to join the effort.

Why did Rabbi Salanter find it so important to trouble both himself
and others in order to influence Grodzinski's position? It may be that
he was pained by the fact that his own son-in-law did not share his
views on such a fundamental issue, but over and above the personal
motivation, Salanter would seem to have acted out of the awareness
that it was necessary to create a united front of Orthodox leadership to
defeat Guenzburg's initiative.

Salanter's choice of means by which to carry out his goal entailed
an inner conflict, as we learn from the testimony of Yaakov Lifschitz,[95]
who recounts a letter sent by the St. Petersburg *gevir*, Meir Friedland,[96]
to Rabbi Spector in 1882. Friedland, presumably acting in concert with
Guenzburg, attempted to convince Rabbi Spector to support the latter's
initiative. Evidently, in light of the failure of the rabbinical seminaries
established by the government in the 1840s, Guenzburg and his cohorts
realized that they needed the support of some of the leading rabbis in
Russia.

Lifschitz relates that, during the summer of 1882, Rabbi Israel
Salanter traveled from Koenigsberg to Kovna in order to speak with
him on the subject of the Guenzburg initiative and expressed his astonishment that the wealthy Jews of St. Petersburg saw fit, during such a
stressful period, to "make breaches in the wall of religion, and fissures
in Jewish unity. . . ." Salanter said that he was at a loss as to how to
react to this, since an open struggle against the nobility was likely to
harm the interest of Russian Jewry as a whole. On the other hand, in
light of the serious dangers inherent in Guenzburg's plan, it was impossible to sit idly by and do nothing. How, then, was one to act? Was
it desirable for the representatives of the Orthodox public to appeal
directly to the Russian government to express their opposition to the
creation of a rabbinical seminary? Or was it preferable to approach
Baron Guenzburg by peaceable overtures and attempt to persuade him
to abandon the project? Salanter thought the latter path preferable:
first, because a direct appeal to the regime was liable to upset the
representative status of the *gevirim* as spokespersons for Russian Jewry;
second, a complaint to the authorities would seriously injure the prestige of the *gevirim* and bring about division and controversy among the
camps. Thus, only the second path was left—that is, to attempt to
convince Guenzburg himself. Salanter suggested that Rabbi Spector
begin this effort, and protest to Baron Guenzburg against his plan; the

rabbis of the other communities would join in the protest thereafter. But Salanter expressed the fear that Rabbi Spector might be reluctant to take this assignment upon himself, lest it sour his good relations with the wealthy nobility of St. Petersburg.

In light of these considerations, Rabbi Israel's appeal to Yaakov Lifschitz becomes more understandable. The latter was known as a stubborn fighter against the Haskalah generally and against the plan to establish a rabbinical seminary in particular.[97] Moreover, as a confidant and assistant of Rabbi Spector, Lifschitz might be able to influence his opinion. Salanter preferred to move Rabbi Spector to action through Lifschitz, rather than address him directly, because he realized that it would be considered undignified were the rabbi of Kovna to act in such an important public matter at the instigation of another prominent rabbinic figure. But were this instigation to come from his adviser, close at hand, that would clearly be different. Indeed, Salanter's plan worked well. Lifschitz encouraged Rabbi Spector to write a letter of protest to "the princes of the children of Israel in St. Petersburg."[98] In this letter, dated August 1882, Rabbi Spector argues that the rumors about the plan to establish a rabbinical seminary had aroused memories among the public of the seminaries established by the government, "which had already made irreparable breaches in the walls of our holy Law. . . ." There could therefore be no doubt that the new initiative would likewise upset the broad public and bring about severe controversy and division. There was no need for the establishment of such an institution in practice for, unlike previous times, knowledge of the vernacular and general education were now widespread even among the Orthodox. Rabbi Spector goes on to argue that, even if one were to find a few prominent rabbis who would be willing to give their backing to this new institution—a possibility that he finds extremely doubtful—even then the broader public would not be prepared to recognize the authority of its graduates. Therefore, the "nobility of the children of Israel" ought to forego this plan.

Rabbi Spector's letter was intended to serve as the spearhead for extensive protest activities, and it appears that Rabbi Salanter was successful in moving many of the rabbis of Russia to join in with Rabbi Spector's protest. We know something of Rabbi Salanter's involvement in the organization of these protest activities from a number of letters that he sent to Lifschitz in the fall of 1882, after he returned to Koenigsberg.[99] Among other points, Salanter advised Lifschitz to organize an appeal of rabbis to Rabbi Spector, requesting that he protest to Guenzburg. This was evidently intended to strengthen Rabbi Spector's authority as the representative of the Orthodox public to Baron Guenzburg and his friends. In one letter, Salanter is undecided as to the tone that the rabbis ought to take in their letter of protest directed toward Guenzburg directly. He initially thought it preferable to write in a moderate and gentle tone, but he now fears that there may not be enough time to "go gently," so one ought to be sharper and more outspoken. In another letter, Rabbi Israel discusses the possibility that written protests will not be sufficiently effective, and that it would be necessary to send a delegation to St. Petersburg. In such a case, one must choose qualified people, providing them with enough money to remain in St. Petersburg for as long as necessary to carry out their mission. In a later letter, which evidently came in response to Lifschitz's optimistic opinion, Rabbi Israel warns that one must remain on one's guard. The fact that, even though they had closed the rabbinical seminaries, the government retained the order requiring the rabbis to possess general education, was likely to serve as an official excuse in assisting the Jewish aristocracy to carry out their plan.

In brief, in his letters to Lifschitz, Salanter appears as one who, despite living far away, continued to be the moving spirit of the struggle. Not only did he follow developments in detail, but he took a decisive role in formulating policy and in activating those who carried it out. As was his usual way, Salanter acted by means of emissaries who were close to the focus of events, whom he activated through the power of his personal authority and his sound advice. It is characteristic that Rabbi Israel's directives were not confined to general principles, but related to the details of tactical considerations. In addition, it is nearly certain that Salanter's contacts with Yaakov Lifschitz were but one facet of an extensive and far-reaching activity, in the course of which he activated other individuals. We learn of the extent of the protest that Rabbi Israel succeeded in arousing and its results from a letter sent by the Haskalah author Judah Leib Katzenelson (1846–1917) to Ahad Haam in January 1894.[100] In this letter, Katzenelson relates that he had participated in a committee organized in 1881 by the Society for the Promotion of Culture, whose function it was to formulate a program for the establishment of a rabbinical seminary. Katzenelson goes on to say that, when the Society wished to carry out this program, "thousands of letters came from all over the Jewish Diaspora to Baron Guenzburg, urging him not to go along with the contumacious ones of the generation, who wish to destroy the religion of Israel." Under the influence of these protest letters, Baron Guenzburg withdrew his support for the plan, a stance that he maintained despite repeated protests from his friends prevailing upon him to renew his efforts for its realization.

It is interesting that Salanter thought that, alongside these protest activities, there was also need for informational activities,[101] so that the wealthy Jews would cease their initiative, not only under pressure, but out of inner understanding and conviction. He therefore initiated the publication of a collection of essays devoted to presenting the various arguments against the establishment of a rabbinical seminary in Russia. The collection, edited by Lifschitz, was published in Warsaw in 1884 under the title *Divrei shalom ve-'emet*.

UNDERLYING Rabbi Salanter's struggle against the attempt to establish a rabbinical seminary in Russia was a certain principled understanding of the proper means of cultivating rabbis, which he had already formulated at the beginning of the 1860s. As elaborated above, he posed three main requirements to those who wished to serve as teachers of halakhah: (1) extensive knowledge both of the Talmud and of the halakhic literature of the early authorities, his approach being that one may not rely upon the rulings of the later authorities alone in deciding the halakhah; (2) intellectual acuity by means of which one is able to analyze sources and arrive at a halakhic ruling through deduction and analogy; and (3) ethical qualities, which guarantee one's loyalty to the truth of Torah.[102] Examination of Salanter's writings at the beginning of the 1880s, denigrating the rabbinical seminaries, reveals that he judges and evaluates them according to these same criteria.

As Salanter wrote to his son-in-law,[103] an institution whose avowed purpose is to prepare its students to become rabbis as a profession and source of income is unable to implant a deep spiritual commitment to the Torah within the soul of the young person, as is required of teachers of halakhah. This being so, the graduates of the rabbinical seminaries are unable to stand up to the pressures placed upon them, and are therefore liable to permit that which is forbidden according to the law of the Torah. Shortly thereafter, Rabbi Israel repeated this argument in a letter to Rabbi Yaakov Eliezer Haves.[104] Salanter also thought that the rabbinical seminaries were unable to train scholars capable of issuing halakhic rulings based upon the Talmud, for two reasons: first, the devotion of a significant part of the curriculum to general knowledge left insufficient time for Torah study[105] and, second, due to the relatively small amount of time devoted to Torah and the practical orientation of the rabbinical seminaries, the emphasis was transferred from theoretical study of the Talmud to the Codes literature. The result of this tendency was the inability of their students to understand the halakhah on the basis of the talmudic discussion, and their mistaken impression that it is sufficient to know the rulings of the later authorities in order to clarify the halakhah.[106]

Along with these basic considerations, Salanter's attitude toward the rabbinical seminaries was based upon an additional element, rooted in his own life experiences in Germany and his relatively close acquaintance with neo-Orthodoxy. Since, according to both direct and indirect testimonies, Salanter greatly admired the work of the neo-Orthodox leaders in Germany,[107] the question arises as to whether he thought it desirable to utilize the same approach among Russian Jewry as well. Indeed, there were those who inferred from his positive attitude toward neo-Orthodoxy in Germany that he held a similar position with respect to Russian Jewry.[108] Rabbi Israel utterly rejected any such conclusion, as can be seen in the memoirs of Rabbi Reines:

> . . . . I entered into conversation with the Gaon, our teacher, Rabbi Israel Salanter. . . . During the course of the conversation, we got onto the subject of the position of the rabbinate in our country, and he said the following:
> "What shall we do with the rabbis in our country, who do not know their place and time? See, there has now been printed in *Ha-levanon* . . . a story entitled 'Suess Oppenheim,' whose source is the German language paper *Israelit*, published in Maintz by Rabbi Lehmann, and the translation was done by a certain rabbi in our country who is among the well-known rabbis. It is clear in my eyes that the intention of the righteous Rabbi Lehmann in [publishing] this story was for the sake of Heaven, and it may be that this story will be effective for the Germans. Nevertheless, it is not fitting for a rabbi from our country to copy such a story, for in the final analysis it deals with matters of love."
> And the Gaon went on to say "I [will illustrate] how much the rabbis in our country ought not to follow the ways of the rabbis of Germany by telling you one incident. When I was in Berlin I visited the seminary of Rabbi Azriel Hildesheimer . . . and I went to visit the school for girls . . . where I saw a spacious room with a large table in the middle, around which there sat grown girls, and the [above-mentioned] rabbi sat at the head of the table giving them a lesson in *Shulhan 'Arukh*. . . . It is clear to me that the rabbi's intentions are for the sake of Heaven, and the thing is praiseworthy in my eyes beyond any doubt, for all of the students who listened to his teaching will be proper [religious] women, who will fulfill all the mitzvot a woman is required to perform and educate their children according to the ways of the Torah and the faith, so that one can say with absolute and complete certainty that this learned rabbi is doing a thing beyond value. Nevertheless, let a rabbi in our country attempt to create a school of this type, they would insult him

and chase him away; and there is no doubt that he would be forced to cease practicing the rabbinate, for he would no longer be suited for it.[109]

It is therefore clear that for Salanter what was appropriate to the unique circumstances of Germany was not at all appropriate to Russia. Yet from Reines's account it is not even clear whether Salanter considered neo-Orthodoxy in Germany and the traditional Orthodoxy of Russia as two alternative approaches of equal value, each of which was suitable to its particular place, or whether he considered one or another superior in absolute terms. The answer to that question, together with some explicit remarks about Hildesheimer's rabbinical seminary, appears in a letter by Salanter written in 1880:

> To his honor Rabbi Dr. Hildesheimer, may he and the members of his household live and be blessed with goodness:
>
> I have received the letter from the honorable *Gaon* written on the Eve of the Sabbath . . . but I am unable to fulfill the request of a great man such as he—may the likes of him multiply in Israel. The rabbinical seminary of the honorable Torah personality is a great thing, beyond all praise, for strengthening Torah and the fear of God, and it is located in Germany. But in Russia the situation of the rabbinate is still based upon the old system, and we hope that it will so continue for many years, with God's help. For thank God, there are many who devote themselves to Torah exclusively, and are prepared to become *gedolim* (may they multiply). And I fear to represent his *bet-midrash*, in which science is the main thing and Torah is secondary, as a model for them, lest I perform a sin, Heaven forbid. Generally speaking, there is no legitimate reason for one to speak of temporal life as a good thing.
>
> His friend, who sends his greetings and respects;
> Israel of Salant, known as Lipkin[110]

Salanter thus answers in the negative to Rabbi Hildesheimer's request that he recommend the rabbinical seminary under his leadership to the Jews of Russia for their support. The refusal is striking, in light of the fact that Rabbi Yitzhak Elhanan Spector had composed an enthusiastic letter of recommendation on behalf of Hildesheimer, encouraging the wealthy Jews of Russia to contribute to his institution.[111] *Inter alia*, Rabbi Spector wrote that Hildesheimer's seminary trains "Torah scholars of outstanding piety." He even states in this letter—without any reservation or criticism—that young people from Russia are flocking to this seminary. Salanter himself does not deny the high level of

Hildesheimer's seminary—so long as it refers to the German milieu; within Russia, it is preferable to continue to train rabbis on "the old basis." Salanter justifies the superiority of the traditional method with the statement that exclusive devotion to Torah, without the admixture of general culture, is a precondition for cultivating *gedolei Torah*. At the end of his letter, Salanter alludes to what he thinks is an additional weak point of Hildesheimer's seminary: the combination of "worldliness" and Torah implies a certain willingness to compromise with the requirements of temporal life at the expense of eternal life—that is, dedication to Torah study. Therefore, Rabbi Israel thought that the traditional method of training rabbis, as practiced in Russia, was preferable, while that of neo-Orthodoxy in Germany was only acceptable after the fact. He also states this position in a letter to Rabbi Naphtali Ehrmann, one of his closest associates in Germany, following the promulgation of the new conscription law in Russia in 1874. According to this edict, those individuals having general education were granted far-reaching concessions and Rabbi Ehrmann evidently suggested, in light of this, that Russian Jewry adopt the system of preparing rabbis followed in Hildesheimer's seminary in Berlin. Salanter replied to that suggestion:

> Although according to the new law about military service for the educated—each one according to his level—[their] service will be greatly shortened, and there will be other concessions, and the majority will go into general studies, out of necessity; nevertheless, [among] those who cling to the Torah at present, we [could] have enough new rabbis for the next thirty years. For this reason, we ought not to speak [of doing] in the manner of the Germans, for through this it has nearly become forgotten to the world that it [that is, their form of Torah training] is inadequate. . . .[112]

Salanter justified his refusal to recommend that the wealthy Jews of Russia support the rabbinical seminary in Berlin on the grounds that his words might be interpreted as implying support of this model within Russia itself. This was not an idle fear on his part, for there were those who were in favor of establishing a rabbinical seminary under Orthodox auspices in Russia who might have seen in the seminary of Rabbi Hildesheimer living proof of the fact that it was possible to train rabbis who were both pious and educated within the framework of this kind of institution. Salanter's remarks were directed against such a possibility.[113]

One must not conclude from the above that Rabbi Israel unqualifiedly rejected involvement in *Wissenschaft* and "sciences." Even though we have not found any explicit formulation of his position on this matter in his writings, we may infer it in light of his behavior. Salanter read German, if not fluently, and studied scientific literature in a number of areas.[114] His guiding principle in this matter was that *Wissenschaft* and "sciences" were to be treated as "handmaidens" (that is, auxiliary disciplines) to the study of Torah. In this respect, Salanter followed a path that had been accepted by a certain group among the learned elite of Mitnaggedic society since the time of the Gaon of Vilna.[115] It would appear that Salanter thought that, just as he was able to study science without requiring the formal framework of a general education, so other *talmidei hakhamim* did not need institutions of this type, but could acquire whatever general knowledge they needed by means of independent study.

To conclude this discussion, Rabbi Israel Salanter's struggle against the program for establishing a rabbinical seminary, and his efforts to strengthen *Kollel Ha-Perushim* in Kovna, are two sides of the same coin. While Salanter understood the rabbinical seminary as an institution embodying a deviation from the traditional way of training rabbis, he saw the *kollel* as an instrument for the perpetuation of this path under new circumstances. Rabbi Israel thought that talented young people who devoted themselves for years to *Torah li-shemah* and who, over the course of these years, acquired both the ability to study and the requisite quality of purity, may then prepare themselves for rabbinic office by independent study of the literature of the *poskim* needed for this. Indeed, there were no formal study arrangements in *Kollel Ha-Perushim*. In practice, the young *lomdim* were scattered among the various study houses of Kovna where they studied by themselves,[116] the function of the *kollel* being confined to providing them with the means of existence.

Alongside his activities to strengthen the economic basis of the *kollel*, Salanter attempted to encourage talented young men to dedicate themselves to rabbinic office. A typical expression of Salanter's promotion of this matter may be seen in one of his letters:

> . . . Particularly in our day, when rabbis are few in number, it is fitting that every God-fearing [person] seek with all his strength to study and to arrive at the goal of [being qualified for] halakhic ruling. This is the fulfillment of each person who presently devotes himself to the Torah. The main thing is to prepare oneself to be qualified as a rabbi and a righteous teacher according to his level. . . . I will repeat my words at this time, that this is the goal of *yira'h* and study *li-shemah*: to be vigilant and to achieve the goal of the rabbinate.[117]

This goes beyond the personal guidance of close disciples—the above-cited letter contains a programmatic call, directed toward the entire population of young *lomdim*, wherever they may be. Moreover, Salanter no longer hesitates to state explicitly that at this time what ought to be considered as *Torah li-shemah* is study with the aim of the rabbinate. In light of the fear that the public would be left without qualified rabbis, it is no longer advisable to respect the desire of individuals to achieve perfection through the path of *Torah li-shemah*. Under the new circumstances, study for the rabbinate is transformed from a necessary evil into a positive goal toward which one ought to strive: "The highest level in the study of the Torah is study in order to know and to teach in Israel by law and halakhah. . . ."[118] Salanter so wished to elevate the status of the rabbinate that he was forced to justify his own refusal to serve in the rabbinate: "And he further said that the reason he did not accept any rabbinic [post] was because of specific reasons which kept him [from it]; in any event, had he foreseen the future as it now is, he would have prepared himself for this with all his strength."[119]

Thus, all of Salanter's activities mentioned here—the publication of the journal *Tevunah*, his participation in the establishment and development of *Kollel Ha-Perushim* in Kovna, and the struggle against the attempt to establish a rabbinical seminary—point in one direction, namely: the strengthening of the traditional Torah elite. In this way, Rabbi Israel sought to bolster the ability of Orthodox society in Russia to withstand the growing process of secularization in the '60s and '70s of the nineteenth century.

18
The Mussar Doctrine, 1859–81

DURING the 1860s and '70s, Rabbi Israel Salanter's thinking took on a new dimension of profundity and complexity, due to his recently found awareness of the phenomenon of the unconscious. Salanter also exhibited a certain literary efflorescence during this period, expressed in letters 6, 7, and 8 in *Sefer or yisra'el*, which were in effect Mussar sermons from the end of the '50s; in the *derushim* published in the periodical *Tevunah* during the early '60s; in various letters from the '60s and '70s; and in Salanter's final literary work, the "Treatise for the Strengthening of Those Who Study Our Holy Torah," published in *Sefer 'ez peri* in 1880. These writings, while extending over a period of about twenty years, are all characterized by the idea that left the strongest impression on Rabbi Salanter's thought from this period—namely, the distinction between the conscious and the unconscious.

Tikkun ha-middot: The Improvement of Character Traits

One of the central themes of Salanter's thought throughout the period under discussion was *tikkun ha-middot* (character training), with most of the sermons published in *Tevunah* in 1861 being devoted to this subject. To begin with, Rabbi Israel attempts to disabuse his readers of the deterministic view of human nature, replacing it with a more optimistic approach:

> Do not say that what God has made cannot be altered, and that because He, may He be blessed, has planted within me an evil force I cannot hope to uproot it. This is not so, for the powers of a human being may be subdued, and even transformed. Just

> as we see regarding [the nature of] animals, that man is able to
> tame them and bend their will to his will . . . and also to
> domesticate them . . . so has man the power to subdue his own
> evil nature . . . and to change his nature toward the good
> through exercise and practice (see *Heshbon ha-nefesh*).[1]

At the base of Salanter's remarks concerning *tikkun ha-middot* is the
assumption that we are able to alter our personality traits for the better.
The analogy with animal training, borrowed from Rabbi Mendel Lefin's
Sefer heshbon ha-nefesh,[2] is intended not only to demonstrate the truth
of this axiom, but also to provide a hint of the means that can be
utilized in order to train character.

The possibility of activity deliberately aimed at changing a human
being's nature is already discussed in *Iggeret ha-mussar*, as we have
seen.[3] However, the discussion of *tikkun ha-middot* in the periodical
Tevunah differs from that which preceded it in a number of respects.
First, it is the most detailed and systematic discussion that Salanter
devoted to the subject. Moreover, even though in *Iggeret ha-mussar*
Salanter also considered the possibility of changing patterns of natural
behavior, he did not deal there with *tikkun ha-middot* in the precise
sense of the concept, as the discussion there was conducted within the
framework of the concepts of commandment and transgression. What
he proposed there was a system of studying and repeating halakhot,
intended to bring about the observance of mitzvot and the avoidance
of sins by the use of one's natural inclination. He speaks here of *tikkun
ha-middot* in terms of reshaping the fundamental contents of the soul,
by uprooting such negative qualities as anger, severity, and pride, and
by developing such good qualities as patience and modesty. Finally, it
is notable that the first time the subject of character training was mentioned in Salanter's writings was after he came to know about the
phenomenon of the unconscious, and was in relation to it.

By transferring his discussion from the realm of mitzvah and
transgression to that of character training, Salanter moved the focus
from isolated, external manifestations of behavior to their underlying
psychological motivations. This change raises the question of the theological meaning given by Rabbi Israel to *tikkun ha-middot*. How did he
picture the role of character training within the overall scheme of the
service of God? I will attempt to explicate Salanter's stance concerning
the theological meaning of *tikkun ha-middot* in comparison with the
characteristic outlooks of philosophical Mussar literature, on the one
hand, and kabbalistic Mussar literature, on the other.

In philosophical Mussar literature, the problem of *tikkun ha-middot* is discussed in terms of the assumption that a given combination of psychological traits embodies the ethical good. Thus, for example, Rabbi Saadyah Gaon thought that the ethical good is embodied in the proper harmony among the thirteen functions of the soul. Following Plato, Rabbi Saadyah Gaon thought that *intellectual cognition* is the element of the psyche whose task it is to fix the appropriate place in the life of the soul of each of the thirteen qualities. Intellectual cognition is meant to judge these matters in terms of the benefit or harm inherent in each of the tendencies of the soul.[4] This approach, which sees the embodiment of the ethical good in a certain balance of the traits of the soul, likewise underlies the Aristotelian doctrine of the golden mean adopted by Maimonides. According to this doctrine,

> Good deeds are such as are equibalanced, maintaining the mean between two equally bad extremes, the too much and the too little. Virtues are psychic conditions and dispositions which are midway between two reprehensible extremes, one of which is characterized by an exaggeration, the other by a deficiency.[5]

Thus, the ethical good is itself embodied in the very balance between the two extremes. Maimonides tries to demonstrate that the principle of mediation is consistent with the ethics of the Torah,[6] although he does not argue that the Aristotelian ethical principle and the system of the commandments are identical in contents. In the Fifth Chapter of his *Shemonah perakim* he gives the religious justification for his own ethical theory, portraying ethical perfection as a necessary precondition for the pure knowledge of God, which is the ultimate goal of Divine worship.[7]

There seems to be a certain degree of resemblance, with regard to the religious significance of *tikkun ha-middot*, between the stance characteristic of kabbalistic Mussar literature and that of philosophic Mussar literature. Like the latter, kabbalistic Mussar literature also tends to see the embodiment of the ethical good in a certain quality of the tendencies of the soul. But unlike the utilitarian harmony of Rabbi Saadyah Gaon, or the principle of the Golden Mean advocated by Maimonides, kabbalistic Mussar encouraged the quality of asceticism and maximal apathy toward the values of worldliness and its acquisitions.[8] Moreover, just as for Maimonides ethical perfection is a necessary precondition for the achievement of the ultimate goal of Divine service—namely, philosophical knowledge of God—in kabbalistic Mussar ethical perfection is understood as needed for the attainment of what it regarded as the highest level: *devekut*, or mystical attachment to God.[9]

But along with the points of similarity, there are also striking differences. While in philosophical Mussar literature the *middot* are presented as a separate and distinct system from that of the mitzvot, kabbalistic Mussar tends to bring out the strong connections between the two. Thus, for example, in *Sefer sha'arei kedushah*, by Hayyim Vital (sixteenth-century Safed Kabbalist, leading disciple of Rabbi Isaac Luria), the connection between the mitzvot and the *middot* is explained in light of the structure of the soul. The human body is composed of 248 limbs and 365 sinews, totaling 613 organs, corresponding to the 613 mitzvot. There are 613 spiritual organs of the intellective soul, each one of which is embodied in the corresponding bodily organ. The activity of the bodily organs is controlled by the power of the organs of the soul. But between the intellective soul and the body is the "lowly soul," in which the *middot* dwell. On the basis of this schema, Rabbi Vital defines the relationship between the mitzvot and the *middot* as follows:

> Therefore the *middot* are not included in the 613 *mitzvot*, but they are essential preparations for the 613 *mitzvot*, in their performance or negation, because the intellective soul is unable to fulfill the *mitzvot* by means of the 613 organs of the body save by means of the intermediate [that is, lowly] soul, which is joined to the body itself. . . .[10]

That being so, the *middot* are a kind of a vessel, by whose means alone the soul can cause the organs of the body to fulfill the mitzvot.

In addition to this structural explanation, *Sha'arei kedushah* contains detailed discussions of the relation between specific evil traits and the complex of transgressions likely to stem from them; the evil trait is depicted in these discussions as the spiritual source of specific sins.[11] Moreover, alongside the discussion of the evil traits, the author of *Sha'arei kedushah* describes a separate category, which he calls "forbidden traits,"[12] which are essentially sins. Their inclusion under the rubric of *middot* leads to a certain blurring of the line distinguishing between *middot*, on the one hand, and transgressions, on the other.

Although Salanter's writings contain no explicit discussion of the religious meaning of *tikkun ha-middot*, his views on the subject may be inferred from the overall context of his discussion of other subjects. First, it is clear that he did not see the ethical good as embodied in a harmony of the functions of the soul—as found, for example, in Rabbi Saadyah Gaon and Maimonides. Nor does he think that ethical perfection need be expressed in apathy toward worldly things, as is the position of kabbalistic Mussar. In Salanter's writings generally, and in his discussions of *tikkun ha-middot* in particular, there is no indication

Maimonides

that any normative meaning is attached to an ethical principle independent of the concepts of mitzvah and transgression. Therefore, one ought to return to a definition proposed earlier in this book: In Rabbi Salanter's opinion, ethical perfection is expressed in the maximal response to the commandments of the Torah. That being so, what religious significance is there to *tikkun ha-middot?* How does he justify transferring one's attention from acts of omission and commission— that is, the rubric of commandments and transgressions—to the characteristics of the soul, which are not directly subject to the discussions and rulings of the halakhah? It seems that this is dealt with in two ways. First, there is an attempt within Salanter's writings to subsume various character traits under the categories of mitzvah and *'averah* (sin). Thus, for example, he writes: "A bad trait is a very great transgression, for the sages greatly stressed the punishment for it; and a good trait is a great mitzvah, for the sages dwelt long on its high value."[13] In referring to the position of the Sages with regard to character traits, he quotes such sayings as: "Whoever is angry is subjected to all kinds of [punishment in] Gehinnom [Hell]. . . ."[14] That and similar sayings are not intended as categorical halakhic rulings, but rather as ethical guidelines or advice. Thus, even though it is doubtful whether Salanter would have included the various character traits within the formal enumeration of the 613 mitzvot, he nevertheless clearly wished to invoke the authority of the Sages in this matter, to the extent that he makes it into a subject of reward and punishment, like other mitzvot. This tendency is strikingly seen in remarks cited in his name by his disciple, Rabbi Naphtali Amsterdam:

> . . . . We heard from him once, when he [discussed] at length the obligation incumbent upon a person not to stand [too much] on his rights, saying that this is a positive commandment of the Torah. When a person hears another insult and embarrass him, he is required at that very moment to love him and to do him good, in place of the evil which his fellow did to him. As it is spoken in the Torah, "to Him you shall cling" [Deut. 10:20], which the Sages interpreted, "that is—to cling to His ways. Just as He does not stand upon his rights, so shall you do, etc." As is written in [Moses Cordovero's] *Sefer tomer devorah*, that we have found regarding the traits of the Holy One, blessed be He, that [even] at the moment that a man sins before God, He does much good for him, for even at the moment of sin He causes life to flow to him. For [were he to be] without His flow for even a moment, he would be destroyed and lost, Heaven forbid. . . . And a man is required to do thus, for if not he violates

a positive precept of the Torah, like *tefillin* and *zizit* and the like.[15]

But while Salanter wished to lend the normative status of mitzvot and transgressions to the character traits, there is no doubt that the significance attached to *tikkun ha-middot* went beyond that. It would seem that in principle he understood *tikkun ha-middot* as the shaping of the personality in a manner appropriate to the commandments of the Torah. By creating harmony between the characteristics of the soul and the demands of the halakhah, the psychological obstacles hindering man from serving God are removed, thereby paving the way for the maximal response to God's commandments. This approach forms the background for the following statement by Salanter:

> There are two kinds of [character] transmutation: one, in which man turns the powers of his soul to the good, so that the power of evil is totally uprooted and not seen at all. To accomplish this, it is insufficient for man to improve his general will, to long for the good and to despise evil, but he must seek the means of correcting each individual trait of his soul. This is required in the case of the rational [ethically self-evident] commandments, pertaining to man and his fellow. . . . The second way involves the "transmutation" of his general will, to love and to heed that which comes out from the mouth of God in the traditional commandments [ritual or ceremonial law reflecting arbitrary, Divine will] known to us by revelation, and to seek out and reduce the power of the appetite in each detail. . . .[16]

From the distinction drawn between the "two kinds of transmutation," it is clear that *tikkun ha-middot* relates to the realm of mitzvot between people, and not to those between a person and God, as it is in the interpersonal realm that such traits as arrogance or humility, anger or patience—which are the objects of *tikkun ha-middot*—are expressed. At the same time, it is clear that Salanter does not simply wish to identify the *middot* with the realm of mitzvot between people; rather, the relationship between these two distinct systems is one of interdependence. *Tikkun ha-middot* creates the psychological framework that fosters and makes possible the observance of the mitzvot between people. On the other hand, there are no specific traits of the soul whose correction as such will assure the fulfillment of the mitzvot between a person and God. It is nevertheless both possible and desirable that one work at correcting one's soul so as to fit the commandments of the Torah in this area, and by means of "correction of his general will to love and to observe that which emanates from the mouth of God," or, to use our language, by cultivating a psychological tendency to wish to fulfill all of the mitzvot.

To summarize, one may say that, in Salanter's view, the theological significance of *tikkun ha-middot* is anchored in the concepts of mitzvah and transgression in two different ways: the tendency to define the *middot* themselves within the framework of these concepts, and the attribution of instrumental significance to the *middot*—that is, that *tikkun ha-middot* prepares the soul to fulfill the entirety of the mitzvot between one person and another. We thus find that Salanter's outlook on this question approximates that of *Sefer sha'arei kedushah*.

Rabbi Israel explained the instrumental nature of *tikkun ha-middot* by means of a distinction between two concepts: the subjugation of the Evil Impulse (*kibbush ha-yezer*) and the correction or transmutation of the Evil Impulse (*tikkun ha-yezer*). The former denotes the reining in and curbing of the appetites by the power of the will, while the latter concept is used in a parallel sense to *tikkun ha-middot*. The uniqueness of Salanter's approach to this question may be seen by means of comparison with the positions taken, respectively, by Maimonides and the author of *Sha'arei kedushah*. Maimonides deals with this question in his *Shemonah perakim*,[17] where he attempts to overcome the contradiction between the position of the philosophers and that of the classical talmudic Sages. According to the philosophers, the "saintly individual [that is, one whose character is refined to begin with] who does good, and who [naturally] desires and longs for it," is preferable to the "man of self-restraint," who overcomes his Evil Impulse and performs "praiseworthy deeds" even though he "desires iniquity and longs for it." The Sages, on the other hand, hold that:

> He who desires iniquity and craves for it [but does not do it] is more praiseworthy and perfect than the one who feels no torment at refraining from evil. . . . Furthermore, they command that man should conquer his desires. . . . Rabbi Simeon ben Gamliel summed up this thought in the words, "Man should not say, 'I do not want to eat meat together with milk' . . . but he should say, 'I do indeed want to, yet I must not, for my Father in Heaven has forbidden it.' "[18]

Maimonides resolved this contradiction by means of the famous distinction between the rational and the traditional commandments. The position of the philosophers, which prefers the "saintly person" whose character is innately good over the individual who exercises self-restraint, refers to the rational commandments. It is clear in such a case that "a soul which has the desire for and lusts after such misdeeds, is imperfect; that a noble soul has absolutely no desire for any such crimes and experiences no struggle in refraining from them. . . ." The approach of the Sages, which sees the one who "overcomes his spirit"—that is, he who controls his longing in the face of God's commandment—as superior, refers to the revealed commandments, "since were it not for the Law, they would not at all be considered transgressions. Therefore, the rabbis say, that a person should permit his soul to entertain the natural inclination for these things, but that the Law alone should restrain him from them."[19]

In this respect, Rabbi Hayyim Vital's position in *Sha'arei kedushah* is quite different. Unlike Maimonides, who thinks that one does not give absolute preference to either *kibbush ha-yezer* or *tikkun ha-yezer*, because each is preferable in its particular realm, Vital establishes a clear and unequivocal hierarchy between the two:

> The rule that follows, is that one who fulfills the 613 mitzvot while the Evil Impulse is within man, and he overcomes it, is called a *zaddik* [a righteous man]; but one who fulfills them through the utter negation of the Evil Impulse, which indicates the acquisition of the good traits as a part of his nature, is called a *hasid gamur* [a perfect saint].[20]

The author of *Sha'arei kedushah* expresses an absolute preference for the *hasid*—that is, the person whose character is perfect as such—because the goal toward which such a person strives is that of asceticism and withdrawal from the world. To this end, an ascetic way of life, based upon a psychological attitude of indifference and equanimity toward this world and its possessions, is clearly superior. From that point of view, there is also no reason to draw a distinction between "rational" and "traditional" mitzvot. From the rationalistic point of view of Maimonides, on the other hand, the correspondence between the tendencies of the soul and that which follows from the intellect—that is, the rational mitzvot—is extremely important; this correspondence is not at all required in the case of the traditional mitzvot. But despite the difference between the position of Maimonides and that of Rabbi Hayyim Vital, there is nevertheless a common denominator between them: wherever they prefer *tikkun ha-middot* above *kibbush ha-yezer*—a preference that, according to Maimonides, is confined to the realm of the rational mitzvot, while in Vital it covers the entire spectrum of Divine service—both of them attribute value to this preference.

Against the background of both the differences and similarities between these positions, the uniqueness of Rabbi Israel Salanter's approach stands out. It differs from the kabbalistic approach in that it does not claim asceticism to be the goal of ethical improvement. On the contrary, Rabbi Israel believes that the deliberate attempt at *tikkun ha-middot* must be performed in relation to a social-worldly context or, in his language, *be-milei de-'alma* (in worldly things), as opposed to asceticism.[21] It is precisely in this context that people may anticipate those ethical trials for which, in order to stand up to them properly, they must make efforts to improve their character. On the other hand, Salanter's approach also differs from that of Maimonides in that his point of departure is not philosophical-rationalistic, but psychological-existential. Therefore, even if he does agree with Maimonides that *tikkun ha-middot* pertains specifically to the rational commandments— that is, those pertaining to human beings and their fellows—he is in no way prepared to forego the attempt to reshape the tendencies of the soul with regard to the realm pertaining to people and God as well. Thus, Salanter's position differs both from that of Maimonides and that of Rabbi Hayyim Vital in that, to the extent that he does prefer *tikkun ha-yezer* to *kibbush ha-yezer*, this is not a choice of values, but a functional choice, as explained below. The instrumental character of *tikkun ha-middot* in Salanter's approach is reflected in the fact that he does not see *kibbush ha-yezer* and *tikkun ha-yezer* as two different stages or levels of ethical perfection, but as two systems of ethical education and improvement that complement one another.

At the beginning of his discussion of these two concepts, Salanter notes the superiority of *tikkun ha-yezer*. While one who has succeeded in subjugating his *yezer* many times is still liable to fall into sin, one who has transmuted it is no longer exposed to the pull of the appetite because "the spirit of his appetite is given over to his intellect, to love righteousness and not to desire its opposite." Further on in his remarks, Salanter points out to us the exact significance of this preference: "[T]his is the entire [purpose] of man, to uproot every evil attribute and characteristic from his heart, for so long as he is not cleaned from their filth, even if he overcomes his Impulse many times, he will fall into their net. . . ."[22] It must nevertheless be emphasized that the preference of *tikkun ha-yezer* over *kibbush ha-yezer* is not a value judgment, because Salanter does not see the presence of the appetites within the human personality as an ethical defect per se. The religio-ethical status of a person is not fixed by the innate inclinations of the soul, but by the manner in which that person confronts them. Rabbi Israel's preference for *tikkun ha-yezer* is thus a functional, tactical one: One whose negative traits have been transmuted is stronger and more resistant to the temptations of the appetite and the *yezer*. Subjugation and transmutation of the *yezer* are therefore understood as two different ways of withstanding ethical trials. But in addition to this functional judgment, Salanter places the two within a chronological framework. In the first stage of ethical growth, one is liable to struggle with the *yezer*, in the sense of *kibbush ha-yezer*, while later on "he will gradually advance to the stage of controlling his spirit. . . ."[23] Ethical improvement is thus depicted as a graded path with two levels on which we are expected to progress over the course of time from a relatively lower level to the higher and more certain one.

At a later stage of his discussion, Salanter qualifies these earlier comments, so that the hierarchical unequivocal structure described above becomes more complex. This new stage of the discussion opens with the warning that even those who have achieved the level of *tikkun ha-yezer* cannot entirely forego the need to subjugate the *yezer*. Although they have uprooted the evil from their hearts, new dangers may arise as the result of a powerful, unforeseen situation. For example, a person who is extremely patient and has seemingly totally conquered his tendency to get angry cannot be certain that, given some major personal catastrophe that he is unable to withstand, he may nevertheless fall prey to anger.[24] This warning is based on the possibility that the forces of the personality hidden within the depths of the unconscious may suddenly burst forth to the conscious realm in the wake of some external stimuli.[25]

In light of such a possibility, one can no longer regard *tikkun ha-yezer* as a final position and as a permanent attainment. Even those who have successfully devoted themselves to improving their character traits cannot be certain that they may not once again be forced to confront the struggle for *kibbush ha-yezer*. Indeed, there is a fear that such a person may now find it difficult to struggle with the Impulse and restrain it, "for the habit of subduing it which he once possessed has been uprooted from within him . . . as he has not made use of it for a long time, since the time that he came to enjoy the attribute of 'correction.' "[26]

Rabbi Israel goes on to suggest a new understanding of the interrelationship between *kibbush ha-yezer* and *tikkun ha-yezer*. These are no longer thought of as two levels, to be acquired sequentially, but as two different approaches to the problem of ethical improvement, which are both necessary and complementary. Certainly, one must persist in *tikkun ha-yezer*, since those whose character faults have been transmuted can conduct their lives in an ethical manner without the enormous psychological effort demanded by subjugation of the *yezer*; however, one may not rely exclusively upon *tikkun ha-yezer*, but must continue to practice *kibbush ha-yezer* in order to assure an effective line of defense in case of emergency.[27]

In his continuing treatment of this problem, Salanter faced a new question: To which stage of human life is each of these two methods appropriate? In answering this question, Rabbi Salanter reverses the previously suggested chronological order. *Tikkun ha-middot*, which had at first been described as a later stage, is now seen as suitable to youth and adolescence, whereas subjugation of the *yezer* is more appropriate to maturity and old age. Salanter's argument for this is based on a number of factors. *Kibbush ha-yezer* involves a concentrated spiritual effort, demanding great powers of forbearance. As such, it is appropriate to more mature individuals, whose endurance and tolerance for suffering have developed as the result of the trials of life and the struggle for survival. *Tikkun ha-yezer*, on the other hand, is more suitable to young people, whose personalities are still flexible and capable of change.[28] Salanter elsewhere mentions another reason for this:[29] The young man, who does not yet need to earn a living, enjoys a certain psychological calm and peace allowing for introspection and self-examination, careful planning of his actions, and the use of devices and various other means needed in order to transmute his traits. The older person, who must confront the pressures, temptations, and trials of practical life, lacks the emotional space necessary for serious work on his character. It seems reasonable to assume that Salanter was guided by these considerations in choosing the educational tactic to be taken in various contexts. It is certainly not accidental that the subject of *tikkun ha-middot* enjoyed detailed discussion on the pages of *Tevunah*, which was to a great extent intended for young *lomdim*, while it was played down, and at times not mentioned at all, in those writings and letters directed at the public of *ba'alei batim*.[30]

The mind plays an important role in the correction of the traits, according to Salanter, as it makes the decisions concerning the nature of both good and bad attributes. He refers here to common sense—that is, reflection based neither on logical reasoning nor empirical evidence. Salanter assumes an identity between the decisions of common sense and the ethical norms demanded by the Torah in the interpersonal realm. While he does not directly justify this assumption, it may be explained on the basis of a combination of ideas that Salanter does formulate explicitly. On the one hand, he claims that the *middot* relate to the realm between people and their fellows; on the other hand, he agrees with the outlook that states that the mitzvot between people are rational mitzvot—that is, commandments that would be required by the intellect even had they not been included in the Torah. On the basis of these assumptions, Salanter states that the "man of self-restraint" is one "the spirit of whose appetites is given over to his intellect, to love righteousness and not to desire its opposite."[31] In other words, *tikkun*

ha-middot means shaping the tendencies of the soul in accordance with the command of the intellect. There is an apparent closeness on this point between the outlook of Rabbi Salanter and the typical stance of philosophical Mussar literature. Unlike the latter, however, Salanter related rather skeptically to the power of intellectual cognition to impose its decisions upon the other powers of the psyche. Moreover, he thought that one ought to treat the intellect itself with suspicion, as it is a commonplace event that emotional drives may overwhelm the intellect and enslave it to their needs. For that reason, only common sense, "which is not corrupted or enchained by the forces of the psyche, whose tendencies are generally towards evil,"[32] can fulfill this function with regard to *tikkun ha-middot*.

We have thus far spoken about the function of common sense in distinguishing between good and evil traits. However, common sense also continues to fulfill a multivalent function within the framework of the educational process of *tikkun ha-middot*, first of all, by means of self-contemplation, whose function it is to locate and to distinguish the evil traits. Salanter again raises the demand for self-reflection, which we first encountered in his discussion of worldly wisdom,[33] in this connection, but here it refers to a deeper and more penetrating kind of self-reflection. The focus of this process is no longer the appetites, but rather the essential character traits. It must be emphasized that this contemplation is directed not only toward the *middot*, but also toward the various stimuli likely to awaken them.

The process of self-examination and identification of character faults is followed by the decisive and most difficult stage in the training of character: the attempt to break the negative traits and to implant and cultivate positive ones. The mind has an important contribution to make at this stage, as well—through mental devices. Before attempting to determine the nature of these devices, we must remember the common view of habit as a means of correcting the *middot*. According to this conception, which is first found in Greek ethics[34] and appears frequently in Jewish ethical literature,[35] a given pattern of behavior may become second nature by frequent repetition. We have already mentioned the theoretical basis for this assumption,[36] which Salanter took from Lefin's *Heshbon ha-nefesh*. But those Mussar authors who extolled habit as a tool of character training did not give much thought to the problematics involved in the use of this technique in practice. For example, it is quite possible that one attempting to change his character traits by means of habit will find it difficult to impose the decision of his will upon his actual behavior. How, then, will it be possible for him to repeat the desired behavior over and over again sufficiently in order to convert it into second nature? It seems to me that the function of mental devices may be understood in relation to this problem: They are designed to strengthen will power, to enable it to overcome the negative traits until they are uprooted from the personality.

We now examine the nature of these mental devices, through a number of examples from the testimony of Rabbi Naphtali Amsterdam, who describes what he heard from his teacher:[37]

> I once asked him for a cure for the trait of anger and short-temperedness, and he answered, "The cure is for a person to constantly bear in mind to be a good person, to do good to others. . . . So that when a person awakens in his soul loving-kindness, and doing good to people, and becomes known as a good person who does good to all, this will make it easier for him to keep himself from anger and short-temper. . . ."

This device is based upon a line of thought typical of Salanter as an educator, one that we have already encountered several times during the course of our discussion—namely, the use of social pressure to motivate individuals to act as they should. In this case, Salanter suggests awakening and directing social pressure by the deliberate cultivation of a self-image that elicits certain definite expectations from society. The psychological tendency to respond to our social environment and to fulfill the role that it imposes upon us in accordance with our image is meant to conflict with negative traits and defeat them.[38]

Another example of a mental device that Rabbi Amsterdam heard from Rabbi Israel is the following one:

> I once asked him for a cure for the trait of impatience, and he answered that a person should reflect upon the ways of the world and the caravans of the merchants. For example, a distinguished merchant whose custom it is to go about in pleasant clothing and beautiful adornments, in a white collar and the like; when he is confronted with a great cause for concern in his business, such as having to pay a large debt . . . and he does not have [the money], he leaves his house for the marketplace with anxiety on account of his great concern. Is it likely that at such a time he will take care as to whether his collar is on straight? He will certainly not pay any heed to such vain things. So is this matter, for a person must always reflect upon his great debt in the service of God, to God and to people, to improve himself and to improve the world, for this is the whole purpose

of his coming into the world. And this great care of his soul has
the power to thrust behind his back his vain thoughts to be
impatient with his fellow.

Salanter here again makes use of the same rhetorical device whose
efficacy he frequently noted in his writings: the use of the parable taken
from everyday life. By means of these parables, it is possible to convert
abstract truths, which reside in the back of our consciousness, into
concrete certainties affecting the entire spiritual existence of the individual. The above parable, and others like it, are able to cultivate in
our consciousness a new evaluation of our relationships with other
people. In accordance with this evaluation, a significant change will
come about in the order of priorities and in the understanding of the
relative significance of various events.

The third and last device cited by Rabbi Amsterdam is also directed
against the trait of impatience or severity:

> . . . . that a person should bear in mind three principles of the
> halakhah. . . . First, that the prohibition against stealing which
> appears in the Torah applies not only to actual theft, in which
> a person takes his fellow's money or belongings, but that any-
> thing which contradicts the civil law found in the section *Hoshen
> Mishpat* of the *Shulhan 'Arukh* is also theft. Second, that accord-
> ing to the law found in the *Hoshen Mishpat*, it makes no differ-
> ence whether he takes from his neighbor a garment which had
> always been his, or if he gives his neighbor a garment as a gift
> . . . and afterwards takes away that same garment. This too is
> literally theft. The third principle is that a grudge against one's
> neighbor is also subject to the laws in the Talmud and in the
> *Shulhan 'Arukh, Hoshen Mishpat*, and that one who bears a
> grudge against his neighbor, where this is forbidden by law, is
> also culpable of theft. . . . On the basis of these principles, when
> a person is truly convinced of them in his heart, whenever
> another person does him wrong or crosses him, he may conquer
> his tendency to impatience by thinking in his heart or saying
> aloud that he forgives that person entirely. It then becomes
> forbidden by law to hold a grudge or complaint against that
> person. In this way, he will allay the hatred and impatience that
> he bears in his heart. . . .

This device, which according to his own account Salanter himself used
in his youth, is typical of a scholar. The familiarity with the halakhah
and the speculative ability to manipulate a legal argument combine
here to place upon the negative trait of severity the full seriousness and
force of the laws of theft. In this manner, the deeply ingrained repug-

nance against violating the prohibition on theft is marshaled in order to help the individual overcome the trait of impatience.

The common denominator of all of the various devices described here is the attempt to reawaken the forces and tendencies dormant within the soul, utilizing their hidden strength to foster the correction of the *middot*. The trick thus entails an element of guile, as it displaces a given psychological tendency to redirect it toward the realm in which it encounters and conquers an evil trait, or develops and strengthens a positive characteristic. In the background of these and similar devices lies the analogy between animal training and the ethical education of human beings—an analogy that Salanter borrowed from Lefin's *Heshbon ha-nefesh*. According to this analogy, the personality, which is the object of moral education, is parallel to the animal to be trained, and the mind, which directs the process of moral training, is analogous to the animal trainer. Just as an animal trainer must ensnare the animals through guile, awakening their animal instincts and directing these into desired channels, the minds of those human beings who wish to improve their own character traits must guide the impulses and tendencies of the personality into the desired channels for purposes of ethical education.

Rabbi Israel's concept of moral education as an individual process, in which we each must act in accordance with our own personality and the circumstances dictated by our environment, is even more true with regard to transmutation of the *middot*.[39] This would seem to be the reason why Salanter does not much discuss the practical aspect of *tikkun ha-middot* in his writings, since detailed instructions in these matters must be personal;[40] even the mental devices described above were based upon the verbal instructions that Salanter gave to one of his disciples. In one of his letters to Rabbi Isaac Blazer, Salanter described an interesting example of a dilemma involving *tikkun ha-middot*, requiring a solution anchored in the individual situation and practical experience of the person involved:

> Generally, in the powers of the human soul one is not to operate by analogy. There is a person who will find a particular thing easy for him, and another thing very difficult for him to attain. Regarding the difficult thing, he must go about it gradually and over a long period of time, together with [sustaining] his longing to acquire it quickly. These are two opposing forces, both of which a person must touch. For if the longing will cease, then the labor will weaken, and if the longing become very strong he will do it hastily, so that the labor will hardly be accomplished at all, and it will not bear fruit, Heaven forbid. The wise-hearted

person, who reflects upon himself, will understand how to me-
diate between them without any fixed boundary.[41]

The dilemma depicted here is rooted in the tension between the intense
drive and impatient longing to correct one's ethical faults, and the
gradual and protracted character of the process of ethical correction. In
light of this dilemma, Salanter cautions against fixed and rigid directives, in the sense of "a fixed boundary." Only those individuals who
directly bear the burden of psychological confrontation involved in
tikkun ha-middot can determine for themselves the proper balance between these two extremes. By its nature, this must be based upon self-
examination and the drawing of conclusions from accumulated experience.

The Unconscious and Ethical Education

The most striking development in Salanter's psychological
theory during this period pertained to the distinction between "dark"
forces and "bright" or "clear" forces within the human psyche—a
distinction largely parallel to that in modern psychology between the
unconscious and the conscious. This similarity has moved some authors
to herald Salanter as having preceded Freud in discovering the unconscious.[42] However, he made no claim of originality, explicitly stating
that he borrowed this concept from "the scholars of the forces of the
human soul."[43] There were, in fact, a number of nineteenth-century
thinkers who preceded Freud in discovering the unconscious life of the
mind,[44] and there has recently even been an interesting discovery relating to the exact source that apparently influenced Salanter—namely,
Immanuel Kant, who in one of his tractates discusses the phenomenon
of the unconscious, using the identical terminology as was later used
by Salanter.[45] Whether Kant's influence was direct or indirect, his
discussion seems to have been the source from which Salanter drew
the distinction between dark and bright powers.[46] Of course, the refutation of his "discovery" of the unconscious does not detract from the
originality and creativity he displayed in his use of these new concepts
and in their incorporation within his thought.

In tracing the development of Salanter's awareness of the unconscious, as expressed in the distinction between dark and clear forces,
Yohanan Silman observes:

> The transition from psychology to discussion of the unconscious
> realms of the psyche took place in Rabbi Israel during the course
> of an organic and continuous intellectual development. The very

> possibility of the existence of "habits" implies the existence of
> a level of the psyche in which individual acts and desires are
> submerged and combine into "habits." This level is necessarily
> an unconscious one, as consciousness does not preserve its con-
> tents over a long period of time, while the very existence of
> "habits" requires the continuity of the impressions of isolated
> acts.[47]

Silman alludes to the possibility that Rabbi Salanter was close to recognizing the existence of the unconscious level of the psyche even
before reaching a clear conceptual formulation of the phenomenon.
This theory would seem to be confirmed in light of two facts, which
are explained below: Rabbi Salanter's relation to Rabbi Mendel Lefin's
Heshbon ha-nefesh, and the reference to the unconscious in that same
book.[48] But Lefin only mentions this phenomenon in passing, and does
not give it a clear and mature conceptual expression. Therefore, Salanter
did not explicitly relate to it in the earlier stages of his own thought.
At the same time, Salanter's use of the theory of the accumulation of
impressions in the mind, which he borrowed from Lefin, strengthens
the conjecture that the concept of an unconscious level of the psyche
was not foreign to him. It should therefore not be surprising that, upon
encountering the concepts coined by Kant, he adopted them and incorporated them into his own thought.

Salanter's principal discussions of the unconscious appear in three
sources: the article published at the beginning of the 1880s in *Sefer 'ez
peri*; the *derushim* that appeared in the periodical *Tevunah* during the
latter half of 1861; and the letter printed in *Sefer or yisra'el* as letter 6.
The date of composition of this letter was omitted, but on the basis of
certain signs it is possible to state with near certainty that it was composed in 1859, that is, about two years after Salanter moved to Prussia.[49] This is therefore his first explicit discussion of the unconscious.
An additional argument supporting this assumption is that, if we compare the terms used by Rabbi Salanter in his various discussions of the
unconscious, we find that, while in letter 6 he still uses the terms
"dark" and "bright" forces—citing the German original in paren-
theses—in the other sources cited above, these terms are no longer
used. It would therefore seem that Salanter was still under the influence
of the German source at the time that he wrote letter 6. In this connection, he also cited the "scholars of the forces of the human soul" as
the source from which he drew these new concepts. When he returned
to the subject of the unconscious in his later writings, he coined Hebrew
terms for this purpose, which were no longer dependent upon the
German original.[50]

How did Salanter understand the unconscious and its significance for moral education? The division of the psychological life into those levels revealed to our consciousness and those concealed from it, presents, according to Salanter, both in the emotional and intellectual realms. Insofar as this refers to the moral improvement of the human being, Salanter's interest is concentrated on the emotional aspects of the unconscious. The example he chose to explain the phenomenon of the unconscious to his readers was that of the process of learning to read a new language. At first, a student must invest considerable effort to combine the strange letters into words and the words into sentences—an effort that takes place on the conscious level. At a later stage, the student is able to read fluently without any special effort, because the entire process of combining letters into words and words into sentences now occurs in the unconscious. In light of this example, Salanter states: "The same is true of the powers of arousal of the soul: there are bright powers and dark ones. The dark forces are stronger and perform their functions powerfully and with little stimulus."[51]

In the final sentence, Salanter describes two traits that in his view characterize the feelings belonging to the realm of the unconscious: first, that they are immeasurably stronger than those in the realm of the conscious; second, the emergence of the dark powers from their concealment in the depths of the soul into consciousness is the result of external stimuli, with even a small stimulus sufficient to release powerful dark forces. He uses a familiar example drawn from human experience to illustrate this point: "A parent's love for his children is dark, and in most cases the person himself does not consciously feel it, but even a small stimulus awakens it to a burning passion."[52] What are the external stimuli capable of making the dark forces emerge into the consciousness from the hidden recesses of the soul? In the case of parents' love for their children, the feelings of love burst forth when they become aware of some danger threatening their offspring. More generally, Rabbi Israel decribes the "awakening," or stimulus, as an event or phenomenon in a person's immediate environment, bearing some relation to a specific force hidden in the depths of the soul. In other words, the stimulus is a concrete point of contact between the hidden emotion and the realm of the conscious.

The significance of this phenomenon for ethical education is based on the fact that both the appetites and the *middot* are rooted in the unconscious realm of the soul.[53] In practice, Rabbi Israel understands the unconscious as a hidden storehouse of psychological forces, identical in content to those known to us from consciousness. The same appetites and traits as are found in the conscious realm are permanently present in the hidden depths of the soul, until some external stimulus awakens them, causing them to be revealed.

It should seemingly be possible to recognize and identify the powers hidden in the depth of the soul by examination of how they reveal themselves in the conscious realm. However, Salanter cautions against the delusion that one can reconstruct a picture of the unconscious by means of analogy with what is known to us of the conscious psyche: For the powers of the human psyche move from the earlier to the later, from the depths of the roots of the heart to their manifestations. And there are many external reasons to cause some force, which in its source is small (as compared with the other forces), to expand and be revealed. For this reason, those who look with the eye of their understanding from the later to the earlier will greatly err in their judgment of the roots of the powers that bring about pain and pleasure.[54]

The picture of the unconscious, as reflected in the conscious realm, is neither complete nor balanced. Because the degree and power of the conscious manifestations of the soul's various unconscious powers are not determined by their relative weight, but by "external causes," examination of the conscious level of the psyche reveals no more than a small portion of the unconscious. In light of this conclusion, the threat posed to the possibility of ethical perfection by the appetites and the negative traits becomes more real, as the process of self-examination advocated by Salanter as a preventive measure cannot possibly uncover and locate all of the possible dangers buried in the depths of the soul.

In the following passage, Salanter notes the danger inherent in the evil traits being latent in the depths of the soul:

> For habit and nature change for extraneous reasons, as they are forced to do by another force opposed to that. Such is the case of the person who is diligent in his studies out of habit and nature, but who has a hidden potential which longs for money; this potential is not recognized, for he has no path to it, for his situation and ways are not those of trade, and he never in his life saw money. As a result, this potential has nothing to which it can attach itself, for the powers of a man, so long as they have no concrete thing upon which to hold, are hidden away in the depths of the soul, and are not seen or known outside. Therefore, if there will be some reason for him to seize on, in order to engage in commerce for the needs of his household and so on, this potential of the pursuit of money may burst forth, until he will nearly neglect his studies completely due to this potential—something which he would not have believed about himself in any circumstance, that he could so neglect his studies.[55]

Thus, the evil forces concealed within the unconscious are liable to bring about a revolutionary change in a person's way of life—if the external cause to arouse them presents itself. Even those patterns of behavior that are habit are likely to become changed from one extreme to the other, for the devotion to Torah study was a deeply rooted habit in the life of that scholar. Nevertheless, once presented with the opportunity to engage in commercial activity, he suddenly began to pursue gain.

The example of the scholar who is transformed into an avaricious tradesman is used to illustrate the possibility that a serious disparity may at times exist between a given individual's overt behavior patterns, which have been fashioned by the surrounding environment, and the attributes embedded in the depths of the psyche, which circumstances have not given the opportunity to find expression. In the following passage, Salanter refers to this phenomenon, its causes, and its potential dangers:

> One must realize that man's internal and external powers are distinct from one another. A given person may possess very good external forces, while his internal ones may be very evil; while at times, the opposite may be the case. For the basic foundation of the external forces is education. An individual who was raised and educated by honest and pious parents and teachers, and among pious people, will be shaped in such a way that his external forces will reflect the path of ethics and justice, even though his internal forces may remain evil, as they were at birth. . . . At times, the opposite may be true. The external forces will be evil, because he was educated by parents and teachers who rejected the ethical way, and because he associated with bad people, although his innate internal forces may be extremely good. Thus, we sometimes see a person renowned for piety who, in response to some powerful factor acting upon him at a certain time, is easily turned towards evil, because his inner nature is evil. This strong force arouses these evil forces within him, until they outweigh his good external forces, and so he moves from one extreme to the other. And at times the opposite may also take place. . . .[56]

The potential gap between the inner and outer forces of the soul is presented here in its full sharpness, so that one may even encounter an extreme situation in which education and environment act upon a person in a direction totally different from that person's natural inclination. Salanter would seem to have chosen to emphasize this extreme possibility in order to illustrate a certain potential danger: even one who has consolidated a regular, ethically positive way of life, and whose behavior patterns seem to be the result of positive psychological traits, may undergo a radical transformation, if changed circumstances bring about the liberation of those forces hitherto restrained in the depths of the soul. In light of this discovery, the challenge of ethical education becomes deeper and more complex, and the inner forces of the unconscious personality become the principal object of the effort at ethical self-improvement.

Salanter, in his writings, defines two ways of dealing with the appetites and negative traits concealed in the depths of the soul. The first method does not attempt to cause any change in these powers; its whole purpose is to curb, or at least to diminish, the negative effects likely to flow from them. This goal may be accomplished:

> provided [a person] sets his mind to penetrate to the depths of his heart to perceive the general forces within himself, which are likely to dominate his outer self as the result of a small stimulus, and he applies his understanding to them, in order to quell them somewhat so that they not go with quite such great rapidity, until he will have the power to restrain his spirit.[57]

Thus, despite the limitations of self-examination discussed above, Salanter continues to advise that it be practiced. Although it is impossible to expose fully the forces hidden in the depths of the soul, it can at least identify those forces that have on previous occasions broken through the threshold of consciousness. The identification of these forces and of the external causes that arouse them enable one to take appropriate preventive action, though in light of the awareness of the phenomenon of the subconscious and its implications, self-examination and preventive action lose some of the importance earlier ascribed to them.

The second way of dealing with the appetites and the negative traits found in the realm of the subconscious is more radical, in that it attempts to bring about a qualitative change within the soul. This is based on the assumption that, even if we are unable to examine or act upon our subconscious directly, we may still affect it indirectly—that is, through appropriate actions on the level of the conscious. One activity of this type is *hitpa'alut* (intense emotional excitement). The nature of *hitpa'alut* and its advantages for ethical education are explained by Salanter by means of a comparison with intellectual activity:

> The mind may discover hidden wisdom . . . awakening both the knowledge and the initiative to search out and to ask, and clarifying those things which are in doubt. The root of *hitpa'alut* is to open the closed heart, to fill it with the layers of understanding which are known to man, but have not penetrated to his inner self. This is because study of the ways of straightening

the character traits and purifying the psychic powers differs from the study of Torah or any other science. In the latter, the object of knowledge and the man who has the knowledge are two separate entities, and knowledge of them is merely stored away within man. . . . This is not so with regard to the *middot* and the purification of the psychic powers. . . . Not by knowledge of these alone does man live to conduct his affairs on the level paths of their teachings, unless the information is ensconced in his heart and, bound and linked in man, they become an [inseparable] unity. The way of acquiring them is by means of the doctrine of *hitpa'alut*, whose path and potency it is to bring blessing into the heart of man, leaving behind some gleanings in man even after it has ceased.[58]

The comparison with intellectual knowledge demonstrates the superiority of *hitpa'alut*: whereas the knowledge or insight gained by means of the intellect is stored in the consciousness or in the memory, *hitpa'alut* leaves an impression upon the very personality itself. Salanter explains the distinction between the intellect and *hitpa'alut* as follows: By its very nature, the process of intellectual awareness involves the dissipation of psychic energy, as the intellect examines the subject under discussion from different angles, clarifying various possible solutions. *Hitpa'alut*, by contrast, is characterized by the maximum concentration of the psychic powers on one specific sensation. This focusing of emotional energy on one point momentarily obscures all other sensations of the psyche and weakens their gravity.

Rabbi Israel believed that the effect of *hitpa'alut* was not limited to the conscious realm, but that it penetrates and leaves an impression on the subconscious:

Also in the inner-most, hidden recesses of the human psyche, around whose deep-rooted forces all of man's actions and longings revolve . . . there, too, the power of *hitpa'alut* comes to rest (albeit scarcely recognized or felt), to gather strength, until the rest of man's powers are pushed aside by it, and nearly extinguished (until the right time, when an arousing spirit shall come upon them that they spread forth, to be seen and known).[59]

We see that, insofar as we can speak about the influence of *hitpa'alut* upon the psyche, these processes take place simultaneously in both the conscious and subconscious realms. However, as stated explicitly in the last passage quoted, those powers pushed aside and weakened by *hitpa'alut* may again be strengthened when and if one is exposed to the appropriate stimuli. How, then, can one guarantee that this process of *hitpa'alut* will have the desired long-lasting results? One could say, by repeated experiences of *hitpa'alut*, because, although the impression of a one-time experience of *hitpa'alut* is liable to disappear with time, the quantitative impression of many experiences of this type in the aggregate will bring about a qualitative difference in the soul. In practice, this change takes place through a gradual, extended, and subconscious process. Salanter feels the need to encourage those who follow in this path:

> Let him not be discouraged when he sees that no impression is left in his heart, for he should surely know that his excitement was not in vain, but left a blessing not perceived by the sensory organs, until they multiply, and then they take root to bring forth a righteous fruit. Like the drops of water which, if they fall drop by drop over the stone for many days and years, will wear it away, even though the first drop was not even felt. . . .[60]

But the question of *hitpa'alut* still needs to be explained from two aspects: What are the contents of this experience and by what means may it be aroused in a disciplined and controlled manner? Salanter dealt with these questions in two different contexts, referring to the distinction between that type of *hitpa'alut* intended to correct the *middot* and that intended to deal with the appetites. The latter is to be eradicated by means of Mussar study. Salanter had repeatedly advised the study of Mussar by *hitpa'alut*, but now its significance is explained in terms of the theory of the subconscious—namely, that the experience of *hitpa'alut* by Mussar study leaves an impression on the subconscious level of the personality. Thus, impressions that accumulate in the wake of Mussar study implant in the depths of the soul "dark forces to aid in the struggle with the appetite."[61] He refers here to subconscious positive forces that are able to curb, or even to submerge and eradicate, subconscious appetites. Although he does not describe in this context the specific content of these forces, one may assume that he is referring to the dark forces expressing the longing to fulfill God's commandments.[62]

Whereas the form of *hitpa'alut* that is intended to eradicate the appetites is of a general character, that meant to affect *tikkun ha-middot* is more specific, directed toward the particular trait meant to be eradicated or cultivated. Thus, for example, one who wishes to rid himself of the trait of pride and supplant it by modesty is instructed to engage in repeated states of *hitpa'alut*, the content of which is to devalue his own personal traits in comparison with those of others. Such *hitpa'alut* will gradually diminish the attribute of pride, until it ultimately disappears completely.[63] The same holds true for the correction of other bad traits. In each case, the contents of *hitpa'alut* must be suited to the particular quality being addressed.[64] This is performed by the repetition of suitable rabbinic sayings, where the very act of repetition, the raising of the voice, and the special melody all contribute to the emotional excitation.

We have found that Salanter's awareness of the phenomenon of the subconscious did not bring about any radical change in the educational means that he advised, and that all those that he had already suggested at an earlier stage of his thought—self-examination, preventive actions, the study of Mussar through *hitpa'alut*, and the repetition of rabbinic sayings—continued to discharge a significant function. However, based on his new conception of the nature of the psyche, Salanter understood the significance and functioning of these techniques in a new light. From this, one may perhaps draw this conclusion about the development of Salanter's system: It was a process in which practical insights preceded theoretical speculation. Thus, means that were developed through practical experience and that proved their effectiveness in practice were not displaced by the new theory, but were reinterpreted in light of it.

To conclude this discussion, we may say that the inclusion of the theory of the subconscious in Salanter's Mussar doctrine refined and sharpened tendencies that were already present. The optimistic view that it is possible to bring about guided and controlled change in the human psyche now takes on a new dimension of depth, because Salanter applies it even to the subconscious. On the other hand, the pessimism expressed in perpetual self-doubt apropos the power of the appetite and the negative traits is also sharpened, since even one who has developed positive behavior patterns lives under the constant suspicion that evil forces hidden in the depths of the soul may suddenly break forth in response to some external cause and destroy the structure so painstakingly built up. It follows from this that a person cannot complete the process of ethical perfection through a concentrated, one-time effort. Ethical education is a process that one undergoes in all stages of life and throughout all transformations. In truth, Rabbi Israel Salanter understood ethical education as an ongoing way of life.

Epilogue

THE PICTURE of Rabbi Israel Salanter that emerges from the body of this book is primarily that of a teacher, educator, thinker, and leader. However, the personal dimension in his image remains obscure. Very little information pertaining to his personal life is available, either in his letters and his writings or in the numerous accounts about him. The silence of the sources on this matter suggests that Rabbi Israel was an extremely private and restrained individual, who did not reveal his personal world to others. We do not know whether this was an innate feature of his personality, or whether he consciously adopted it by means of deliberate effort. In either event, it is in keeping with his outlook regarding the importance of restraint and self-discipline in human life.

It may also be that this phenomenon reflects the fact that the personal dimension in Salanter's life was greatly limited. He rejected material comfort and quiet family life in favor of his public mission. At the same time, insofar as this pertained to his relations with others, he did not neglect those small details that constitute the life of the individual. Rabbi Salanter personally fulfilled the principle of "a trait and its opposite," which he advocated in his teaching on *tikkun ha-middot*.[1] While practicing a degree of asceticism in his own life, he revealed responsibility and sensitivity for the material well-being of others.[2]

We know little about Rabbi Israel's relations with the members of his family.[3] His wife and children remained in Lithuania when he moved to Prussia in 1857,[4] his youngest son then being about eleven years old. Rabbi Israel used to visit his family in Lithuania for periods of several weeks or, at times, months,[5] and likewise maintained contact with them by mail.[6] In the letters to his son Yitzhak, who was later to serve in the rabbinate, Rabbi Israel included Torah novellae that he came upon in the course of his study.[7] He presumably intended by this to encourage him to do well in his studies. His letters to his son-in-law, Rabbi Eliyahu Eliezer Grodzinski of Vilna, were primarily devoted to matters of public concern. Even though Rabbi Israel's letters to the members of his family, or at least those that are extant, are succinct and restrained, they still contain a sense of his warm personal feelings. Thus, for example, in a letter to his son concerning communal matters, he added a few words in Yiddish to his granddaughter: "Dear Granddaughter Leah, It made me very happy to see your own handwriting, so please write me again in your own hand. Your grandfather who wishes you much good, Israel."[8]

If Rabbi Israel generally refrained from exposing his feelings regarding personal matters in public, he was forced to deviate from this practice in the case of his youngest son, who became a scientist.[9] As a youth, Yom Tov Lipman Lipkin displayed brilliant talents in the field of mathematics. Even though he had not received a formal secular education on the elementary and secondary levels, he was accepted into the University of Koenigsberg at the age of seventeen. Young Lipkin completed his studies in Vienna, where he received his doctorate. From Vienna he went to St. Petersburg, where he received fame and honor because of a certain technological invention. The scientific success of the young Lithuanian Jew attracted the attention of the Jewish Maskilim in Russia, and the correspondent of *Ha-maggid* reported to his readers of the nineteen-year-old Lipkin's return to Kovna following a period of absence to study abroad. To this report, the publisher of *Ha-maggid* added the following note:

> This outstanding enlightened young man is the son of the famous rabbi and great *Ga'on*, known in the gates of the multitude, our teacher Rabbi Israel Salanter, may he long live, from Kovna. . . . And it is also an honor to his righteous father, the *Ga'on*, that he did not prevent his son from acquiring wisdom in the university, so that Torah and wisdom might be united in his son, to the glory of our people.[10]

A few weeks later, the following letter from Salanter appeared on the pages of *Ha-maggid*:

> Kovna, Adar 5625 [March 1865]. As the truth is a lamp to the feet of the righteous who walk about in the land, I am obligated to make it known before the people that the honor is not mine, as was written [in the report] concerning my son (in the pages

of *Ha-maggid*, no. 7), but the opposite is the case. The thing is very much to my dislike, and my heart is saddened concerning the path which my son wishes to pave for himself. Whoever loves his soul and is able to speak to the heart of my son, to change the desire of his spirit not to go against the spirit of my heart and my will, will do a great favor to a downcast one such as I am this day.

He who seeks faithfully, Israel of Salant.[11]

Salanter's reaction was intended to totally nullify any attempt to use his authority to legitimate the path of the Haskalah. At the same time, his words explicitly express the pain, anguish, and helplessness that he felt. Salanter's willingness to reveal his personal pain on the pages of this journal was presumably a result of his desire to display to the broader public his vigorous dissent from the path chosen by his son. He may also have hoped that one of the readers would answer his call and influence his son to return to the straight path.

An additional incident, in the course of which Rabbi Israel's profound relation to the members of his family was revealed, concerned a grandson who was involved with Haskalah. Salanter's letters to Rabbi Naphtali Ehrmann, which were published a few years ago, contain considerable information on this subject. Unfortunately, the editor deleted some material from and introduced inaccuracies into these letters, so that the reader cannot understand what the two rabbis are talking about.[12] After examination of the original manuscripts of these letters, as well as the drafts of Rabbi Ehrmann's replies,[13] the following picture appears: Rabbi Shmuel Adler, Rabbi Israel's oldest son, who lived in Kovna and made his living from trade, had a son who went to Germany in 1873 in order to study in a high school for trade. Salanter was troubled by the fear that the boy would eat nonkosher meat while living in a foreign city, and he therefore prevailed upon him to promise that he would eat only kosher meat. The grandson acceded to his grandfather's request, on the condition that his father would add to the living stipend that he sent him, to cover the additional expense of kosher meat. While in Kovna at the end of 1873, Rabbi Israel made efforts to convince his son to fulfill the young grandson's request. But after a certain period of time, Salanter informed Rabbi Ehrmann of his suspicions that the grandson was eating nonkosher food, because his father, "who is not among the God-fearing people," had not fulfilled his promise.[14] Salanter thereupon went into action. He first arranged that his grandson would eat at the table of a family who observed *kashrut* (the Jewish dietary laws), but this arrangement did not last long; the boy complained that the meals he was served there were not to his liking. Rabbi Israel then sought ways of sending him kosher meat, which he could cook as he saw fit. In the course of the various efforts made in this direction, Rabbi Israel enlisted the help of his student and friend, Rabbi Naphtali Ehrmann, as well as of other acquaintances. In reading the exchange of letters between Rabbis Israel and Ehrmann on this matter, one sees Rabbi Israel as a practical man of action, who paid attention to the smallest detail and examined every possible means of attaining his goal. More than anything else, one is struck by the firmness of his decision to do everything in his power to prevent his grandson from eating *treif* (not in accordance with *kashrut*).

In effect, Rabbi Salanter personally experienced what was undergone by many Russian Jewish families during that period, whose children abandoned the traditional study house to flock after the "light" of the Haskalah. This occurrence, which in many cases involved the abandonment of the yoke of mitzvot, was understood by the families of those young people as a severe, inconsolable blow. But, unlike those who observed mourning for their alienated children and became estranged from them, Salanter made efforts to maintain contact with his son and grandson and to return them insofar as possible to what he perceived to be the proper path.

Moving back into the public realm, it can be seen that Rabbi Israel Salanter was among those individuals whose image has been depicted in different and at times contradictory ways. In the eyes of the Orthodox public, Rabbi Israel was seen as a Torah giant whose main uniqueness, in relation to other *gedolei Torah*, lay in his worldview, his projects, and his personal achievements in the realm of *yir'ah*. His students, friends, and all those who knew him close up saw another side to his personality: a powerful and uncompromising fighter who confronted whatever he thought of as threatening the integrity and validity of the tradition. Among the Haskalah writers, there were those who identified him as one of their outstanding opponents, while there is a tendency on the part of others to portray him as a supporter of their views. For example, the publisher of *Ha-maggid* tried to attribute to Rabbi Israel a view that advocated the integration of Torah with *Wissenschaft*.[15] Even Salanter's forceful and unequivocal denial on the pages of *Ha-maggid* did not discourage a similar attempt a few years later.

In 1868, Joseph Gibianski published a report in *Ha-meliz* describing in detail a sermon allegedly given by Rabbi Israel in one of the communities of Lithuania. In the words placed in his mouth by Gibianski, Salanter appears as an outright propagandist on behalf of Haskalah, calling for a reorganization of the spiritual and cultural life of the Jewish community. The lesson to be derived from Salanter's "sermon" is summarized by Gibianski in the following words:

> If the *Gaon*, the glory and crown of Israel, head of the righteous and pious faithful ones of our generation, counseled thus on behalf of the Haskalah, what shall the other rabbis in our land answer, who do not reach to the ankles of that great *Gaon*? . . . O generation, you see the light sown upon us . . . for the cloud has also departed from above the tabernacle of the Torah, and over the house of Israel the light of the morning shall rise. . . .[16]

Several weeks after Gibianski's column was published, a response appeared in the pages of *Ha-meliz* under the title, "A Question of Rabbi Israel against Rabbi Israel."[17] The author of this response cast doubt upon the authenticity of Gibianski's account, as it diametrically opposed the position articulated by Salanter himself on the pages of *Ha-maggid*. But even this serious rebuttal did not end the controversy. Moshe Lilienblum came to the defense of the beleagured Gibianski,[18] first of all expressing surprise at the editor of *Ha-meliz*, who saw fit to publish a report questioning Salanter's image as a supporter of Haskalah. Lilienblum replied thus, not because of any deep conviction of the accuracy of that image, but for another reason: "Even if it were the case that Gibianski lied, what will you lose if the Orthodox readers believe in his words? And what good will it bring if they do not believe in them? For they will not consent to teach their children the language of the country!" As for the substantive issue, Lilienblum argued that he knew that Rabbi Israel had instructed his students to learn the vernacular and to be loyal subjects of their king. Regarding Salanter's reservations as to the path chosen by his son, this was not directed against his involvement with science within the borders of Lithuania, but only against the son's going abroad to study in Prussia.

How are we to understand the attempt to present Salanter as a supporter of Haskalah? There is no doubt that this attempt was a reflection of the Maskilim's awareness of the immense authority Salanter enjoyed within the Orthodox community. But why did the Maskilim use Salanter and not some other Torah figure of similar prestige and authority? It would seem that there were some aspects of Salanter's personality, expressed in his public activity, that gave a certain basis for his image as a Haskalah supporter. These features included the fine sensitivity that Salanter showed toward the suffering of the weaker segments in society; the criticism he directed toward the failures of his contemporaries in the field of interpersonal relationships; his tendency to act outside of institutional frameworks; and the openness and originality that he demonstrated in the cultivation of new educational tools and methods. To these must be added the fact that Rabbi Israel generally refrained from direct and explicit polemics against the Haskalah. It also seems reasonable to assume that Salanter's extended residence in Germany, the center of the Haskalah, as well as his close connections with the leaders of neo-Orthodoxy there, contributed to his image as a supporter of Haskalah.

Did the Maskilim themselves believe in this picture of Salanter, or did they fabricate it consciously for propaganda purposes? It is difficult to answer that question in an unequivocal manner. It would seem that some of them were prepared to encourage the dissemination of this image, even though they knew that it did not reflect the true opinions of Salanter, while others presumably adopted it in all innocence. In either event, the repeated attempts of some Haskalah authors to find support for their worldview in the positions of Rabbi Israel Salanter indicate to what extent his image differed from that of the majority of Orthodox leadership in the latter half of the nineteenth century.

IN REFLECTING on the origins of Rabbi Israel Salanter's Mussar doctrine as embodied in the teachings and path of the Gaon of Vilna, Rabbi Hayyim of Volozhin, and Rabbi Zundel of Salant, they are seen to be marked by a dialectical tension of continuity and of change. In a certain sense, the roots of Rabbi Salanter's thought were to be found in the spiritual heritage of these personalities. Like them, he championed the centrality of Torah study as a value, and its dependence upon the devotion of effort and attention to the cultivation of *yir'ah*. Rabbi Israel's approach to the ways in which one does battle with the Evil Impulse was likewise influenced by them; similarly, Salanter followed in the path of these same people by the very fact of addressing himself to the question of the relation and balance between Torah and *yir'ah*. But alongside these elements of continuity, we find aspects of innovation and change in Mussar teaching, which distinguished it from its predecessors. This was expressed in the shift of focus from the specific context of the circles of *lomdim* to broader society; in placing the problematics of Mussar in the psychological rather than the theological realm; in the conscious ignoring of the concepts and ideas of the Kabbalah, which is indicative of the decrease in the importance of theosophic speculation as against the growing interest in humankind's existential situation; and in the creation of a naturalistic psychological theory concerning the nature of the Evil Impulse, and the development of educational methods based upon this theory.

This being so, in seeking new and more effective ways of dealing with the problem of ethical education, Rabbi Israel was influenced, whether directly or indirectly, by certain ideas that had gained currency in eighteenth- and nineteenth-century European thought. This was expressed not only in the shift of the center of gravity of Mussar to the psychological realm and the new understanding of the psyche, but in the optimistic assumption that human beings are capable of improving the character of their psyche, if they would only use appropriate methods of doing so, namely, the fruit of the human intellect. This assumption entailed a demand that was also characteristic of the thinking of the new age: that people must take the primary initiative and responsibility for the battle against the Evil Impulse—and this in place of the traditional tendency to emphasize the element of Divine assistance. The modern spirit is also recognizable to an extent in Salanter's stance regarding earthly existence. The Gaon, Rabbi Hayyim, and Rabbi Zundel all thought that any ascent in one's spiritual level depended upon the denial of worldly values. Salanter did not dissent from that view, and even followed it to some extent; however, the great sensitivity he displayed toward the material suffering of the lower classes, as well as his advocacy of activism in the economic realm, would suggest that he departed somewhat from the above outlook toward a new and more modern valuation of earthly existence.

Rabbi Israel had not initially intended to make any innovations as far as the goals of Divine service were concerned, for he understood Mussar as a tool, the entire purpose of which was to help people to submit themselves more fully to the demands of the halakhah. But after the fact, the new elements embodied in Mussar teaching went beyond the realm of means and did leave their impression upon the contents of Divine service. In truth, the Mussar system created a new model of the pious person. The Mussar devotees—or ''Mussarniks,'' in the popular idiom—differed from the traditional Lithuanian scholars in that they saw ethical improvement as a matter of central importance, to which one was to devote time and spiritual resources. Even though devotion to ethical improvement is not understood by the Mussar devotee as opposed to the centrality of Torah study, it led in practice to a certain erosion of its status. This stemmed not only from the need to divide one's time and psychic energies between these two activities, but from the fact that ethical achievement now became an important criterion with regard to a person's standing in terms of Divine service generally.

The spiritual world of the Mussar devotee is stretched between two opposing poles: on the one hand, the optimistic belief that, through appropriate means of Mussar education, we may reshape anew the attributes of our psyche, and on the other hand, an intense pessimism as to our ability to act in light of the demands of the halakhah, due to the power of the drives that move us to commit sin and their ability to dominate our understanding and to prevent honest self-criticism. From both these poles, the Mussar devotees were subject to undertake far-reaching tasks and to judge themselves harshly.

Even though the Mussar devotees perceived their goal and final test in the performance of the mitzvot, they tended to move the center of gravity of Divine service toward the realm of psychological events. But this redirection toward the life of the psyche is not concerned with assuring the *kavvanah* meant to accompany the act of mitzvah, or with religious emotions of any other sort. The focus of the Mussar devotees' service is rather upon the struggle over the very control of the forces of their soul, which in turn dictate their patterns of behavior and response. While kabbalistic teaching required the Jew to take part in the mighty struggle in the metaphysical sphere between the forces of holiness and those of the *Sitra Ahra* (Other Side), Mussar teaching transferred this powerful drama of the battle of good and evil to inside the human soul. One of the most striking signs of Mussar devotees is their adamant stand in this perpetual struggle.

There are those who have noted a similarity between Mussar teaching and Hasidism, on the basis of the role played in Mussar teaching by emotional excitation within the framework of ethical education. Even though one ought not to negate the significance of this general similarity, one must take care not to confuse or obscure the substantial differences between the two systems. Hasidism—at least that whose outstanding spokesmen were the Baal Shem Tov, the Maggid of Mezheritch, and his disciples—understood the performance of the mitzvot, as well as ethical perfection, as means toward the sublime goal of mystical cleaving to God; Mussar teaching does not acknowledge any religious value above and beyond that of the maximal fulfillment of the mitzvot themselves. From this difference in their understanding of the ultimate purpose of Divine service, there likewise follows a difference in the attitude of the two systems toward humankind's existential framework.

In the writings of the Maggid of Mezheritch and his disciples, one commonly finds such concepts as "the casting off of corporeality," "the negation of existence," and "the transformation of the I into nothingness." These concepts reflect the assumption that what separates people from God is their self-consciousness, and of course the earthly existence within which they are confined. The *hasid* yearns to reach unmediated contact with the Divine realm by a conscious and deliberate effort to negate his own autonomous being and to break through the boundaries of his earthly existence. We find the opposite of this approach in the doctrine of Rabbi Israel Salanter: The goal of ethical education is to attain the maximal degree of self-control specifically within the earthly context in which we exist. The accomplishment of such a goal demands self-contemplation, through which one comes to recognize and understand the "I" in its psychological depths.

The difference between Hasidism and Mussar teaching is also striking in terms of the desired relation toward the act of sin. One of the innovations of Hasidism was expressed in its reserved attitude toward the emotions of sadness and regret aroused in the wake of the deed of sin. Hasidism saw the fostering of these emotions as the counsel of the Evil Impulse, which sought to prevent one from serving God. Constant self-examination, invoking feelings of sadness and regret, does not square with the spiritual mood required of one who wishes to achieve mystical closeness to God. In Salanter's thought, we find the exact opposite: self-examination, self-suspicion, and the fear of sin are central features of the religious personality that Salanter wished to cultivate.

Another major area of difference between the two movements was that of leadership, a difference expressed both in the understanding of the spiritual level of the leader and in the nature of that leadership. In Hasidism, the *Taddik* was understood as one graced with a soul possessing unusual qualities, and therefore not subject to sin. The "descent of the *Taddik*," demanded by his responsibility to the people, is expressed in sinful thoughts or in a spiritual connection with sinners, but never in actual sinful deeds. As against this, in the Mussar teaching of Rabbi Salanter, even the *Taddik* is not without an Evil Impulse, nor is he exempt from struggling with it. Moreover, the higher the level of Divine service reached by a person, the more stringent the criteria against which he is expected to measure himself. The *Taddik* is therefore a person marked by such strict self-criticism that he is able to discover hidden sins—that is, sins that are seemingly so trivial that an ordinary person would not notice them at all.

The difference between Hasidism and the Mussar movement with regard to the mode of functioning of the leader is rooted both in their respective understanding of the goal of Divine service and in their understanding of the nature of the leader. The Hasidic leader, by means of his mystical-psychic connection with his followers, is able to lift them up to a higher spiritual level and connect them to the upper worlds. The Hasidic *Taddik* thereby serves, not only as a personal example and guide, but as a kind of bridge by which the ordinary Hasidim are able to realize the sublime value of *devekut*. From the viewpoint of the Mussar movement, on the other hand, the function of the spiritual leader is confined to providing guidance to individuals in their efforts toward ethical improvement. The leader is able to arouse and stimulate, to present a personal example and to give advice. But in the final analysis, each of us stands alone with our urges, and upon us alone is imposed the task of conquering them. The experience of spiritual elevation, which may come about through the inspired example of the leader or through the feeling of community of Mussar followers, may assist the individual in battling the *yezer*. But ultimately, this experience can never serve as a substitute for the battle itself, which takes place within the soul of the individual.

THE FOUNDATION and growth of the Mussar movement are among the striking manifestations of the crystallization of Orthodoxy within Russian Jewry. In view of the growth in the influence of the Haskalah movement in the 1840s, Rabbi Israel concluded that the existing frameworks of traditional society were incapable of continuing to assure the force and integrity of the tradition. Ethical improvement, in the unique method of Mussar teaching, was meant to strengthen the power of the individual to withstand the new circumstances. In a certain sense, Salanter wished to shift the burden of responsibility for the existence of the tradition from the communities, whose spiritual and cultural homogeneity had begun to be challenged, to the shoulders of the individuals, who found support and encouragement in the fellowship of the new movement. Furthermore, Salanter saw in the improvement of ethical norms in the interpersonal realm the answer required by halakhah itself to the economic and social distress that weighed heavily upon Russian Jewry during that period.

Unlike German neo-Orthodoxy, which sought to overcome the crisis of the tradition by means of a synthesis of "Torah with worldliness," Salanter attempted to restore the vitality of the tradition, by cultivating its own inherent values. At the same time, he did not hesitate to use innovative tools and methods that reflected the spirit of the times. It may be that it was precisely this note of innovation that attracted to the Mussar movement individuals who had to some extent or another been exposed to the influence of Haskalah, but who wished to remain loyal to the tradition. Rabbi Israel's willingness to adopt and cultivate new methods and patterns in order to protect and strengthen the values of the tradition was not only expressed in Mussar teaching and in the organization of the Mussar movement, but in all of his public activity. This tendency, like the stubbornness of his struggle and his unwillingness to compromise—even for tactical reasons—were among the salient characteristics that made his image stand out in the human scenery of Orthodox leadership in Russia in the second half of the nineteenth century.

Rabbi Israel Salanter's biography is marked by the profound gap between the recognition and honor he enjoyed for his great Torah knowledge and *yir'ah*, and the actual response of the public to his Mussar message. Despite his extensive efforts, he did not succeed in turning the Mussar movement into a widespread and influential movement. Moreover, from the very beginning his initiatives encountered fierce opposition on the part of prominent personalities in the rabbinic leadership. The failure of the Mussar movement to attract the masses of Lithuanian Jews to its ranks would seem to be rooted, first and foremost, in the severity of the demands that he presented to the individual Jew. The cool response of the rabbinic leadership stemmed from its fears of sectarian splits within Lithuanian Jewry. These were presumably nurtured by the lessons of the precedent of Hasidism. In addition, the opponents of the Mussar movement probably feared that it would cause damage to the position of Torah study. Salanter's belief that it would be possible to halt the threat to the tradition more successfully by means of the movement he founded was not accepted by the majority of the Orthodox leadership, perhaps because the natural reaction aroused by this threat to the tradition was greater adherence to existing patterns and structures, whereas Salanter hoped to protect the tradition by means of tools and patterns that involved an element of innovation.

But what Rabbi Israel did not succeed in accomplishing during his own lifetime, his disciples and their disciples in turn succeeded in doing after his death. At the end of the nineteenth century, the Mussar movement shifted the focus of its activity to the realm of the yeshivot. Mussar yeshivot were founded, and efforts were undertaken to introduce Mussar teaching into the established yeshivot.[19] These steps encountered severe opposition from the supporters of the Haskalah, on the one hand, and from influential circles within the rabbinic establishment, on the other.[20] However, the Mussar movement emerged victorious from its confrontation with its opponents. Not only was the way of the Mussar yeshivot seen as legitimate, but even those yeshivot that had originally expressed reservations concerning this path began to adopt it. These developments took place after it was clearly shown that Mussar teaching was most successful in the struggle against Haskalah influences. That being so, toward the end of the nineteenth century the Mussar movement became the leading force in the Lithuanian yeshivot, and as such a highly influential factor within the Orthodox public generally. But the task that this movement was to fulfill in the future in the world of Russian Jewry would not have been possible without the foundations laid by Salanter.

The great strides taken by the Mussar movement in the realm of the yeshivot may be explained by the fact that the quest for ethical wholeness particularly suits youth as an age group. The demands of the Mussar movement, which repelled the more mature public by their severity, were accepted as an exciting challenge by the yeshiva students. Moreover, at the end of the nineteenth century, enlightened Jewish youth in Russia were characterized by a mood of radicalism, whether social radicalism or national radicalism. In such a cultural climate, the Mussar movement provided Orthodox youth with avenues of expression for religious radicalism.

In practice, the influence of the Mussar movement went beyond the boundaries of the yeshivot that adopted it. This fact found interesting expression in a remark of Rabbi Eliezer Gordon, one of the students of Salanter, who for many years headed the yeshiva at Telz. In his eulogy for Rabbi Israel Salanter, Rabbi Gordon said that the obligation to mourn him applied both to the adherents of the Mussar movement and to its opponents: to the former group, because he paved a new way for them in the fear of God; to the latter, because he forced them to prove that it was possible to be a God-fearing Jew even without embracing the Mussar doctrine.[21]

Notes

Introduction

1. The literature devoted thus far to the biography of R. Israel Salanter and his thought is relatively small. The involvement of critical scholarship in this area has been even more limited. Those books and articles that were available to me have been specified in the notes that accompany the body of this work. I would like here to note two works whose contribution seems to me to be particularly significant: (1) Dov Katz, *Tenu'at ha-mussar: toldoteha isheiha ve-shitoteiha* [*The Mussar Movement: Its History, Personalities and Systems* (Hebrew)], 5 vols. (Tel Aviv, 1945). The first volume of this set is devoted almost entirely to Rabbi Israel Salanter. One cannot overestimate the importance of Rabbi Katz's contribution in gathering together the numerous sources that shed light upon the biography of Salanter. However, being himself a product of the Mussar movement and a fervent admirer of its founder, Katz's descriptions tend toward idealization, which does not always stand up in the light of criticism; (2) *Kitvei rabbi yisrael salanter* [*Writings of Rabbi Israel Salanter* (Hebrew)], edited, with introduction and notes, by Mordecai Pechter (Jerusalem, 1973). Pechter includes in this edition the principal writings of Rabbi Israel. His use of full Hebrew orthography, with contemporary-style punctuation and explanatory notes, is of great value to everyone interested in Salanter's thought. Pechter's introduction includes a biographical survey and a comprehensive and insightful discussion of Salanter's Mussar teaching.

2. In contemporary Hebrew, the term *Mussar* is used in a sense more or less synonymous with the Western concept of "ethics." In biblical wisdom literature, the word refers to a punishment or verbal rebuke directed against a negative act, while in medieval Hebrew literature it refers to proper interpersonal behavior.

3. *Yir'ah*—literally, "fear," here signifying "the fear of God." In this part of our discussion, the concept of *yir'ah* is used in the widely accepted sense found in the literature of the period—that is, to refer to a sublime religio-ethical level that was seen as an ideal in the traditional Jewish society.

Chapter 1

1. See *Tevunah; kevuzat hiddushei torah mi-hakhmei u-gedolei yisra'el*, ed. R. Israel Salanter (Memel and Koenigsberg, 1861–62), 3, note.

2. See Eliezer Rivlin, *Ha-zaddik r. yosef zundel mi-salant ve-rabotav* (Jerusalem, 1927), 129.

3. *Sefer or yisra'el*, including a collection of letters of R. Israel Salanter with various additions by R. Isaac Blazer, ed. R. Isaac Blazer (Vilna, 1900), 30.

4. Ibid., 24. R. Naphtali Amsterdam, who was one of R. Salanter's closest disciples, likewise attests to R. Israel's connection to this lineage (ibid., 124).

5. See Dov Katz, *Tenu'at ha-mussar, toldoteha isheha ve-shitoteha*, 5 vols. (Tel Aviv, 1967), 1: 86–87. For the proofs cited by Katz regarding the genealogy of the Mussar movement, see pp. 87–92.

6. Ibid., 92.

7. N. Lamm, *Torah li-shemah, Torah for Torah's Sake in the Works of Rabbi Hayyim of Volozhin and His Contemporaries* (New York, 1989).

8. Ibid., 287–90.

9. Ibid., 290–91.

10. Ibid., 291–93.

11. The periodicals *Ha-meliz* and *Ha-zefirah* were among the main forums for this struggle. For a detailed survey of this controversy, see Dov Katz, *Pulmus ha-mussar* (Jerusalem, 1972). Katz's work in effect constitutes a defense of the Mussar movement against its critics, and contains as well a valuable concentration of source material relating to the controversy.

12. R. Isaac Blazer published an announcement in the pages of *Ha-meliz* in 1897 (no. 167) that he was about to publish a book containing the writings of Rabbi Israel Salanter. Both the wording and timing of this announcement suggest that the book was intended to serve as a reply to the criticism of the Mussar movement. As I have mentioned, *Sefer or yisra'el* was published in 1900, and the above announcement would seem to refer to it.

13. My remarks here are not intended as criticism of Lamm's work, as the historical development of the Mussar movement was not intended as the subject of his discussion.

Chapter 2

1. For a comprehensive list of the writings of the Vilna Gaon, as well as a fairly detailed list of the secondary literature concerning him, see Isaac J. I. Dienstag, "Rabbi Elijah of Vilna; A Bibliographical List" [Heb.], *Talpiyot* 4 (1949): 269–356. Of the secondary literature, the book by Bezalel Landau, *Ha-gaon he-hasid mi-vilna* (Jerusalem, 1965), is deserving of particular mention for its broad scope and the numerous sources cited. The figure and activity of the Gaon have not yet received a comprehensive and exhaustive explanation in the historical literature. Of the little that has been done, particularly deserving of note is the article by Hayyim Hillel Ben-Sasson, "The Personality of the Gaon of Vilna and His Historical Influence" [Heb.], *Zion* 31 (1966): 39–86, 197–216. The question of the nature and role of *yir'ah* in the Gaon's teaching has not been discussed thus far in the critical literature, except in connection with other questions. The detailed discussion here, as far as I know, is the first of its kind.

2. Alongside this title, found extensively in the writings and documents of the Gaon's contemporaries, one also finds the single word, *he-hasid*, used as a title for the Gaon.

3. See Ben-Sasson, "The Personality of the Gaon," 41–45.

4. See R. Bahya ibn Paquda, *Hovot ha-levavot*, ed. Mahbarot le-Sifrut (Tel Aviv,

1964), *Sha'ar ha-perishut*, 522ff., and ibid., the beginning of *Sha'ar ahavat ha-shem*, 555–56; Mordecai Pechter, "The Homiletical and Ethical Literature of the Sages of Safed in the 16th Century and their Principal Ideas" [Heb.], Ph.D. diss., Hebrew University, 1976, 430–35.

5. See R. Elijah ben Shlomo Zalman (that is, the Gaon), *Sefer aderet eliyahu*, Deut. 1:1.

6. See R. Elijah ben Shlomo Zalman, *Iggeret ha-ger'' 'a* (this is the ethical will that the Gaon intended for his family when he was about to go to the Land of Israel), first published in *Kuntres 'alim li-terufah* (Minsk, 1836). The sources and quotations cited below are from the version of *Iggeret ha-ger'' 'a* found in *Siddur ishei yisra'el 'al-pi derekh ha-ger''a* (Jerusalem, n.d.), 561–64.

7. Things in this spirit are very common in *Iggeret ha-ger''a*; see also *Sefer tosefet ma'aseh rav* (Jerusalem, 1896), *She'iltot*, sec. 97.

8. *Be'ur ha-ger'' 'a le-mishlei*, on Prov. 23:30.

9. Ibid., 21:19.

10. See *Iggeret ha-ger'' 'a*, 563.

11. See R. Joshua Heschel Levin, *Sefer 'aliyot eliyahu* (Vilna, 1856), 65–67.

12. Ibid., 65, n. 36.

13. Ibid., 66, and elsewhere. The two notable occasions on which the Gaon abandoned his practice of withdrawal and took part in public polemics—namely, during the controversy surrounding the rabbi of Vilna and the struggle against Hasidism—appear to be the exceptions that prove the rule.

14. Ibid., 70ff. It is significant that those who were not among his close disciples who were privileged to be received by him noted this as an unusual occasion. Thus, for example, R. Yehezkel Feivel of Dretschin writes in the introduction to his *Sefer toldot adam* (Dührnfurt, 1801), ". . . in the first half of the month of Adar 5557 [that is, March, 1797], I was called to go to the home of our master, the Gaon . . . and God gave me grace and kindness in his eyes until I merited to speak with him five times. . . ."

15. See Levin, *Sefer 'aliyot eliyahu*, 67–68; see also the Introduction by R. Hayyim of Volozhin to *Sifra di-zeni'uta 'im perush ha-ger'' 'a* (Vilna and Horodna, 1820). Cf. the Introduction, by R. Issachar Baer b. Tanhum, to *Sefer ma'aseh rav* (Vilna and Horodna, 1832), cited in J. L. Maimon, *Toldot ha-ger'' 'a* (Jerusalem, 1970), 344, for a description of the Gaon's intense relation to the study of Torah.

16. *Sefer ma'aseh rav*, sec. 14.

17. *Sefer tosefet ma'aseh rav*, *Sheiltot*, sec. 47; cf. secs. 48, 49.

18. Ibid.

19. See also ibid., sec. 68.

20. Introduction to *Ma'aseh rav*, in Maimon, *Toldot ha-Ger'' 'a*, 343–44.

21. *Be'ur ha-ger'' 'a le-mishlei*, on Prov. 22:5.

22. Ibid.

23. Ibid., 24:31.

24. Ibid., 11:16.

25. Cf. R. Hayyim Vital, *Sefer sha'arei kedushah*, Pt. 1: Sec. 1.

26. *Iggeret ha-ger''a*, 563.

27. See *Be'ur ha-ger'' 'a le-habakkuk*, 2:4; compare *Sefer sha'arei kedushah*, Pt. 1: sec. 2.

28. *Iggeret ha-ger'' 'a*, 563.

29. See *Be'ur ha-ger'' 'a le-mishlei*, 11:22.

30. Ibid., 4:15.

31. Ibid., 20:18.
32. Ibid., 1:23.
33. *Sefer ma'aseh rav*, sec. 60.
34. *Iggeret ha-ger'' 'a*, 564.
35. Ibid.
36. Ibid.
37. *Be'ur ha-ger'' 'a le-mishlei*, 4:4.
38. See R. Shmuel Melzen, *Sefer even shelemah* (Vilna, 1890), 70.
39. *Hanhagot ve-'ezot*, recorded by R. Aaron Zelig Lifschitz, a disciple of R. Hayyim of Volozhin, in MS London Fedro 1,14 (in the Institute for Microfilmed Hebrew Manuscripts, No. 8800, sec. 115).
40. R. Elijah ben Shlomo Zalman, *Be'ur aggadot le-masekhet bava kama*, chap. 8, s.v. "shitin tikhlei."
41. *Be'ur ha-ger'' 'a le-mishlei*, 2:5.
42. Ibid., 19:2.
43. Ibid., 1:7.
44. Ibid., 24:31.
45. This is the wording of the Tosafot to Ta'anit 7a, and similar to that of Nazir 23b, Pesahim 50b, Berakhot 17a; cf. Rashi on Berakhot 17a.
46. *Be'ur ha-ger'' 'a le-mishlei*, 23:1.
47. See Melzen, *Even shelemah*, 80. For other remarks criticizing those who study to attain honor, see *Be'ur ha-ger'' 'a le-mishlei*, 12:8; 31:30.
48. Melzen, *Even shelemah*, 77.
49. *Be'ur ha-ger'' 'a le-mishlei* 15:16–17; 17:1. The Gaon's strict stand concerning study "for ulterior motivations" is similar to that adopted in *Sefer hasidim*, Parma version, sec. 753.
50. See R. Israel of Shklov, Introduction to *Pe'at ha-shulhan* (Jerusalem, 1959), 5. In his introduction to *Sifra di-zeni'uta 'im perush ha-ger'' 'a*, R. Hayyim of Volozhin writes: "and he himself [that is, the Gaon] said that R. Isaac Luria left room for him to do this."
51. See the illuminating testimony of R. Abraham Simhah of Amzislav, the nephew of R. Hayyim of Volozhin, who heard the things directly from R. Hayyim in the name of the Gaon: R. Moses Hayyim Luzzatto, *Sefer derekh tevunot la-ramha''l* (Jerusalem, 1880), 38.
52. Ben-Sasson, "The Personality of the Gaon," 46.

Chapter 3

1. A comprehensive and exhaustive biography of R. Hayyim remains to be written. A brief biographical sketch appears in the book of R. Moshe Shmuel Shmukler-Shapiro, *Toldot rabbenu hayyim mi-volozhin* (Vilna, 1900). For a discussion of the worldview and educational theory of R. Hayyim, see Yonah Ben-Sasson, "The Spiritual World and Teaching of the Founders of the Lithuanian Yeshivah" [Heb.], in *Hinukh ha-adam ve-ye'udo* (Jerusalem, 1967). For a comprehensive and detailed discussion of R. Hayyim's teaching against the background of other tendencies in the thought of the time, see Norman Lamm, *Torah li-shemah be-mishnat rabbi hayyim mi-volozhin uve-mahshevet ha-zeman* (Jerusalem, 1972). For a discussion of his activity in its historical context, see I. Etkes, "The Doctrine and Activity of R. Hayyim of Volozhin as the Reaction of 'Mitnaggedic' Society to Hasidism" [Heb.],

PAAJR 38–39 (1972): 1–45. In chap. 4, I summarize my main conclusions from that article, treating more extensively those topics that pertain to the specific subject of the present work.

2. R. Hayyim's unique position is implied in many sources of the period. See, for example, the introduction of the Gaon's sons to *Shulhan 'arukh: orah hayyim 'im be'ur ha-ger'' 'a*; R. Hayyim's letter concerning the founding of the yeshiva, first published in *Ha-peles* 3 (1902): 140–43; Shmukler-Shapiro, *Toldot rabbenu hayyim*, 162–68; and other sources.

3. On the book *Nefesh ha-hayyim*, its editions, structure, and date of composition, see Lamm, *Torah li-shemah*, 38–56. The references and quotations to *Nefesh ha-hayyim* in the present work are based upon the 1874 Vilna edition.

4. Lamm surveys the different opinions concerning the underlying motivations of R. Hayyim's work, and concludes that the reaction to Hasidism played only a secondary role in this matter (see Lamm, *Torah li-shemah*, 57–64). For a detailed critique of this opinion, see my review of the above work in *Kiryat sefer* 50 (1975): 638ff.

5. Hayyim Hillel Ben-Sasson's conclusion that the Gaon's commentary on Proverbs (*Be'ur ha-ger'' 'a le-sefer mishlei*) was possibly "his anti-hasidic manifesto," seems to me unconvincing. See Ben-Sasson, "The Personality of the Gaon," 204.

6. On R. Hayyim's relationship with the Gaon, see Ben-Sasson, "The Personality of the Gaon," 198–200; Lamm, *Torah li-shemah*, 2–8.

7. The Gaon's relationship to Hasidism, and the task he fulfilled in the struggle against it, are implied in the documents gathered by Mordecai Wilensky in *Hasidim u-mitnagdim*, 2 vols. (Jerusalem, 1970). For a description of the struggle against Hasidism under the leadership of the Gaon, see Simon Dubnov, *Toldot ha-hasidut* (Tel Aviv, 1960), 114–17, 138–50. For a discussion of the motivations of the Gaon's war against Hasidism, see Ben-Sasson, "The Personality of the Gaon," 204–12, and see now my article, "The Gaon R. Elijah and the Beginning of Opposition to Hasidism" [Heb.], in the forthcoming Shmuel Ettinger Festschrift.

8. In sec. 6 of the anti-Hasidic pamphlet *Zemir 'arizim* (Wilensky, *Hasidim u-mitnagdim*, 1: 64), it is related that the Gaon decided to launch an organized struggle against Hasidism on the basis of the consideration that the Hasidim "are heretics and that one pushes them down [into the pit] and does not take them up"—a reference to the halakhah in Avodah Zarah 26b. Confirmation of this testimony appears in the letter of R. Shneur Zalman of Lyady quoted there, 40, in a note.

9. R. Menahem Mendel of Vitebsk and R. Shneur Zalman of Lyady testified that they were rejected by the Gaon when they sought to defend Hasidism in his presence. See Wilensky, *Hasidim u-mitnagdim*, 1: 95, 198.

10. R. Hayyim refers to the Hasidim as "those who seek the closeness of God"— *Nefesh ha-hayyim*, 75.

11. R. Hayyim's moderation with regard to Hasidism is a fact agreed upon by all of the authors who dealt with the subject. One exception to this is Isaiah Tishby, who believes that R. Hayyim's moderate expressions in *Nefesh ha-hayyim* are not directed toward Hasidim per se at all, but only toward those "drawn after Hasidism" (*gerurei hasidut*). See I. Tishby, "The Source of the Saying 'The Holy One blessed be He, the Torah and Israel are One' in Luzzatto's Commentary to the *Idra rabba*" [Heb.], *Kiryat sefer* 50 (1975): 487, n. 32. See my reaction to Tishby's hypothesis in *Kiryat sefer* 50 (1975): 638, n. 1.

12. See Lamm, *Torah li-shemah*, 9–10.

13. The Gaon decided to initiate a struggle against Hasidism after he received a report from his followers in Shklov concerning a debate in the course of which the Hasidim were unable to answer the criticisms of their opponents. See Wilensky, *Hasidim u-mitnagdim*, 1: 64.

14. It appears from a number of sources that R. Hayyim had direct contact with Hasidim and Hasidism. Hayyim Meir Heilmann, who studied in the Volozhin yeshiva in his youth, testifies that many Hasidim "who held fast to their Hasidism" studied in the yeshiva, and that R. Hayyim drew them close. R. Hayyim was likewise accustomed to receive in his home various distinguished Hasidic leaders who passed through Volozhin. Once, R. Israel Yaffeh, the publisher of *Shivhei ha-besht* (the hagiographical account of the life of the Baal Shem Tov) and a follower of R. Shneur Zalman of Lyady, spent Shabbat at R. Hayyim's home, during which the latter asked him to say "words of Torah" that he had heard from his teacher. Heilmann further relates that R. Isaac, the son of R. Hayyim, used to read Hasidic works and would even at times incorporate ideas that he found there within the sermons that he delivered before the yeshiva students; see Hayyim Meir Heilmann, *Beit rabbi* (Berditchev, 1902), 10. On the visit of one of the great Hasidic leaders to R. Hayyim's home and the words of Torah that he said in his presence, see Isaac Sobalski's notes in *He-assif* (1888), 45. On an attempt by R. Hayyim to cooperate with a certain Hasidic *rebbe* in a matter related to the decrees of the Russian government, see Yaakov Lifschitz, *Zikhron ya'akov*, 3 vols. (Eretz Yisrael, 1968), 1: 27–28. It is well known that R. Hayyim undertook a trip through the Jewish communities of White Russia, where Hasidism was extremely prevalent. His impressions of Hasidism from that trip may be reflected in his remarks in *Nefesh ha-hayyim*, 75: ". . . and with my own eyes I saw a certain region in which this [i.e., the preference for study of Mussar works above halakhic studies] had spread so much that in most of Study Houses they have only Mussar works, and one cannot even find one complete set of the Talmud." For another explicit reaction to his unmediated meeting with Hasidism, see *Nefesh ha-hayyim*, 74. On R. Hayyim's reaction to one of the members of his family who became a Hasid, see *Hanhagot ve-'ezot*, 1: sec. 44. This relative may be the "grandson" of R. Hayyim, of whom it is told that he tended toward Hasidism. See Yizhak Isak Ha-Kohen, *Sefer sha'arei yizhak* (Warsaw, 1902), among the letters of the author's son, at the end of the book.

15. On the crisis within the circle of the learned in the wake of the strengthening of Hasidism, see Etkes, "R. Hayyim of Volozhin," 7–16.

16. See *Nefesh ha-hayyim*, 75, and the discussion of this phenomenon below.

17. On the innovations of Hasidism concerning the subject of *devekut*, see Gershom Scholem, "Devekut, or Communion with God," *The Review of Religion* 14 (1949–50): 115–139; reprinted in his *The Messianic Idea in Judaism and Other Essays* (New York, 1971), 203–27.

18. See n. 15 above.

19. This applies to the multitude. Nevertheless, R. Hayyim encourages those individuals capable of doing so also to study kabbalistic literature. See Aryeh Leib Frumkin, *Toldot eliyahu* (Vilna, 1900), 18; Lifschitz, *Zikhron ya'akov*, 1: 87; *Keter rosh: orhot hayyim*, sec. 60; Appendix to *Siddur ishei yisra'el 'al-pi derekh ha-ger'' 'a*, 575.

20. In R. Isaac b. R. Hayyim of Volozhin's introduction to *Nefesh ha-hayyim*, 7, he relates that even the sermons that his father gave verbally were generally based upon the *Zohar* and Lurianic writings, although he was in the habit of concealing

their kabbalistic source. However, R. Hayyim would occasionally reveal his kabbalistic sources for some specific reason.

21. See I. Tishby, *Mishnat ha-zohar* (Jerusalem, 1957), 1: 265ff.; E. Gottleib, "The Theological and Mystical Element of the Understanding of Man's Purpose in Kabbalah" [Heb.], in *Mehkarim be-sifrut ha-kabbalah* (Tel Aviv, 1976), 29–37. [Originally published in *De'ot* 33 (Winter 1966/67): 143–48.]

22. *Nefesh ha-hayyim*, 81. For a more detailed discussion of R. Hayyim's view concerning the influence of Torah study in the upper worlds, see Etkes, "R. Hayyim of Volozhin," 21–27.

23. On the kabbalistic elite in the late Middle Ages, see Jacob Katz, *Tradition and Crisis* (Glencoe, Ill., 1961), 219–24.

24. On the integration of *devekut* with Torah study, see Etkes, "R. Hayyim of Volozhin," 28–31.

25. On the relationship of Hasidism to Torah study, see J. Weiss, "Torah Study at the Beginnings of Hasidism" [Heb.], *Ha-doar* (1965): 615–18; id., "Torah Study in the System of R. Israel Baal Shem Tov" [Heb.], *Tif'eret yisrael, sefer yovel li-khevod r. yisra'el brody* (London, 1967), 151–69; Rivka Schatz-Uffenheimer, *Ha-hasidut ke-mistikah* (Jerusalem, 1968), 157–67.

26. See *Nefesh ha-hayyim*, 76.

27. Ibid. For more details concerning R. Hayyim's polemic with the Hasidic interpretation of the concept *Torah li-shemah*, see Etkes, "R. Hayyim of Volozhin," 27–28.

28. The reference is evidently to the remarks of R. Hannina b. Dosa in Avot 5:9: "Whosoever's fear of sin precedes his wisdom, his wisdom shall be sustained; whosoever's wisdom precedes his fear of sin, his wisdom shall not be sustained. He used to say: Whosoever's deeds are greater than his wisdom, his wisdom is sustained; whosoever's wisdom is greater than his deeds, his wisdom is not sustained."

29. See Meshullam Feibush Heller, *Sefer yosher divrei emet* (Munkatsch, 1905), 11b.

30. Ibid., 12a.
31. Ibid., 12a–b.
32. *Nefesh ha-hayyim*, 75.
33. Ibid.
34. Ibid.
35. Ibid.
36. Ibid., 57.
37. Ibid., 77.
38. Ibid., 79.
39. Ibid., 77.
40. Ibid., 36.
41. Ibid., 79.

42. See *Ruah hayyim; perush rabbi hayyim mi-volozhin le-pirkei avot* (Vilna, 1859), chap. 1., Mish. 1, s.v. "hem amru."

43. *Nefesh ha-hayyim*, 78.

44. This subject is explained in greater detail below.

45. On R. Hayyim's approach to halakhah, and his relation to the Gaon on that subject, see Zvi Kaplan, *Me-'olamah shel torah* (Jerusalem, 1974), 9–49.

46. This problem is explored in an article by J. Weiss, "The Beginning of the Growth of the Hasidic Path" [Heb.], *Zion* 16 (1951): 88–103.

47. On "service in corporeality," see I. Tishby and J. Dan, "Hasidut," *Ha-enze-klopedyah ha-'ivrit* (1965), 17: 808–09.

48. See *Nefesh ha-hayyim*, 58; see also, *Hanhagot ve-'ezot*, Pt. 1, sec. 41.

49. See *Nefesh ha-hayyim*, 71–72.

50. *Sefer tosefet ma'aseh rav, She'iltot*, sec. 71.

51. *Nefesh ha-hayyim*, 38; cf. 69.

52. Ibid., 47.

53. For detailed examples of his teaching on the way to achieve prayer with *kavvanah* by the method of levels, see Etkes, "R. Hayyim of Volozhin," 41–42. The approach taught by R. Hayyim has a definite mystical coloration.

54. See *Nefesh ha-hayyim*, 70.

55. Ibid.

56. Ibid., 71.

57. Ibid., 86–87.

58. On the founding of the yeshiva in Volozhin and the innovations entailed in its organization, see Etkes, "R. Hayyim of Volozhin," 16–21.

59. The pamphlets are the *She'iltot* (see *Sefer tosefet ma'aseh rav*); *Hanhagot ve-'ezot* (see chap. 2, n. 39, in this volume); and *Keter rosh; orhot hayyim* (above, n. 19).

60. The use of the term *hasid* in this context does not refer to the Hasidic movement, but to the outstanding level of an individual in the service of God. This term was widely used in Mitnaggedic circles in reference to the Gaon. R. Zundel of Salant was likewise referred to by the disciples of R. Israel Salanter by the title *hasid* (see *Or yisrael*, 124).

61. See *Sefer tosefet ma'aseh rav, She'iltot*, secs. 27, 44, 46, 51, 62–67, 68. See also *Hanhagot ve-'ezot*, Pt. 1, sec. 61, 127; Pt. 2, sec. 20.

62. See *Ruah hayyim*, chap. 2, Mishnah 4.

63. See *Hanhagot ve-'ezot*, Pt. 2, sec. 15.

64. See BT, Bezah 16a.

65. See *Ruah hayyim*, chap. 1, Mishnah 14.

66. *Sefer tosefet ma'aseh rav, She'iltot*, sec. 71.

67. See H. Tschernovitz (Rav Tsa'ir), *Toldot ha-poskim* (New York, 1948), 3: 210ff.

68. See above, chap. 2, n. 20.

69. R. Issachar Ber b. Tanhum, *Sefer ma'aseh rav*, in Maimon, *Toldot ha-ger'' 'a*, 343–44.

70. See R. Hayyim of Volozhin's *haskamah* (approbation) to *Ma'aseh rav*.

71. Several traditions are recorded in the name of the Gaon in the pamphlets in which R. Hayyim's disciples recorded his counsels. However, the author of *Ma'aseh rav* turned to R. Hayyim directly with the request that he confirm the reliability of the book's contents (see n. 70).

72. Introduction of R. Hayyim to *Shulhan 'arukh; orah hayyim, 'im be'ur ha-ger'' 'a*.

73. *Sefer tosefet ma'aseh rav, She'iltot*, sec. 89. Evidence that R. Hayyim set forth the customs of the Gaon as an example to be followed by his disciples may be seen from Rivlin, *Ha-zaddik r. yosef zundel*, 147, sec. 13.

74. See *Sefer tosefet ma'aseh rav, She'iltot*, sec. 120.

75. See R. Hayyim's instructions to his disciples, ibid., secs. 98, 114, 125.

76. Ibid., sec. 26.

77. Ibid., sec. 15. See also the remarks of R. Saul Katzenellenbogen in his

haskamah to *Nefesh ha-hayyim*, stating that R. Hayyim was accustomed "to sacrifice himself to fulfill every word of the rabbis. . . ."

78. *Sefer tosefet ma'aseh rav, She'iltot,* secs. 35, 36.

79. Ibid., sec. 41.

80. Ibid., sec. 78.

81. Similar to Hasidism, and perhaps due to its influence, R. Hayyim seems to have objected to the overemphasis upon worry and sadness because of one's sins, because he feared that worry might itself bring one to sin. Ibid., sec. 36.

82. Ibid., sec. 43.

83. See, e.g., ibid., secs. 32, 57, 58.

84. Ibid., sec. 34.

85. See *Hanhagot ve-'ezot,* Pt. 1, secs. 31, 104.

86. See *Sefer tosefet ma'aseh rav, She'iltot,* secs. 96–99.

87. Ibid., secs. 31, 37, 23. As mentioned above, *Nefesh ha-hayyim* includes detailed instructions concerning *kavvanah* during prayer.

88. See *Sefer tosefet ma'aseh rav, She'iltot,* sec. 42.

89. *Ruah hayyim,* chap. 1, Mishnah 6, s. v. "aseh lekha rav."

90. See *Sefer tosefet ma'aseh rav, She'iltot,* sec. 76.

Chapter 4

1. A biographical sketch of R. Zundel Salant appears in Rivlin, *Ha-zaddik r. yosef zundel.* Rivlin also published in this book several manuscript letters of R. Zundel. Dov Katz likewise provides an extended portrait of R. Zundel on the basis of various traditions; see Katz, *Tenu'at ha-mussar,* 1: 93–136.

2. See Rivlin, *Ha-zaddik r. yosef zundel,* 8, 9. Rivlin stresses that R. Zundel continued to serve as an halakhic teacher in Jerusalem even after a number of prominent rabbis settled there. See also Katz, *Tenu'at ha-mussar,* 1: 97, n. 9.

3. *Tevunah,* 3, note.

4. Examples are cited below.

5. Rivlin, *Ha-zaddik r. yosef zundel,* 27, in letter 2; the same is repeated in letter 3.

6. The pamphlet is quoted by Rivlin, *Ha-zaddik r. yosef zundel,* 50–51.

7. Ibid., 5. Rivlin notes that R. Zundel refused to accept money from the *halukah* (monies raised abroad for scholars living in the Land of Israel) even while in Jerusalem.

8. See R. Naphtali Amsterdam's remarks in *Sefer or yisra'el,* 122–23. R. Naphtali Amsterdam was also from Salant, so that his information concerning R. Zundel was evidently based upon both what he had heard from the elders of the city and what he heard from R. Israel Salanter.

9. Ibid., 124.

10. See Rivlin, *Ha-zaddik r. yosef zundel,* 13–15; Katz, *Tenu'at ha-mussar,* 1: 113–14.

11. See R. Naphtali Amsterdam's testimony in *Sefer or yisra'el* (n. 8).

12. See *Sefer or yisra'el,* 31.

13. Rivlin, *Ha-zaddik r. yosef zundel,* 50.

14. Ibid., 50–51.

15. See the story brought by R. Naphtali Amsterdam, *Sefer or yisra'el,* 123.

16. See Rivlin, *Ha-zaddik r. yosef zundel,* 27.

17. Ibid., 61–62.

18. Ibid., 25. In the continuation of the letter to his son, 25–26, R. Zundel cites certain things in this same spirit in the name of R. Hayyim. This understanding of Divine Providence, along with the emphasis upon *bitahon*, seems to have played a role in the guidance R. Hayyim gave to his disciples.

19. Ibid., 26.

20. Ibid.

21. Ibid.

22. Ibid., 59–60.

23. Ibid., 26–27.

24. R. Zundel's writings include listings of the practices of the Gaon and of R. Hayyim. See Rivlin, *Ha-zaddik r. yosef zundel*, 100–19. In his halakhic responsa, he also relied upon the writings of the Gaon and the instructions of R. Hayyim; ibid., 41–46.

25. Reported by R. Naphtali Amsterdam, who heard them from R. Israel Salanter. See *Sefer or yisra'el*, 122–23.

26. R. Zundel's remarks concerning the Evil Impulse appear in a letter quoted by Rivlin, *Ha-zaddik r. yosef zundel*, 34–39.

27. Ibid., 38.

28. Ibid.

29. Ibid.

30. Ibid., 38–39.

31. *Sefer or yisra'el*, 124.

32. Ibid.

33. See *Hanhagot ve-'ezot*, Pt. 1, sec. 34.

34. See the approbations (*haskamot*) by R. Abraham Abli and R. Saul Katzenellenbogen to *Sefer nefesh ha-hayyim*.

35. R. Zundel was not the only one among R. Hayyim's students to allocate greater importance to the cultivation of *yir'ah* than was required by his teacher's doctrine. A striking example of this tendency is to be seen in R. Samuel b. Joshua Zelig, who was among the students of R. Hayyim in Volozhin, served in the rabbinate in the communities of Ahalinov and Iliya, and was noted for his work, *Minhat shmuel le-masekhet berakhot*, published in Vilna in 1842. His connection with the dominant tendencies in the Volozhin yeshiva may already be seen in the introduction to that work. R. Samuel's stance concerning the relation between Torah and *yir'ah* is formulated in a small pamphlet written in 1856, after his immigration to the Land of Israel, where he spent a year in "isolation" in Hebron. This pamphlet, also entitled *Minhat shmuel*, has been published as an appendix to the photo edition of R. Pinhas b. Judah's *Keter torah* (Jerusalem, 1968). This pamphlet is based upon the argument that Torah and mitzvot are insufficient in themselves; one who wishes to overcome the Evil Impulse and cling to God must devote intensive effort to ethical improvement and repentance. Within the framework of this struggle with the Evil Impulse, R. Samuel recommends that one periodically devote a day exclusively to self-isolation, fasting and taking an account of the condition of one's soul. On this day, certain special prayers and confessions should be recited, preferably those that one wrote oneself rather than standard texts. In addition, R. Samuel advocates that one set aside an entire year for contemplation, devoted entirely to ethical and spiritual improvement and repentance. Among other things, he recommends that during this year one spend less time in halakhic studies and instead devote the bulk of one's time to the study of Mussar works. In light of these remarks, R. Samuel again warns that one not pay heed to the advice of the Evil Impulse, which argues that "Torah

study is equivalent to them all. . . . ," as this rule only refers to one who has already acquired the quality of *yir'ah*. In general, R. Samuel's doctrine of *yir'ah* reflects the influence of R. Hayyim, while in many points it is similar to the path of R. Zundel, the common denominator being that they both advocate the cultivation of *yir'ah* over and above that recommended by R. Hayyim.

On the basis of what has been said above, there is room for the conjecture that, despite its personal stamp, R. Zundel's unusual piety may be seen as part of a more general tendency that developed within the circle of the *lomdim*, whose roots are anchored in the exemplary model of the Gaon of Vilna and the educational path of the Volozhin yeshiva. However, as I have said, the strengthening of the yeshiva and the revival of Torah study prepared the ground for a greater emphasis upon *yir'ah*.

Chapter 5

1. See Hillel Noah Maggid Steinschneider, *'Ir vilna* (Vilna, 1900), 128; on the text of Salanter's tombstone, ibid., 132.

2. *'Ir vilna* mistakenly states that he was born in Telz. Katz, *Tenu'at ha-mussar*, 1: 138, n. 4, corrects this error to show that his birthplace was Zager.

3. See Frumkin, *Sefer toldot eliyahu*, 1. On Rabbi Zeev Wolf, see Levi Ovzinski, *Toldot yeshivat ha-yehudim be-courland* (Vilna, 1912), 56ff.

4. See Yaakov Mark, *Bi-mehizatam shel gedolei ha-dor* (Jerusalem, 1958), 61.

5. See Shmuel Rosenfeld, *Rabbi yisra'el salanter: hayav pe'ulotav ve-talmidav* (Warsaw, 1911), 9.

6. See David Bonimowitz, *Sefer mikhtav me-eliyahu* (Vilna, 1902), 13.

7. See Rabbi Meir Sterlitz, *Mi-bet meir* (Jerusalem, 1937), 2: 3.

8. *Or yisra'el*, 31.

9. As has been mentioned, *Or yisra'el* was published in 1900, and should be seen as a kind of apologetic response of the Mussar movement in light of the opposition that rose against it in the 1890s. Indeed, in that portion of the book written by R. Isaac Blazer, the polemical tendency to prove the value of Mussar study is particularly strong.

10. *Or yisra'el*, 124.

11. One should note that R. Naphtali Amsterdam first mentioned the repetition of Rabbinic dicta, a fact ignored by R. Isaac Blazer. In general, the testimonies of R. Naphtali seem to be more exact than those of R. Blazer.

12. *Tevunah*, 3, in a note.

13. R. Zundel was born in 1786; see Rivlin, *Ha-zaddik r. yosef zundel*, 3.

14. *Tevunah*, 3.

15. However, R. Israel later changed his mind on this point, as discussed below.

16. See Y. Rimon and Y. Z. Wasserman, *Shmu'el be-doro* (Tel Aviv, 1961), 8–9.

17. See Katz, *Tenu'at ha-mussar*, 1: 147.

18. See R. Isaac Blazer's comments in *Or yisr'ael*, 111.

19. See Katz, *Tenu'at ha-mussar*, 1: 147, quoting R. Shmuel Schenker.

20. The assumption that it is a mark of piety for scholars to abstain from serving in the rabbinate was also common among the students of R. Israel. See *Or yisra'el*, 112.

21. The significance of the decision not to study Kabbalah, the third "decision" taken upon himself by R. Israel, is explained below.

22. See *Or yisra'el*, 111.

23. See R. Yehiel Ya'akov Weinberg, *Seridei esh* (Jerusalem, 1969), 4: 286.

24. *Or yisra'el*, 111.

25. See Katz, *Tenu'at ha-mussar*, 1: 145–46. This statement is connected by Katz with R. Israel's decision not to become a recluse.

26. Ibid., 146.

27. Ibid., 147–148.

Chapter 6

1. See the text of R. Israel's appointment as *ra''m* at R. Meile's yeshiva in Vilna, in Steinschneider, *'Ir vilna*, 128–29, n. 3; see also the account of R. Israel's son, R. Isaac Lipkin, "Concerning the Path and Activities of Our Master, the Light of Israel from Salant, of Blessed Memory" [Heb.], *Tevunah* (Jerusalem, 1941), 7: 75, sec. 2.

2. Max Lilienthal, who visited Vilna at the beginning of the 1840s, estimated that some 30,000 Jews lived in the city at the time. See David Philipson, *Max Lilienthal; Life and Writings* (New York, 1915), 261. A letter from the community of Vilna to Moses Montefiore in 1846, published by S. Ginzburg, *Historische Verk* (New York, 1937), 2: 293–98, states that there were then 40,000 Jews in the city.

3. The unique status of Vilna as a Torah center appears in many contemporary sources. See, for example, the rhetorical description by Isak Meir Dick, *Ha-oreah*, (Vilna, 1846), 5–6. See also the letter written in 1840 by R. Abraham b. Joseph Zakheim in M. A. Ginzburg, *Devir* (Vilna, 1844), 102ff.

4. See on this below, chap. 10.

5. Evidence concerning the poverty of the Jewish masses in Vilna is cited below, in chap. 11.

6. Some claim that R. Israel moved to Vilna following the invitation to serve as teacher in R. Meile's yeshiva. See the Introduction in R. Mordecai b. Asher Klatzki (Meltzer), *Sefer tekhelet mordekhai* (Vilna, 1889), 14; this likewise follows from the remarks of R. Isaac Blazer in *Or yisra'el*, 109; it seems to me that Dov Katz similarly interprets it in *Tenu'at ha-mussar*, 1: 148. On the other hand, Steinschneider, in *'Ir vilna*, 123, claims that R. Israel lived in Vilna for a certain period of time even before he was invited to serve as a teacher. This version is confirmed by the account of R. Israel's son, who relates that, "when he came to Vilna from Salant, in about 1840, he intended to go to eat at the home of a different householder every day, saying that he did not want to be different from any other young scholar . . ."—Lipkin, "Concerning the Path," sec. 2. It therefore follows that Salanter came to Vilna by himself, as an "ascetic" young man who ate "days" at the homes of various householders; only some time later, after he received the position at the yeshiva of R. Meile, did his family join him.

7. See *Or yisra'el*, 109.

8. See the Introduction in R. Shmuel Lovtzer, *'Olat shmu'el* (Vilna, 1901), iv.

9. On R. Mordecai b. Asher Klatzki, known as Meltzer, see Steinschneider, *'Ir vilna*, 122–26. For more details concerning R. Mordecai, as well as R. Meile's yeshiva, see Meltzer, *Tekhelet mordekhai*, 19–20; Hillel Noah Steinschneider, "On the History of One of the Rabbis" [Heb.], in *Ozar ha-sifrut* (Krakow, 1892), 4: 533–34.

10. Meltzer, *Tekhelet mordekhai*, 13–14.

11. Ibid., 21. Below, the author describes several incidents from which it is clear that R. Mordecai Meltzer and R. Israel Salanter respected one another. Ibid., 22, sec. 21; 23, sec. 26.

12. Steinschneider, *'Ir vilna*, 123–24.

13. Salanter's document of appointment is quoted in Steinschneider, *'Ir vilna*, 128, n. 3. It was dated 6 Ellul 5600 (September 1839).

14. Most of the authors who have written about the life of R. Israel Salanter have followed *'Ir vilna* in their description of this incident, and have at times even sufficed with quoting it exactly. See Rosenfeld, *Rabbi Yisrael Salanter*, 15–16; cf. "R. Israel Salanter, The History of His Life and Activity" [Heb.], in *Ha-yehudi* (New York, 1937), 2: 57–69; Zvi Hirsch Ferber, "'Zvi yisra'el'" [Heb.], in *Sha'arei zion* (Jerusalem and Kislev-Shevat, 1932/33), 30–31. Several authors close to the Mussar movement conceal the fact that R. Israel's entering into service as a teacher at R. Meile's yeshiva involved a certain injury to the status of R. Mordecai Meltzer. The tension between these two figures is interpreted by them entirely in favor of R. Israel—that is, that the majority of the students followed him due to his greater popularity, and that he later relinquished the office out of pity for R. Mordecai. See Weinberg, *Seridei esh*, 4: 288; Katz, *Tenu'at ha-mussar*, 1: 149.

15. See Steinschneider, *'Ir vilna*, 124, 129.

16. See Meltzer, *Tekhelet mordekhai*, 14, sec. 13; Introduction to Lovtzer, *'Olat shmu'el*.

17. See Menahem Mendel Zalmanovitz, *Zikhron hillel* (Vilna, 1902), 15–17; Mark, *Bi-mehizatam*, 31ff.

18. The term *yeshiva* was used in Lithuania during this period to refer to a variety of institutions of Torah learning that differed from one another considerably in their degree of organizational development. There were yeshivot that were outstanding in the physical plant available to them, in the internal division into classes, in the way in which the students' needs were met, in methods of fund-raising, etc. At the other extreme, a group of *lomdim* who gathered in one of the study houses to hear a lecture (*shi'ur*) on a regular basis might in some cases also be designated as a yeshiva. We hardly know anything about the structure of the yeshiva of R. Israel in Zarzecze, but it seems likely that it was closer to the latter type.

19. See Ferber, *"Zvi yisra'el,"* 30.

20. R. David Luria of Bikhov (Harada"l) was well known in his day as a great Torah scholar, and the most important rabbis addressed him with halakhic questions. At the same time, he was also learned in *Wissenschaft des Judentums* literature, and was outstanding for his public activity. His relative, Shmuel Luria, wrote a brief biographical sketch of him, which is appended to the second edition of R. David Luria's work, *Kadmut sefer ha-zohar* (Warsaw, 1887). See also Steinschneider, *'Ir vilna*, 157–59; Saul Ginzburg, *Ketavim histori'im* (Tel Aviv, 1944), 28ff.

21. *Or yisra'el*, 100.

22. Lovtzer, *'Olat shmu'el*, Introduction. These things were formulated by R. Hanokh Agus, the son-in-law of R. Samuel Lovtzer, so that it constitutes second-hand information.

23. Lipkin, "Concerning the Path," 75.

24. See Steinschneider, *'Ir vilna*, pp. 185–88.

25. Ibid., 129. Hillel Noah Steinschneider was born in Vilna in 1829 and died there in 1904. He was prominent in his day as an expert researcher in the personalities of Vilna. Most of his information and findings on this subject were gathered in the book *'Ir vilna*, published in 1900. He examined and gathered many documents pertaining to the life of the community, and also laid the groundwork for the Strashun Library. His information is generally reliable and accurate.

26. Steinschneider writes that *Heshbon ha-nefesh* was published in 5604 (i.e., 1843/44), while the title page states that it was published in 5605 (1844/45). The

inexactitude may stem from the fact that the non-Jewish date cited on the title page is 1844.

27. The last edition of *Sefer tikkun middot ha-nefesh* prior to the 1845 Vilna edition was that published in Linvell, 1807. *Sefer heshbon ha-nefesh* was first printed in 1808. The tradition that R. Israel Salanter was involved in the printing of *Sefer heshbon ha-nefesh* was accepted in the circle of the Mussar movement, which again reprinted the book later on: *Sefer heshbon ha-nefesh* (Keidan, 1937), published by the Association of Slobodka Students in Lithuania. Katz, *Tenu'at ha-mussar*, 155, likewise attributes the initiative for the printing of *Sefer mesillat yesharim* to R. Israel. This book was published in Vilna in 1844 without any identification of the publisher, so it is possible that R. Israel was in fact involved in the publication of this book.

28. The above quotation is from R. Shneur Zalman Hirshowitz's introduction to *Sefer even yisra'el*. Even the citation of the years and places in which the sermons were given is included in this introduction. See also Salanter's letter of agreement to the publication of the sermons following the Introduction. *Sefer even yisra'el* was first published in Warsaw in 1883, and enjoyed subsequent editions. The sermons appear according to the order of the weekly Torah readings. The fact that there are many readings for which no sermons exist does not necessarily mean that there were interruptions in R. Israel's activity as a preacher, since R. Shneur Zalman himself testifies that he heard and recorded only a portion of the sermons.

29. Steinschneider, *'Ir vilna*, 129. It would seem that these remarks by Steinschneider refer to the same period of which R. Shneur Zalman testifies, as he hints that this occurred prior to Moses Montefiore's visit to Vilna, which took place during the month of Iyyar 5606 (May 1846).

30. See, for example, the beginning of Sermon 3 in *Even yisra'el*, whose point of departure is a contradiction between two statements of R. Joshua b. Levi, although in both cases R. Joshua b. Levi's remarks are strictly aggadic and there is no contradiction between them whatsoever in terms of their contents. The "contradiction" to which R. Israel points only exists by virtue of a nicety of *pilpul*.

31. *Iggeret ha-mussar* was first published as an addendum to R. Moses Cordovero's *Tomer devorah* (Koenigsburg, 1858).

32. Weinberg, *Seridei esh*, 288.

33. Vol. 1, 152–53.

34. These outlines characterize his activity during the 1850s, when he lived and was active in Kovna. On the activities of R. Israel as a *maggid* in the community of Kovna, see below. During that period, those students, they and their students, who found the Mussar yeshivot, and from whom R. Weinberg gleaned his data about R. Israel, attached themselves to him.

35. Steinschneider, *'Ir vilna*, 129.

Chapter 7

1. See L. Ginzberg, "Rabbi Israel Salanter," in *Students, Scholars and Saints* (Philadelphia, 1945), 163–81; Katz, *Tenu'at ha-mussar*, 1: 130–245; Zvi Kurzweil, "The Psychological Roots and the Educational Meaning of the Mussar Movement According to the Writings of R. Israel Salanter" [Heb.], in *Hinukh ha-adam ve-ye'udo* (Jerusalem, 1967), 217–28; *Kitvei r. yisrael salanter*, ed. Mordecai Pechter (Jerusalem, 1972), Introduction.

2. Silman's article differs on this point; see Yohanan Silman, "The Doctrine of the Soul in the Thought of R. Israel Lipkin (of Salant)" [Heb.], *Bar-ilan, sefer ha-*

shanah 11 (1973): 288ff., in which the author notes the transition to the psychology of the unconscious as an advanced stage in the development of Salanter's thought.

3. See the Introduction to his book *Even yisra'el*, and see also R. Shneur Zalman's note at the end of Sermon 6. The quotations from *Even yisra'el* are all taken from the 1954 Jerusalem edition.

4. Thus, for example, the idea of the Mussar house that R. Israel established in Vilna may be more clearly understood in light of these letters.

5. See Rivlin, *Ha-zaddik r. yosef zundel*, 65, n. 1. Among R. Zundel's writings there also appears a copy of the *kavvanot* for prayer from *Nefesh ha-hayyim*, based upon a kabbalistic approach; ibid., 54–58. Apparently, a number of R. Hayyim's students were involved in Kabbalah. The positive attitude toward Kabbalah of his son, R. Isaac, is clearly seen in a gloss he added to the first pages of *Nefesh ha-hayyim*. In the same gloss, he also polemicizes against those who mock "the faithful ones of Israel" because of their belief in kabbalistic principles; ibid., 24. Another disciple of R. Hayyim, R. Samuel of Ohalinov, included in a small Mussar book that he composed in 1856 instructions for those who wished to begin the study of Kabbalah. He especially recommends this study in light of "those who argue on the basis of human intellect," who, according to him, had multiplied in his generation. See Ben Joshua Zelig, *Minhat shmu'el*, 36.

6. See *Even yisra'el*, Sermon 3.

7. See above, chap. 5.

8. See H. E. Zaitchik, *Sefer ha-me'orot ha-gedolim* (New York, 1953), in the section on R. Israel Lipkin of Salant, sec. 185.

9. Ibid., sec. 186.

10. From a letter written in 1850 to his friend and disciple, R. Elijah of Kartinga, quoted by Shraga ha-Kohen Willman, *Iggerot u-mikhtavim me-'et ha-gaon r. yisra'el mi-salant* (New York, 1970), 28, letter 6. Hillel Goldberg, in his book, *Israel Salanter: Text, Structure, Idea* (New York, 1982), devotes an excursus to the question: "Did Israel Salanter Study Philosophy and Kabbalah?" (pp. 209–19). He engages there in a detailed polemic with my position, marshaling evidence of his own to support the conclusion that Salanter did in fact study Kabbalah. After a careful study of his arguments, I remain convinced of the validity of the position presented here. Even if we assume that Goldberg is correct—namely, that Salanter did study and know Kabbalah—and we admit, for the sake of argument, that he was expert in all the various branches of Kabbalah, what is the significance of it? The crucial question for anyone who wishes to characterize and to analyze the thought of Salanter is whether, and to what extent, his thought was influenced by the Kabbalah. Goldberg has not brought any proof likely to upset my conclusions on this matter. Incidentally, the seemingly most conclusive text cited by Goldberg in fact supports my stand. I refer to the following sentences from R. Isaac Blazer: "[H]e [Salanter] evidently also knew a great deal in esoteric matters, for he also possessed books of Kabbalah, and he would at times search diligently to acquire one of the books of Kabbalah; but due to his humility, his way in holy matters was not to speak of this with any person, and therefore his path in this matter is unknown to us" (*Or yisra'el*, 119). It follows from these remarks that Salanter did not give any expression in his contacts with his students to what he had learned, if he in fact did learn, of kabbalistic literature. But the most conclusive proof that Salanter's thought was not influenced by Kabbalah are his own writings. See on this Mordecai Pechter, "R. Israel Salanter Seen in a New Light" [Heb.], *Tarbiz* 53 (1984): 636.

11. For a general discussion of the genre of Mussar literature, see Isaiah Tishby

Mussar (handwritten)

and Joseph Dan, *Mivhar sifrut ha-mussar* (Tel Aviv, 1971), General Introduction; Joseph Dan, *Sifrut ha-mussar veha-derush* (Jerusalem, 1975); id., *Encyclopaedia Judaica,* s.v. "Ethical Literature."

12. See the Introduction in *Sefer hovot ha-levavot,* ed. Mahbarot le-Sifrut (Tel Aviv, 1964), 68ff.

13. See *Sefer hasidim,* ed. Margaliot, sec. 1, and many others; Cf. Hayim Soloveitchik, "Three Themes in the Sefer Hasidim," *AJS Review* 1 (1976): 311–57; Ivan G. Marcus, *Piety and Society; The Jewish Pietists of Medieval Germany* (Leiden, 1981), 21–36.

14. See above, chap. 2, n. 5.

15. See Ze'ev Gries, "The Hasidic *Hanhagot* Literature as an Expression of Leadership and Ethos" [Heb.], Ph.D. diss., Hebrew University, 1979.

16. A typical example of this type is R. Jonah Gerondi's *Sefer sha'arei teshuvah.*

17. The characterization of Mussar literature presented here obviously suffers from gross generalization and oversimplification, but it is only intended to serve as background to emphasize the uniqueness of R. Israel Salanter in this context. On R. Israel's innovation in his understanding of the problem of Mussar, compare Pechter, 39.

18. See *Iggeret ha-mussar* in *Kitvei r. yisrael salanter,* ed. Mordecai Pechter (Jerusalem, 1972), 118.

19. *Even yisra'el,* Sermon 8, p. 38 in note. Ibid., also the text of the sermon.

20. See *Even yisra'el,* Sermon 8, p. 34.

21. ". . . the wide-spread appetite to love that which is momentarily desirable for ignoring the aftereffects even if they end up being bitter"—*Iggeret ha-mussar, Kitvei,* 117. See also *Even yisra'el,* Sermon 8, p. 34, note.

22. "Therefore fear of God rules over everything: over the appetite, which it imprisons in the strength of its power, that it not overstep its bounds except for what is necessary and permitted. . . ."—Pechter, *Kitvei,* 208.

23. See *Even yisra'el,* Sermon 8, p. 38; Sermon 6, p. 26.

24. *Even yisra'el,* Sermon 2, p. 7.

25. In this respect, the difference between the Gaon of Vilna and R. Hayyim of Volozhin, who understand the *yezer ha-ra'* as the emissary of the *Sitra Ahra,* and Salanter, is striking. It becomes clear below that at a certain stage R. Israel admitted that the activity of the Evil Impulse was also influenced by the "power of impurity," although by this he did not retreat from his basic approach.

26. See, for example, the interpretation of *yir'ah* in Nahmanides's *Iggeret ha-mussar.*

27. See *Sefer hasidim,* ed. Margaliot, sec. 164, pp. 169–70.

28. See chap. 3, "Sha'ar 'avodat ha'elohim," in Ibn Paquda, *Hovot ha-levavot,* 220–21; H. M. Luzzatto, *Sefer mesillat yesharim* (Jerusalem, 1964), chap. 4, p. 22; chap. 24, p. 120; the sermon by R. Eleazar of Worms, cited in Dan, *Sifrut ha-mussar veha-derush,* 139.

29. *Even yisra'el,* Sermon 2, p. 7.

30. R. Israel arrived at this conclusion on the basis of "searching and proof." See *Even yisra'el,* Sermon 4, p. 21.

31. See Ibn Paquda, *Hovot ha-levavot,* "Sha'ar 'avodat ha'elohim," Opening, chaps. 1, 3.

32. R. Israel did not explicitly formulate this distinction, although it clearly follows from the overall context of his remarks.

33. See Pechter, *Kitvei,* 211.

34. Pechter, *Kitvei*, 114.

35. R. Israel may have preferred to use the concept of imagination here under the influence of the definition of "the imaginative part" in the first chapter of Maimonides's *Shemonah perakim*.

36. Pechter, *Kitvei*, 200.

37. R. Naphtali Amsterdam relates that R. Israel instructed him to divide the time allotted to Mussar study between study with concentration and study *be-hitpa'alut*. See *Sefer or ha-mussar* (B'nai Barak, 1965), 2: 62–63.

38. " . . . For this is [the goal of] all the labor of man for His service, may He be blessed—to think and to contemplate the fear of God, with the fear of His punishment, by means of Mussar books and legends of the rabbis, until he hear with his ears and virtually see with his eyes the great punishment, in quantity and quality. . . ."—*Iggeret ha-mussar* in Pechter, *Kitvei*, 117.

39. See Pechter, *Kitvei*, 203, 212; *Sefer or ha-mussar*, 1: 14.

40. See R. Isaac Blazer's description of the method of Mussar study *be-hitpa'alut* as introduced by R. Israel Salanter, in *Or yisra'el*, 32–33. See also the remarks of R. Yehoshua Heller, one of R. Israel's disciples, in *Sefer divrei yehoshu'a* (Vilna, 1846), 23; cf. Rosenfeld, *Rabbi Yisrael Salanter*, 27–28.

41. *Sefer or ha-mussar*, 1: 114.

42. See the Epilogue of this book for the similarities and differences between the Mussar system and the path of Hasidism.

43. This technique is well known from the history of religions generally, and is particularly widespread in groups with a mystical inclination. Again, the closest parallel that comes to mind in the Jewish context is the use of song and dance in Hasidism.

44. *Sefer or ha-mussar*, 2: 62, 65.

45. See Pechter, *Kitvei*, 203. For this same reason, Salanter made extensive use of allegories in his sermons.

46. Pechter, *Kitvei*, 202–03.

47. See Pechter, *Kitvei*, 216–18; *Or yisra'el*, 36.

48. One of the goals of "Mussar study" is "to break the heart and to purify it somewhat of its pollution . . ."—Pechter, *Kitvei*, 205.

49. *Sefer hayyei ha-mussar* (B'nai Barak, 1964), 2: 155.

50. *Sefer or ha-mussar*, 2: 10–11.

51. See Pechter, *Kitvei*, 208–09.

52. Ibid., 203.

53. Ibid., 209.

54. Cf. Ibid.

55. Ibid., 210.

56. Ibid.

57. This motif is particularly prominent in the five letters written by R. Israel in 1849. Ibid., 200–13.

58. See *Even yisra'el*, Sermon 2, p. 8.

59. "Involvement in worldly matters will teach one its affairs and their rules. Each person according to his particular nature will acquire his wisdom [in worldly matters] . . . involvement in the ways of [Divine] service will teach one its processes"—Pechter, *Kitvei*, 210.

60. "For just as in matters of economic life and trade a person must initially guard himself more against loss of the investment than toward the pursuit of profit, so in the service of the Creator it is certainly preferable to look upon that form of

service which is least likely to entail loss, even though it is not the best [possible] way, than pursuit of a higher level of service which is more likely to lead to loss."— *Even yisra'el*, Sermon 2, p. 6.

Chapter 8

1. Pechter, *Kitvei*, 200; cf. 201.
2. Ibid., 201.
3. Ibid., 203.
4. Ibid., 204–05.
5. Unlike the formulae generally used for beginning letters during that period, which were filled with ceremonial titles of respect, R. Salanter's letters to his disciples open with the words "my friends," or "my brethren and comrades," etc.
6. Pechter, *Kitvei*, 203.
7. Ibid., 201–02.
8. Ibid., 201.
9. Ibid., 202.
10. Ibid., 204.
11. Ibid.
12. Ibid., 205.
13. Ibid., 211.
14. Ibid., 208.
15. A number of authors agree: see Mark, *Bi-mehizatam*, 66; Rosenfeld, *Rabbi Yisrael Salanter*, 15; H. H. Ben-Sasson, "The Mussar Movement in Lithuania in the 19th Century—Indications of Inner Crisis" [Heb.], *World Congress of Jewish Studies*, vol. 1 (Jerusalem, 1952); S. Bialovolski, "Torah Centers in Lithuania" [Heb.], *Yahadut lita* (Tel Aviv, 1960). We attempt here to document and to elaborate this theory.
16. Pechter, *Kitvei*, 238.
17. *Tevunah*, 3, note.
18. From a letter signed by R. Gershon Mendel Ziv, in an article entitled "Le-ma'an da'at," published in *Ha-meliz* 155 (1897). R. Gershon Mendel Ziv was the rabbi of Plongian and was evidently close to Salanter. The latter asked him to spread the study of Mussar among the people of his city. See Willman, *Iggerot u-mikhtavim*, Letter 55, 73.

Chapter 9

1. R. Zundel was accustomed to copying for himself selected chapters from various books. There is also a copy of several chapters from *Sefer heshbon ha-nefesh* among his manuscripts. See Rivlin, *Ha-zaddik r. yosef zundel*, 148.
2. See, for example, *Mesillat yesharim*, chap. 5, concerning the effect of *hitpa'alut*; compare the beginning of chap. 10 with Salanter's remarks concerning "hidden" sins. Two strongly stressed motifs in *Mesillat yesharim*, which are also of central importance in R. Israel's doctrine, are self-examination and the use of the power of habit.
3. Salanter's position on this matter is discussed at length in chap. 11.
4. See above, chap. 7, sec. 1 and n. 10.
5. A number of passages copied from kabbalistic works have been found in the manuscript of R. Zundel. See Rivlin, *Ha-zaddik r. yosef zundel*, 145ff.

6. See Pechter, *Kitvei*, 123–24. This position of R. Israel is discussed in greater detail in chap. 13.

7. Ibid.

8. H. E. Zaitchik, *Sefer ha-me'orot ha-gedolim* (New York, 1953), 66.

9. Ibid., 101.

10. For a comprehensive survey of this controversy, see Katz, *Pulmus ha-mussar*.

11. See, for example, the essay "Le-ma'an da'at," *Ha-meliz*, no. 155 (1897). For evidence of the fact that the opponents of the Mussar movement already relied upon R. Hayyim's position in the 1870s, see R. Shmuel Meltzen's introduction to his book, *Even shelemah* (Vilna, 1873).

12. Salanter himself testified to the decisive influence of his contacts with R. Zundel upon his own involvement in Mussar.

13. On Lefin's biography and lifework, see Israel Vinlez, "R. Menahem Mendel Lefin of Satanow" [Heb.], *Ha-'olam* 4, nos. 39–42 (1925); Joseph Klausner, *Historyah shel ha-sifrut ha-'ivrit ha-hadashah* (Jerusalem, 1953), 1: 224–53; Israel Zinberg, *A History of Jewish Literature* (New York and Cincinnati, 1975), 6: 275–80; Raphael Mahler, *Divrei yemei yisra'el; dorot aharonim*, 4: 71–88 [English translation: *A History of Modern Jewry, 1780–1815* (London, 1971), 587–600]; Hillel Levine, *Menahem Mendel Lefin*, Ph.D. diss., Harvard University, 1974.

14. See Hillel Levine, "Between Hasidism and Haskalah: On a Concealed Anti-Hasidic Polemic" [Heb.], in *Perakim be-toldot ha-hevrah ha-yehudit . . .* [J. Katz Festschrift] (Jerusalem, 1980), 182–91.

15. For a detailed discussion of Lefin's translation, see Zinberg, *Jewish Literature*, 9: 215ff.

16. Vilna, 1845; Warsaw, 1852; Warsaw, 1894; Berditchev, 1925; Keidan, 1937. The last-mentioned edition was republished a number of times in photo-offset.

17. See the introduction to the book by R. Yizhak Isaac Sher.

18. See Menahem Mendel Lefin, *Sefer heshbon ha-nefesh* (Keidan, 1937), 20–29. The remarks are cited here with extreme brevity.

19. It seems to me that the first one to note this connection was Zeev Yavitz, in his work, *Toldot yisra'el* (Tel Aviv, 1963), 14: 9. See also Vinlez, "R. menahem mendel lefin," 819; Klausner, *Historyah*, 1: 232–33; Zinberg, *Jewish Literature*, 6: 279; Mahler, *Divrei yemei yisra'el*, 6: 77 [*Modern Jewry*, 594]; A. R. Malachi, "Benjamin Franklin and Hebrew Literature" [Heb.], *Ha-doar* 35 (1957): 238–39; Nissan Waksman, "A Forgotten Book" [Heb.], *Shanah be-shanah* (1969), 303–15; M. G. Glenn, *Israel Salanter* (New York, 1953), 115–19.

20. See Benjamin Franklin, *Autobiography* (New York, 1941), 128ff.

21. This is based upon the testimony of Samuel Yaakov Bick, a close friend of Lefin, in his letter in *Kerem hemed*, 1: 97, and according to the testimony of Lefin himself, cited in Vinlez, *R. menahem mendel lefin*, 800, 819. Lefin evidently read the *Autobiography* in French translation [B. Franklin, *Mémoire de la vie privée* (Paris, 1791)].

22. ". . . The traditional concepts of Judaism are interwoven with the prevailing spirit and worldview at the close of the eighteenth century. The foundation of Jewish ethics appear here not in mystical or pilpulistic-rabbinic garb but in more modern forms. In explaining the principles he set forth, Lefin not infrequently introduces arguments from the natural sciences and bases himself on the psychology and the physiology of the senses."—Zinberg, *Jewish Literature*, 6: 279.

23. ". . . But Mendel Lefin added his own 'Chapters on Morals' and 'Selections' to Franklin's concepts of chastity and the art of cultivating virtue. These incorporated

a vast collection of psychological problems and new philosophical ideas (such as those of Locke and Kant), although he also occasionally employed ancient and medieval philosophical terminology (for example, Plato and Maimonides)."—Mahler, *Modern Jewry*, 594.

24. See above, n. 13. Levine explains in detail Lefin's views as a moderate Maskil, who in some respects follows the characteristic ideas of the European Enlightenment, while at the same time attempting not to undermine the authority of the tradition. On the social background of *Sefer heshbon ha-nefesh*, see Levine, "Between Hasidism and Haskalah"; and id., "Dwarfs on the Shoulders of Giants; A Case Study in the Impact of Modernization on Social Epistemology of Judaism," *Jewish Social Studies* 40 (1978): 63–73.

25. See Klausner, Zinberg, Mahler, Malachi, Waksman, and Glenn, as cited above in notes 13 and 19.

26. Gotlober's evidence on this subject is confined to the following remarks: "And we also saw and heard that there were established circles which behaved according to *Sefer heshbon ha-nefesh* and which practiced improvement of their character traits in accordance with it"—*Ha-maggid*, no. 40 (1873): 364.

27. Waksman does not cite the source upon which he relies for the attribution of the list to R. Israel. Neither in the writings of Salanter nor in the accounts of his disciples is there any mention made of these traits.

28. See Glenn, *Israel Salanter*, 119.

29. This assumption is explained below.

30. What we state below is based primarily upon *Heshbon ha-nefesh*, 14–15, 30–35.

31. Lefin may have chosen to use concepts that were familiar from medieval Jewish ethical literature, with the intention that his book would be accepted by the Jewish public in Eastern Europe. For the same reason, Lefin gave his book a traditional character by peppering it with biblical verses and Rabbinic dicta.

32. *Heshbon ha-nefesh*, 14.

33. This refers to the thirteen chapters devoted to traits that one ought to correct; see pp. 30–35. For a more detailed explanation of the theoretical premises underlying his device, see the section entitled *Likkutim*, esp. pp. 100ff.

34. Ibid., 30.

35. Ibid., 31.

36. Ibid.

37. Ibid., 33.

38. Lefin would seem to have incorporated in *Sefer heshbon ha-nefesh* various ideas that are taken from numerous other sources. It is almost certain that he was influenced, among others, by the following authors and works: John Locke, *An Essay Concerning Human Understanding*; Etienne Bonnot de Condillac, *Trait de Sensations*; David Hume, *A Treatise on Human Nature*.

39. On the development of the understanding of the psyche in seventeenth- and eighteenth-century European thought, see J. M. Baldwin, *History of Psychology* (New York and London, 1913); R. S. Peters, *Brett's History of Psychology* (London and New York, 1953); E. Cassirer, *The Philosophy of the Enlightenment* (Boston, 1965), 93–133.

40. The presentation of the problem in this light is characteristic of European thought from Locke onward. See Peter Gay, *The Enlightenment: An Interpretation* (New York, 1966), 2: 176.

41. See Baldwin, *History of Psychology*, 2: 1–2.

42. It seems to me that Lefin was particularly influenced by Hume regarding

this matter. Cf. "A Dissertation on the Passions," in David Hume, *Essays* (London, 1875), 2: 139–66.

43. This view is current in Greek philosophy, and again became accepted in the eighteenth century. Thus, for example, Hume writes: "There is implanted in the human mind a perception of pain and of pleasure as the chief spring and moving principle of all its actions"—D. Hume, *A Treatise on Human Nature* (London and New York, 1962), 119.

44. See *Heshbon ha-nefesh*, 35; compare David Hartley, *Observation on Man; His Frame, His Duty and His Expectations* (Gainesville, Fla., 1966), Book 1, sec. 1, prop. 4.

45. See Peters, *Brett's History of Psychology*, 500.

46. Compare on this point secs. 8–10 in *Heshbon ha-nefesh*, 17, with Salanter's sermon in *Even yisra'el*, 38, note. Compare also the use made by Salanter of the concept of *dimyon* (imagination) at the beginning of *Iggeret ha-mussar*, in Pechter, *Kitvei*, 114, with the description of the imagination in *Heshbon ha-nefesh*, 100, sec. 200.

47. This subject is explicated below, chap. 18; and see Pechter, *Kitvei*, 125.

48. The use made by R. Israel of this theory is discussed below. See Pechter, *Kitvei*, 217.

49. *Heshbon ha-nefesh*, 106.

50. I will devote a special discussion to the role of the subconscious in Salanter's thought; see below, chap. 18.

51. See *Heshbon ha-nefesh*, 12, 13, 17, 19, etc.

52. See *Heshbon ha-nefesh*, 20.

53. See, for example, Pechter, *Kitvei*, 201, and *passim*.

Chapter 10

1. See Rosenfeld, *Rabbi Yisrael Salanter*, 5–8, 15; A. A. Friedman, *Le-toldot kitat ha-mussara'im* (Jerusalem, 1926), 3–4; Glenn, *Israel Salanter*, 23.

2. See Immanuel Etkes, "Compulsory Enlightenment as a Crossroads in the History of the Haskalah Movement in Russia" [Heb.], *Zion* 43 (1978): 264–313. On the program of the Russian Haskalah, see I. Etkes, "Te'udah be-yisra'el—Between Change and Tradition" [Heb.], Introduction to Isaac Ber Levinsohn's *Te'udah be-yisra'el* (Vilna and Horodna, 1828 [Photo edition: Jerusalem, 1977]), 3–19.

A recently published study shedding new light on the history of Russian Jewry during the reign of Nicholai I is Michael Stanislawski, *Tsar Nicholas I and the Jews: The Transformation of Jewish Society in Russia, 1825–1855* (Philadelphia: The Jewish Publication Society, 1983). It follows from this instructive study that the changes that came about in Jewish society in Russia during this period were more far-reaching than had been set forth by the previous historiography. In principle, Stanislawski's conclusions strengthen the interpretation given in this chapter concerning the relationship between the growth of the Haskalah and the establishment of the Mussar movement.

3. Max Lilienthal was an educator and Reform rabbi. Educated in Germany, Lilienthal was called upon by the Jewish community of Riga in 1839 to establish and direct a modern school. Following his success in this task, the Russian education minister, Sergei Uvarov, appointed him as his advisor in matters of Jewish Enlightenment. He was asked to draw up a comprehensive plan for the reform of traditional Jewish education, and was sent by Uvarov to persuade the communal leadership

to support this project. In 1844, Lilienthal left Russia secretly, and one year later immigrated to the United States, where he served as a Reform rabbi.

4. Most historians who have dealt with this question tend to minimize the results of the establishment of government schools for Jewish children. Stanislawski, on the other hand, claims that both in terms of scope, and particularly in terms of their influence upon the process of growth of the intelligentsia in Russian Jewry, this phenomenon was one of great consequence. See Stanislawski, *Tsar Nicholas I and the Jews*, 97–122.

5. On other manifestations that may be described as Orthodox reactions to the strengthening of the Haskalah, see Stanislawski's discussion, ibid., 148–54.

6. Moses Montefiore was a philanthropist and intercessor on behalf of Jewish interests. Together with other members of his family, Montefiore conducted a brokerage firm on the London exchange. He was knighted by Queen Victoria, and in 1824 left most of his business involvements in order to devote himself to community activities and to the protection of Jewish rights. He filled various important positions in Jewish organizations in England, and journeyed abroad to various Jewish communities in distress; he was particularly noted for his intercession in the Damascus Affair. He visited Palestine several times, and acted on behalf of economic productivization of the Jewish settlements there.

7. See Mahler, *Divrei yemei yisra'el*, 5: 141.

8. The Damascus Affair was the best known and most notorious anti-Jewish blood libel of the nineteenth century. In 1840, a Capuchin friar and his Moslem servant disappeared in Damascus. The Christians accused the local Jews of murdering the two to use their blood for baking matzot. The authorities arrested several leading figures of the Jewish community, and extracted from them "confessions" by the use of torture, as a result of which several died. News of the affair upset the entire Jewish world, particularly that of Western Europe, which was then at the height of the process of Emancipation. A delegation, including Moses Montefiore, his secretary Louis Loewe (Eli'ezer Ha-Levi), Adolphe Cremieux, and Salomon Munk went to Egypt to convince Muhammed Ali to obtain the release of those Jews being held. Montefiore and his secretary continued to Constantinople, where they received a *firman* from the sultan declaring the blood libels fallacious and prohibiting the trial of Jews on such charges.

9. A detailed description of Montefiore's reception in Vilna and the itinerary of his visit in this city appears in Dick, *Ha-oreah*. See also the description given by Ginzburg, *Devir* (Vilna, 1862), 98–108.

10. Yaakov Lifschitz states this in the name of his grandfather, who was a contemporary. See Lifschitz, *Zikhron ya'akov*, 1: 153–54.

11. Ibid., 1: 154.

12. See Dick, *Ha-oreah*, 7.

13. *Ibid.*, 32.

14. Ibid., 34.

15. Lifschitz, *Zikhron ya'akov*, 1: 156.

16. Ibid., 156–57.

17. See Dick, *Ha-oreah*, 16.

18. See ibid., 37. This sermon by Loewe was translated into Hebrew by Samuel Joseph Fühn, and published under the title *Sefer masa' eliezer* (Vilna, 1847).

19. See Dick, *Ha-oreah*, 30–31.

20. A polemical response to the Maskilic motifs in Loewe's sermons appears in a sermon delivered in honor of Montefiore by R. Shlomo Zalman, the *Maggid*

Mesharim of Vilna, published under the title *Sefer tiff'eret moshe* (Warsaw, 1884). See Etkes, "Compulsory Enlightenment," 303–04.

21. Lifschitz, *Zikhron ya'akov,* 1: 154–55.

22. Dick, *Ha-'oreah,* 25.

23. These accusations are frequently repeated in the letters of the Maskilim. See M. A. Ginzburg, *Ha-moriyah* (Warsaw, 1878), 46–47; see also Etkes, "Compulsory Enlightenment," 275.

24. On the history of the Vilna Rabbinical Seminary, see Judah Slutzki, "The Rabbinical Seminary in Vilna" [Heb.], *He-'avar* 7 (1960): 29ff.; A. Shohat, *Mossad "ha-rabbanut mi-ta'am" be-russiah* (Haifa, 1976), chap. 1.

25. See Slutzki, "The Rabbinical Seminary," 30; B. Z. Dinur, "The Historical Image of Russian Jewry and the Problems of its Research" [Heb.], *Zion* 22 (1957): 104.

26. See the letter of Isaac ben-Ya'akov to Y. B. Levinsohn [Heb.], in *Ha-kerem* (1888), 43.

27. See ibid., 42; cf. Noah H. Rosenblum, "On the World-View of Adam Ha-Cohen" [Heb.], *Perakim* 3 (1963): 141.

28. See Slutzki, "The Rabbinical Seminary," 33.

29. Some authors claim that R. Salanter was offered the post of head of the rabbinical seminary (Ozvinsky, *Toldot yeshivat,* 61; Weinberg, *Seridei esh,* 4: 290; Katz, *Tenu'at ha-mussar,* 1: 163). However, this version seems to me somewhat exaggerated, the position offered Salanter being in fact that of lecturer in Talmud. See the letter of Isaac ben-Ya'akov in *Ha-kerem* (1888): 42; Barukh Ha-Levi Epstein, *Sefer mekor barukh* (New York, 1954), Pt. 2: 1084; and also the letter of H. L. Katzenellenbogen to Y. Katzenelson, December 1948, in the Ginzburg Archives.

30. The earliest description of this event, followed by the majority of authors, appears in Steinschneider, *'Ir vilna,* 130.

31. See the letter of Isaac ben Ya'akov in *Ha-kerem* (1888): 42.

32. Ibid.

33. Ya'akov Lifschitz explains the appeal to R. Israel in this spirit. See Lifschitz, *Zikhron ya'akov,* 1: 176.

34. This theory is developed by Rabbi Yehiel Ya'akov Weinberg, *Seridei esh,* 4: 290.

35. See the discussion on this phenomenon in the Epilogue of the present work. Salanter's stand concerning the rabbinical seminary engaged a number of Haskalah authors in a later period, some of whom blamed the eventual failure of the institution on R. Israel's refusal to teach there. See Israel Bernstein, "To Hasten Redemption" [Heb.], *Ha-shahar* 10 (1880): 230ff.

36. Emil Benjamin, *R. Israel Lipkin Salant; Sein Leben und Wirken* (Berlin, 1899), 10. A similar reply was given by Salanter to the Kovna Maskil, Dr. Zvi Hirsch Apteker; see Lifschitz, *Zikhron ya'akov,* 1: 177.

37. This approach of Salanter's is discussed in greater depth below.

38. Ben Ya'akov argues in his letter to Levinsohn that Adam Ha-Cohen implanted an attitude of contempt for the Talmud in his students at the seminary. See *Ha-kerem* (1888): 43.

39. Ben-Ya'akov relates that R. Zvi Hirsch Katzenellenbogen taught his students Talmud with Alfasi, *Rosh* and *Tur* (i.e., the major medieval codifiers, primarily of the Spanish school, omitting the dialectical-analytical commentaries and glosses of the Tosafistic and French schools, or of the later German and Polish schools); see *Ha-kerem* (1888): 42. The pragmatic tendency reflected in this program of study was

likewise expressed in the stress upon Maimonides's *Mishneh torah* and the *Shulhan 'arukh*. Those who were preparing for the rabbinate concentrated upon those tractates that were particularly useful for halakhic rulings, such as Gittin, Niddah, and Hullin, and on *Yoreh de'ah* (see Slutzki, "The Rabbinical Seminary," 33).

40. Salanter's stand on this issue is discussed at length in chap. 14.

41. Cited in Ozvinski, *Toldot yeshivat*, 61, where the quote is given in the name of R. A. Demant, who was a student of Salanter at Zarzecze.

42. Ibid., 61–62.

43. Avot 2:2, the precise wording being: *Yafeh talmud torah 'im derekh erez . . .* ("Excellent is the study of Torah together with way of the world. . . .").

44. *'Even yisra'el*, 16, note.

45. In *Divrei shalom ve-'emet*, N. H. Wesseley uses the concept *derek-erez* both as a synonym for manners and ways of behavior, and in the broader sense of that which he calls *Torat ha-'adam* (the Torah of Man).

46. See, for example, Levinsohn, *Te'udah be-yisra'el*, 159.

47. *'Even yisra'el*, 16, note.

48. Ibid.

49. Wilmann, *Iggerot u-mikhtavim*, letter 65, pp. 71–73.

Chapter 11

1. Shmuel Haggai has already observed the connection between the social distress of the period and the founding of the Mussar movement in his article, "The Historical Background of the Mussar Movement" [Heb.], *Mahanayim* 81 (Iyyar 1963): 70–75. However, Haggai was content to point out the fact of economic distress and did not attempt to base his explanation upon the writings and activities of Salanter.

2. In my description of the economic and social distress of Russian Jewry during the period of Nicholai I's rule, I relied upon the comprehensive discussion by Mahler, *Divrei yemei yisra'el*, 5: 13–145. To a large extent, my description relies upon two documents that describe the situation in the 1840s. I refer to two letters addressed to Moses Montefiore in 1846: one by R. Mordecai Gimpel Yaffe, the rabbi of Ostian at the time, and the other by the community of Vilna. The former was published in *Sefer zikhronot mordekhai* (Warsaw, 1913), 30–41; the latter (referred to below as "Letter of Vilna Community") was published by Ginzburg, *Historische Verk*, 2: 293–98. A final section of the "Letter of Vilna Community" was printed under the heading "Sof davar" (postscript), in Dick, *Ha-'oreah*, 44–47. From Dick's hints (ibid., 17), it would appear that this passage was formulated by Adam Ha-Cohen.

3. See Philipsohn, *Max Lilienthal*, 261–62.

4. See "Letter of Vilna Community" in Ginzburg, *Historische Verk*, 294. For a striking expression of the sense of disappointment and frustration rampant among the Jews of Vilna in light of the disappearance of their sources of livelihood and the growth of poverty, see ibid., 295, as well as the postscript to the above-mentioned letter, in Dick, *Ha-'oreah*, 44–47.

5. See Mahler, *Divrei yemei yisra'el*, 5: 118–20. The satiric work by Isaac Ber Levinsohn, *'Olam hefker*, includes severe accusations concerning the economic exploitation of the poor people by the communal leaders.

6. See Mahler, *Divrei yemei yisra'el*, 5: 121–22.

7. See on this matter I. Levitats, *The Jewish Community in Russia* (New York, 1943), 46–68; and see now also the detailed discussion by Stanislawski, *Tsar Nicholas I and the Jews*, 13–34.

8. This tendency is clearly reflected in the list of candidates for conscription in the community of Minsk from 1827. See Mahler, *Divrei yemei yisra'el*, 5: 284–85, Appendix 4. It follows from Stanislawski's study that the role of the communal leadership in carrying out the conscription edict led to a loss of faith in its leadership by the masses of the people.

9. The terrible suffering of those kidnapped and of their families is described in the memoirs of several contemporaries. See A. S. Friedberg, "Memories from my Childhood" [Heb.], in *Sefer ha-shanah* 3 (Warsaw, 1902); Judah Leib Levin (Yahal-a"l), "The Kidnapped" [Heb.], in *Efer ha-yovel je-nahum sokolow* (Warsaw, 1904).

10. See Elijah Cherikover, "The Jewish Masses, the Maskilim and the Regime During the Reign of Nicholai" [Heb.], in *Yehudim be-'itot mahpekhah* (Tel Aviv, 1957), 107ff.

11. See Friedberg, "Memories," 86–87; cf. Epstein, *Mekor barukh*, Pt. 1, 967–68.

12. Ya'akov Lifschitz, who describes the history of the Jews of Russia from the viewpoint of the Orthodox camp, attempts to defend its leadership; however, he does not deny the facts themselves, but only tries to soften their severity somewhat (see Lifschitz, *Zikhron ya'akov*, 1: 102–27). R. Baruch Epstein, on the other hand, who also reflects the world of the learned class in his memoirs, is not afraid to admit the ethical failure of its leadership (see Epstein, *Mekor barukh*, Pt. 1, 967–68).

13. See Friedberg, "Memories," 86–87.

14. Additional evidence for the fact that unemployment was more severe in Vilna than elsewhere appears in a passage from a letter by Marcus Mendelsohn, sent in 1845 from Vilna to Yaakov Katzenelson, who then lived in Minsk: "... But my friend! Happy are you that you have abandoned accursed Vilna (would that I also did not know it). Happy you are, that you will not see the inhabitants of the city, including your own friends, crushed under the heavy yoke of [earning a] livelihood which does not suffice even to quiet their hunger. I am fed up with the life of this unfortunate city. . . .'' Further on, the author describes in greater detail the suffering of various individuals from the circle of the Maskilim. (The letter is extant in the Ginzburg Archives, housed in the Manuscript Department of the Jewish National Library in Jerusalem.)

15. See *Even yisra'el*, Sermon 7, p. 30; the beginning of Sermon 1; Sermon 2, p. 8.

16. *Even yisra'el*, Sermon 3, pp. 14–15.

17. *Nefesh ha-hayyim*, 25.

18. Willman, *Iggerot u-mikhtavim*, letter 20, p. 40. While this letter is admittedly late, from 1864, the stance expressed therein seems to match what we have found from the sources known to us from our period.

19. Ibid, letter 6, pp. 27–28.

20. Ibid.

21. The passage below is from *'Even yisra'el*, Sermon 3, p. 11.

22. Ibid.

23. Ibid., 11–12.

24. Ibid. For an additional example, see ibid., Sermon 4, p. 17.

25. Ibid., Sermon 8, p. 36.

26. Ibid.

27. Avot 2:5.

28. The stories about R. Israel Salanter have been gathered and published in a number of places. The earliest collection, which consists in part of first-hand evidence, was printed by R. Isaac Blazer in *Or yisra'el*, mainly in the section entitled

"Netivot or," 109–24. An important collection is also contained in Yaakov Mark's biographical sketch of R. Salanter, first published in his book, *Gedoylim fun unzerer tsayt* (New York, 1927). The present author made use of the Hebrew version, *Be-mehizatam shel gedolei ha-dor* (Jerusalem, 1958). Several anecdotes were published in the periodical *Sha'arei zion*, nos. 3–5 (Jerusalem, 1933): 54–65. An impressive collection of stories is brought by Dov Katz in the first volume of his *Tenu'at ha-mussar*. In addition to the stories that he gathered from earlier written sources, he cites a number of others that he himself heard from various personalities within the circle of the Mussar yeshivot. One should also mention the extensive collection of anecdotes published in *Sefer ha-me'orot ha-gedolim*. Unfortunately, this editor was not careful to cite the stories exactly as they appear in the sources from which they were gathered. On the value of these stories as a source of information concerning the authentic image of R. Israel, see Pechter, *Kitvei*, 26, n. 11.

29. See Bava Kamma 30a.

30. See Katz, *Tenu'at ha-mussar*, 1: 353.

31. See Mark, *Bi-mehizatam*, 68.

32. Cited by Katz, *Tenu'at ha-mussar*, 1: 383, from the manuscript of R. Simhah Zeisel Ziv. On this matter, see also the testimony of R. Isaac Blazer, *Or yisra'el*, 117.

33. See Lipkin, "Concerning the Path," 76. There are additional stories according to which Salanter considered the act of waking those who were sleeping as theft.

34. See *Sha'arei zion*, nos. 3–5 (Jerusalem, 1933): 59, from a letter of Yehiel Mikhel Tukutzinski, who heard this story from a disciple of Salanter's.

35. Lipkin, "Concerning the Path," 75–76.

36. *Or yisra'el*, 112.

37. There are numerous testimonies to this aspect of his personality. See, e.g., Katz, *Tenu'at ha-mussar*, 1: 358; Mark, *Bi-mehizatam*, 69.

38. *Or yisra'el*, 118.

39. See Mark, *Be-mihizatam*, 88.

40. Katz, *Tenu'at ha-mussar*, 1: 371.

41. *Or yisra'el*, 117–18.

42. See Zaitchik, *Sefer ha-me'orot ha-gedolim*, sec. 7, p. 49.

43. See Mark, *Bi-mehizatam*, 70.

44. See Zaitchik, *Sefer ha-me'orot ha-gedolim*, secs. 38, 41, pp. 60–61; *Sha'arei zion*, nos 3–5 (Jerusalem, 1933): 57; Katz, *Tenu'at ha-mussar*, 1: 357–58. For more on Salanter's attitude toward servants, see id., *Tenu'at ha-mussar*, 1: 355; *Sha'arei zion*, nos 3–5 (Jerusalem, 1933): 56.

45. See Steinschneider, *'Ir vilna*, 130.

46. The following description concerning R. Israel Salanter's activities during the period of the epidemic is primarily based upon the memoirs of R. Isaac Lipkin, "Concerning the Path," pp. 74–76.

47. *Or yisra'el*, Letter 22, p. 67. The letter was published without any date; it seems likely that it was written in 1855, when the cholera epidemic struck Russia a second time.

48. Lipkin, "Concerning the Path," 75.

49. Steinschneider, *'Ir vilna*, 130.

50. I refer to the story by David Frishman, "Three Who Ate" [Heb.], in his *Kol kitvei* (1950), 131–34. The above version of *'Ir vilna* was also followed by Rosenfeld, *Rabbi Israel Salanter*, 17, and is also that accepted by Katz *Tenu'at ha-mussar*, 1: 159–61. Baruch Epstein cites a similar version, marked by even greater dramatization (*Mekor barukh*, 2: 1012).

51. To be considered culpable of violating Yom Kippur under Torah law, one

must consume a certain minimum quantity of food (about 30 g.) or drink (about 40 cc.) within a period of no more than nine minutes. Those who needed to eat or drink on Yom Kippur in order to alleviate danger were therefore instructed to eat less than these quantities at any given time; cf. *Shulhan 'arukh, Orah hayyim* 618: 7–8.

52. See Mark, *Bi-mehizatam*, 68.

53. Lipkin, "Concerning the Path," 76.

54. See Pechter, *Kitvei*, 121. Among other things, he writes there that: ". . . Does not [the removal] of anything which, according to the Torah, belongs to one's fellow constitute theft, and [does not one thereby] violate the prohibition of 'thou shalt not steal'. . . . And we see that in our great sinfulness the *lomdim*, and even those who are [called] God-fearing, are not as careful as they ought to be concerning this prohibition. . . ."

55. See M. Levin, *'Erkei hevrah ve-kalkalah ba-ideologia shel tekufat ha-haskalah* (Jerusalem, 1975).

Chapter 12

1. A contemporary account, confirming that Salanter's move from Vilna to Kovna was essentially a flight, appears in a letter of the Maskil, Hayyim Leib Katzenellenbogen, to his friend Yaakov Katzenelson. This letter, sent from Vilna on December 22, 1848, states, among other things, that, "Rabbi Gershon Cohen is rumored to have been appointed instructor in Talmud at the Rabbinical Seminary, instead of the Salanter, who fled to Kovna. . . ." (The letter is preserved in the Ginzburg Archives, File 17/4.) From the wording used in this letter, it would appear that Rabbi Israel's flight to Kovna was fresh news.

2. See the detailed discussion above, in chap. 8.

3. See *Or yisra'el*, the beginning of letter 1, p. 41; the beginning of letter 3, p. 44; the end of letter 3, p. 45; the beginning of letter 5, pp. 46–47.

4. *'Or yisra'el*, 113.

5. *Sefer 'or ha-mussar*, 1:78. Dov Katz accepts the reading of R. Naphtali Amsterdam (*Tenu'at ha-mussar*, 1:177), but does not distinguish between earlier and later phases of this incident. He only relates to Salanter's activity as a *maggid mesharim* after extensively describing his activities in the *kloiz* of R. Zvi Nevyozer (*Tenu'at ha-mussar*, 1:170–176), while in fact R. Israel became active in this *kloiz* only after he was forced to abandon the post of *maggid*, as explained below.

6. R. Mordecai Eliasberg, *Sefer shevil ha-zahav* (Warsaw, 1897), xii.

7. *Sefer 'or ha-mussar*, 1:78.

8. I discuss below the motivations for Salanter's resignation from this office.

9. See Willman, *'Iggerot u-mikhtavim*, letter 65, pp. 71–73; cf. *'Or yisra'el*, letter 11, p. 59. We already found this position expressed in Salanter's letters from 1849.

10. "Even one preoccupied with business affairs may easily go to the Mussar house, particularly on the holy Sabbath" (*'Or yisra'el*, 49). ". . . One can easily see that to go to the Mussar house occasionally during [the penitential month of] Elul is a very easy thing . . . and when a person goes to the Mussar house, this is a great and awesome factor, which has the power to bring about serious and weighty consequences" (*Or yisra'el*, 52).

11. Ibid., p. 59.

12. See ibid., letters 6, 7, 12.

13. See ibid., letter 6, pp. 49, 50.

14. Details concerning the location of the Mussar House in Kovna appear in Katz, *Tenu'at ha-mussar*, 1:176, n. 20.

15. A. A. Friedman writes concerning those who attended the Mussar House in Kovna: "The first to attend the house were those who came from the party of merchants, such as the Gordon brothers, Shlomo Azinski, Reuven Avenski, and others from this group, who constituted the majority and most important. . . . " ("Li-pelagot yisra'el," in *Ha-meliz*, no. 108 (1897). Dov Katz adds several other names, including members of the family of the *gevir* R. Zvi Hirsch Nevyozer (see Katz, *Tenu'at ha-mussar*, 1:177, n. 23).

16. *Ha-meliz*, no. 137 (1897), contains an announcement supporting the Mussar yeshivot. The announcement, which appeared under the heading "Meha'ah gel-uyah" ("An Open Protest"), was signed by ten *ba'alei batim* from Kovna. See Rosenfeld, *Rabbi yisrael salanter*, 53ff., on the hold of the Mussar movement in Kovna during the 1880s.

17. On the renewal of Jewish settlement in Kovna, see D. M. Lippman, *Le-toldot ha-yehudim be-kovna u-slobodka* (Keidan, 1934), 194ff.

18. See Hayyim V. Heschel, "The Jewish Community in Kovna" [Heb.], in *Keneset yisra'el*, ed. Shaul Pinhas Rabinowitz (Warsaw, 1888), 164.

19. Compare Friedman's description of the origins of the Mussar movement in Kelm: A. A. Friedman, *Sefer ha-zikhronot* (Tel Aviv, 1926), 78.

20. On R. Elijah's activity in this area, see Mark, *Bi-mehizatam*, 10.

21. Willman, *'Iggerot u-mikhtavim*, letter 65, p. 73.

22. M. A. Dolitzki, *Mofet le-rabbim* (Frankfurt am Main, 1892), 10–11. Wissotzky's memoirs were formulated in this book by the writer M. Dolitzki, who was among the regular visitors at his home and was even supported by him.

23. R. Mazeh relates in his memoirs that the time spent by Wissotzky in R. Salanter's presence had a profound influence upon the former's personality and way of life. See R. Ya'akov Mazeh, *Zikhronot* (Tel Aviv, 1936), 1:130–31.

24. Heikel Lunski, *Min ha-getto ha-vilna'i* (Vilna, 1921), 11–12.

25. On the biography and personality of the Kelmer Maggid, see *Luah ahi'asaf* (1901), 389; A. H. Zayanshik, *Ha-zefirah*, no. 247 (1899); Ben Zion Eisenstadt, *Dor rabanav ve-sofrav* (Vilna, 1900), 53–54; Mark, *Bi-mehizatam*, 222–36; Mazeh, *Zikhronot*, 3: 126ff.; Katz, *Tenu'at ha-mussar*, 2:395–407.

26. See, e.g., J. L. Gordon in *Allgemeine Zeitung des Judentums* 25 (1861): 169.

27. See Ben Zion Eisenstadt, *Dor rabbanav ve-sofrav*, 53–54.

28. Mazeh, *Zikhronot*, 3:127.

29. Taken from the biographical sketch of the life of R. Israel Salanter by his grandson, R. David Sidarsky, typewritten and preserved at the Jewish National Library, Schwadron Collection, Autograph Israel Lipkin (the passage quoted is from p. 10). Generally speaking, Sidarsky followed in the footsteps of earlier authors, his contribution to his grandfather's biography being rather limited. Compare also *Ha-meliz* (1883): 126, in the section "*Alon bakhut.*"

30. Willman must have miscopied the word *matende* from the manuscript, which is meaningless. He evidently intended to write *metoda*—i.e., a system of teaching.

31. Willman, *Iggerot u-mikhtavim*, letter 33, p. 47. Willman copied from a corrupt manuscript, for which reason his text is fragmentary and incomplete.

32. Dov Katz was rather inaccurate in quoting that section from the above letter, which describes the method of study that Salanter observed within that group of artisans, describing it as a "special method" invented by R. Israel in order to make literate people of these artisans (see Katz, *Tenu'at ha mussar*, 1:179).

33. Ben Zion Eisenstadt, *Dor rabbanav ve-sofrav*, 53.

34. See Katz, *Tenu'at ha-mussar*, 2:395–407.

35. Ibid., 396.

36. The only book written by the Kelmer Maggid is *Tokhehot hayyim* (Vilna, 1897).

37. See, for example, ibid., 32, 33, 34.

38. See, for example, how the Kelmer Maggid elaborated in the description of the sufferings in Hell to be expected by those who do not fix appointed times to study Torah; ibid., Sermon 5, p. 67ff.

39. The Maggid devotes considerable space in his book to explaining the obligation of Torah study, but does not at all advocate the study of Mussar works. (See his *Sefer tokhehot hayyim*, especially Sermons 4 and 5.)

40. See Katz, *Tenu'at ha-mussar*, 4:17–175.

41. See ibid., 17.

42. See, for example, Rosenfeld, *Rabbi Yisrael Salanter*, 32, and cf. Louis Ginzberg, "Rabbi Israel Salanter," in his *Students, Scholars and Saints*, 157, and following him, Glenn, *Israel Salanter*, 45.

43. Katz, *Tenu'at ha-mussar*, 1:178–79.

44. Ibid., 181.

45. Ibid., 2:405.

46. Ibid., n. 13. For Gordon's article, see above, n. 26, pp. 168–70.

47. Dov Katz may have erred by relying upon Y. Mark without examining the original article by Gordon. Mark himself attributes the founding of Mussar houses to the Kelmer Maggid, relying upon Gordon, albeit the figure "tens" is Katz's contribution to this story (see Mark, *Bi-mehizatam*, 227–28).

48. R. Hayyim Zvi Hirsch Broide, *Lakahat Mussar Haskel*, *Ha-meliz*, no. 120 (1897).

49. In his article, "Le-ma'an da'at," *Ha-meliz*, no. 143.

50. See *Mikhtevei avraham mapu*, ed. Ben Zion Dinur (Jerusalem, 1970), 19.

51. This supposition is based upon R. Israel's contact with R. Gershon Mendel Ziv, the rabbi of Plongian, concerning the dissemination of Mussar study in that community (see Willman, *Iggerot u-mikhtavim*, letter 65, p. 73).

52. Yehiel Ya'akov Weinberg, *Li-ferakim* (Warsaw, 1936), 399, in a note.

53. This is of course an error; R. Israel first arrived in Kovna only at the end of 1848.

54. Lippman, *Le-toldot ha-yehudim*, 202.

55. Ibid., n. 1; *Mikhtevei avraham mapu*, Introduction, 15.

56. See S. Ginzburg, "Abraham Mapu" [Heb.], *He-'avar* #1 (1918): 96–101. See also Klausner, 3: 294–95.

57. See *Mikhtevei avraham mapu*, 19, 22. Mapu describes R. Gediel as a clever scholar, a charismatic preacher who inspired his audience, an extremist, and an "Orthodox" zealot. See *Kol kitvei mapu* (Tel Aviv, 1955), 223, 228, 233, etc.

58. The reference is to the traditional *heder*.

59. That is, the above-mentioned R. Elijah Levinsohn of Cartinga.

60. Salanter.

61. *Mikhtevei avraham mapu*, 19–20.

62. Ibid., Introduction, 15.

63. See above, n. 26.

64. We have already discussed above the taking root of the Haskalah in Vilna, Kovna, and Rosein. Mitava, the central city of Courland, was within the zone of

influence of the German culture, so that its Jews were affected by the tendencies of the Jewish Haskalah in Germany. On the Haskalah in Zager, see Y. Slutzki, "Dr. Max Mandelstamm" [Heb.], *He-'avar* (1957) 4:56ff.

65. See Baal Makhshoves (Israel Elyashev), "Gerobin" [Heb.], *He-'avar* #1 (1918): 107–16; 2:89–107.

66. Ibid., 1:108.

67. Evidence for this may be seen in the fact that R. Leib Shapira, who served as rabbi of Kovna from 1849 until his death in 1854, headed the opposition. Further proof of this appears in the testimony of R. Naphtali Amsterdam, cited below, from which it follows that opposition already arose during the period in which R. Salanter served as *maggid*. It will be shown below that R. Israel resigned from the position of *maggid* in 1851.

68. See Lippman, *Le toldot ha-yehudim*, 224–27.

69. Among them: R. Yehoshua Heschel Eliaszon, rabbi of Yanova and a close friend of R. Leib Shapira; R. Yeshayah, the rabbi of Salant; R. Abraham Shmuel of Rosein, who served as rabbi of Kovna following R. Shapira's death; see Friedman, "Li-pelagot yisra'el"; Rosenfeld, *Rabbi Yisrael Salanter*, 32.

70. See Eliasberg, *Sefer shevil ha-zahav*, xiii.

71. Cited by Friedman, above (n. 15), in the name of R. Alexander Lapidot, who heard these remarks from R. Israel Salanter himself.

72. Ibid.

73. See "Shivrei ra'ayonot," *Ha-meliz*, no. 109 (1897).

74. This quip was widely known and quoted in numerous sources. See, for example, Lippman, *Le toldot ha-yehudim*, 228, n. 2; Ginzburg, *Students, Scholars and Saints*, 157.

75. These remarks are cited by R. Meir Feimer in his article, "From a Private Letter" [Heb.], *Ha-meliz* no. 101 (1897).

76. *Or yisra'el*, letter 13, p. 60.

77. These ideas are discussed below, in chap. 13.

78. "Hasidim of Zamot" is a sarcastic designation for the Mussar devotees, Zamot being the region of Lithuania of which Kovna is the capital. "Hasidim of Galicia" refers to the followers of the Hasidic movement, an important nineteenth-century center of which was in Galicia.

79. Above, n. 48.

80. This tendency received institutional expression in the Mussar yeshivot, where the status of the *mashgiah* was higher than that of the *rosh-yeshivah*.

81. Concerning these tendencies in the writings of the opponents of Hasidism, see the manifesto *Zemir 'arizim ve-harvot zurim*, brought by Wilensky, *Hasidim u-mitnagdim*, 1:37–69. See also the polemic letter of R. Abraham Katzenellenbogen to R. Levi Yizhak of Berditchev, ibid., 123–31.

82. See note 81.

83. See Moshe Hayyim Ephraim of Sudylkow, *Sefer degel mahaneh ephraim, parashat yitro* (Jerusalem, 1963), s.v. "ve-khol ha'am ro'im et ha-kolot," 111.

84. See *Sefer 'or ha-mussar*, 1:114.

85. See n. 68. R. Manashe of Ilyah sought to bring about changes in Jewish society in the spirit of the Haskalah, and was even persecuted for it. See Mordecai Plongian, *Ben porat* (Vilna, 1858).

86. In the eyes of the Haskalah authors, this rabbi was the archetypal "reformist" rabbi. See Reuben Asher Broides, *Ha-dat veha-hayyim* (Jerusalem, 1974), 1:96.

87. The influence of the young R. Mordecai was based, as far as we can tell, on his being the son-in-law of the wealthy R. Markel, one of the richest Jews in Kovna.

An expression of his wealth is seen in the fact that he built a study house with his own money, wherein he established ten Torah scholars whom he fully supported. Moreover, R. Markel's house served as a lodging for Moses Montefiore when he visited Kovna. See Eliasberg, *Sefer shevil ha-zahav*, vii, ix.

88. See Steinschneider, *'Ir vilna*, 130; Katz, *Tenu'at ha-mussar*, 1:170.

89. Rabbi David Bonimowitz, the biographer of R. Elijah Levinsohn of Cartinga, relates that in 1867, in the wake of the sudden decline in his business, R. Elijah told him that, "Since the Gaon R. Israel Salanter ceased to be the *maggid* in Kovna, I have supplied all the needs of his household, and this amounts to about 800 rubles a year. Now that I am no longer able to do so, I must reveal this to you, so that we may take counsel together how to get [money] for him. . . . " (Bonimowitz, *Sefer mikhtav me-'eliyahu*, 54). This testimony is confirmed by R. Isaac Blazer, who writes that, after R. Israel left his office in the Kovna community, "He was forced to accept benefit from others. And his livelihood was provided by one of the outstanding ones of his greater disciples" (*Or yisra'el*, 113). This clearly refers to the selfsame R. Elijah, who was already a disciple-colleague of R. Israel's in his Salant days. On this point, see also Mark, *Bi-mehizatam*, 10.

90. R. Isaac Blazer testifies that "that *zaddik* was pained all his days" because of being supported by others. He also brings a story that expresses this pain. See *'Or yisra'el*, 113.

Chapter 13

1. The quotations from *Iggeret ha-mussar* are taken from *Kitvei*, Pechter edition.
2. *Kitvei*, 117.
3. See ibid., 114–15.
4. Ibid., 117.
5. Ibid., 118.
6. See, for example, the beginning of letter 1 in *Or yisr'ael*, 41.
7. *Kitvei*, 118.
8. Ibid., 119.
9. Ibid.
10. Ibid., 120.
11. See the remarks cited in this context by R. Naphtali Amsterdam in the name of his teacher, in *Sefer'or ha-mussar*, 1:17.
12. *Kitvei*, 123.
13. Ibid.
14. R. Isaac Blazer states that R. Salanter taught his students to "to pray together in public concerning the spiritual Evil Impulse, to remove the heart of stone from our flesh . . . " See *'Or yisra'el*, 121. On prayer as a tool against the spirit of impurity, see also *'Or yisra'el*, letter 14, pp. 60–61.
15. The question of study of halakhot as a means of ethical education is discussed below.
16. *Kitvei*, 123–24.
17. R. Naphtali Amsterdam brings an argument in the name of Salanter that diminishes even further the status of Torah study as a means of struggle with the Evil Impulse. On the basis of the Rabbinic dictum, "Torah, while one studies it, protects one" (Sotah 21a), he concludes that only while a person is actually engaged in studying Torah does it offer protection from the Evil Impulse. See *Sefer 'or ha-mussar*, 1:117.
18. *Kitvei*, 119.

19. *Even yisra'el*, Sermon 8, p. 34.

20. That is to say, the butcher is by habit so pious that even if he has already invested in a carcass, if he discovers reason to think it might be ritually impure he will pursue the point, risking considerable financial loss (*Kitvei*, 120–21).

21. See above, chap. 9.

22. See, for example, letter 10, *'Or yisra'el*, 58.

23. *Kitvei*, 120–21.

24. The term refers both to the outstanding rabbinic authorities in any given generation and, in the context of Torah study, as here, to the literature of Codes, such as R. Yitzhak Alfasi's *Hilkhot ha-rif*, R. Jacob ben Asher's *Arba'ah turim*, R. Joseph Caro's *Shulhan 'arukh*, and Maimonides's *Mishneh torah*. These works present authoritative rulings on the entire gamut of halakhic subject matter in systematic, authoritative format, and were studied and referred to as standard legal texts.

25. *Kitvei*, 121–22.

26. *'Or yisra'el*, letter 21, p. 67. See also: Rabbi Hayyim Yizhak Lipkin, *Torat r. yisra'el mi-salant* (Tel Aviv, 1954), Pt. 2, p. 61.

27. Introduction to *Tevunah*, in note.

28. See *Kitvei*, 124.

29. Ibid., 115.

30. Ibid.

Chapter 14

1. The *kloiz* itself was established in 1851 (see Lippmann, *Le-toldot ha-yehudim*, 202). An indication that R. Salanter began to operate in the *kloiz* in that same year is to be found in a biographical sketch of R. Yeruham Yehudah Leib Perlman, who was among his students during that period. Perlman's biographer relates that he was born in 1835, married at the age of thirteen, was supported by his father-in-law for three years, and then traveled to Kovna where he became a student at Salanter's *kloiz*. This would have been in 1851. See *Sefer ben-'oni; kinah ve-hesped 'al r. yeruham yehudah leib perlman*, by his brother, Binyamin Bishke (Vilna, 1896), Introduction.

2. See ibid.; Eliasberg, *Sefer shevil ha-zahav*, xii; R. Naphtali Amsterdam's article in *Ha-levanon*, no. 37 (1879).

3. Sketches of these personalities are included in Mark, *Bi-mehizatam*. On the abortive attempt to establish an official rabbinate in New York City in the 1890s involving R. Jacob Joseph, see Abraham J. Karp, "New York Chooses a Chief Rabbi," *AJHQ* 44 (1955):129–98.

4. See the autobiographical testimony of R. Kalonymus Ze'ev Wissotzky, in Dolitzki, *Mofet le-rabbim;* the sketch of R. Yeruham Leib Perlman, above, n. 1; and the biographical information on R. Eliezer Gordon, below.

5. Based upon the letter of R. Eliezer Gordon, published in *Sefer ish yerushalayim*, ed. M. Ostrovsky (Jerusalem, 1937), 67–69.

6. Thus, for example, it states in the introduction to Bishke, *Sefer ben-oni*, that "there was a large assembly of *talmidei-hakhamim* in Kovna at that time. . . . "

7. See Lifschitz, *Zikhron ya'akov*, 2:8.

8. See below, chap. 17, in the discussion of the *Kollel ha-perushim*.

9. Rosenfeld, *Rabbi Yisrael Salanter*, 22. So also Lifschitz, in the comments cited above; Mark, *Bi-mehizatam*, 76; and Katz, *Tenu'at ha-mussar*, 1:170.

10. A detailed discussion of this appears below, in chap. 17.

11. See Glenn, *Israel Salanter*, 50.

12. The periodical *Tevunah* is discussed below, in chap. 17.

13. The quotations that follow are from the introduction to *Tevunah* (Memel and Koenigsburg, 1861–62).

14. Generally speaking, this concept is used in the sense of the purification of consciousness from thoughts of sin, particularly during prayer.

15. This evidently refers to such figures as R. Judah Loeb (the Maharal) of Prague, R. Ephraim Lontschitz, R. Isaiah Horowitz (the Shelah), and the like, who strongly attacked *pilpul*. See S. Assaf, *Mekorot le-toldot ha-hinukh be-yisra'el* (Tel Aviv, 1925), 1:48–51, 62–63, 65–66.

16. On the method of *pilpul*, which spread throughout the yeshivot of Eastern Europe at the end of the Middle Ages and was a target of sharp criticism, see M. Breuer, "The Rise of *Pilpul* and *Hilluk* in Ashkenazic Yeshivot" [Heb.], in *Sefer ha-zikaron la-rav yehiel weinberg* (Jerusalem, 1970), 241ff.; I. Ta-Shma, "Tosaphot Gornish" [Heb.], *Sinai* 68 (1971) 153ff.; H. Z. Dimitrovsky, "On the Method of Pilpul" [Heb.], in *Sefer yovel li-khevod shalom baron* (Jerusalem, 1975), 111ff.

17. Salanter evidently refers here to the words of the Talmud in Eruvin 13a, Megillah 6b and 25a, Nazir 59b, etc. However, one ought to note the difference between the sharp words allowed by the Sages and the *pilpul* defended by Salanter. The Talmud there speaks about cases in which the rabbi deliberately distorts or confuses things before his students in order to sharpen their minds—that is, to encourage them to ask questions, to think in a critical manner, etc.; while R. Israel proposes allowing the students themselves to create clever novellae, even if these are not faithful to the true meaning of the text, in order to develop their intellectual abilities.

18. One should stress that R. Salanter did not include in his discussion any definition or detailed example of *pilpul*, the use of which he wished to defend. It is doubtful whether his understanding of this concept was identical with the methods of reasoning and analysis designated by the terms *pilpul* and *hilluk* in the late Middle Ages. While R. Israel stressed, both here and elsewhere, the importance of extensive, wide-ranging knowledge, *pilpul* and *hilluk* were based upon close analysis of the *sugya* itself, without drawing comparisons with other talmudic sources. Cf. Dimitrovsky's instructive article, "On the Method of Pilpul." In any event, from the totality of Salanter's remarks in the introduction to *Tevunah*, it seems that *pilpul* was a form of speculation providing wide range for acumen, even if sometimes at the price of faithfulness to the truth of the *sugya*.

19. For a typical example of criticism of *pilpul* by the circle of the students of the Gaon, see Feivel, *Sefer toldot 'adam*, 11b ff.

20. See Zvi Kaplan, "On the Way of R. Hayyim of Volozhin in Halakhah" [Heb.], in his *Me-'olamah shel torah* (Jerusalem, 1974), 9ff. We have already discussed the connection between Salanter's attempt to refrain from *pilpul* and the influence of the Volozhin yeshiva in connection with R. Israel's relationship to R. Zundel of Salant (see chap. 5, above).

21. See I. Etkes, "The Gaon of Vilna and the Haskalah—Image and Reality" [Heb.], in *Perakim be-toldot ha-hevrah ha-yehudit . . .* [J. Katz Festschrift] (Jerusalem, 1980), 192–217.

22. Introduction to *Tevunah*, 3.

23. See above, chap. 10, n. 19.

24. See *Ha-maggid* 5 (1861):289; *Ha-carmel* 1 (1861):265.

25. These incidents are explained below.

26. *Aharonim*, literally, "the latter ones," is a term used to refer to the figures

and works from the later Middle Ages onward, such as R. Moses Isserles (*Rama*, 1525?–72), R. Mordecai Jaffe (*Levush*, ca. 1535–1612), R. Joel Sirkes (*Bayit hadash* or *Ba''h*, 1561–1640), R. Solomon Luria (*Yam shel shlomo* or *Maharshal*, 1510?–74), and R. Joseph Caro himself (1488–1575). The term is used in contradistinction to the *rishonim* (the "earlier ones"), which refers to the authorities of the High Middle Ages. While there is no clear cut-off date between the two periods, the *rishonim* is generally understood as referring to those figures who flourished in Spain and Franco-Germany, while the main center of the *aharonim* was in Germany, Poland, and Russia.

27. Israel Salanter, et al., *Sefer 'ez peri* (Vilna, 1881), 23.

28. See Willman, *Iggerot u-mikhtavim*, letter 63, p. 70.

29. See ibid., letters 51, 52, pp. 65–66.

30. R. Naphtali Amsterdam's article, above, n. 2.

31. *Or yisra'el*, 111.

32. The following citations from the letters are from the text printed in Lipkin, *Sefer torat r. yisra'el mi-salant*, Pt. 2:59–60. Three of the letters were also published by Willman, *Iggerot u-mikhtavim*, 37–38.

33. Lipkin, *Sefer torat r. yisra'el mi-salant*, Pt. 2:60; Salanter writes likewise in the first letter, ibid., 59.

34. Ibid.

35. Ibid., 60.

36. Ibid., 59.

37. Ibid.

38. This refers to letters 18, 19, and 20 in *Or yisra'el*, 64–66. However, in the published version the name of the recipient of the letters is omitted. Dov Katz identifies him as R. Isaac Blazer; see Katz, *Tenu'at ha-mussar*, 2:222. On the basis of the contents of these letters and their formulation, this identification would seem to be correct.

39. *Or yisra'el*, 112.

Chapter 15

1. *Or yisra'el*, 121.

2. Further on, in the continuation of his words, R. Blazer again observes that Salanter's sermons lasted for several hours.

3. Introduction to *Tevunah*, 4.

4. *Sefer kokhvei 'or* (Jerusalem, 1974), letter 21, p. 246. *Kokhvei 'or* contains Mussar essays from the *nachlass* of R. Yitzhak Blazer, published by his descendants. There are numerous letters at the end of the book, some written by Blazer himself and others received from his friends R. Simhah Zissel of Kelm and R. Naphtali Amsterdam. Some of these letters were previously published in periodicals, but the majority are published there for the first time.

5. According to this testimony of R. Amsterdam; R. Blazer writes similarly in *Or yisra'el*, 121.

6. See the letter by R. Naphtali Amsterdam, above, n. 4.

7. Pechter, *Kitvei*, 213–14.

8. *Sefer kokhvei 'or*, 187.

9. *Or yisra'el*, 121.

10. Amsterdam states this in a letter to his son—see *Sefer or ha-mussar*, 1:247.

11. See, e.g., *Or yisra'el*, letter 2, p. 42.

12. See n. 10.

13. *Or yisra'el,* 121.

14. A detailed discussion of *tikkun ha-middot* in Salanter's thought appears below, chap. 18.

15. *Or yisra'el,* letter 19, p. 65.

16. Ibid.

17. Ibid., 66.

18. In the essay, "Le-ma'an da'at," Ha-meliz 155 (1897).

19. This is the same R. Gershon Mendel whom Salanter asked to disseminate Mussar study when he served in the rabbinate in Plongian; see Willman, *Iggerot u-mikhtavim,* letter 65, p. 73.

20. In R. Naphtali Amsterdam's letter, *Sefer or ha-mussar,* 1:247.

21. Bishke, *Sefer ben-oni,* 4.

22. One may infer the nature of these conversations from the letters exchanged among R. Israel's disciples after they left the *kloiz.* See, for example, *Sefer kokhvei 'or,* 213.

23. Salanter's views on this matter are explained in chap. 8.

24. *Sefer kokhvei 'or,* 189.

25. Ibid., 213.

26. Cf. ibid.

Chapter 16

The sources for Salanter's life and activity during the period of his study in Germany are relatively few and poor. The main sources upon which I relied for writing this chapter were the following: Benjamin, *Rabbi Israel Lipkin, Salant;* Rabbi Dr. Ehrmann, "Rabbi Israel Salanter . . . ," *Der Israelit,* no. 21 (1883); Mark, *Bi-mehizatam;* and various letters of R. Israel published in Willman, *Iggerot u-mikhtavim.* The exchange of letters between Salanter and Rabbi Dr. Naphtali Ehrmann is of special importance. Willman has published most of Salanter's letters to Ehrmann, but with errors and omissions, which are noted below. Professor Mordecai Breuer of Jerusalem, who owns the original letters of Salanter to R. Ehrmann, made them available to me, for which I wish to thank him. I found copies of R. Ehrmann's replies in the blank space left in R. Salanter's letters. Ehrmann's letters, in addition to containing interesting information in their own right, shed light upon Salanter's letters.

1. See Mark, *Bi-mehizatam,* 77; and Steinschneider, *'Ir vilna,* 130.

2. Mark, *Bi-mehizatam,* 78. Mark cites these remarks in the name of R. Elijah Levinsohn of Cartinga, who heard them from R. Salanter.

3. On R. Jacob Zvi Mecklenburg and his role in the struggle against religious reformers, see David Druck, "The Gaon R. Jacob Zvi Mecklenburg" [Heb.], *Horev* 4 (1937):171–79.

4. See Benjamin, *Rabbi Israel Lipkin Salant,* 16.

5. On the Jewish community in Memel, see Yosef Shulman, "Memel" [Heb.], in *Yahadut lita* (Tel Aviv, 1967), 3:233–81; Dr. Shmuel Grinhoiz, "Memel" [Yiddish], in *Lita* (New York, 1951), 1:1427–38.

6. On the abandonment of religious observance as a common phenomenon in the communities of Prussia at the beginning of the 1860s, see *Ha-maggid* 7 (1861):43, report from Halberstadt.

7. Two of Salanter's major supporters were the wealthy traders, Elijah Baer

Fischel and Binyamin Heinemann. The latter made a special room in his home available to Salanter to serve as a place for prayer and study. See Benjamin, *Rabbi Israel Lipkin Salant*, 17.

8. On Salanter's activity in Memel, see ibid., 17–18.

9. See Katz, *Tenu'at ha-mussar*, 1:184.

10. On the celebration of the completion of the study of the entire Talmud in a fraternity founded by R. Israel in Memel, see *Ha-maggid* 13, no. 26 (1869).

11. See Katz, *Tenu'at ha-mussar*, 1:185, n. 10. One of the outstanding students of Salanter during this period was R. Yitzhak b. Shmuel Meltzen; see on him *Yahadut lita*, 3:68.

12. See Mark, *Bi-mehizatam*, 77.

13. See Ehrmann, "Rabbi Israel Salanter." Salanter's host in Berlin was Dr. Judah Sternheim, who placed his apartment and library at his service. See Benjamin, *Rabbi Israel Lipkin Salant*, 18.

14. See Ehrmann, "Rabbi Israel Salanter."

15. See ibid.; Benjamin, *Rabbi Israel Lipkin Salant*, 18; Willman, *Iggerot u-mikhtavim*, letter 39, p. 55.

16. This subject is discussed in detail below, chap. 18.

17. See Benjamin, *Rabbi Israel Lipkin Salant*, 24.

18. This episode was related by R. Azriel Hildesheimer in his eulogy for R. Israel Salanter. See Meir Hildesheimer, "On the Image of R. Azriel Hildesheimer" [Heb.], *Sinai* 54 (1963/64):87, n. 116.

19. See Benjamin, *Rabbi Israel Lipkin Salant*, 27–28.

20. Tuviah Preshel, in his article, "Rabbi Israel Salanter and the Translation of the Talmud into the Hebrew Language" [Heb.], *Ha-doar* 53 (1974):555, notes that Rosenfeld, and following him Dov Katz and other authors, erred in attributing to R. Salanter a plan for the *translation* of the Talmud into Hebrew, his original intention being the composition of a new *commentary* to the Talmud.

21. In 1893, ten years after Salanter's death, announcements appeared in the Jewish press concerning a new society founded in London whose purpose was the publication of a new commentary to the Talmud. Among the heads of this society was Dr. Judah Sternheim, who had been close to Salanter. This attempt was also unsuccessful; see in this connection Preshel, "Rabbi Israel Salanter."

22. See Etkes, "The Gaon of Vilna and the Haskalah," 192–215.

23. For a detailed discussion of the periodical *Tevunah*, see below, chap. 17.

24. A detailed account concerning R. Salanter's notes from these classes (*shi'urim*) is cited below, chap. 17.

25. See Ehrmann, "Rabbi Israel Salanter."

26. Ben Usiel (pseud.), *Iggerot Zafon: Neunzehn Briefe über Judentum* (Altona, 1836). [English: *Iggerot Tzafon: The Nineteen Letters on Judaism*, trans. B. Drachman (New York, 1960).]

27. Salanter's stance on the approach of *Torah 'im derekh eretz* and his opinion of the activity of Rabbis Hirsch and Hildesheimer are explained in greater detail in chap. 17.

28. See n. 26.

29. According to the MS owned by Professor M. Breuer; see above, n. 1.

30. This evidently refers to the journal *Monatsschrift für Geschichte und Wissenschaft des Judenthums*, published under the editorship of R. Zechariah Frankel. See Willman, *Iggerot u-mikhtavim*, letter 33, p. 47.

31. See n. 30.

32. From the draft of R. Ehrmann's response to Salanter's letter of 16 Shevat 5634 (February 1874)—Willman, *Iggerot u-mikhtavim*, letter 33. These remarks refer to the period of Ehrmann's residence in Carlsruhe.

33. This opinion is strengthened by Salanter's reply (Willman, *Iggerot u-mikhtavim*, letter 33), in which he describes, among other things, a method of disseminating Torah among artisans.

34. *Ha-peles* 1 (1900):139.

35. The author of this sketch signed with the pseudonym *Ayalah Sheluhah* (a hind let loose), an obvious allusion to R. Ehrmann's first name, Naphtali, as per Gen. 49:21.

36. This refers to R. Ehrmann's reply to Salanter's letter, published by Willman in *Iggerot u-mikhtavim* as letter 68. In this letter, Salanter notes that he had sent R. Ehrmann his responsum concerning the question of mixed dancing.

37. About 1876.

38. *Ha-levanon* 15 (1879):46.

39. Mark, *Bi-mehizatam*, 80–81.

40. Willman, *Iggerot u-mikhtavim*, letter 32.

41. Ibid., letter 40.

42. Ibid., letter 50.

43. Ibid., letter 47.

44. Mark, *Bi-mehizatam*, 82.

45. See Benjamin, *Rabbi Israel Lipkin Salant*, 19.

46. See Mark, *Bi-mehizatam*, 83; Rosenfeld, *Rabbi Yisra'el Salanter*, 40–41.

47. This subject is not mentioned at all in Salanter's letters from the period of his stay in Paris.

48. See *Ha-maggid* 26 (1882):276.

49. Ibid.

50. The subject of this controversy is explained below.

51. Willman, *Iggerot u-mikhtavim*, letter 53.

52. R. Hillel Milikovski, known as Salanter, was one of R. Israel's students in Vilna. Through R. Israel's intervention, R. Hillel was appointed rabbi of the town of Salant. R. Hillel's biographer relates that R. Israel sent him a letter of rabbinic appointment from Paris together with 1,000 rubles for traveling expenses, but R. Hillel rejected the proposal because he did not wish to migrate to a foreign land. See Zalmanovitz, *Zikhron hillel*, 21–22.

53. See *Ha-maggid* 26 (1882):276.

54. See ibid., 380.

55. See S. L. Zitron, "The War of the Dynasties in the Volozhin Yeshivah" [Heb.], *Reshumot* 1 (1925):123–25. On Salanter's support of a periodical published by R. Joshua Heshel Levin, see below, chap. 17.

56. See Mark, *Bi-mehizatam*, 84.

57. See *Ha-maggid* 26 (1882):276, 380. R. Lewin's intention of migrating to the Land of Israel was never realized, and he died in Paris in Autumn 1883. See Frumkin, *Toldot eliyahu*, 26.

58. *Ha-maggid* 26 (1882):276.

59. Ibid., 333.

60. Ibid., 343.

61. Ibid., 380–81.

62. See Willman, *Iggerot u-mikhtavim*, letters 49, 50. In these letters Salanter asks Ehrmann, who at the time lived in Troyes, to prepare a place where he would be

able to stay for a period of time, because his stay in Paris involved much suffering on account of the poor state of his health. I do not know whether this trip ever took place. In a letter sent by Salanter from Paris to his daughter and son-in-law in Vilna (Willman, *Iggerot u-mikhtavim*, letter 54), he describes an accident in which he fell from a height and was injured.

63. See Benjamin, *Rabbi Israel Lipkin Salant*, 19. R. Meir Lebush Malbim served during the last years of his life as the rabbi of the Polish and Russian émigré community in Koenigsberg, where he died in 1880 (see Mark, *Bi-mehizatam*, 129–33).

64. See Broides, *Vilna ha-zionit*, 12.

65. Evidence indicating that R. Israel Salanter was neither among the supporters nor the opponents of *Hibbat Zion* appears in a letter by Y. D. Frumkin, cited by A. Druyanow, *Ketavim le-toldot hibbat zion ve-yishuv erez-yisra'el* (Tel Aviv, 1932), 3:410–11.

Chapter 17

1. See Lifschitz, *Zikhron ya'akov*, 2: 115, 127–28.

2. Lifschitz describes Salanter as "the right-hand pillar in all matters pertaining to the welfare of the community, with all the efforts of his strength. . . ."—ibid., 3: 80. Among other things, Salanter was involved in the struggle against the edict of the government concerning the *melamdim* (school teachers) (see ibid., 2: 127–28) and took part in the consultations that preceded the rabbinical conference of 1879 (see below, n. 109).

3. See H. Seton-Watson, *The Decline of Imperial Russia, 1855–1914* (New York, 1966), 41–73.

4. On Alexander II's policy toward the Jews, see S. M. Dubnow, *History of the Jews in Russia and Poland* (Philadelphia, 1916), 2: chap. 18; L. Greenberg, *The Jews in Russia* (New York, 1976), 1: chaps. 6, 7.

5. See Greenberg, *The Jews in Russia*, 1: chap. 9; Dubnow, *History of the Jews*, 2: chap. 20; Judah Slutzki, *Ha-'itonut ha-yehudit-russit ba-me'ah ha-tesha' 'esreh* (Jerusalem, 1971), esp. chap. 1.

6. According to the information given by Slutzki, *Ha-'itonut*, 27, the number of Jewish students in the Russian gymnasia increased from 159 in 1853 to 547 in 1863, to 2,405 in 1870, 4,674 in 1875, and 7,999 in 1880. The number of Jewish students in the universities increased from 129 in 1864 to 556 in 1880.

7. See Gideon Katzenelson, *Ha-milhamah ha-sifrutit bein ha-haredim veha-maskilim* (Tel Aviv, 1954); Lifschitz, *Zikhron ya'akov*, 2: 75ff.

8. See Shmuel Ettinger, "The Ideological Background of Anti-Semitic Literature in Russia" [Heb.], in his *Ha-antishemiut ba-'et ha-hadashah* (Tel Aviv, 1979), 110ff.

9. This is the opinion voiced by Ya'akov Lifschitz, *Zikhron ya'akov*, 2: 99, which seems to have been widespread among the Orthodox public at the time.

10. See, e.g., N. M. Shaikevitz, *Shirei Shm''r ve-zikhronotav* (Jerusalem, 1952), 60, 72–74.

11. The Orthodox point of view in this conflict is reflected in the memoirs of Ya'akov Lifschitz, *Zikhron ya'akov*, 2, esp. 75ff.

12. See Katzenelson, *Ha-milhamah*.

13. See Lifschitz, *Zikhron ya'akov*, 2: 99ff.

14. See, for example, his article serialized in *Ha-meliz* 7 (1867): 35–36, 39–43.

15. See Joseph Salmon, "The Beginnings of Reform in the Yeshivot of Eastern Europe" [Heb.], *Molad* 27 [N.S. 4] (1971): 161–72.

16. See Lifschitz, *Zikhron ya'akov*, 2: 95.

17. The individual issues of *Tevunah* do not give the date or month of publication. The fact that twelve issues appeared over a period of three months is attested to by R. David Sidersky, R. Salanter's grandson, in the introduction to *Sefer imrei binah* (Warsaw, 1878). The first four issues were published in the late summer of 1861 (end of 5621) at the press of August Stobbe in Memel; the remaining eight were printed at the beginning of the following Hebrew year at the press of Albert Rasbach in Koenigsberg. For further details about *Tevunah*, see I. Etkes, "*Tevunah*— The First Rabbinical Periodical in Eastern Europe" [Heb.], *Kiryat sefer* 54 (1979): 371–83.

18. See Abraham Yitzhak Bromberg, *Mi-gedolei ha-torah veha-hasidut; xvi. ha-gaon rabbi yosef sha'ul natanson* (Jerusalem, 1960).

19. See Yehudah Aharon Kluger, *Toldot shlomoh* (Lemberg, 1868).

20. See Ya'akov Lifschitz, *Toldot yitzhak* (Warsaw, 1896).

21. See *Yahadut lita*, 3: 65.

22. See ibid., 56; Benjamin Yafeh, *Ha-rav mi-yahud* (Jerusalem, 1957).

23. See Hayyim Karlinski, *Ha-rishon le-shoshelet brisk* (Jerusalem, 1984); and cf. *Yahadut lita*, 3: 72.

24. See Mordecai Nadav, "The History of the Community of Pinsk" [Heb.], *Pinsk* (Tel Aviv and Haifa, 1973), 1: 285–87.

25. See ibid., 290–92.

26. See Aryeh Leib Frumkin, *Toldot hakhmei yerushalayim* (Jerusalem, 1929), Pt. 3, 269, 273.

27. The following are the names of the contributors to *Tevunah* who are not mentioned above: R. Yehiel Heller, rabbi of Plongian; R. Zvi Hirsch Kalischer, rabbi of Tohren; R. Mordecai Eli'ezer Kovner of Vilna; R. Eliyahu, rabbi of Gridtz (Posen district); R. Moshe Filchenfeld, rabbi of Rogozn; R. Morim b. Moshe, rabbi of Kobrin; R. Baruch Rosenfeld of Galob; R. Hayyim b. Meir Berlin, *moreh-zedek* in Mohilev; R. Yehoshua b. Aharon Heller of Plongian.

28. *Ha-maggid* began publication in the summer of 1856 in the city of Lyck in Eastern Prussia, near the Russian border. The publisher of the weekly, Eliezer Lipman Zilberman, was a native of Koenigsberg who was educated in Lithuania. The editor, David Gordon, was likewise a Lithuanian Jew.

29. He stated this explicitly in a third announcement, cited below.

30. *Peleitat sofrim*, ed. Yehoshua Heshel Levin (Volozhin, 1863), in a note to the editor's introduction.

31. Indeed, R. Israel expressed support of Levin's project in *Ha-karmel*, no. 37 (1863): 296–97.

32. See Katz, *Tenu'at ha-mussar*, 1: 186ff.

33. Both this quotation and those below are from the editor's introduction to the first number of *Tevunah*, pp. 2–4.

34. See above, chap. 14.

35. Introduction to *Tevunah*, p. 4.

36. See Yitzhak Rafael, "*Peleitat sofrim* with *Safah la-ne'emanim*" [Heb.], *Areshet* 1 (1959): 327ff.

37. See ibid., 358. R. Salanter's letter was written on 1 Adar 5611 (about March 1851). The letters of the other rabbis cited by Rafael are also from the 1850s.

38. See Etkes, "Compulsory Enlightenment," 312.

39. See S. L. Citron, "Impressions Concerning the History of the Hebrew Press" [Heb.], *Ha-'olam* 6 (1912): *passim*. See also *Luah ahi'asaf* 13 (1923): 240ff.

40. One should note that *Tevunah*, as a periodical combining Torah and Mussar, enjoyed several revivals at the initiative of later generations of Salanter's disciples. *Tevunah* was published under the editorship of Yisrael Zissel Dvortz in the 1920s in several cities of Europe, as well as in the early '30s in Jerusalem. An additional reincarnation of *Tevunah*, also in Jerusalem, took place in the 1940s.

41. See Katz, *Tenu'at ha-mussar*, 1: 192–99.

42. Ibid., 192–93.

43. The sources in question are Moshe Reines, *Akhsaniot shel torah*, no. 1 (Cracow, 1890), 21–35; Lifschitz, *Zikhron ya'akov*, 3: 222–26; Friedman, *Sefer ha-zikhronot*, 129–33.

44. Lachman's contribution was noted in the contemporary press. See "Koenigsberg," *Ha-levanon* 15, no. 16 (1879): 127; "Ve-ha-hokhmah me-'ayin timaze," *Ha-levanon* 15, no. 27 (1879): 209. On the personality of Eliezer Yaakov Haves, see Weinberg, *Le-ferakim*, 221.

45. Reines, *Akhsaniot shel torah*, 21.

46. Ibid., 27.

47. Ibid., 27–28.

48. R. Hayyim Hillel's father, R. Eliezer Yitzhak Fried, was the son-in-law of R. Yizhak, son of R. Hayyim of Volozhin. He even briefly headed the yeshiva, between the death of R. Yitzhak and the appointment of Naphtali Zvi Berlin, as *rosh-yeshivah* (1849–52). See Eliezer Lioni, "The History of the 'Etz Hayyim Yeshivah in Volozhin and its Leaders" [Heb.], in *Sefer volozhin*, ed. E. Lioni (Tel Aviv, 1970), 154. On R. Eliezer Yitzhak's appointment as *rosh-yeshivah*, see ibid., 109.

49. See M. Zinowitz, *'Ez hayyim; toldot yeshivat volozhin* (Tel Aviv, 1972), 290.

50. The *Natziv* writes thus in a letter cited by Reines, *Akhsaniot shel torah*, 27, where he evidently cites the letters of R. Lapidot and of the dignitaries of the Yanishok community.

51. From the letter of the *Natziv* to R. Ya'akov Reines, quoted there, p. 28.

52. Lifschitz, *Zikhron ya'akov*, 3: 223.

53. See ibid., 222.

54. As mentioned, R. Moshe Alexander Lapidot was among the *lomdim* in R. Salanter's *bet midrash* in Zarzecze; see above, chap. 6.

55. See above, n. 20.

56. Lifschitz, *Zikhron ya'akov*, 3: 224.

57. Katz, *Tenu'at ha-mussar*, 1: 197.

58. See Willman, *Iggerot u-mikhtavim*, letter 45. Willman copied the letter from the manuscript. Part of this letter is also printed in *Or yisra'el*, 56.

59. The letter is cited, without any date, by the editor of *Sefer 'ez peri* (Vilna, 1881), at the end of R. Israel's article, on pp. 23–24.

60. Ibid.

61. See Katz, *Tenu'at ha-mussar*, 1: 198.

62. We learn this, among other things, from R. Salanter's letter to R. Eliezer Ya'akov Haves; brought by Willman, *Iggerot u-mikhtavim*, letter 51, pp. 64–65. It follows from Salanter's letter that Haves was accustomed to consult with him concerning the use of the money that he raised in support of Torah students.

63. *Sefer 'ez peri*, 23.

64. See *Yahadut lita*, 3: 39.

65. See Lifschitz, *Zikhron ya'akov*, 3: 225–26.

66. Katz, *Tenu'at ha-mussar*, 1: 198.

67. There was a strong sense of closeness between R. Israel and his son-in-law, who participated in that gathering. We have already discussed the relationship between R. Lapidot and Salanter, above.

68. See Katz, *Tenu'at ha-mussar*, 2: 229.

69. See ibid., 228. We learn about the fund-raising campaign for the *kollel* from a letter of the *Natziv* from August 1880, in which he expresses the fear that the agents of the *kollel* acting throughout Lithuania will harm the income of the Volozhin yeshiva. R. Berlin even expresses the opinion that these agents are acting without the agreement of R. Yitzhak Elhanan Spector. See Reines, *Akhsaniot shel torah*, 26. In the spring of 1881, R. Abraham Shenkar arrived in Frankfurt to solicit money on behalf of the *kollel* from the wealthy Jews there. It would appear that he was not overly scrupulous as to the means used, as in a letter of introduction obtained by Shenkar from R. Samson Raphael Hirsch, *Kollel Ha-Perushim* was described as an institution that conveyed to its students Torah combined with general education. See Mordecai Breuer, "The Approach of Torah and Worldliness in the Teaching of R. Samson Raphael Hirsch" [Heb.], *Ha-ma'ayan* 2 (1969): 27–28.

70. See Rosenfeld, *Rabbi Yisra'el Salanter*, 51–53.

71. Ibid.

72. See Katz, *Pulmus ha-mussar*, chaps. 2, 3.

73. On the role played by *Kollel Ha-Perushim* in the Orthodox struggle against *Hibbat Zion*, see Joseph Salmon, "The Book *Shivat Zion* and its Historical Background" [Heb.], *Eshel be'er shev'a* 2 (1980): 331ff.

74. For a detailed summary of the public discussion on this subject, see Shohat, *Hossad ha-rabbanut mi-ta'am*, 61–98. I mention here only the main conclusions based upon the discussion of Shohat.

75. See Slotzki, "The Rabbinical Seminary in Vilna," 29ff.; Shohat, *Mossad ha-rabbanut mi-ta'am*, 16–26.

76. See the letters of Isaac b. Ya'akov to R. Yitzhak Baer Levinsohn, "'Olam ha-'assiyah" [Heb.], in *Ha-kerem* (Warsaw, 1887), 41–49.

77. See Shohat, *Mossad ha-rabbanut mi-ta'am*, 26–38.

78. For a typical expression of the Maskilic vision of the 1840s of a new type of rabbinate, which would spread the message of Haskalah among the public, see the letter of S. Y. Fünn to Bezalel Stern, *Ha-pardes* 3 (1897): 150–56.

79. See Shohat, *Mossad ha-rabbanut mi-ta'am*, 16ff.

80. See Y. L. Rosenthal, *Toldot hevrat marbei ha-haskalah be-eretz russyah mi-shenat hityasdutah trk''d 'ad shenat trm''v*, 2 vols. (St. Petersburg, 1885–90).

81. See Shohat, *Mossad ha-rabbanut mi-ta'am*, 61–65.

82. The positive attitude of the Maskilim toward the Breslau Seminary would seem to have been rooted in their sympathy with the approach to Judaism of Zacharias Frankel. Eliezer Zvi Zweifel, in *Shalom 'al yisra'el* (Zhitomir, 1873), Pt. 4: 50–51, 61, relates that both he and other Maskilim "of the remnants of the older generation" identified with Frankel's approach.

83. The positions of the rabbis as presented below are based upon Shohat, *Mossad ha-rabbanut mi-ta'am*, 71–73.

84. On the question of the status of the traditional rabbinate during the latter half of the nineteenth century, see I. Etkes, "The Relationship Between Talmudic Scholarship and the Institution of the Rabbinate in Nineteenth Century Lithuanian Jewry," in *Scholars and Scholarship: The Interaction Between Judaism and Other Cultures*, ed. Leo Landman (New York: Yeshiva University Press, 5750/1990), 107–32.

85. See Shohat, *Mossad ha-rabbanut mi-ta'am*, 82, 89–93, n. 89.

86. See *Ha-levanon* 16, no. 32. Harkabi's article is quoted by Ya'akov Lifschitz, *Divrei shalom ve'emet*, 9–10.

87. See Ben Zion Dinur, "Ignatyev's 'Plans' for the 'Solution of the Jewish Problem' and the Assembly of the Communal Representatives in St. Petersburg in 1881–82" [Heb.], *He-'avar* 10 (1963): 5–60.

88. See Lifschitz, *Zikhron ya'akov*, 3: 125.

89. The letter, dated Koenigsberg, December 1882 (Monday of Sect. *Mikez*, 5643), is cited by Lifschitz in *Zikhron ya'akov*, 3: 131.

90. See Willman, *Iggerot u-mikhtavim*, letter 52, pp. 65–66.

91. R. Eliyahu Eliezer participated in the rabbinical gathering sponsored by the government in 1879, as well as in the gathering of communal representatives called by Baron Guenzburg in the wake of the pogroms. R. Eliyahu Eliezer also conducted in his own home consultations among the rabbis who gathered in Vilna to prepare for the rabbinic assembly of 1879. See on this: Yitzhak Yaakov Reines, "Zikharon ba-sefer," in *Shenei ha-me'orot* (Pietrkov, 1913), 46.

92. It is quite possible that the above meeting of R. Israel with Baron Guenzburg in Paris preceded his exchange of letters with R. Yitzhak Elhanan and with his son-in-law. It may also be that this exchange of letters came about in light of information concerning the committee appointed by the Society for the Advancement of Culture in that same year, 1881, to formulate a practical plan for a rabbinical seminary. See J. L. Katzenelson, "Mah she-ra'u 'einai ve-sham'u oznay," in Buki ben Yogli (pseud. for Katzenelson), *Zihronot me-yemei hayyai* (Jerusalem, 1947), 225–26.

93. The letter is cited by Lifschitz, *Zikhron ya'akov*, 3: 132.

94. The author of *Dorot rishonim*, who came out strongly on the pages of *Ha-levanon* against the plan to found a rabbinical seminary in Russia. See Shohat, *Mossad ha-rabbanut mi-ta'am*, 83–86.

95. See Lifschitz, *Zikhron ya'akov*, 3: 125–33.

96. One of the wealthy Jews in St. Petersburg, brother of the prominent *gevir* Aryeh Leib Friedland. The latter corresponded with a number of the outstanding rabbis in Russia, whom he attempted to convince to support reform in the training of rabbis. See Abraham Yitzhak Katz, "Moshe Aryeh Leib Friedland and his Famous Library" [Heb.], *Perakim* 3 (1963): 169ff.

97. One may assume that R. Israel knew of the articles published by Lifschitz in *Ha-levanon* on this subject.

98. The letter is cited by Lifschitz in *Zikhron ya'akov*, 3: 127–29.

99. The five letters, written during the Fall of 1882, are brought by Lifschitz in *Zikhron ya'akov* iii, 131–32. Lifschitz first printed these letters in his book, *Mahzikei ha-dat* (Pietrkov, 1903), 11–12.

100. See Y. L. Katzenelson, "Mah she-ra'u 'einei" *(op cit.,* n. 92), 225–26.

101. See Lifschitz, *Zikhron ya'akov*, 3: 129–30.

102. See above, chap. 14.

103. See above in this chapter.

104. The letter to Haves was dated Paris, June 28, 1881, and deals with the preferred way of using the money that Haves had raised to support Torah students. The following are the main sections pertinent to our subject: "In my opinion it is a criminal thing to include the God-fearing ones of Ashkenaz in this, even if nearly the whole world is sustained by a few pious ones from abroad. For this is their way, that the basis of the study be as a spade with which to dig ... and this is a root bearing gall and wormwood, to raise up those who will permit forbidden things,

Heaven forbid. [But] we will follow what has been our habit since youth, that those who study and those who support them [do so] to raise up great ones in Torah, and afterwards, for lack of any [other] livelihood, they make it to be a spade. But then the little which they learned for that spade [i.e., studies directed toward the rabbinic title] is negated by the majority [i.e., studied *li-shemah*].—Willman, *Iggerot u-mikhtavim*, letter 51, p. 65.

105. This follows from the letter of R. Salanter to R. Azriel Hildesheimer, cited below.

106. The following are the remarks made by R. Salanter in his letter to Lifschitz, dated January 20, 1883: ". . . . The basis for the lack [i.e., of the rabbinical seminary] is that through this there may, Heaven forbid, be negated the capability of study for halakhic ruling. For our eyes see in Germany, even among a number of the great ones of the God-fearers, this matter is almost completely forgotten, in thinking that it is sufficient to rule in halakhic matters to have knowledge of the *Shulhan 'arukh* and to be God-fearing. But it is not thus, for those who know the nature of [Torah] study and of halakhic ruling, thank God this knowledge has not yet been extinguished among the older generation, that for halakhic ruling one needs people who are great in learning. . . ." (Lifschitz, *Zikhron ya'akov*, 3: 132).

107. See the testimony of R. Reines below concerning what he heard from R. Salanter regarding this matter, as well as Salanter's letter to R. Azriel Hildesheimer. See also M. Breuer, "The Approach of Torah" (*op cit.*, n. 69). Breuer notes that Hirsch's disciples "drew strength and encouragement from the position of the founder of the Mussar movement . . . regarding the approach of *Torah 'im derekh eretz.*" See M. Hildesheimer, "Documents Concerning the Founding of the Rabbinical Seminary in Berlin" [Heb.], *Ha-ma'ayan* 14, no. 2, n. 87, (1974): 35–36.

108. I found two letters addressed to Salanter's son, R. Aryeh Leib Lipkin, in the Manuscript Department of the Jewish National Library in Jerusalem (Folder 40 1378). The letters—one from 1887 and the other from 1894—were evidently written by the St. Petersburg *gevir*, Aryeh Leib Friedland (see above, n. 96), who corresponded with many contemporary rabbinic figures, whom he tried to persuade to reform Jewish education generally and the training of rabbis in particular. The letters to R. Lipkin also deal with this question, the main focus of the dispute between them being upon the question of what R. Salanter would have done concerning this matter had he still been alive. Among other points, Friedland notes Salanter's favorable attitude toward German neo-Orthodoxy. The following are two characteristic passages:

> . . . . In 1865, when I was in Frankfurt-am-Main, I found his honour your father the Gaon . . . and he spoke in praise of the rabbi of that place, S. R. Hirsch, saying that by the spirit of his wisdom and his pure piety . . . he turned the hearts of the people of his congregation towards his desire that they walk in the paths of righteousness . . . until it became a faithful city, filled with righteousness, and this is a sign and proof [of] the great goodness stored up for the congregation in particular and the nation in general, if its leaders will direct it to walk uprightly in the spirit of knowledge and fear of God. . . .
>
> . . . . Perhaps this was also the intention of your father, the Gaon, in his many travels to different communities in the land of Germany—that he might see with his own eyes the new ways in education, established by the wise men of Germany, in which the

darkness is pushed away before the light not by means of a strong
hand. He therefore wished to improve the situation of the education
for Torah and wisdom in our land as well, in the spirit of the wise
men of Ashkenaz. . . .

Further on, Friedland writes that he has no doubt that, were Salanter still alive,
he would wholeheartedly support the reform in education. He supports this view
by a rumor "from a reliable source," stating that during his last days R. Salanter
regretted having opposed the rabbinical seminary established by the goverment in
the 1840s. It would seem that, among the moderate Maskilim, there was a widespread image of Salanter as a supporter of the neo-Orthodox trend in Germany,
supporting its realization even in Russia. Evidently, these people wished to find
support for their own position in a prominent authority such as R. Israel, but they
did not really know him well. How is it possible to square this image with the major
role played by Salanter in the struggle against the rabbinical seminary in the early
'80s? The answer may be found in the fact that R. Israel operated mainly behind
the scenes, so that his position was not necessarily clearly known to the public.

109. Reines, "Zikharon Ba-sefer" (*op cit.*, n. 91). The conversation between R.
Reines and R. Salanter took place some time before the rabbinical gathering of
1879.

110. The letter is cited in the article by Azriel Hildesheimer, "Between the Two
Luminaries of the Generation" [Heb.], *Ha-zofeh* (21 Shevat 5723 [February 1963]).

111. The letter is cited in the article by M. Hildesheimer (*op cit.*, n. 107), 34–
37.

112. Willman, *Iggerot u-mikhtavim*, letter 69: 75–76.

113. See above, in this chapter, the letter to his son-in-law, R. Eliyahu Eliezer
Grodzinski, and see also the letters quoted in notes 104, 106.

114. In a letter to R. Dr. Ehrmann from 1876, R. Salanter writes, among other
things: "I heard that in Berlin [one can acquire] antique books very cheaply, and I
wish to acquire various works concerning logic, which speak about the details of
this science, and perhaps also in other fields, such as jurisprudence and medicine,
etc. For even though my knowledge of German is very weak, perhaps by skimming
through various authors and various disciplines, it will become easier for me to
glean the information needed for the study of knowledge of our Talmud. Will [H]is
[H]onor pardon me for requesting that he write to Berlin concerning this and that
he inform me. . . ."—Willman, *Iggerot u-mikhtavim*, letter 39, p. 55.

115. See Etkes, "The Gaon of Vilna and the Haskalah," esp. 214ff.

116. See Hayyim Tschernovitz (Rav Tsa'ir), *Pirkei hayyim* (New York, 1954),
129ff.

117. Willman, *Iggerot u-mikhtavim*, letter 64: 71.

118. *Sefer 'ez peri*, 23. One must be careful as to how one understands these and
similar statements, bearing in mind that they were addressed to young people who
had already spent much time over the course of years in the study of *Torah li-
shemah*. It is only thereafter that R. Salanter encourages them to engage in study
directed toward preparation for the rabbinate.

119. Lipkin, *Torat r. yisra'el mi-salant*, Pt. 2: 62.

Chapter 18

1. *Kitvei*, 125.
2. Lefin, *Heshbon ha-nefesh*, 14–15.

3. See above, chap. 13, and *Kitvei*, 120ff.

4. See Tishby and Dan, *Mivhar sifrut ha-mussar*, 9–11.

5. Maimonides, *Shemonah perakim*, beginning of chap. 4. [English translation: Joseph I. Garfinkle, *A Maimonides Reader*, ed. I. Twersky (New York and Philadelphia, 1972), 367–68.]

6. See ibid., further along in chap. 4.

7. See ibid., chap. 5; Eliezer Schweid, *'Iyunim bi-shemonah perakim la-rambam* (Jerusalem, 1965), 96–104. J. Guttman has shown that, in the concluding chapter of the *Guide of the Perplexed*, ethical perfection becomes the end rather than merely a means to Divine service. However, he does not think that the Maimonidean doctrine as a whole ought to be interpreted on the basis of those isolated places in which he proposed this view. See J. Guttman, *Dat u-mad'a* (Jerusalem, 1955), 96–97; and see also what Y. Dan has written on this subject, *Sifrut ha-mussar*, 114–15.

8. See Pechter, "The Homiletical and Ethical Literature of the Sages of Safed," 430ff. See also Vital, *Sha'arei kedushah*, Pt. 1, Gate 3; Luzzatto, *Mesillat yesharim*, chap. 26.

9. See *Kitvei*, and Vital, *Sha'arei kedushah*, Pt. 1, Gate 2.

10. *Sha'arei kedushah*, Pt. 1, Gate 2.

11. Ibid., Pt. 2, Gate 4.

12. Ibid., Pt. 2, Gate 5.

13. *Kitvei*, 165.

14. Nedarim 22a. Salanter himself cited this passage there as an example.

15. *Sefer or ha-mussar*, 1: 77–78.

16. *Kitvei*, 130.

17. Chap. 6.

18. Ibid.; Maimonides, *Shemonah perakim*, chap. 6. [English: Garfinkle, *A Maimonides Reader*, 377.] The Rabbinic quotation is from *Sifra*, Lev. 20:26.

19. Maimonides, *Shemonah perakim*, chap. 6. [English: ibid., 378.]

20. *Sha'arei kedushah*, Pt. 1, Gate 3. The citation here is based upon the 1967 B'nai Barak edition, pp. 20–21; and see there the entire discussion in the third Gate.

21. See *Kitvei*, letter 20, p. 249.

22. Ibid., 125–26.

23. Ibid.

24. Ibid., 128.

25. We return to this matter later at greater length.

26. *Kitvei*, 128.

27. See ibid., s. v. "la-zot mah tov," and see also on this matter the passage from a letter of R. Salanter quoted in Katz, *Tenu'at ha-mussar*, 1: 283.

28. See *Kitvei*, 132–33.

29. See the Introduction to *Tevunah*, 4.

30. Thus, for example, in *Iggeret ha-mussar; Kitvei*, 114–24.

31. *Kitvei*, 126.

32. Ibid., 135.

33. See above, chap. 7.

34. See Henry Sidgwick, *Outlines of the History of Ethics* (London, 1946), 43–44.

35. See Maimonides, *Shemonah perakim*, chap. 4; Luzzatto, *Mesillat yesharim*, chap. 9, and elsewhere.

36. Chap. 9.

37. The following quotations are taken from the "notes" of R. Naphtali Amsterdam in *Sefer or ha-mussar*, Vol. 1: 76–78.

38. R. Salanter wrote to his young nephew in the same spirit: "For him, the

principle of 'study for its own sake' means that he should study 'not for its own sake'—that is, so that he may be seen as a great one by other people. . . . And if God, be He blessed, will merit that he be accepted as a great one in Torah among people, all of the details of the service of God will be easy for him . . . and it is a reliable principle for a person to seek for himself some device so that the service of God not be too heavy for him."—*Lipkin, torat r. yisra'el mi-salant,* Pt. 2: 60. Salanter therefore suggests that his nephew demonstrate his attainments in the study of Torah, particularly his attainments in erudition, so as to acquire a reputation as a "great one in Torah." It will thereafter be easier for him to be punctilious in "details of the service of God," as this punctiliousness will be a natural response to the expectations imposed upon him by society.

39. See *Kitvei,* 125, 128.

40. See in this connection above, chap. 15.

41. *Kitvei,* letter 20, p. 249.

42. Thus, for example, R. Yehiel Yaakov Weinberg wrote as follows concerning this subject: "It has already been pointed out to us that the scientific discovery concerning the life of the soul beneath the threshold of consciousness, which at the time astonished thinkers throughout the world . . . this new teaching first came from the mouth of R. Israel Salanter, of blessed memory. . . . R. Israel Salanter preceded Freud by seventy or eighty years."—Weinberg, *Seridei 'esh,* Pt. 4, 333.

43. *Kitvei,* 216–17. M. Pechter already noted this in his introduction to Salanter's writings, *Kitvei,* 39, n. 2. Pechter mentions there a number of authors who, like R. Weinberg, saw Salanter as preceding Freud in this matter.

44. See L. L. Whyte, *The Unconscious Before Freud* (London, 1962).

45. See Yizhak Ahren, "Rabbi Israel Salanter und das Unbewisste," *Udim* 6 (1975–76): 9–11.

46. It clearly follows from a letter of R. Israel from 1876 that he read German, and even displayed interest in scientific literature in this language. See Willman, *Iggerot u-mikhtavim,* letter 39, p. 55.

47. Yohanan Silman, "The Theory of the Psyche in the Thought of R. Israel Lipkin (of Salant)" [Heb.], *Sefer bar-ilan* 11 (1973): 295.

48. See above, chap. 9.

49. This statement is based upon the following considerations: (1) In letter 6, *Kitvei,* 218, there appears a motif that was first formulated in *Iggeret ha-mussar,* which was printed in 1858. But while in *Iggeret ha-mussar* these ideas are seen as an innovation, in letter 6 they are presented as something well known. It follows that this letter was written following the publication of *Iggeret ha-mussar.* (2) Letters 6, 7, 8 (*Kitvei,* 213–32) constitute one literary unit, on the basis of their contents and style, which were written more or less together. While letters 6 and 7 appear without any date, at the end of letter 8 there appears the date, "Rosh Hashanah Eve, 5620," that is, the fall of 1859.

50. In *Sefer 'ez peri,* R. Salanter makes use of the concepts "external and internal forces" (*kohot hizoniot u-penimiot*). See *Kitvei,* 169.

51. *Kitvei,* 217.

52. Ibid.

53. See ibid., 149, 217.

54. Ibid., 164.

55. Ibid., 245.

56. Ibid., 173.

57. Ibid., 165.

58. Ibid., 148.
59. Ibid., 149.
60. Ibid., 150–51.
61. Ibid., 150.
62. Ibid., 130.
63. Ibid., 149.
64. Ibid., 150.

Epilogue

1. For a discussion of the concept of "a trait and its opposite," see the Hebrew edition of this book: I. Etkes, *R. yisra'el salanter ve-reshitah shel tenu'at ha-mussar* (Jerusalem, 1982), 320–21.

2. On the interest and worry displayed by Salanter concerning the condition of his relatives' affairs, see Willman, *Iggerot u-mikhtavim*, letter 20, p. 40; letter 33, p. 48. From the exchange of letters between Salanter and R. Naphtali Ehrmann (see this volume, chap. 16, n. 1), it follows that Salanter made efforts to find an appropriate marriage partner for this student of his. An episode demonstrating the use of "a trait and its opposite" in Salanter's behavior is included in the description given by Aryeh Leib Frumkin, concerning a meeting between his father, R. Shmuel of Kelm, and Salanter. See Frumkin, *Toldot eliyahu*, 72.

3. R. Israel had two daughters and four sons: Malka Hinda, who married R. Eliyahu Eliezer Grodzinski of Vilna; Shmuel Adler, who lived in Kovna and practiced trade; Aryeh Leib, who served as the rabbi in the city of Brezneh; Hodah Libbe, the wife of R. Aharon Sidarski of Grodna; Yitzhak, who served as rabbi in the towns of Kroz and Prosnitz; and Yom Tov Lipman Lipkin, who became a scientist—from David Sidarski, "Biographical Sketch of R. Israel Salanter" [Heb.], Jewish National Library, Schwadron Collection, Autograph Lipkin Israel.

4. R. Israel's wife, Esther, lived in the home of her eldest daughter in Vilna, where she died in Ellul, 5631 (August/September 1871).

5. This statement is based upon examination of the places and dates cited in R. Israel's letters. This examination reveals that, generally speaking, his visits to Lithuania occurred during the summer months. On an extended visit of R. Israel to his daughter Hodah Libbe, who lived in Grodna, see the sketch by Yosef Gibianski, in *Ha-meliz* 8, no. 3 (1868): 20–21.

6. See on this the publisher's introduction to *Sefer hut ha-meshulash* (Jerusalem, 1904), a collection of the halakhic responsa of R. Salanter, his father, and his son R. Yitzhak. Only some of R. Israel's letters to his family are extant, and these are included in the collection of letters published by S. Willman.

7. See the introduction to *Sefer hut ha-meshulash*.

8. Ibid.

9. See S. T. Margaliot, "The Life of the Sage Dr. L. Lipkin" [Heb.], *Ha-zefirah* 2, no. 11 (1875); see also *He-assif* 1 (1885): 259–62.

10. *Ha-maggid* 7 (1865): 49.

11. Ibid., no. 11: 83.

12. See Willman, *Iggerot u-mikhtavim*, letter 34, p. 45. The second line reads: "and he has already written me . . . ," while the original MS reads, "my grandson wrote me . . ."; letter 31, p. 46, line 2 reads, "the letter of my friend from Stralsond, . . ." while the MS reads, "the letter of my grandson from Stralsond . . .";

letter 68, p. 75, contains the following deletions: in line 1, the words "my grandson"; in line 2, "his father"; in line 3, "my grandson"; and in line 4, "his father."

13. See above, chap. 16, n. 1.

14. See Willman, *Iggerot u-mikhtavim*, letter 32, p. 46. In this letter the editor has also omitted the words, "his father," which appears in the source prior to the words, "is not among the God-fearing ones."

15. This was not the first attempt of its kind. *Ha-maggid* 5, no. 21 (1861): 116, contains a sketch by Aryeh Leib Frumkin devoted to R. Issar Einhorn, a student of Salanter's who went to Germany at his teacher's advice to study medicine. Frumkin emphasizes that, even though Einhorn received a general education and was a successful physician, he continued to observe mitzvot strictly and to study Torah regularly. The lesson derived by Frumkin from Einhorn's life is expressed as follows: "How false is the opinion of those who say that it is impossible for a Jewish person to combine wisdom and faith, *yir'ah* and understanding."

16. *Ha-meliz* 8, no. 3 (1868): 20–21.

17. Ibid., no. 11: 82–84.

18. Ibid., no. 17: 129, in "Letter to the publisher."

19. The growth and development of the Mussar yeshivot has not yet been described in the historical literature. Dov Katz's multi-volume book, *Tenu'at ha-mussar*, contains important material on this subject.

20. On the struggle between the Mussar movement and its opponents at the end of the nineteenth century, see Katz, *Pulmus ha-mussar*.

21. An instructive example of the correctness of R. Gordon's statement is to be seen in the reaction of the *Hazon 'ish* (R. Avraham Yeshayahu Karelitz) to the Mussar movement. He was among the outstanding opponents of the Mussar movement, and engaged in severe polemics with it—see his *Sefer hazon 'ish; 'al inyanei emunah u-bitahon ve-'od* (Jerusalem, 1954), esp. chap. 3. The *Hazon 'ish* simultaneously attempted to create an alternative path for the development of the ethical level of the Jew, by means of Torah study.

Bibliography

Ahren, Yizhak. "Rabbi Israel Salanter und das Unbewisste." *Udim* 6 (1975–76): 9–11.

Anonymous. "R. Israel Salanter, the History of his Life and Activity" [Hebrew]. In *Ha-yehudi*. New York, 1936.

Assaf, S. *Mekorot le-toldot ha-hinukh be-yisra'el*. Tel Aviv, 1925.

Bahya ibn Paquda. *Hovot ha-levavot*. Ed. Mahbarot le-Sifrut. Tel Aviv, 1964.

Baldwin, J. M. *History of Psychology*. New York and London, 1913.

Ben-Sasson, Hayim Hillel. "The Mussar Movement in Lithuania in the 19th Century—Indications of Inner Crisis" [Hebrew]. In *World Congress of Jewish Studies*. Vol. 1. Jerusalem, 1952. 446–49.

——. "The Personality of the Gaon of Vilna and His Historical Influence" [Hebrew]. *Zion* 31 (1966): 39–86, 197–216.

Ben-Sasson, Yonah. "The Spiritual World and Teaching of the Founders of the Lithuanian Yeshivah" [Hebrew]. In *Hinukh ha-adam ve-ye'udo*. Jerusalem, 1967. 155–216.

Benjamin, Emil. *Rabbi Israel Lipkin; Sein Leben und Wirken*. Berlin, 1899.

Bialovolski, S. "Torah Centers in Lithuania" [Hebrew]. *Yahadut lita*. Tel Aviv, 1960.

Bishke, Binyamin. *Sefer ben-'oni; kinah ve-hesped 'al r. yeruham yehudah leib perlman*. Vilna, 1896.

Blazer, Yitzhak. *Sefer kokhvei 'or*. Jerusalem, 1974.

Bonimowitz, David. *Sefer mikhtav me-eliyahu*. Vilna, 1902.

Breuer, Mordecai. "The Rise of *Pilpul* and *Hilluk* in Ashkenazic Yeshivot" [Hebrew]. In *Sefer ha-zikaron la-rav yehiel weinberg*. Jerusalem, 1970. 241–55.

——, "The Approach of Torah and Worldliness in the Teaching of R. Samson Raphael Hirsch" [Hebrew]. *Ha-ma'ayan* 9, no. 1 (1969): 1–16; no. 2 (1969): 10–21.

Broides, Reuben Asher. *Ha-dat veha-hayyim*. Jerusalem, 1974.

Broides, Yitzhak. *Vilna ha-zionit ve-'askaneha*. Tel Aviv, 1939.

Bromberg, Abraham Yitzhak. *Mi-gedolei ha-torah veha-hasidut; xvi. Ha-gaon rabbi yosef sha'ul natanson*. Jerusalem, 1960.

Caro, Joseph. *Shulhan 'arukh: orah hayyim 'im be'ur ha-ger''a*. Numerous editions.

Cassirer, E. *The Philosophy of the Enlightenment*. Boston, 1965.

Cherikover, Elijah. "The Jewish Masses, the Maskilim and the Regime During the

Reign of Nicholai" [Hebrew]. In *Yehudim be-'itot mahpekhah*. Tel Aviv, 1957. 107–26.

Citron, S. L. "Impressions Concerning the History of the Hebrew Press" [Hebrew]. *Ha-'olam* 6 (1912).

Cordovero, Moses. *Tomer devorah*. Koenigsberg, 1858.

Dan, Joseph. *Sifrut ha-mussar veha-derush*. Jerusalem, 1975.

———. "Ethical Literature." *Encyclopaedia Judaica* 6: col. 922–32.

Dick, Isaac Meir. *Sefer ha-oreah*. Vilna, 1846.

Dienstag, Isaac J. I. "Rabbi Elijah of Vilna; A Bibliographical List" [Hebrew]. *Talpiyot* 4 (1949): 269–356.

Dimitrovsky, Hayyim Z. "On the Method of *Pilpul*" [Hebrew]. In *Sefer yovel li-khevod shalom baron*. Jerusalem, 1975. 111–81.

Dinur, Ben-Zion. "The Historical Image of Russian Jewry and the Problems of its Research" [Hebrew]. *Zion* 22 (1957): 93–118.

———. "Ignatyev's 'Plans' for the 'Solution of the Jewish Problem' and the Assembly of the Communal Representatives in St. Petersburg in 1881–82" [Hebrew]. *He-'avar* 10 (1963): 5–60.

Dolitzki, M. *Mofet le-rabbim*. Frankfurt am Main, 1892.

Druck, David. "The Gaon R. Jacob Zvi Mecklenburg" [Hebrew]. *Horev* 4 (1937): 171–79.

Druyanow, A. *Ketavim le-toldot hibbat zion ve-yishuv erez-yisra'el*. Tel Aviv, 1932.

Dubnow, S. M. *History of the Jews in Russia and Poland*. 4 vols. Philadelphia, 1916.

Dubnov, Simon. *Toldot ha-hasidut*. Tel Aviv, 1960.

Ehrmann, Herz. "Rabbi Israel Salanter. . . ." *Der Israelit*, no. 21 (1883).

Eisenstadt, Ben-Zion. *Dor rabanav ve-sofrav*. Vilna, 1900.

Eliasberg, Mordecai. *Sefer shevil ha-zahav*. Warsaw, 1897.

Eliashiv, Israel, "Baal Makhshoves" (pseud.). "Gerobin" [Hebrew]. *He-'avar* 1 (1918): 204–32.

Elijah ben Shlomo Zalman, the "Vilna Gaon." *Be'ur aggadot le-masekhet bava kama*. Koenigsberg, 1856.

———. *Be'ur ha-ger" 'a le-habakkuk*. Jerusalem.

———. *Be'ur ha-ger" 'a le-mishlei*. Shklov, 1798.

———. *Iggeret ha-ger" 'a*. [First published in *Kuntres 'alim li-terufah*. Minsk, 1836.]

———. *Sefer aderet eliyahu*. Jerusalem, 1905(?).

Epstein, Barukh Ha-Levi. *Sefer mekor barukh*. New York, 1954.

Etkes, Immanuel. "Compulsory Enlightenment as a Crossroads in the History of the Haskalah Movement in Russia" [Hebrew]. *Zion* 43 (1978): 264–313.

———. "*Te'udah be-yisra'el*—Between Change and Tradition" [Hebrew]. Introduction to *Te'udah be-yisra'el*. By Isaac Ber Levinsohn. Jerusalem, 1977. Photo edition of Vilna, Horodna, 1828. 3–19.

———. "*Tevunah*—The First Rabbinical Periodical in Eastern Europe" [Hebrew]. *Kiryat sefer* 54 (1979): 371–83.

———. "The Doctrine and Activity of R. Hayyim of Volozhin as the Reaction of 'Mitnaggedic' Society to Hasidism" [Hebrew]. *PAAJR* 38–39 (1972): 1–45.

———. "The Gaon R. Elijah and the Beginning of Opposition to Hasidism" [Hebrew]. In *Transition and Change in Modern Jewish History* (Shmuel Ettinger Festschrift). Jerusalem, 1987. 439–58.

———. "The Gaon of Vilna and the Haskalah—Image and Reality" [Hebrew]. In *Perakim be-toldot ha-hevrah ha-yehudit . . .* (J. Katz Festschrift). Jerusalem, 1980. 192–217.

———. "The Relationship Between Talmudic Scholarship and the Institution of the Rabbinate in Nineteenth Century Lithuanian Jewry." In *The Interaction Between Judaism and Other Cultures.* Ed. Leon Landman. New York, 1990. 107–32.

Ettinger, Shmuel. "The Ideological Background of Anti-Semitic Literature in Russia" [Hebrew]. In *Ha-antishemiut ba-'et ha-hadashah.* Tel Aviv, 1979. 99–144.

Ferber, Zvi Hirsch. "Zvi yisra'el" [Hebrew]. In *Sha'arei zion.* Jerusalem: Kislev-Shevat, 1932/33.

Franklin, Benjamin. *The Autobiography of Benjamin Franklin.* New York, 1941. [Original French translation: *Mémoire de la Vie Privée.* Paris, 1791.]

Friedberg, A. S. "Memories from my Childhood" [Hebrew]. *Sefer ha-shanah* 3 (1902): 82–101.

Friedman, A. A. *Le-toldot kitat ha-mussara'im.* Jerusalem, 1926.

———. *Sefer ha-zikhronot.* Tel Aviv, 1926.

Frishman, David. "Three Who Ate" [Hebrew]. In *Kol kitvei david frishman,* part I. Warsaw and New York, 1929. 123–31.

Frumkin, Aryeh Leib. *Sefer toldot eliyaha.* Vilna, 1900.

———. *Toldot hakhmei yerushalayim.* Jerusalem, 1929.

Fünn, S. Y. Letter to Bezalel Stern. *Ha-pardes* 3 (1897): 150–56.

Gay, Peter. *The Enlightenment: An Interpretation.* New York, 1966.

Ginzberg, Louis. "Rabbi Israel Salanter." In *Students, Scholars and Saints.* Philadelphia, 1945. 145–94.

Ginzburg, Mordecai Aharon. *Devir.* Vilna, 1844.

———. *Devir.* Vilna, 1862.

Ginzburg, Saul. "Abraham Mapu" [Hebrew]. *He-'avar* I (1918): 96–101.

———. *Historische Verk.* New York, 1937. [Hebrew translation: *Ketavim histori'im.* Tel Aviv, 1944.]

Glenn, M. G. *Israel Salanter.* New York, 1953.

Goldberg, Hillel. *Israel Salanter: Text, Structure, Idea.* New York, 1982.

Gottleib, Ephraim. "The Theological and Mystical Element of the Understanding of Man's Purpose in Kabbalah" [Hebrew]. In *Mehkarim be-sifrut ha-kabbalah.* By Ephraim Gottleib. Tel Aviv, 1976. 29–37.

Greenberg, L. *The Jews in Russia.* New York, 1976.

Gries, Ze'ev. "The Hasidic *Hanhagot* Literature as an Expression of Leadership and Ethos" [Hebrew]. Ph.D. diss., Hebrew University, 1979. [Published as *Sifrut ha-hanhagot: toldoteha u-mekomah be-hayyei hasidei r. yisra'el ba'al shem tov.* Jerusalem, 1989.]

Grinhoiz, Shmuel. "Memel" [Yiddish]. In *Lita,* vol. 1. New York, 1951. 1427–38.

Guttman, J. *Dat u-mada'.* Jerusalem, 1955.

Haggai, Shmuel. "The Historical Background of the Mussar Movement" [Hebrew]. *Mahanayim,* no. 81 (Iyyar 1963): 70–75.

Hartley, David. *Observation on Man; His Frame, His Duty and His Expectations.* Gainesville, Fla., 1966.

Hayyim ben Isaac of Volozhin. *Hanhagot ve-'ezot.* Recorded by R. Aaron Zelig Lifschitz, in MS London Fedro 1,14. Institute for Microfilmed Hebrew Manuscripts, No. 8800, sec. 115.

———. *Nefesh ha-hayyim.* Vilna, 1824.

———. *Ruah hayyim; perush rabbi hayyim mi-volozhin le-pirkei avot.* Vilna, 1859.

———. Introduction to *Sifra di-zeni'uta 'im perush ha-ger''a.* Vilna, Horodna, 1820.

Heilmann, Hayyim Meir. *Beit Rabbi.* Berditchev, 1902.

Heller, Meshullam Feibush. *Sefer yosher divrei emet.* Munkatsch, 1905.

Heller, Yehoshua. *Sefer divrei yehoshu'a.* Vilna, 1846.

Heschel, Hayyim V. "The Jewish Community in Kovna" [Hebrew]. In *Keneset yisra'el.* Ed. Shaul Pinhas Rabinowitz. Warsaw, 1888.

Hildesheimer, Azriel. "Between the Two Luminaries of the Generation" [Hebrew]. *Ha-zofeh* (February 1963).

Hildesheimer, Meir. "Documents Concerning the Founding of the Rabbinical Seminary in Berlin" [Hebrew]. *Ha-ma'ayan* 14/2: 12-37.

———. "On the Image of R. Azriel Hildesheimer" [Hebrew]. *Sinai* 54 (1963/64): 67-94.

Hirsch, Samson Raphael (pseud., Ben Usiel). *Iggerot Zafon: Neunzehn Brief uber Judentum.* Altona, 1836. [English translation: *Iggerot Tzafon: The Nineteen Letters on Judaism.* Trans. B. Drachman. New York, 1960.]

Hume, David. "A Dissertation on the Passions." In *Essays.* Vol. 2. London, 1875. 139–66.

———. *A Treatise on Human Nature.* London and New York, 1962.

Israel of Shklov. Introduction to *Pe'at ha-shulhan.* Jerusalem, 1959.

Issachar Baer ben Tanhum. Introduction to *Sefer ma'aseh rav.* Vilna, Horodna, 1832.

———. *Sefer tosefet ma'aseh rav.* Jerusalem, 1896.

Judah ben Samuel he-Hasid. *Sefer hasidim.* Ed. R. Margoliot. Jerusalem, 1957.

Kaplan, Zvi. "On the Way of R. Hayyim of Volozhin in Halakhah" [Hebrew]. In *Me-'olomah shel torah.* Jerusalem, 1974. 9–43.

Karelitz, Avraham Yeshayahu. *Sefer hazon 'ish; 'al inyanei emunah u-bitahon ve-'od.* Jerusalem, 1954.

Karlinski, Hayyim. *Ha-rishon le-shoshelet brisk.* Jerusalem, 1984.

Karp, Abraham J. "New York Chooses a Chief Rabbi." *AJHQ* 44 (1955): 129–98.

Katz, Abraham Yitzhak. "Moshe Aryeh Leib Friedland and His Famous Library" [Hebrew]. *Perakim* 3 (1963): 169–91.

Katz, Dov. *Pulmus ha-mussar.* Jerusalem, 1972.

———. *Tenu'at ha-mussar, toldoteha isheha ve-shitoteha.* 5 vols. Tel Aviv, 1967.

Katz, Jacob. *Tradition and Crisis.* Glencoe, Ill., 1961.

Katzenelson, Gideon. *Ha-milhamah ha-sifrutit bein ha-haredim veha-maskilim.* Tel Aviv, 1954.

Katzenelson, Judah Leib. "Mah she-rau 'einai ve-sham'u oznay." In *Zihronot me-yemei hayyai.* By Buki ben Yogli (pseud.). Jerusalem, 1947.

Klatzki (Meltzer), Mordecai b. Asher. *Sefer tekhelet mordekhai.* Vilna, 1889.

Klausner, Joseph. *Historyah shel ha-sifrut ha-'ivrit ha-hadashah.* Jerusalem, 1953.

Kluger, Yehudah Aharon. *Toldot shlomoh.* Lemberg, 1868.

Kurzweil, Zvi. "The Psychological Roots and the Educational Meaning of the Mussar Movement According to the Writings of R. Israel Salanter" [Hebrew]. In *Hinukh ha-adam ve-ye'udo.* Jerusalem, 1967.

Lamm, Norman. *Torah li-shemah be-mishnat rabbi hayyim mi-volozhin uve-mahshevet ha-zeman.* Jerusalem, 1972. [English translation: *Torah li-shemah, Torah for Torah's Sake in the Works of Rabbi Hayyim of Volozhin and His Contemporaries.* New York, 1989.]

Landau, Bezalel. *Ha-gaon he-hasid mi-vilna.* Jerusalem, 1965.

Lefin, Menahem Mendel. *Sefer heshbon ha-nefesh.* Kaidan, 1937. [First published in Lvov, 1808.]

Levin, Joshua Heschel. *Sefer 'aliyot eliyahu.* Vilna, 1856.

Levin, Judah Leib (Yahala"l). "The Kidnapped" [Hebrew]. In *Yehudim be-'itot mah-pekhah.* Tel Aviv, 1957.

Levin, M. *'Erkei hevrah ve-kalkalah ba-ideologia shel tekufat ha-haskalah.* Jerusalem, 1975.

Levine, Hillel. "Menahem Mendel Lefin." Ph.D. diss., Harvard University, 1974.

———. "Between Hasidism and Haskalah: On a Concealed anti-Hasidic Polemic" [Hebrew]. In *Perakim be-toldot ha-hevrah ha-yehudit . . .* (J. Katz Festschrift). Jerusalem, 1980.

———. "Dwarfs on the Shoulders of Giants; A Case Study in the Impact of Modernization on Social Epistemology of Judaism." *Jewish Social Studies* 40 (1978): 63–72.

Levinsohn, Isaac Ber. *Te'udah be-yisra'el.* Vilna, Horodna, 1828.

Levitats, I. *The Jewish Community in Russia.* New York, 1943.

Lifschitz, Ya'akov. *Divrei shalom ve-emet.* Warsaw, 1884.

———. *Mahzikei ha-dat.* Pietrkov, 1903.

———. *Toldot yitzhak.* Warsaw, 1896.

———. *Zikhron ya'akov.* 3 vols. Eretz Yisra'el, 1968.

Lioni, Eliezer. "The History of the 'Etz Hayyim Yeshivah in Volozhin and its Leaders" [Hebrew]. In *Sefer volozhin.* Ed. E. Lioni. Tel Aviv, 1970.

Lipkin, Hayyim Yizhak. *Torat r. yisra'el mi-salant.* Tel Aviv, 1954.

———. "Concerning the Path and Activities of Our Master of Israel from Salant, of Blessed Memory" [Hebrew]. *Tevunah* 1, no. 7 (1941).

Lippman, D. M. *Le-toldot ha-yehudim be-kovna u-slobodka.* Keidan, 1934.

Loewe, Louis. *Sefer masa' eliezer.* Trans. Samuel Joseph Fühn. Vilna, 1847.

Lovtzer, Shmuel. *'Olat shmuel.* Vilna, 1901.

Lunski, Heikel. *Min ha-getto ha-vilna'i.* Vilna, 1921.

Luzzatto, Moses Hayyim. *Sefer derekh tevunot la-ramha''l.* Jerusalem, 1880.

———. *Sefer mesillat yesharim.* Jerusalem, 1964.

Mahler, Raphael. *Divrey yemey yisra'el; dorot aharonim,* vol. 6. Tel Aviv, 1976. [English translation: *A History of Modern Jewry, 1780–1815.* London, 1971.]

Maimon, Judah Leib. *Toldot ha-ger'' 'a.* Jerusalem, 1970.

Maimonides, Moses. *A Maimonides Reader.* Ed. I. Twersky. New York and Philadelphia, 1972.

Makhshoves. See Eliashiv.

Malachi, A.R. "Benjamin Franklin and Hebrew Literature" [Hebrew]. *Ha-doar* 35 (1957): 238–39.

Mapu, Abraham. *Kol kitvei mapu.* Tel Aviv, 1955.

———. *Mikhtevei avraham mapu.* Ed. Ben Zion Dinur. Jerusalem, 1970.

Marcus, Ivan G. *Piety and Society; the Jewish Pietists of Medieval Germany.* Leiden, 1981.

Margaliot, S. T. "The Life of the Sage Dr. L. Lipkin" [Hebrew]. *Ha-zefirah* 2, no. 11 (1875).

Mark, Yaakov. *Gedoylim fun Unzerer Tsayt.* New York, 1927. [Hebrew translation: *Bi-mehizatam shel gedolei ha-dor.* Jerusalem, 1958.]

Mazeh, R. Yaakov. *Zikhronot.* Tel Aviv, 1936.

Meltzer. See Klatzki.

Melzen, Shmuel. *Sefer even shelemah.* Vilna, 1890.

Moshe Hayyim Ephraim of Sudylkow. *Sefer degel mahaneh ephraim, parashat yitro.* Jerusalem, 1963.

Moshe Yitzhak, Maggid of Kelm. *Tokhehot hayyim.* Vilna, 1897.

Nadav, Mordecai. "The History of the Community of Pinsk" [Hebrew]. In *Pinsk.* Vol. 1. Tel Aviv and Haifa, 1973.

Ovzinski, Levi. *Toldot yeshivat ha-yehudim be-kurland.* Vilna 1912.

Pechter, Mordecai. "The Homiletical and Ethical Literature of the Sages of Safed in the 16th Century and their Principal Ideal" [Hebrew]. Ph.D. diss. The Hebrew University, Jerusalem, 1976.

———. "R. Israel Salanter Seen in a New Light" [Hebrew]. *Tarbiz* 53 (1984): 621–50.

Peleitat sofrim. Ed. Yehoshua Heshel Levin. Volozhin, 1863.

Peters, R. S. *Brett's History of Psychology.* London and New York, 1953.

Philipson, David. *Max Lilienthal; Life and Writings.* New York, 1915.

Pinhas ben Judah. *Keter torah.* Jerusalem, 1968.

Plongian, Mordecai. *Ben Porat.* Vilna, 1858.

Preshel, Tuviah. "Rabbi Israel Salanter and the Translation of the Talmud into the Hebrew Language" [Hebrew]. *Ha-doar* 53 (1974): 555.

Rafael, Yitzhak. "*Peleitat sofrim* with *Safah la-ne'emanim*" [Hebrew]. *Areshet* 1 (1959).

Reines, Moshe. *Akhsaniot shel torah,* no. 1 (Cracow, 1890): 21–35.

Reines, Yitzhak Yaakov. "Zikharon ba-sefer." In *Shenei ha-me'orot.* Pietrkov, 1913.

Rimon, Y., and Y. Z. Wasserman. *Shmu'el be-doro.* Tel Aviv, 1961.

Rivlin, Eliezer. *Ha-zaddik r. yosef zundel mi-salant ve-rabotav.* Jerusalem, 1927.

Rosenblum, Noah H. "On the World-View of Adam Ha-Cohen" [Hebrew]. *Perakim* 3 (1963): 141–67.

Rosenfeld, Shmuel. *Rabbi yisrael salanter: hayav pe'ulotav ve-talmidav.* Warsaw, 1911.

Rosenthal, Y. L. *Toldot hevrat marbei ha-haskalah be-eretz russyah mi-shenat hityasdutah trk''d 'ad shenat trm''v.* 2 vols. Petersburg, 1885–90.

Salanter, Israel. *Kitvei r. yisra'el salanter.* Ed. Mordecai Pechter. Jerusalem, 1972.

———. *Sefer imrei binah.* Ed. David Sidarsky. Warsaw, 1878.

———. *Sefer or yisra'el.* Ed. R. Isaac Blazer. Vilna, 1900.

Salanter, Israel, et al. *Sefer 'ez peri.* Vilna, 1881.

———. *Sefer hut ha-meshulash.* Jerusalem, 1904.

Salmon, Joseph. "The Beginnings of Reform in the Yeshivot of Eastern Europe" [Hebrew]. *Molad* 27 [N.S. 4] (1971): 161–73.

———. "The Book *Shivat zion* and its Historical Background" [Hebrew]. *Eshel be'er sheva'* 2 (1980): 331–53.

Schatz-Uffenheimer, Rivka. *Ha-hasidut ke-mistikah.* Jerusalem, 1968. [English translation: *Hasidism as Mysticism.* Jerusalem and Princeton, 1993.]

Scholem, Gershom. "Devekut, or Communion with God." *The Review of Religion* 14 (1949–50): 115–39.

———. *The Messianic Idea in Judaism and Other Essays.* New York, 1971.

Schweid, Eliezer. *'Iyunim bi-shemonah perakim la-rambam.* Jerusalem, 1965.

Sefer hayyei ha-mussar. B'nai Barak, 1964.

Sefer ish yerushalayim. Ed. M. Ostrovsky. Jerusalem, 1937.

Sefer or ha-mussar. B'nai Barak, 1965.

Sefer tifferet moshe. Warsaw, 1884.

Sefer zikhronot mordekhai. Warsaw, 1913.

Seton-Watson, H. *The Decline of Imperial Russia, 1855–1914.* New York, 1966.

Shaikevitz, N.M. *Shirei shm''r ve-zikhronotav.* Jerusalem, 1952.

Shmukler-Shapiro, Moshe Shmuel. *Toldot rabbenu hayyim mi-volozhin.* Vilna, 1900.

Shohat, Azriel. *Mossad ha-rabbanut mi-ta'am be-russyah.* Haifa, 1976.

Shulman, Yosef. "Memel" [Hebrew]. *Yahadut lita.* Tel Aviv, 1967. 281–83.

Sidarski, David. "Biographical Sketch of R. Israel Salanter" [Hebrew]. Jewish National Library, Schwadron Collection, Autograph Lipkin Israel.

Siddur ishei yisra'el 'al-pi derekh ha-ger''a. Jerusalem, n.d.

Sidgwick, Henry. *Outlines of the History of Ethics.* London, 1946.

Silman, Yohanan. "The Theory of the Psyche in the Thought of R. Israel Lipkin (of Salant)" [Hebrew]. *Bar-ilan, sefer ha-shanah* 9 (1973): 288–304.

Slutzki, Judah. *Ha-'itonut ha-yehudit-russit ba-me'ah ha-tesha' 'esreh.* Jerusalem, 1971.

———. "Dr. Max Mandelstamm" [Hebrew]. *He-'avar* 4 (1957): 56–76.

———. "The Rabbinical Seminary in Vilna" [Hebrew]. *He-'avar* 7 (1960): 29–48.

Soloveitchik, Haym. "Three Themes in the Sefer Hasidim." *AJS Review* 1 (1976): 311–57.

Stanislawski, Michael. *Tsar Nicholas I and the Jews: The Transformation of Jewish Society in Russia, 1825-55.* Philadelphia, 1983.

Steinschneider, Hillel Noah Maggid. *'Ir vilna.* Vilna, 1900.

———. "On the History of One of the Rabbis" [Hebrew]. *Ozar ha-sifrut.* Krakow, 1892. 531–41.

Sterlitz, Meir. *Mi-bet meir.* Jerusalem, 1937.

Ta-Shma, I. "Tosaphot gornish" [Hebrew]. *Sinai* 68 (1971).

Tchernowitz, Hayyim (Rav Tsa'ir). *Pirkei hayyim.* New York, 1954.

———. *Toldot ha-poskim.* New York, 1948.

Tevunah; kevuzat hiddushei torah mi-hakhmei u-gedolei yisra'el. Ed. R. Israel Salanter. Memel and Koenigsberg, 1861–62.

Tishby, I. "The Source of the Saying 'The Holy One blessed be He, the Torah and Israel are One' in Luzzatto's Commentary to the *Idra rabba*" [Hebrew]. *Kiryat sefer* 50 (1975): 480–92.

Tishby, I. and Joseph Dan. *Mivhar sifrut ha-mussar.* Tel Aviv, 1971.

———. "Hasidut." *Ha-enzeklopedyah ha-'ivrit* 17 (1965): 808–09.

Tishby, I. and F. Lachover. *Mishnat ha-zohar.* 2 vols. Jerusalem, 1957.

Vinlez, Israel. "R. Menahem Mendel Lefin of Satanow" [Hebrew]. *Ha-'olam* 4, nos. 39–42 (1925).

Vital, Hayyim. *Sefer sha'arei kedushah.* Bnei Braq, 1967.

Waksman, Nissan. "A Forgotten Book" [Hebrew]. *Shanah be-shanah* (1969): 303–15.

Weinberg, Yehiel Ya'akov. *Seridei esh.* 4 vols. Jerusalem, 1969.

Weiss, Joseph G. "The Beginning of the Growth of the Hasidic Path" [Hebrew]. *Zion* 16 (1951): 88–103.

———. "Torah Study at the Beginnings of Hasidism" [Hebrew]. *Ha-doar* (1965).

———. "Torah Study in the System of R. Israel Baal Shem Tov" [Hebrew]. *Tiferet yisra'el sefer yovel li-khevot r. yisra'el brody.* London, 1967. 151–69.

Whyte, L. L. *The Unconscious Before Freud.* London, 1962.

Wilensky, Mordecai. *Hasidim u-mitnagdim.* 2 vols. Jerusalem, 1970.

Willman, Shraga ha-Kohen. *Iggerot u-mikhtavim me-'et ha-gaon r. yisra'el mi-salant.* New York, 1970.

Yafeh, Benjamin. *Ha-rav mi-yahud.* Jerusalem, 1957.

Yavitz, Zeev. *Toldot yisra'el.* Tel Aviv, 1963.

Yehezkel, Feivel. *Sefer toldot adam.* Duhrnfurt, 1801.

Yizhak Isak Ha-Kohen. *Sefer sha'arei yizhak.* Warsaw, 1902.

Zaitchik, H. E. *Sefer ha-me'orot ha-gedolim.* New York, 1953.

Zalmanovitz, Menahem Mendel. *Zikhron hillel.* Vilna, 1902.

Zelig, Samuel ben Joshua. *Minhat shmuel le-masekhet berakhot.* Vilna, 1842.

Zinberg, Israel. *A History of Jewish Literature.* New York, Cincinnati, 1975.

Zinowitz. *'Ez hayyim; toldot yeshivat volozhin.* Tel Aviv, 1972.

Zitron, S. L. "The War of the Dynasties in the Volozhin Yeshivah" [Hebrew]. *Reshumot* 1 (1925).

Ziv, Gershon Mendel. "Le-ma'an da'at." *Ha-meliz* 155 (1897).

Zweifel, Eliezer Zvi. *Shalom 'al yisra'el.* Zhitomir, 1873.

Index

Make books your companion
Let your bookshelf be your garden—
                                    Judah Ibn Tibbon

to become a member –
to present a gift –

call 1 (800) 234-3151
or write:
The Jewish Publication Society
1930 Chestnut Street
Philadelphia, Pennsylvania 19103

A Jewish Tradition